The
American
Psychological
Association

A
Historical
Perspective

AMERICAN
PSYCHOLOGICAL
ASSOCIATION

Washington, DC

100 YEARS

The
*American
Psychological
Association*

A
*Historical
Perspective*

EDITED BY
RAND B. EVANS
VIRGINIA STAUDT SEXTON
THOMAS C. CADWALLADER

Published by
American Psychological Association
750 First Street, NE
Washington, DC 20002

Copies may be ordered from
APA Order Department
P.O. Box 2710
Hyattsville, MD 20784

Cover design by Paine Bluett Paine, Inc.
Photo section designed by Grafik Communications Ltd.
Typeset by Easton Publishing Services, Inc., Easton, MD
Printed by Braun-Brumfield, Inc., Ann Arbor, MI
Dust jacket printed by York Graphics, York, PA
Technical editing and production by Olin J. Nettles

Photographs:
Photos 1, 7, 20, 24, and 25 courtesy of the Archives of the History of American
    Psychology, University of Akron.
Photo 2 courtesy of the National Library of Medicine.
Photo 3 courtesy of the Library of Congress.
Photos 4, 5, 6, 8, 9, 10, 11, 12, 13, 15, 16, 17, 18, 21, 22, 23, and 28 courtesy of
    the Evans Collection.
Photo 14 courtesy of the Clark University Archives.
Photo 19 courtesy of Ernest R. Hilgard.
Photo 29 by Alan D. Entin

Library of Congress Cataloging-in-Publication Data

The American Psychological Association: a historical perspective/edited by Rand B.
    Evans, Virginia S. Sexton, Thomas C. Cadwallader.
        p. cm.
    Includes index.
    ISBN 1-55798-136-1 (acid-free paper)
    1. American Psychological Association—History.   I. Evans, Rand B.
II. Sexton, Virginia Staudt.   III. Cadwallader, Thomas C.   IV. American
Psychological Association.
BF11.A68   1992
150'.6'073—dc20   91-35825
                                                                              CIP

Printed in the United States of America
First edition

CONTENTS

CONTRIBUTORS

Thomas C. Cadwallader is professor of psychology at Indiana State University, Terre Haute. He is a past president of the APA's Division 26 (History of Psychology) and is the current historian of the Eastern Psychological Association. He has researched extensively on C. S. Pierce and on the development of early laboratories in psychology.

Thomas M. Camfield is professor of history at Sam Houston State University, Huntsville, Texas. He has published, among other things, on the professionalization of psychology and psychology in the First World War.

James H. Capshew is assistant professor in the Department of History and Philosophy of Science at Indiana University. His historical research explores the disciplinary, professional, and cultural dimensions of psychology in the United States.

Meredith P. Crawford founded HUMRRO in 1951 and retired as chairman in 1990. He was formerly professor of psychology and an academic dean at Vanderbilt University. He served as treasurer (1957–1967) and as administrative officer for accreditation (1978–1982) of the APA.

Rand B. Evans is professor and chair of psychology at East Carolina University, Greenville, North Carolina. He is a past president of Division 26, and his research includes pre-Jamesian American psychology, early systematic psychologies in America, and early instruments in psychological research.

Raymond D. Fowler has been the APA's chief executive officer since 1989. He is Professor Emeritus of the University of Alabama. He served as APA treasurer from 1983 to 1986 and as president in 1988.

Ernest R. Hilgard is Emeritus Professor of Psychology at Stanford University. He is a former president of the APA and of Division 26. He has published widely on the history of psychology, and he was a member of the committee that reorganized the APA after World War II.

Michael S. Pallak is vice president for research at the Foundation for Behavioral Health, South San Francisco, California. He is a former executive officer of the APA and was editor of the *American Psychologist*. He has published widely in social psychology and health policy.

Franz Samelson is Emeritus Professor of Psychology at Kansas State University, Manhattan, Kansas. He has published widely on the history of 20th century psychology, including mental testing in World War I, early behaviorism, and the development of authoritarianism theory.

Elizabeth Scarborough is professor of psychology and dean of liberal arts and sciences at Indiana University, South Bend. She is a former president of Division 26 of the APA and has published on the history of women in psychology.

Virginia Staudt Sexton is professor of psychology at St. John's University, New York. She is a former president of the APA's Division 26 and has been closely involved with Psi Chi. She has written widely on the history of psychology, including *History of Psychology: An Overview* with Henryk Misiak.

M. Brewster Smith is Professor Emeritus of Psychology at Stevenson College, the University of California at Santa Cruz. He is a former president of the APA and has been intimately involved in the development of the APA's social conscience.

Michael M. Sokal is professor of history at Worcester Polytechnic Institute and executive secretary of the History of Science Society. He has written extensively on the history of American psychology and the history of American scientific organization, and is completing a biography of James McKeen Cattell.

Gary R. VandenBos is the executive director of the APA's Office of Publications and Communications. He was the first director of the APA's National Policy Studies unit in the late 1970s, and, in the late 1980s, he served one year as the acting chief executive officer of the APA.

FOREWORD

CHARLES D. SPIELBERGER, PhD
100th PRESIDENT OF THE APA

With the publication of this volume, *The American Psychological Association: A Historical Perspective*, we celebrate an occasion of great significance: the centennial anniversary of organized psychology in North America. One hundred years have passed since a small gathering of academicians met on July 8, 1892, in the Worcester, Massachusetts, study of G. Stanley Hall and formed the American Psychological Association.

From these humble beginnings, that organization began to grow, in fitful spurts at the beginning, gathering momentum into a steadily flowing stream, and, since World War II, achieving the status of a veritable ocean of members and affiliates as we enter our Centennial year. At first, reflecting the state of the discipline in its infancy, the membership was drawn from a small group of American educators. Originally grouped under the discipline of philosophy, our founders were involved in the earliest stages of scientific inquiry.

Slowly, as psychological theory and research evolved, practice, which had always coexisted as an integral part of the discipline, began to develop at an astonishing rate. In true developmental style, as the world entered into what we like to call "The Modern Age," American psychology grew through infancy, childhood, and adolescence into what might be considered an early stage of adulthood. Some will, no doubt, strenuously object to this characterization, believing the discipline to still be in its infancy.

From its founding in 1892, the American Psychological Association has played a vital and preeminent role in the development of psychology as a scientific discipline and a sophisticated profession, comprising theory, research, and practice in equal proportions. Although these indispensible components have not always coexisted in easy alliance, it may be said that both the moments of contention and those of sharing and cooperation have contributed to great strides in knowledge and a wonderous range of applications. The history of the American Psychological Association, as it is presented in these pages, clearly reflects this evolution of the discipline as we strive to meet the challenges of our second century.

From that small cohort of a few individuals that founded the Association one hundred years ago to the more than 112,000 current members and affiliates and a governance structure that now encompasses almost 500 men and women, the cast of characters involved in this adventure has increased exponentially. It is with deep appreciation of the entire Association membership, and with respect for the wide diversity of thought, opinion, and experience that it represents, that we have endeavored to set forth this historical record. If lessons are to be learned from history, we might profit from taking this moment in our development and evolution to cast a glance backward and review what has happened to us as an organized group. The time seems appropriate to consider the issues that have united or divided us, slowed our progress, and spurred our growth.

~

This book would not have come into being if it were not for the dedicated efforts of the APA Centennial Task Force, whose members included John Popplestone (chair), Ludy Benjamin, Kenneth B. Clark, Florence Denmark, Laura Furamoto, Gloria Gottesgan, Asher Pacht, Robert Perloff, Mark Rosenzweig, Stanley Schneider, and Virginia Sexton. The Task Force encouraged the editors of this volume and, with the support of the Board of Directors and the Office of Communications, it has come to pass. The attention given to this worthy and ambitious project by such members of the Board as Joseph Matarazzo and Jack Wiggins must be acknowledged, as well as the valuable consultation of such individuals as Michael Sokal and Ludy Benjamin concerning the preparation of history volumes in general.

I remind the reader that history is an ongoing process. What the editors and the contributors to this volume present is a perspective of that process as it has affected and continues to influence all of us who are privileged to be a part of the American Psychological Association. How that process will continue to evolve as the discipline of psychology becomes more differentiated and specialized, with the emergence of trends such as "cognitive science" and "neuroscience" as free-standing academic units, is very difficult to predict. Morever, the potential impact of limited prescription authority for clinicians on psychological models of behavior as well as on professional practice is even more difficult to foretell. With the rapidly advancing technology of our information age, frankly, who can say where psychology will be even a decade from now? It should be noted, however, that we often tend to look at such developments as potentially divisive, neglecting to consider the ways in which they may stimulate, unite, and drive us forward.

The history of the Association, as it is reported in the pages that follow, is certainly not devoid of controversy and obstacles. In point of fact, however, we are here—in fairly robust shape and continuing to grow and prosper! As we enter our second century, our goal as an association must remain what it has always been: to encourage the development of our discipline as a science, to help each other as professionals, and, most important, to lessen human misery and misunderstanding and contribute to enlightened public interest.

February 1992

PREFACE: THE AMERICAN PSYCHOLOGICAL ASSOCIATION AT 100

RAND B. EVANS, VIRGINIA STAUDT SEXTON, AND
THOMAS C. CADWALLADER

The number of institutional centennials during the past decade and those projected in this decade are evidence of the intense activity at the end of the last century concerning disciplinary professionalization. The creation of a national organization is a good indicator of a discipline's seeking independent recognition. The American Psychological Association was surprisingly early in such organizational professionalization in America and certainly early in its own development as an independent, academic, and scientific discipline.

When the American Psychological Association was founded in 1892 in G. Stanley Hall's parlor at Clark University, the new, experimental psychology was still in its infancy in America. Most psychology programs were still housed in departments of philosophy. Only a few laboratories of psychology existed in America, and these were quite rudimentary compared with those found in Europe. Only one American journal devoted to the new experimental psychology existed at the time, the *American Journal of Psychology*, itself founded by Hall only five years earlier. William James's revolutionary *Principles of Psychology* had appeared only two years previously, and, although it remained more philosophical than experimental, it had made the critical distinction between the older American psychologies that related eventually to a soul concept and the new psychology as the study of mind as a naturalistic process.

Because the American Psychological Association began so early in the development of modern psychological thought, its history and development have been tied irrevocably to the development of the field as a whole. For this reason, the breakthroughs, initiatives, controversies, and failures that have punctuated the development of American psychology have also been reflected in the American Psychological Association. The problem that has plagued American psychology from the beginning has been one of definition. What is psychology relative to similar activities in physiology, philosophy, psychiatry, and a number of other disciplines? What is the subject matter of psychology? What are its methods? Is it a science? If so, what kind of science: natural, mental, social, or behavioral? What is the relationship between theoretical psychology and applied psychology, between academic psychology and professional psychology? Without a central, unifying principle, method, or goal, there has never been a satisfactory consensus on these and similar issues. The result has been, periodically, open conflicts, schisms, and revolts. There has hardly been a decade among the past ten decades of the American Psychological Association in which it has not been shaken by at least one of these factors. The ejection of the philosophers and the revolt of E. B. Titchener's Experimentalists at the end of the Association's first decade, the revolt of the applied societies in the 1920s, the founding of the Psychonomic Society in the 1960s, and the recent creation of the American Psychological Society in the 1980s, just to name some major examples, were all results, at least in part, of a failure to find a consensus as to the nature of psychology and, collaterally, the nature of its primary organization.

If anything, psychology is more heterogeneous today than it has been at any other time in the past century, and anything like a consensus as to the nature of psychology seems more distant than ever. Until such time as a unifying principle or consensus is found or until some revolution in scientific knowledge renders the psychological enterprise obsolete, mutual tolerance and good will, not to mention a healthy sense of humor, may be psychology's best tack.

The chapters that make up this centennial volume, written by historians and psychologists alike, bring together the story of the development of the American Psychological Association, cast against the development of American psychology itself. They relate the successes and failures of the organization and its attempts to define both itself and its field. The editors hope that this volume will provide some understanding of the dynamics that have made the Association and American psychology what they are today, and give some insights into what they may become in the future.

I

HISTORY OF THE AMERICAN PSYCHOLOGICAL ASSOCIATION

1

THE HISTORICAL ROOTS OF THE AMERICAN PSYCHOLOGICAL ASSOCIATION

THOMAS C. CADWALLADER

The organizational, or "preliminary," meeting of what was to become the American Psychological Association was convened by G. Stanley Hall at Clark University in Worcester, Massachusetts, on July 8, 1892. That meeting was the consequence of a number of developments in American intellectual thought over more than a century. The main goal of this chapter

This chapter is the consequence of the efforts and assistance of many individuals and institutions, too many, alas, to identify and thank individually. The archivist and archives of all of the institutions discussed here have provided materials directly or indirectly involved in the preparation of the chapter and in the background understanding on which the chapter stands. But two institutions have provided so much material that they require individual acknowledgment. One is Harvard University, specifically the Harvard University Archives and its curator, Harley P. Holden, and staff. The other is Johns Hopkins University, specifically the Ferdinand Hamburger, Jr. Archives and its archivist, Julia B. Morgan, and staff; and the Department of Special Collections and staff, notably Carolyn Smith. The staff of Indiana State University's Cunningham Memorial Library, the staffs of the Indiana University and University of Illinois Libraries, and my graduate assistants have, for over 20 years, contributed heavily to my research and thus to this chapter, as have the authors of many books and articles, only some of whom are cited in this chapter.

Financial support over the years has been provided by the Research Committee of Indiana State University, the American Philosophical Society, and the American Council of Learned Societies. To all of these, I am greatly indebted.

is to show these developments in terms of some of the intertwining paths of 19th-century American psychology, in the broader context of higher education, that created a professional identity conducive to the founding of the American Psychological Association.

OVERVIEW

The intellectual root of the APA lies within American academic psychology. There, two major changes during the 19th century are of significance. The first was psychology's evolution from a philosophic to a scientific enterprise. The major event in this evolution was the adoption of the Fechnerian–Wundtian tradition. This tradition began in Europe with the 1860 publication of *The Elements of Psychophysics* (1860) by Gustav Theodor Fechner (1801–1887). The *Elements* demonstrated that certain psychological questions can be answered by the same techniques used by physiology and physics (i.e., that certain psychological questions fall with the domain of scientific inquiry).

This tradition was furthered and proselytized by Wilhelm Wundt (1832–1920), whose 1874 *Principles of Physiological Psychology* became the intellectual model for perhaps the first three generations of American scientific psychologists. The adoption of the Fechnerian–Wundtian model permitted and perhaps dictated the differentiation of psychology from its parent, philosophy, just as has been done by all disciplines since antiquity, when philosophy encompassed all learning. However, the separation process was only partially accomplished at the founding of the APA[1]; this explains the widely divergent interests and backgrounds of the early members of the Association.

The second change was in the nature of higher education itself, involving the transition of colleges and universities from strictly undergraduate institutions to organizations including and often centering on graduate education. It was from the realm of graduate education, particularly the granting of PhDs, that much of the push for professionalization came in America. One might conceptualize higher education as the soil in which psychology was rooted and in which it eventually flowered.

Three institutions of higher education played major roles in the twin stories of the evolution of psychology and higher education—Yale, Har-

---

[1]In fact, Harvard University, one of the institutions historically most involved in the early development of psychology, did not break completely away from philosophy administratively until 1934.

vard, and Johns Hopkins—although many others also played significant roles.

Yale University's role was in introducing the nation's first graduate programs (including one in psychology) in 1847. This step led to the granting of the first earned PhD degrees (including one in philosophy and psychology) in 1861.

Harvard University's role was in developing an orientation in Fechnerian–Wundtian psychology. Harvard offered the first course in this tradition (in 1875–76); gave the first laboratory demonstrations and began the first "informal" psychology laboratory (in the second half of the 1870s); established the first "trustee-sanctioned" psychology laboratory (which opened in the fall of 1895); and awarded the world's first PhD in psychology (in 1878).

Johns Hopkins University's role was as the first institution to be founded on the notion that graduate education and research were its primary objectives. In keeping with this role, Johns Hopkins established the first productive (but "trustee-antisanctioned"[2]) psychology laboratory (in 1883), the first PhD program in psychology in the Fechnerian–Wundtian tradition (Johns Hopkins's first psychology PhD was awarded in 1886), and the first psychological journal in English in the Fechnerian–Wundtian tradition (*The American Journal of Psychology*, in 1887). Moreover, the model on which the APA was based may well have been provided at Johns Hopkins.

The changes in psychology and higher education that occurred during the 19th century were so large that they may well fit the broad (if not the narrow) definition of *paradigm shifts* outlined in Kuhn's (1970) *The Structure of Scientific Revolutions*.

PSYCHOLOGY'S ANTECEDENT, INTELLECTUAL PHILOSOPHY[3]

During the first half of the 19th century, most American colleges included among their courses one most commonly called "Intellectual Phi-

---

[2]This cumbersome term means that the Johns Hopkins psychology laboratory was not an official laboratory insofar as the University was concerned, in contrast with Johns Hopkins laboratories in biology, chemistry, and physics. Hall was allowed to establish a laboratory but was specifically forbidden to refer to it as such.

[3]I thank Rand B. Evans for supplying most of this section.

losophy" (e.g., *HUCat*,[4] 1825, p. 21). Other titles included "Moral Philosophy," "Mental Philosophy," and "Mental Science." It was from courses such as these that psychology and other social sciences evolved (Bryson, 1932; Evans, 1984).[5]

Intellectual philosophy was usually taught during the senior year, often by the college president. Until well into the second half of the 19th century, most college presidents were clergymen. This generalization held even for state-supported institutions. Early on, the course often had strongly religious and moral purposes. It was a capstone course designed to prepare the student for life in the world outside of the college.

In the late 18th and early 19th centuries, natural sciences had begun their separation from philosophy under the titles "Natural History" (which later became separated into zoology and geology) and "Natural Philosophy" (later physics), although both courses were still common well into the 19th century. The subject matters that were to become psychology, however, were still connected to their philosophical and even theological apron strings, but things began to change during the second decade of the 19th century.

We can precisely date the arrival of philosophical psychology in America. Jerimiah Dummer (1679–1739; the colonial agent for Connecticut in England) solicited aid, including some 900 books for the newly established (1701) Collegiate School, then located in Saybrook, Connecticut. Among the books sent in 1714 were those of the core authors of Britain's Enlightenment (e.g., Francis Bacon [1561–1626], Isaac Newton [1642–1727], and John Locke [1632–1704]). The copy of Locke's *Essay Concerning Human Understanding* (1690) was contributed by Elihu Yale (1649–1721), the Boston-born but English-raised East India Company official for whose substantial gifts the Collegiate School was renamed Yale College in 1718. Yale's copy of Locke was apparently the first in America and directly influenced the thought of several individuals, including two Yale graduates, Samuel Johnson (1696–1772)[6] and Jonathan Edwards (1703–1758), who

---

[4]In the case of university catalogues and annual reports, the following notation will be used: an abbreviation consisting of the institution's initials, such as HU for Harvard University or JHU for Johns Hopkins University, and either Cat for catalogue or Rep for report, plus the year and page numbers (e.g., *HUCat*, 1875–76, p. 77; or *JHURep*, 1885, p. 22). In the case of reports, words such as "annual" or "biennial," or their synonyms, will be omitted. Johns Hopkins has two frequently cited publications, the *Register* and the *Circulars*, that will be abbreviated as *JHUReg* and *JHUCir*. Much of the biographical and chronological material has come from the *Dictionary of American Biography*, *Who Was Who in America*, and the *Dictionary of Scientific Biography*. In the interest of saving trees, they will not be cited.
[5]How long such courses remained in curricula is not known, but Lynchburg College had "Logic, Moral Philosophy and Ethics" as late as 1909–10 (Lynchburg College, 1989).
[6]This is Samuel Johnson of Connecticut, later president of Kings College, now Columbia. He is not to be confused with the English Samuel Johnson of Boswell's biography.

were to be forces in America's "new learning" in general, and philosophical psychological thought in particular, during the 18th century (Ellis, 1973; Evans, 1984). Locke's *Essay* would be immensely influential in the development of the structure of courses dealing with the study of the human mind (Evans, 1984, pp. 22–26).

Locke's *Essay* began to lose favor in the early part of the 19th century because of the influence of the writings of Thomas Reid and other members of the Scottish realist school of philosophy. Their books were first imported by and used in the new colleges set up across America by the Presbyterian Church, then elsewhere.[7] The contents of Reid's *Essays on the Intellectual Powers of Man* (1785) and *Essays on the Active Powers of the Human Mind* (1788) are almost completely psychological (Evans, 1984, p. 38). Courses in American colleges grew to be organized around the contents of the texts used (Snow, 1907, p. 129).

By the second decade of the 19th century, American professors who taught mental philosophy and intellectual philosophy courses began to work up their class notes and to publish them as their own textbooks. Thomas Upham (1799–1872) of Bowdoin College in the frontier of Maine published one of the most successful of these under the title *Elements of Intellectual Philosophy* (1826). Upham's book, later expanded and renamed *Elements of Mental Philosophy* (1831), was used widely in American colleges well into the 1870s. Other popular and influential authors of intellectual and mental philosophies included Francis Wayland (1799–1865) of Brown University, Joseph Haven (1816–1874) of Amherst Colege and the Chicago Theological Seminary, and Noah Porter (1811–1892) of Yale. These authors were all influenced more or less by the Scottish realists, but their books were often genuinely eclectic, drawing from European as well as British authors. Later, writers like Laurens P. Hickok (1798–1888) would introduce the German idealist position (Hickok, 1848, 1854).

EARLY PSYCHOLOGY TEXTS

It was apparently because of texts used in these early intellectual philosophy courses that the term *psychology* began to replace the term *intellectual philosophy*. Fay (1939/1966), who identified and discussed early

---

[7]Only nine colleges founded between Harvard in 1636 and the American Revolution survived to 1930 (Tewksberry, 1932). Six of those were under the control of Presbyterians. By 1851, two thirds of the permanent colleges in the United States were directly or indirectly under the control of Presbyterians (Evans, 1984, p. 33; Tewksberry, 1932, pp. 58, 60, 92). Later, the efforts of other denominations and the increase of state-supported colleges and universities reduced the percentage of Presbyterian-related institutions.

texts and their authors, claimed that the first text published in the United States, indeed in the English language, to include the word *psychology* in its title was *Psychology, or a View of the Human Soul, Including Anthropology* published in 1840 by Frederick A. Rauch (1806–1841), founder and president of Marshall College (1836–1841), now Franklin and Marshall College. Rauch had come to the United States from the University of Heidelberg, where he had been a professor. His book was written from a Hegelian perspective.

However, in 1834, Caleb Sprague Henry (1804–1884) published *Cousin's Elements of Psychology: Included in a Critical Examination of Locke's Essay on the Human Understanding, and in Additional Pieces*. Victor Cousin (1792–1867) was a French philosopher and historian. Henry was a Congregational and Episcopalian minister and subsequently a—probably *the*—professor of philosophy at Bristol University (a no-longer-extant institution, near Philadelphia) and later at New York University. Presumably, Henry used his text at Bristol and New York Universities. Henry's, rather than Rauch's, appears to be the earliest book published in the United States that contains the word *psychology* (Vande Kempe, 1983).

The use of the terms *mental philosophy* and *intellectual philosophy* remained dominant, however, until after the time of the American Civil War.

THE HIGHER EDUCATION BACKGROUND

Psychology, under such terms as *intellectual philosophy*, *mental philosophy*, and *mental science*, was well established in the undergraduate curriculum by the mid-19th century. Over the next few decades, the term *psychology* began to replace the older terms, but the development of psychology as an independent discipline had to await the development of a graduate educational framework.

Early 19th-Century Higher Education

At the beginning of the 19th century, the university in the modern sense had not yet developed. The contrast between the early 19th-century American college and today's university may be seen by a brief look at Harvard College in 1837–38. In 1837, Harvard College had 10 professorships (4 of which were vacant that year) and 4 tutors (a tutor was assigned to an entering class of students and remained with that class through graduation). In 1837, there were 219 undergraduate students and a single "resident graduate." An additional 172 students were enrolled in Harvard's professional schools: Divinity, Law, and Medical, each with its own faculty. By the standards of the time, Harvard was a large institution.

In 1837–38, all courses at Harvard College were prescribed.[8] The small size of colleges during this time meant that their organizational structure was quite different from that of today's much larger institutions. Because there was often only a single professor in an academic area, there was no concept of a department, nor usually any rank other than professor. In 1837–38, only one member of the Harvard faculty held a PhD degree[9]; all other Harvard College faculty held master of arts degrees, which at the time were "good conduct," not earned, degrees.

Harvard in 1837–38 was not markedly different from Harvard in 1801–02, but things soon began to change. Electives became a permanent part of the curriculum in 1841–42 during the last part of the administration (1829–1845) of Josiah Quincy (1771–1864), and Harvard's first earned master's degrees were awarded in 1869.

Graduate Work

The movement toward graduate education in America deserves particular attention. Prior to the American Revolution, graduate education was minimal in America. Medical instruction began in 1765 at the College of Philadelphia (now the University of Pennsylvania) and in 1767 at King's College (now Columbia University). Before the American Revolution, colonists looked to Europe for medical education, and it was well into the 19th century before American institutions turned out large numbers of medical doctorates. By then, however, Americans had begun to look to Europe for advanced training in nonmedical areas, particularly the arts and sciences.[10] Thus, as the century went on, increasing numbers of Americans went to Europe for graduate training in the arts and sciences, and as the value of the PhD began to be appreciated, American institutions began to think of offering graduate training here.

As was the case at Harvard, most graduate degrees granted during the first three quarters of the 19th century in American colleges were unearned

---

[8]However, earlier, during the administration (1810–1828) of John Thornton Kirkland (1770–1840), electives had been introduced.

[9]*PhD* was then abbreviated *P.D.* This was the Professor of Latin, Charles Beck (1798–1866), whose doctoral degree had been awarded in 1823 by the University of Tübingen.

[10]Edward Everett (1794–1865; Harvard, B.A., 1811) was the first American to earn a European PhD (in Göttingen, 1817). He was also the first American-born Harvard faculty member (1815–26) to hold this degree. He later became Harvard's president (1846–49).

"good conduct" degrees. The conditions for awarding the master of arts degree at Harvard, for example, were as follows:

> The Degree of Master of Arts is conferred in course, on the payment of the usual fee, on every Bachelor of Arts of three years' standing, who shall, in the interval, have sustained a good moral character. Graduates of longer standing many also have the Master's Degree upon the same condition. In both cases, application should be made at the Steward's office, either personally or by letter, as soon as the second day before Commencement. The fee, including the Diploma, is five dollars, payable in advance (*HUCat*, 1869–70, p. 47).

(Apparently, 3 years of good conduct were not enough to establish credit at Harvard!)

The 1847–48 Yale *Catalogue* announced the formation of a new "Department of Philosophy and the Arts," or in today's terminology, a "Graduate School of Arts and Sciences." The Yale "Department" was intended to provide "resident graduates and others, with the opportunity of devoting themselves to special branches of study either not provided for at present, or not pursued as far as individual students may desire" (*YUCat*, 1847–48, p. 42). It was to be over a decade before Yale awarded the PhD degree, however.

The first PhD degree to be awarded in the United States was granted in 1851 by the University at Lewisburg (Bucknell University since 1886), but the degree was an honorary one. Honorary PhD degrees were routinely awarded until late in the 19th century.[11]

In 1861, Yale was the first institution to award earned PhD degrees. Of the first three PhD degrees awarded, one was in philosophy and psychology. Soon other institutions began to offer PhD degrees: New York University awarded a PhD in 1866, the University of Pennsylvania in 1871, and Cornell University in 1872. Harvard announced its Doctor of Philosophy and Doctor of Science programs in the spring of 1872 and a year later awarded two PhDs and one ScD degree.

The transition from undergraduate to graduate training was hardly dramatic. For example, Harvard did not announce any new courses in conjunction with the doctoral degrees; the requirements for the PhD included passing a "thorough examination" on the chosen course of study and writing a "satisfactory thesis" (*HUCat*, 1871–72, 2nd ed., p. 110).

STATUS OF PSYCHOLOGY IN ACADEMIC CURRICULA

The first appearance of a course titled "Psychology" in an American college or university was in 1840 at Marshall College. The title of the course

---

[11]The fifth President of the APA, G. S. Fullerton, received an honorary PhD from Muhlenberg in 1892. (For a history of academic degrees, see Eells, 1963.)

had been changed by its teacher, Frederich Augustus Rauch, from "Intellectual Philosophy." Rauch, as mentioned previously, had just published his lectures for the course under the title *Psychology; or, A View of the Human Soul, Including Anthropology* (Rauch, 1840) in the same year. Rauch was German and the use of the term *Psychologie* in Germany was quite common in the 1830s.

First Graduate Work and PhD Involving Psychology

As noted earlier, in 1847 Yale began a new "Department of Philosophy and the Arts." Included among the descriptions of the new "Department's" faculty members' areas of specialization was the following: "Professor Porter will instruct in Psychology, Logic and the History of Philosophy" (*YUCat*, 1847–48, p. 43). In other words, graduate work in psychology was available at Yale starting in 1847–48 (no graduate courses were listed for any discipline until 1886–87). The opportunity for graduate work in psychology at Yale in 1847–48 was the first in the country, albeit in the preexperimental, philosophical psychology (the first opportunity for graduate work in the "new" Fechnerian–Wundtian psychology would be at Harvard in 1875–76, as discussed later). The opportunity for graduate work in psychology at Yale was to expand into the opportunity for doctoral work beginning in the 1860–61 year, as mentioned earlier.

The "Professor Porter" of the 1847–48 Yale announcement was Noah Porter (1811–1892), a Congregational minister, Professor of Moral Philosophy and Metaphysics, and, later, president of Yale (1871–86). Porter had joined the Yale faculty only one year prior to the announcement of the formation of Yale's Department of Philosophy and the Arts.

Porter had spent half a year in 1853 in Europe studying with Adolf Trendelenberg (1802–1872), who also taught John Dewey (1859–1952) and Franz Brentano (1838–1917; see Evans, 1984; Fay, 1939/1966). He presented a British psychology mixed with German idealism. Presumably, it was Porter who supplied the term *psychology* in the description of his offerings, which remained in the Yale catalogue until 1881–82.

As discussed earlier, in 1861 Yale became the first American institution to grant earned PhD degrees. That PhD in "Philosophy and Psychology" (Rosenberg, 1961) was for Eugene Schuyler (1840–1890), but no copy of Schuyler's dissertation is extant, and even its title is unknown (Rosenberg, 1961). Schuyler had received his Yale bachelor of arts only 2 years previously. Schuyler must have done his graduate work under Noah Porter, because there was no other philosopher or psychologist at Yale until the arrival in 1881 of George T. Ladd (1842–1921; *YUCat*, 1881–82, p. 50). Some years after Ladd's arrival, Yale awarded, in 1889, a PhD that was unambiguously for work in psychology to William O. Krohn (1868–1927), one of the 26 original APA members. Ladd, whose initial title was Professor of Mental and Moral Philosophy, was a genuinely transitional figure in American psychology, publishing the first psychological textbook influenced by Wundt's new psychology, *Elements of Physiological Psychology* (Ladd, 1887). He would later be influential in the establishment of Yale's laboratory of psychology under the direction of E. W. Scripture (1864–1945).

Harvard and the Progress of Psychology

In 1839–40, James Walker (1794–1874), who had just become the Alford Professor of Natural Religion, Moral Philosophy, and Civil Polity at Harvard, used both Henry's English translation of *Cousin's Elements* and Locke's *Essay* in one of his courses. Walker subsequently edited two widely used philosophical psychology texts. One, which appeared in 1850, was an edition of Thomas Reid's *Essays on the Intellectual Powers of Man*, in which the opening sentence of Walker's preface specifically referred to Reid's "psychology." Perhaps Henry's *Cousin's Elements of Psychology* had sensitized Walker to the term *psychology*. Regardless of the source, Walker was, by 1850 at least, differentiating between the usual philosophical terminology of his day and *psychology*. Walker's other edited work was *Elements of the Philosophy of the Human Mind* by Dugald Stewart (1753–1828), which appeared in 1854.

It was probably Walker who was responsible for labeling a course "Psychology" in the 1850–51 Harvard *Catalogue's* "Tabular View of the Hours of Recitations and Lectures" (pp. 45–47). The text for this junior-year course was Reid's *Essays*, presumably the edition Walker had just edited. Walker clearly recognized that psychology was a different branch of philosophy than intellectual philosophy. For the second term of the academic year, the "Tabular View" lists "Intellectual Philos[ophy]" as meeting for 2 days a week for seniors. For this course, the texts were *Analogy* by Samuel Butler (1835–1902), of *Erehwon* fame, and *Evidences of Christianity* by William Paley (1743–1805). The separate listings and the different texts for the two courses show unmistakably that Walker differentiated psychology from intellectual philosophy. Walker continued to teach these two courses (and others) until he became president of Harvard in 1853.[12]

Walker was replaced in the Alford chair by Francis Bowen (1811–1890), who held it until 1889. Presumably, it was Bowen who was re-

---

[12]The "Tabular View" continued as above through the 1855–56 year. Starting in 1856–57, the entries were simply "Phil." or "Philos." I, II, or III; "Logic" was listed separately (*HUCat*, 1856–57, First Term, pp. 34–35).

sponsible for the terminological change from *psychology* back to *intellectual philosophy*. Bowen was a strong supporter of the philosophy of Sir William Hamilton, and his "Philosophy 1" course was almost entirely psychological, albeit philosophical psychology. As we will see below, Bowen would rename his course as "Psychology" again in 1872. Bowen's philosophy courses were in Harvard College, the arts and letters curriculum, but outside of the Harvard College curriculum, psychology made a slightly earlier appearance at Harvard.

Charles W. Eliot (1834–1926) became president of Harvard in 1869. Eliot had taught mathematics and chemistry at Harvard in the Lawrence Scientific School and chemistry at the Massachusetts Institute of Technology for a number of years. His goal, which was successful, was to change the character of Harvard. One of his chief interests was to increase the course offerings beyond those required for the baccalaureate degree. For the 1870–71 year, Eliot greatly expanded the "University Lectures" that had been started in 1863–64 during the administration of his predecessor, Thomas Hill (1818–1891). The 1870–71 University Lectures were "intended for graduates of colleges, teachers, and other competent adults (men or women)" (*HUCat*, 1870–71, p. 108).

Among the University Lectures for 1870–71 was a series taught by Chauncey Wright (1830–1875). Wright was recognized by his contemporaries as a powerful thinker and was among the leading expositors of the Darwinian position in America. Vocationally, however, he was a mathematician employed to do calculations for the *American Ephemeris and Nautical Almanac*.[13] Wright was also the leader of the "Cambridge Metaphysical Club" (see Fisch, 1964; Wiener, 1949), where he importantly influenced two younger members who played large roles in the early history of American psychology, Charles S. Peirce (1839–1914) and William James (1842–1910). The title of Wright's 1870–71 lecture series was "Expositions of the Principles of Psychology From the Text of Bain" (*HUCat*, 1870–71, p. 109). Alexander Bain (1818–1903),[14] a Scot, and his English contemporary Herbert Spencer (1820–1903) held transitional positions in Britain in the history of psychology between the philosophical psychologists in the tradition of Locke, Reid, and Porter and the experimental psychologists in the tradition of Fechner and Wundt.

Wright's Harvard lectures can be seen as moving away from the older

---

[13]He was later given a 1-year appointment as an Instructor in Physics at Harvard (*HUCat*, 1874–75, p. 17).

[14]Bain's major works were *The Senses and the Intellect* (1855), *The Emotions and the Will* (1859), and *Mental Science: A Compendium of Psychology, and the History of Philosophy, Designed as a Text-book for High-Schools and Colleges* (1868). The former two works were later used by William James (*HUCat*, 1878–79, p. 80). The last work was also to be used at Harvard both by the philosopher George Herbert Palmer (*HUCat*, 1873–74, p. 77) and by William James (*HUCat*, 1880–81, p. 82). For more on Wright, see Madden (1963).

philosophical psychologists. Moreover, he was chosen from outside of the members of Harvard College's philosophy "Department." In retrospect, the hiring of an "outsider," particularly one identified with science, to teach psychology was perhaps a harbinger of things to come in the not-too-distant future at Harvard and, subsequently, elsewhere.

Although Wright's Harvard lectures were apart from Harvard College, it was only 2 years later, in 1872, that Francis Bowen would rename his "Philosophy 1" course "Psychology" (*HUCat*, 1872–73, p. 69). The Harvard *Catalogue* entry reads, "Psychology. Locke's essay on the Human Understanding (Selections). Cousin, Philosophie Sensualiste and Philosophie de Locke. Taine, de l'Inteligence. Lectures" (p. 114). It is clear from the texts used that Bowen's "Psychology" was still the old, philosophic psychology under the new name (although William James would also use the English translation of Taine in his early courses). This course in philosophical psychology called "Psychology" continued to be offered, with some variation in the texts and instructors, through the 1877–78 year (*HUCat*, 1877–78, p. 78), when it was taught by George Herbert Palmer. The most significant change regarding psychology at Harvard would come by way of William James, then in the Lawrence Scientific School.

THE FECHNERIAN–WUNDTIAN REVOLUTION COMES TO AMERICA

Harvard was introduced to the "new" experimental psychology of Fechner and Wundt in William James's famous course, "The Relations Between Physiology and Psychology," first offered in the fall term of 1875. This was the first course taught in this country to include the "new" psychology of Fechner and Wundt. James taught this course through the 1877–78 school year. From 1876–77 to 1879–80, James also offered an undergraduate elective course called "Physiological Psychology" in which he used as his text Herbert Spencer's *Principles of Psychology* (1855). Both of these courses were offered in Harvard's "Department" of Natural History in the Lawrence School of Science.

In 1878, over the objections of Francis Bowen, James began to give a course titled "Psychology" in the "Department" of Philosophy of Harvard College. James's text was Taine's (1871) *On Intelligence*, and his course was an elective. The prescribed course for juniors was still the old philosophical psychology course that used Locke's *Essay Concerning Human Understanding* as the text (the instructor was George H. Palmer). James's new course was to foreshadow a shift in his departmental affiliation.

The 1878–79 year showed an important curricular change. James's graduate course, "The Relations Between Physiology and Psychology," was renamed "Physiological Psychology" and was listed along with courses in the Philosophy "Department" rather than with those in the Natural History "Department."

James or Peirce?

One of the major myths in the history of American psychology is that it was William James (1842–1910) who introduced Fechnerian–Wundtian psychology to the United States. For example, Boring (1950) wrote, "James began psychology in America with his recognition of the significance of the new experimental physiological psychology of Germany" (p. 505). To write about the "old" psychology, Fay (1939/1966) titled his book *American Psychology Before William James.* James, however, did not mention Fechner or Wundt in print until early in 1875 in a note in *The Nation* (1875a). For the real introduction of the new psychology to America, we must turn to Charles S. Peirce.

It was in the March 18, 1869, issue of *The Nation* that Fechnerian–Wundtian psychology was introduced to the United States in Charles S. Peirce's (1839–1914) review of Noah Porter's *The Human Intellect* (Peirce, 1869a). Peirce lamented the absence of a treatment of the works of Fechner, Wundt, and others "whose investigations may truly be said to be of more value than all the others put together" (p. 212). In another review, Peirce (1869b) said much the same.

It is clear that Peirce recognized Wundt's importance. In an 1869 letter, Wundt granted Peirce's request (no longer extant) for translation rights to one of Wundt's books.[15] As late as 1896, Peirce unsuccessfully attempted to find a publisher for translations of two unspecified Wundt books (Peirce Papers, L 95, Harvard University).

Peirce is well known as the "father" of pragmatism, James's philosophical mentor, and America's greatest philosopher. Only recently has his role in 19th-century psychology been appreciated (Cadwallader, 1974, 1975). In 1875, Peirce obtained two grants from the National Academy of Sciences (1889, p. 317), to which he was elected in 1877 as an astronomer and physicist. One of the grants was for the study of color; the other was for the comparison of sensations. These may be the world's first grants for psychological research. The results were published in 1877, and they are

---

[15]This letter, designated L 478 (Robin, 1967), is among the Peirce Papers in Harvard University's Houghton Library. No letter to a publisher or translation has been located.

probably the first psychophysical research published in the United States (Cadwallader, 1974). During the early 1870s, Peirce was the only person in the United States *doing* the "new" experimental psychology.

In 1875, Peirce was joined in psychology by his younger friend and protégé, William James. Prior to that date, James was really a physiologist; his only academic degree was an M.D. received in 1869. During the next three years, James suffered from his longest and most famous depression (Perry, 1935, Chap. 19). In the spring of 1873, James taught the physiology portion of a Harvard course, "Comparative Anatomy and Physiology"; he took over the entire course in 1875, after a year in Europe. Copies of some of James's exams from these two courses, as well as those of Thomas Waterman, Jr. (d. 1901), another M.D. who taught the course in 1873–74, when James was in Europe, have been preserved in the Harvard Archives. James's exams are indistinguishable from those of Waterman; both sets of exams were written from the perspective of physiologists, not psychologists.

Prior to 1875, James's publications consisted only of book reviews and occasional "notices" of persons or events, similar to that concerning Wundt (James, 1875a) discussed in the following paragraph. Through these early publications, one can see the development of James's general interests, particularly psychology. His reviews showed three lines of interest in psychological subjects: abnormal psychology (James, 1868, 1873, 1874), parapsychology (1869), and general psychology (1872).

The June 3, 1875, issue of *The Nation* contained a short note by James concerning "two recent appointments in the University of Zurich. One is that of Professor W. Wundt to the chair of philosophy" (James, 1875a, p. 377). The other appointment was of Edward Hitzig (1838–1907), well known for his research with Gustav Fritsch (1838–1927) showing the electrical excitability of cortex. James devoted most of the note to Wundt. He wrote, "Wundt is one of the most learned of German investigators. His own special work has lain most in the line of the senses and in the nervous system, the territory common to mind and matter; and all the elements of his training hitherto unite to make him an eminently well-qualified teacher of mental science" (James, 1875a, p. 377). In the July 1875 *North American Review*, James (1875b) reviewed at length Wundt's recently published *Principles of Physiological Psychology* (Wundt, 1874). James noted that a "new era" in psychology was dawning in Germany. Not only did he review and comment on Wundt and compare him to other writers, but he also voiced his own opinions, some of which would eventually appear in his own *Principles of Psychology*, which appeared 15 years later.

James's 1875–76 and subsequent courses show his shift from physiology to psychology, and so too did his mid-1875 and subsequent publications.

Many of James's post-1875 reviews, and also his short article "The Teaching of Philosophy in our Colleges," published in 1876, show the effects of his recent interest in the "new" psychology. By 1878, he was beginning to publish important psychology papers (e.g., "Brute and Human Intellect" and, by 1879, the seminal papers "Are We Automata" and "The Spatial Quale"). And it was in June of 1878 that James signed the contract for the *Principles of Psychology* (1890). In that same June, G. Stanley Hall received the world's first PhD in psychology from Harvard under James.

Thus, it is clear that, for James, 1875 marked a turning point toward the "new" psychology. Why was 1875 critical in the making of James the psychologist? The answer is clear: James read Wundt's *Physiological Psychology*, and he was convinced, as he had earlier suspected (Perry, 1935, Vol. 1, Chap. 14), that Wundt was on the right track. Although he was later to become disenchanted with Wundt (see Perry, 1935, for the evolution of James's views toward Wundt), in 1875 James saw him as showing the way psychology was to go, and he also saw then, as noted in his review of Wundt, that psychology was "the antechamber to metaphysics" (James, 1875b, p. 195). Such a statement was interestingly prophetical because after James finished *The Principles of Psychology* (1890) and *Psychology* (the "Briefer Course," 1892), he entered the halls of metaphysics and virtually abandoned its "antechamber." One could thus argue that 1875 not only marked James's movement into the "new" psychology, but also foreshadowed his subsequent shift to philosophy proper.

PSYCHOLOGICAL LABORATORIES

The shift in subject matter from philosophical to experimental psychology did not in itself begin the separation of psychology from philosophy, but it brought about the establishment of laboratories. The appearance of laboratories, whether instructional or research in orientation, clearly drew the line between the philosophical psychologists and the new, experimental psychologists.

Harvard

James's 1875–76 course was notable because it had a demonstration laboratory; and soon afterwards, students had hands-on laboratory experience, and James had a small research space from probably 1877 onward

(Harper, 1949, 1950). G. Stanley Hall, who worked with James during 1876–78, also recalled James's research space (Hall, 1923, p. 218).

James published one experiment during this period, "The Sense of Dizziness in Deaf-Mutes" (James, 1882). He had earlier abandoned a line of investigation on the role of the semicircular canals in frogs, as he noted in a footnote to a review published in 1880. Thus, James obviously had some laboratory facilities during the second half of the 1870s; his formal research laboratory would come in the 1880s.

On November 20, 1883, James wrote to the Harvard Corporation (i.e., trustees) asking for the assignment of "a small room to serve as a workshop for the psychological department," for funds ($300) for equipment, and for continued funding. James wanted work space for advanced students and for "the professor" (Box 262, "Official Papers," Charles W. Eliot Papers, Harvard University Archives). The next month, James's request for funds was approved and even increased to $400, but no space was assigned. (Harvard Corporation Minutes, Vol. 13, p. 263). It was only in the spring of 1885 that the Corporation voted to assign and equip two rooms in Lawrence Hall for psychology (Harvard Corporation Minutes, Vol. 13, p. 352).

Beginning with the fall 1885 Harvard *Catalogue*, James's "Advanced Psychology" course ("Philosophy 9") was changed to "Philosophy 9. Special Advanced Study and Experimental Research in Psychology. Mon. 3–5" (p. 95). Additional information about the course was given under "Courses of Instruction" in the report of the Dean of Harvard College (dated December 16, 1886), where it was noted that in addition to "Lectures and theses . . . Laboratory work (about three hours a week)" was also involved (*HURep*, 1885–86, p. 50).

Although the Lawrence Hall Psychology Laboratory never became a very productive laboratory (Harvard turned out no psychology PhDs between Hall in 1878 and Hugo Münsterberg's arrival in 1892), at least two studies may have emanated from it (Delabarre, 1889a, 1889b). These two studies contained footnotes saying they were "Read at" or "Written for the Graduate Course in Psychology at Harvard." In addition to these two studies by Delabarre, it is also possible that Delabarre's observations, referred to in the material he wrote for Volume 2 of James's *Principles of Psychology* (1890, Vol. 2, pp. 13–27; pp. 662–674 of Vol. 2 of the 1981 reprinting), were carried out in the Lawrence Hall Psychology Laboratory.

Although Harvard has long been recognized as having the country's first informal psychology laboratory, recognition should also be given for its having the country's first "institutionally" or "trustee-sanctioned" psychology laboratory, the fall 1885 Lawrence Hall Psychology Laboratory.

Princeton

Princeton University (the College of New Jersey until 1896) was the Scots' intellectual beachhead in America (see Evans, 1984). James McCosh (1811–1894) came from Scotland to Princeton as president in 1868. Although a staunch supporter of the by-then old-fashioned realist philosophy, McCosh was open to new ideas. He himself reported that in 1881 "half a dozen of the younger officers formed a club to study Wundt's work on physiological psychology, and his anatomical experiments were repeated by skillful anatomists with a well-prepared apparatus" (McCosh, 1882).

James Mark Baldwin (1861–1934), later of Johns Hopkins University, earned an A.B. from Princeton in 1884 and, after a semester with Wundt and some teaching, a Princeton PhD in 1887 (Princeton University, 1908). Baldwin later recalled his student days with McCosh:

> McCosh . . . had seized upon the project of scientific psychology as announced in Wundt's Physiologische Psychologie, then just out. . . . Furthermore, I was brought into the circle of interest through the tradition of a course of readings in Wundt, arranged by McCosh, with the demonstrations given by W. B. Scott and H. F. Osborn, young members of the Princeton faculty. (Baldwin, 1930)

In the fall of 1883, Princeton offered a new, one-semester course, "Physiological Psychology." McCosh gave the general lectures; Henry F. Osborn (1857–1935), then a just-promoted professor of comparative anatomy, lectured on the structure of the nervous system; and William B. Scott (1858–1947), then a just-promoted professor of geology, lectured on the physiology of the nervous system. The course description noted that "simple anatomical demonstrations accompany the course" (College of New Jersey *Catalogue*, 1883–84, p. 45).

Starting in 1886–87, only Osborn and Scott were involved; the course material previously offered by McCosh was omitted. For the first time, the catalogue statement included the following: "The demonstrations accompany a laboratory course of practical study and dissection of the brain and examination of microscopic preparations" (Osborn's portion) and "Experiments illustrating nerve action of different kinds accompany this portion of the course" (*CNJCat*, 1886–87, pp. 51–52). This undergraduate course continued into the 1890s. Despite Baldwin's 1887 PhD, no graduate courses in psychology are found in the College of New Jersey *Catalogue* during this period, although courses in philosophy are.

It was at Johns Hopkins, however, that the new laboratory psychology made its most significant impact.

Psychology and Hall's Laboratories at Johns Hopkins University

Perhaps the most important influence on American higher education during the 19th century was the establishment of Johns Hopkins University in 1876. The first president of the new institution was Daniel Coit Gilman (1831–1908), who had been president of the University of California since 1872, although he had previously been chiefly responsible for planning Yale's Sheffield Scientific School, in which he had been Professor of Physical and Political Geography. Gilman was recognized as a leading authority on scientific, technical, and agricultural colleges, and he had surveyed such institutions for the U.S. Commissioner of Education.

Gilman accepted the Johns Hopkins presidency with the understanding that the University would focus on research and graduate training. In May of 1875, Gilman assumed his responsibilities. He and the trustees then turned to locating in both Europe and the United States individuals who would constitute a small, but highly research-oriented, faculty. Gilman's plan was to establish a few first-rate "departments," each with an individual who was already outstanding, or who showed great promise to become so, as professor. The professors were to be assisted by fellows or associates, following the German university model. The sciences and mathematics were prominent in Gilman's plans. An eminent mathematician, the Englishman James J. Sylvester (1814–1897), was recruited as a professor, and laboratories in biology, chemistry, and physics were established.

Instruction began in early October of 1876 with much fanfare. Almost overnight, Johns Hopkins came to be regarded as the leading American university with respect to research and graduate training (Hawkins, 1960; Ryan, 1939; Veysey, 1965). The institutions known today as the leading research institutions followed Hopkins in this direction during the last quarter of the 19th century. Clark University was clearly founded (in 1889) on the model provided by Johns Hopkins, and the "new" University of Chicago (founded in 1892 after the demise of the "old" one in 1886) was also strongly influenced by Johns Hopkins.

By the end of the 19th century, the direction of American higher education had been permanently changed; research and doctoral training was the unquestioned benchmark of a *university*.

Psychology at Hopkins

One notable area of instruction that was missing in 1876 was that of philosophy, which then, of course, encompassed psychology. As early as

1877, however, there was a description of what today would be called a "premed course," prominently including "psychology" as a component (Johns Hopkins University *Official Circulars*, No. 11, June 1877, pp. 1–2).

This and other early announcements spread word about the orientation of the institution and led to a flood of letters of faculty application and nomination. By April 1, 1876, 198 applications had been received (Hawkins, 1960, p. 39). In November of 1875, William James wrote to Gilman strongly endorsing Peirce for, as James put it, "the Chair or Chairs of Logic & Mental Science" (quoted in Fisch & Cope, 1952, p. 363).

In September of 1877, Peirce wrote to Gilman concerning James "for the chair of psychology in the Johns Hopkins University." Peirce, noting that he himself had "made a somewhat profound study of some subjects kindred to psychology," ventured the opinion that

> Every science, before it was a real science, was a theater for empty talk and metaphysical nonsense. Psychology has just left this stage, and is just entering the scientific stage. (quoted in Cope, 1951, p. 615)

In February of 1878, James was invited, and he delivered a series of 10 lectures on psychology at Johns Hopkins under the heading "The Senses and the Brain, and Their Relation to Thought" (*JHUCir*, 1877–78, p. 12).[16]

A month earlier, in January 1878, Johns Hopkins had begun to repair the lack of philosophic courses. George S. Morris (1840–1889), then professor of modern literature at the University of Michigan (but aspiring to a chair in philosophy), gave 20 lectures at Johns Hopkins on the "History of Philosophy" (*JHUReg*, 1877–78, p. 13). A year later, in January 1879, Morris gave 10 more lectures, this time on ethics (*JHUReg*, 1878–79, p. 19).

In February of 1879, James once again wrote to President Gilman concerning a possible appointment in psychology at Johns Hopkins. He again mentioned Peirce and, for the first time, G. Stanley Hall:

> In the psychological line proper, the only workers I know of are Peirce and Hall. Peirce's drawbacks you know. Hall, although a thoroughly original and able worker, is perhaps deficient in the practical and organizing qualities which the J.H.U. especially needs *now* in its professors. (quoted in Cope, 1951, p. 621)

In February of 1879 Hall had recently (the year before) received his PhD in psychology from Harvard. He was then in Germany, where he had

---

[16]This was to be James's only official connection with Johns Hopkins. For James's on-again, off-again interest in a position at Johns Hopkins, see Cope (1951).

gone late in the summer of 1878, first to Berlin and then to Leipzig (Ross, 1972, pp. 80–99), where he became Wundt's first American student. However, Hall did most of his work in other laboratories, notably that of the physiologist Carl Ludwig (1816–1895). He did not return to the United States until the fall of 1880.

In 1878, President Gilman and Peirce discussed the possibility of Peirce being named to a second professorship of physics, but Peirce subsequently said that what he really wanted was an appointment in Logic (Fisch & Cope, 1952). Peirce was appointed Lecturer in Logic on a half-time basis for both terms of the 1879–80 year and was subsequently reappointed through the end of the 1883–84 year. George S. Morris was hired for one full-time term each year, starting in the spring of 1880, and was subsequently reappointed. He last taught in the fall term of 1884–85 (JHUCir, 1884–85, 4, pp. 7, 73).

After Peirce began to teach logic (and also mathematics) at Hopkins, he included much psychology in his teaching, as extant lecture notes show (Ms. 745, Peirce Papers). His publications from this period contained considerable psychological material, regardless of their main subject (e.g., Peirce, 1880).

In addition to logic, Peirce was considered to be in charge of psychology. Under Peirce's leadership, psychology was formally introduced into the Hopkins curriculum in the fall of 1880 (JHUCir, 1879–82, 1, 76) by Allan Marquand (1853–1924), who had received his PhD in logic under Peirce the preceding June and who was a "Fellow-by-Courtesy" during 1880–81.[17]

The second course in psychology was given in the fall semester of 1881 (JHUCir, 1879–82, 1, 157) by Benjamin E. Smith (1857–1913), who was an "Instructor in Mental and Moral Philosophy" (JHUCir, 1879–82, 1, 169) and who is said to have studied with Wundt (Genzmer, 1937). This latter claim is corroborated to some extent by his Metaphysical Club paper "Wundt's Theory of Volition" (JHUCir, 1879–82, 1, 209). Both Marquand's and Smith's courses in psychology at Hopkins were taught before Hall's first appearance there in January of 1882.

Peirce also established the research tradition in psychology at Hopkins: It was Peirce, working with Joseph Jastrow (1863–1944), who did the first psychological research at Hopkins. Jastrow told the story in unambiguous terms in his autobiography:

---

[17]Among the Marquand Papers at Princeton are what appear to be lecture notes for a course in physiological psychology. Marquand received a copy of Wundt's *Principles of Physiological Psychology* on February 26, 1881, just after his semester's teaching assignment was completed.

The first psychological investigation made at Johns Hopkins University was likewise undertaken at Peirce's suggestion. . . . we participated equally as subject and observer. (Jastrow, 1930, pp. 135–136)

The paper by Peirce and Jastrow, "On Small Differences of Sensation," was published in the *Memoirs of the National Academy of Sciences* in 1884 (Peirce & Jastrow, 1884).

Hall at Hopkins

Hall returned from Europe in the fall of 1880 but was unable to obtain a permanent position. He was a "Lecturer on the History of Philosophy" at his alma mater, Williams College, in the falls of 1881 to 1883 (Williams *Catalogue*, 1881–82, 1882–83, & 1883–84, all p. 5). He also gave lectures under Harvard auspices in fall 1881 on pedagogy in Boston, which drew considerable praise. On the strength of these lectures, President Gilman of Hopkins invited Hall to give similar lectures there. Hall suggested that he speak on psychology; Gilman acceded. In January of 1882, Hall gave 10 lectures on psychology at Johns Hopkins. The success of these lectures led to Hall's 3-year appointment as a half-time Lecturer on Psychology; Hall's first semester under this arrangement was that of spring 1883. Both Morris and Hall wanted full-time appointments at Johns Hopkins (Ross, 1972; Wenley, 1917), but Hall was appointed Professor of Psychology and Pedagogics in the spring of 1884, with the appointment effective at the start of the 1884–85 year (Johns Hopkins Trustees Minutes, Vol. 1, p. 218; meeting of April 7, 1884).

The precise circumstances surrounding this appointment are unclear. The Johns Hopkins *Annual Report* for 1884 contains the following statements:

Instruction in Logic, Psychology, Ethics, and the History of Philosophy, has hitherto been given by three lecturers—no one of whom was recognized as the head of the department, and no one of whom devoted himself exclusively to his work in this university. The objections to this arrangement were apparent to all who were interested in these subjects, and when the infelicity was distinctly brought to the attention of the Trustees by *one of the lecturers*, the decision was reached to appoint a professor in the group of philosophical subjects, and to allow the lectureships to terminate at the end of the period for which they had severally been arranged.

   The next step of the Trustees was to make choice of Dr. G. Stanley Hall, late lecturer in Harvard and Williams Colleges, and also in this university, as Professor of Psychology and Pedagogics. He accepted the invitation, and will hereafter reside among us. (JHURep, 1884, p. 9; emphasis added)

Although there seems to be no extant evidence to settle the question as to which lecturer "distinctly brought [the matter] to the attention of the Trustees," it seems likely that it was Hall.

After Hall's appointment as Professor, which was then not only an academic rank but also the equivalent of today's departmental chairperson, both Morris's and Peirce's contracts were allowed to expire.

When the fall 1884 Johns Hopkins term began, Hall was in charge of what was then a two-person department, but Morris was teaching in his lame-duck semester. During the spring of 1885, Hall was the only instructor in psychology and pedagogics; no instruction in logic or philosophy was given.

During the first semester of the 1885–86 year, Henry H. Donaldson (1857–1938) became Instructor in Psychology. He had received a Johns Hopkins PhD in biology the previous June. Donaldson's dissertation research, "On the Temperature Sense," was carried out, however, in the "Psychophysical Laboratory, Johns Hopkins University," as indicated on the first page of the published version (Donaldson, 1885). Donaldson spent the 1886–87 year working in a number of European laboratories (Zurich, Munich, Vienna, and Pavia), but he returned to Hopkins in the fall of 1887 as an Associate in Psychology. Other faculty were added to handle the philosophical aspects of the department as well.

During the 1887–88 year, Edward Cowles (1837–1919), a prominent psychiatrist and, at the time, Medical Superintendent of the McLean Hospital, gave "psychology" lectures in the department. Their subject was "Insistent and Fixed Ideas" (*JHUCir*, 1887–88, 7, p. 7), and they were published in Volume 1 of *The American Journal of Psychology* in 1888.

Hall's Laboratory

Long before Hall arrived for his first full-semester appointment, he had written persistently to President Gilman to secure a faculty position at Johns Hopkins (Ross, 1972, p. 135). Hall wrote to President Gilman as early as July of 1876. After Hall received his PhD and went off to Leipzig, his correspondence clearly shows that he wished to establish a psychology laboratory at Johns Hopkins (vide, e.g., Hall to Gilman, May 3, 1880, Gilman Papers, Johns Hopkins). Almost immediately following his 1882 half-time appointment for 3 years (Johns Hopkins Trustees Minutes, Vol. 1, p. 183, for May, 1, 1882), Hall began to discuss what would be carried out in a "practical course" (i.e., a laboratory course) in psychology (Hall to Nicholas Murray, Gilman's secretary, May 28, 1882, Gilman Papers). In two letters of October 9, 1882, to Gilman, Hall referred to "the psychophysic laboratory" and "the proposed psychophysic laboratory" (Gilman Papers).

After Hall arrived at Johns Hopkins in the spring of 1883 for his first semester-long appointment, he requested an appropriation of $250 for a laboratory. The sum was granted (Johns Hopkins Trustees' Executive Committee *Minutes*, Vol. 1, pp. 178–179, for March 8, 1883). With the funds, as James McKeen Cattell, a student at Hopkins at the time, recalled, Hall "set up a modest laboratory in a private house adjacent to the center of ugly little brick buildings and great men that formed the university" (Cattell, 1928, p. 546; 1943, p. 63). Because Cattell and Hall were together at Hopkins only during the spring semester of 1883, the "modest laboratory" that Cattell described must have been started then. The Executive Committee, upon granting Hall's request for the money to establish the laboratory, added a proviso, "as a caution to Dr. Hall that the Committee is not ready to establish a psycho-physiology laboratory" (Executive Committee *Minutes*, Vol. 1, March 8, 1883, p. 179). That is to say, the Executive Committee of the trustees said that Hall could have the facilities of a laboratory, but that he could not *call* it a laboratory. Johns Hopkins official publications are markedly silent on the use of *psychological laboratory* to refer to Hall's facilities. What was generally said was something like the following from the announcement of Hall's appointment as professor: "He has also been deeply engaged in psycho-physic researches soon to be published. Convenient rooms and suitable apparatus have been provided for this work" (*JHUCir*, 1883–84, 3, p. 95). The de facto psychology laboratory during Hall's Hopkins period was never given formal status by the Johns Hopkins Board of Trustees (i.e., it never became a *de jure* laboratory).

At least one study must have been conducted in the laboratory in the spring of 1883, because Hall and Edward M. Hartwell (1850–1922; PhD at Johns Hopkins, M.D., then an Instructor in Physical Culture at Hopkins) published "Bilateral Asymmetry of Function" in the January 1884 issue of *Mind*.

The "modest laboratory" in the "private house" was used for only a short time. Another psychology laboratory was located in the new Biological Laboratory, which opened in the fall of 1884 (*JHURep*, 1884, p. 94; *JHU-Cir*, 1883–84, 3, p. 85; *Science*, 1884, 3, pp. 350–354).[18] The psychology laboratory remained in the Biological Laboratory building until moved to the Physical Laboratory for the opening of the 1887–88 school year (*JHU-Rep*, 1888, p. 23). At the end of that year, Hall left Johns Hopkins to

---

[18]This description of the Biological Laboratory was presumably written by Henry Newell Martin (1848–1896), Professor of Biology and Director of the Biological Laboratory from 1876 to 1893.

become president-elect of the embryonic Clark University. (For another view of psychology at Johns Hopkins, see Pauly, 1986.)

The Johns Hopkins–Harvard Psychology Laboratories Connection

The date of Hall's establishment of his laboratory at Hopkins predates that of James's formal research laboratory at Harvard. It seems likely that Hall's laboratory was a stimulus to the establishment of James's. At some point following the end of the spring 1883 semester, Hall returned to North Somerville, Massachusetts, where he had been living since returning from Germany in 1880 until he moved to Baltimore late in the summer of 1884 (see, e.g., Hall to Gilman, July 26, 1884, Gilman Papers). North Somerville lies just beyond Cambridge, where Harvard is located and where James lived at the time. The summer of 1883 was one of the few that James spent in Cambridge (James's whereabouts can be reconstructed from Perry [1935], James's correspondence, and similar sources that document James's whereabouts). Because Hall's and James's summer 1883 residences were so close together, it is not surprising that there is no correspondence between them during that period. It seems reasonable to think that Hall would have called on James to tell him about what had happened during the past spring at Johns Hopkins (for Hall's boasting, see Ross, 1972). Surely Hall would have described his new laboratory to James.

James was very loyal to Harvard. In fact, a decade later, in 1895, James and others made strong objections to Hall's inaccurate claims about the role his students played in founding psychology laboratories (Hall, 1895). James specifically responded to Hall's statement that a Clark PhD, Herbert Nichols, had founded the Harvard laboratory. It seems reasonable to hypothesize that it was James's knowledge of the new Johns Hopkins laboratory that led to his requests to the Harvard Corporation in the fall of 1883 and the spring of 1885 for a psychology laboratory.

Both Harvard and Johns Hopkins have legitimate claims with respect to their psychology laboratories. Harvard had the first laboratory demonstrations (during 1875–76), the first "informal" teaching and research laboratory (in the second half of the 1870s; as noted by Harper, 1949, 1950), and the first "institutionally or trustee-sanctioned laboratory" (which opened in the fall of 1885). Johns Hopkins, on the other hand, had the first "productive" psychology laboratory, although it was an "institutionally or trustee-antisanctioned" laboratory, to use some of the terminology suggested earlier (Cadwallader, Noonan, & Wetmore, 1981). Harvard, where Hall received his first formal introduction to the "new" psychology and an exposure to a laboratory orientation in psychology under James, should be honored for its pioneering role with respect to the "new" psychology in general and to the laboratory orientation in particular. Hopkins should be honored for its pioneering role in making a psychology laboratory the vehicle for productive research, for giving instruction in the "new" psychology to many of the first group of APA members and especially to its leaders, and for founding the *American Journal of Psychology*. Both institutions played necessary roles, and both should be honored for their respective contributions.

Other Laboratories

Harvard and Johns Hopkins were not the only institutions with psychology laboratories, of course, but they were the first. By the late 1880s, psychological laboratories began to pop up all over the country. Some, such as the Wisconsin laboratory started by Joseph Jastrow, stemmed from Hall's laboratory at Hopkins. Others were started by individuals with new doctorates in psychology from Europe, where they had taken degrees in the laboratories of Hermann Ebbinghaus (1850–1909) and Wilhelm Wundt (1832–1920).

Indiana University

William Lowe Bryan (1860–1955), after receiving his A.B. from Indiana University in 1884, became an Instructor in Greek at his alma mater. The following year he became Associate Professor of Philosophy. At the end of that year, Bryan went to the University of Berlin, where he studied with Hermann Ebbinghaus (1850–1909), whose pioneering monograph on memory had recently been published (1885, although not translated into English until 1913). Because of the death of his father, Bryan returned to Indiana in the summer of 1887 and that fall was promoted to Professor of Philosophy (perhaps setting the record for speed of promotion to full professor without an institutional move).

When Bryan returned from Germany, he taught a one-semester course in elementary psychology and a year-long course in physiological psychology (Indiana University, *Catalogue*, 1887–88, p. 51). With the training he received from Ebbinghaus as a stimulus, Bryan requested and was granted funds in 1887 (Woodburn, 1940, p. 399) to buy a Hipp chronoscope, which he set up in a classroom in January of 1888. Bryan read a paper "by title," "Investigations in Physiological Time," at the 1888 meeting of the Indiana Academy of Sciences. The 1888–89 Indiana *Catalogue* noted, "A laboratory for investigation in Physiological Psychology has been provided with a small number of superior instruments. The most important of these is Hipp's

Chronoscope with its attachments" (p. 68). The Indiana *Catalogue* for 1892–93 described the "Laboratory for Experimental Psychology" and noted that it had been "established upon a very modest foundation, [in] January 1888, [and was then, in 1892–93] in process of very considerable enlargement" (p. 60). At about the same time, Bryan received a PhD under Hall at Clark (December, 1892; Wilson, 1920; for more on Indiana psychology, see Hearst & Capshew, 1988).

The University of Iowa

In 1887, even before he received his PhD at Johns Hopkins, G. T. W. Patrick (1857–1949) accepted an appointment at his alma mater, the University of Iowa, as Professor of Mental and Moral Science and Didactics. Patrick (1932) described the evolution of the Iowa Psychology Laboratory, recalling that "in the fall of my second year, in 1888, I think, . . . a few of the students met with me to dissect [a sheep's brain]" (p. 412). He also recalled that "during the second year we procured from Germany our first apparatus, consisting of a set of six tuning forks, mounted on resonators, and also a large dissectible model of the human brain, and other models of the brain, ear, and eye" (p. 413). These recollections are to some degree corroborated by expenditures, recorded in the Report of the Secretary of the Iowa Board of Regents for the school year 1888–89, of $15.55 for the Chair of Mental and Moral Sciences (Haddock, 1889, p. 40). These expenditures might have covered the costs of the items Patrick recalled, considering 1888–89 Iowa faculty salaries: For the 1887–88 biennium, all professors, including the Dean of the Collegiate Faculty, received $1,800, with the single exception of the Professor of Engineering, who received $3,000 (Richardson, Burrell, & Rich, 1889, p. 8).

In any case, the Iowa 1890–91 *Catalogue* described "the Psychophysical Laboratory" as having "made thus far, only a beginning" (p. 53). The *Catalogue* went on to list procedures carried out in the laboratory; these were compatible with the apparatus described by Patrick, but it is clear that additional apparatus had also been acquired.

In those early years, Patrick had "one room, used as lecture room, laboratory, seminary room, and private office," as he described it in his "Special Report" in the appendix to the President's Report for 1891–93 (Schaeffer, 1893, pp. 47–48). The 1894–95 *Catalogue* described a new Psychology Laboratory that included "a commodious lecture, library and reading room, and three quiet and well lighted laboratory rooms" (p. 63). Thus, over a span of 7 years, Iowa moved from an informal to a formal laboratory. (For more on psychology at Iowa, see Cantor, 1991.)

The University of Pennsylvania

James McKeen Cattell (1860–1944), while a student at Hopkins, reported to his parents that "Dr. Hall has not acted honorable towards me" (Sokal, 1981, p. 135). Cattell felt that Hall had lied to him about why John Dewey had been given the Philosophy Fellowship (*JHUCir*, 1882–83, 2, p. 155) instead of himself. Much of Cattell's animosity toward Hall in later years may have possibly had its origin here. Cattell left Johns Hopkins and went to Leipzig, where he received his PhD with Wilhelm Wundt in 1886. Cattell then went to the University of Cambridge (England), where he worked independently until the end of 1888 (with a 3-month teaching interlude in Philadelphia; Sokal, 1972).

Cattell was appointed Lecturer on Psycho-Physics at the University of Pennsylvania in October of 1886 (*UPARep*, 1885–87, p. 31), but he did not lecture there until January of 1888. He delivered 10 lectures between January 23 and March 26, 1888 (Sokal, 1981, p. 287). He also gave a lecture series at Bryn Mawr at about the same time (Sokal, 1981, p. 289). During the previous year he had had three pieces of apparatus and brain charts made in Leipzig (Sokal, 1981, pp. 272, 279) for use at Pennsylvania; he was eventually reimbursed by the University (Sokal, 1981, p. 301). These instruments and charts may have been used at least for demonstration purposes during Cattell's 1888 lectures at Pennsylvania (and perhaps at Bryn Mawr). Cattell then returned to Cambridge (for Cattell's adventures in Germany and England, see Sokal, 1981).

Cattell was subsequently appointed Professor of Psychology at Pennsylvania, beginning in January of 1889 (*UPARep*, 1887–89, p. 16). The Annual Report of the Dean of the College Faculty for the year ending October 1, 1889, noted that "the laboratories of Experimental Psychology in Biological Hall are held to be, with a single exception, the best in existence" (*UPARep*, 1887–89, p. 71). Cattell remained at Pennsylvania until he became Professor of Psychology at Columbia.

The University of Wisconsin

Joseph Jastrow (1863–1944), after 2 post-PhD years (at Johns Hopkins, where he had received a PhD in 1886) of unsuccessful efforts to find a permanent position, was appointed Professor of Experimental and Comparative Psychology at the University of Wisconsin in the fall of 1888 (Cadwallader, 1987). Shortly afterward, a laboratory was established (Chamberlin, 1888, pp. 44–45). The next spring, Jastrow was authorized "while in Europe, to order apparatus not exceeding $300" (University of Wisconsin Board of Regents' Minutes, Vol. D; meeting of January 15th,

1889, p. 24). The first "Studies from the Laboratory of Experimental Psychology" at Wisconsin appeared in *The American Journal of Psychology* in early 1890 (Jastrow, 1890). By the end of 1892, over 20 such studies had appeared.

Jastrow was in charge of the psychology exhibit at the 1893 Columbian World Exposition, which (somewhat belatedly) celebrated the tercentenary of the discovery of America; as a consequence of overwork, he had a severe health breakdown (Jastrow, 1930). One consequence of this overwork was that the early productivity of the Wisconsin Psychology Laboratory was not matched for decades.

The University of Nebraska

Harry K. Wolfe (1858–1918) received his PhD under Wundt in 1886, along with Cattell. In 1889, after three years of high school teaching, he became Lecturer in Philosophy at his alma mater, the University of Nebraska, where he immediately established a laboratory. For more on Wolfe (and why he dropped out of the APA for a time), see Benjamin and Bertelson (1975) and Benjamin (1975).

Cornell

The psychological laboratory at Cornell was founded by Frank Angell (1857–1939; not to be confused with James R. Angell of Chicago functionalism fame). Frank Angell had received his PhD with Wilhelm Wundt in 1891 and went immediately to Cornell. J. G. Schurman, who had just moved from the chair of philosophy to become president of Cornell, was seeking an experimental psychologist. He had failed to attract Hermann Ebbinghaus, but succeeded in landing Angell. During the 1891–92 academic year, Angell set up the beginnings of what would become one of the most productive laboratories in America, under the directorship of E. B. Titchener (1867–1927). Angell was attracted to the new Stanford University in California, and Titchener, Angell's friend and classmate in Leipzig, gained the post.

During the final decade of the 19th century, more and more institutions moved to the "new" psychology. Garvey (1929) listed 14 academic psychology laboratories that had been "founded" prior to the APA's founding. Garvey's dates may or may not be accurate—he simply asked the "secretary of the institution," although "the letter was usually referred to someone in the psychology department" (p. 652), to supply such information as the date when the laboratory was established. What was meant by "laboratory" or "established" was not spelled out. The list nevertheless shows how rapidly recognition of the hallmark of the "new psychology," the laboratory, had spread.

THE JOHNS HOPKINS LEGACY TO THE APA: EARLY MEMBERS AND LEADERS

Of the 26 original members of the APA, 16 (62%) had some connection with Johns Hopkins: two full-time faculty members (G. Stanley Hall and Edward H. Griffin); two short-term lecturers (William James and Edward Cowles); eight PhD recipients (Josiah Royce, John Dewey, H. H. Donaldson, Joseph Jastrow, Edmund C. Sanford, James H. Hyslop, William H. Burnham, and George T. W. Patrick); and four non-degree-recipient graduate students (James M. Cattell, James G. Hume, B. I. Gilman, and William Noyes).

The early APA leadership was even more strongly dominated by Johns Hopkins-related individuals. Of the first 11 APA presidents, seven (64%) were Johns Hopkins related (Hall, James, Cattell, Dewey, Jastrow, Royce, and Sanford), as were the first 3 APA secretary-treasurers (Jastrow, Cattell, and Sanford). There were nine Johns Hopkins-related members on the APA Council (equivalent to today's Board of Directors) through 1904 (Cattell, James, Dewey, Griffin, Sanford, Royce, Jastrow, and Patrick).

No other institution had such an input into APA leadership during the APA's first 2 decades. But, of course, during the 1880s very little was going on in psychology anywhere in the United States other than at Johns Hopkins with respect to granting PhDs in psychology-related disciplines.

This early Hopkins-dominated group would form the core of the APA, although some would not always be sympathetic with G. Stanley Hall (see Chapters 2 and 3).

THE MODEL FOR THE APA

In the 1880s, a number of specialized societies, scholarly in general and scientific in particular, were established. Through the first three quarters of the 19th century, scholarly and scientific societies had generally been broad-based (e.g., the American Association for the Advancement of Science, founded in 1848, and the American Social Science Association, founded in 1865; T. L. Haskell, 1977, p. 97). Beginning with the American Chemical Society in 1876, however, discipline-oriented societies began to be founded with increasing frequency (e.g., the American Philological

Society in 1869, the Modern Language Association in 1883, and the American Historical Association in 1884).

It was the American Physiological Society (APS) that was apparently the model for the APA. In May of 1887, the neurologist S. Weir Mitchell (1829–1914), the physiologist (and close friend of William James) Henry P. Bowditch (1840–1911), and the Director of the Johns Hopkins Biological Laboratory, H. Newell Martin (1848–1896), circulated a letter soliciting interest in a proposed society that became the APS. (For the early history of the APS, see Appel, 1987). Two of these three men had close contact with Hall. Martin was Hall's colleague at Johns Hopkins, and it was in Martin's Biological Laboratory (building) that the second Johns Hopkins psychology laboratory was located. Hall had worked in Bowditch's Physiological Laboratory at Harvard, and Bowditch was on Hall's PhD committee.

Both Hall and Joseph Jastrow (who was still at Johns Hopkins, post-PhD, trying to find a permanent position) were among the original 28 members of this early APS, and both were among the 17 who attended the organizational meeting held in December of 1887 at the new physiological laboratory at the College of Physicians and Surgeons in New York.

Just as a large percentage of the early APA membership had some involvement with Johns Hopkins, so did that of the APS. Of the original 28 APS members, 10 had some connection with Johns Hopkins: Eight were physiologists (Appel, 1987, p. 15), and two were psychologists (Hall and Jastrow). Three of the physiologists later became APA members: H. H. Donaldson (1857–1938), T. W. Mills (1847–1915), and William H. Howell (1860–1945).

The APS established a five-member Council to govern the affairs of the society. The Council comprised the president, the secretary-treasurer, and three members (American Physiological Society, 1987, p. 499). Bowditch served as the first president from 1887 to 1889 (and again from 1891 to 1895); Martin served as the first secretary-treasurer, through 1892, and was chiefly responsible for the Society's constitution (Appel, 1987, p. 15). There would certainly have been ample opportunity for Hall to discuss the APS with Martin prior to Hall's departure from Baltimore in the late spring of 1888, and possibly at the Society's meetings, most of which Hall attended.

THE PERSONAL DIMENSION: HALL'S DRIVE TO BE LEADER OF AMERICAN PSYCHOLOGY

It was only a matter of a few months after Hall returned from the first APS meeting in December of 1887 that he received the initial letter from the Clark trustees concerning the presidency of Clark University. Once Hall started considering the presidency, accepting it, going to Worcester, visiting European universities, getting Clark University started, and coping with the death of his wife and young daughter in May of 1890 (Ross, 1972), he was surely far too busy and distracted to consider founding an organization of psychologists.

Hall was an exceptionally ambitious man. When one looks at Hall's career, his post-Johns Hopkins behavior suggests that he was trying to out-Hopkins Hopkins—that is, he tried to go beyond what Hopkins was doing. Thus, whereas Hopkins emphasized research and graduate education, Clark had only research and graduate education. The Clark faculty would not have to divert its attention from what had become, by the mid-1880s, the central concern of the leading educational institutions of the United States, research and graduate education, to what had become the secondary task, undergraduate instruction. In this respect, Hall's efforts were successful (Koelsch, 1987; Ross, 1972).

Hall had the credentials to make him the uncontested leader of the new psychology in America. He had founded one of the early (according to Hall, the first) psychological laboratories in America. He had founded America's first journal devoted to the new psychology and had vehemently attacked the older philosophical psychologies in favor of the new experimental psychology through the journal's pages. Hall's attacks on the philosophical psychologies of Bowen and McCosh, Ladd's *Elements of Physiological Psychology* (1887), and even William James's *Principles of Psychology*, were exceptionally harsh (Evans & Cohen, 1987). Clearly, Hall believed that he was the leader of the new discipline in the United States.

In the early 1890s, Hall probably realized that others—notably James, Cattell, Baldwin, and Jastrow—were becoming increasingly important within American psychology. For example, in 1890, William James published his *Principles*, which, Hall's review aside, was soon considered the harbinger of a new day in American Psychology (Thorndike, 1943). James had also founded psychology laboratories (the first to do so, in his estimation; Evans & Cohen, 1987). Perhaps Hall realized that unless he took definite action to assert his leadership of American psychology, it might pass to someone else.

Another problem emerged for Hall. During Clark's second year (1890–91), financial and other problems began to surface. These problems were exacerbated during the third year; by the spring of 1892, it was widely known that a mass defection of faculty and graduate students would occur at the end of the academic year (Koelsch, 1987). At that point, Hall desperately needed something to provide favorable publicity for both Clark

University and his own prestige. The founding of a new scholarly society on Clark soil would surely supply that.

Certainly by 1892, the time was right for the new psychologists to organize. The number of laboratory-oriented psychologists was sufficient to form such an organization, and it is clear that these new psychologists were at the forefront of the formation of the APA. Others were welcomed into the new society: the old-fashioned philosophical psychologists, those making the often difficult transition between the old and new psychologies, and even metaphysicians and individuals with a more or less amateur interest in psychology. However, as Chapters 2 and 3 will show, that openness would not last. The beginnings of professional competition and personal ambition, both of which contribute heavily to professionalization and to professional organizations, were indeed present in the new association.

ENDVIEW

The changes that took place in psychology during the 19th century were immense. Indeed, the greatest change that has ever occurred in psychology took place during the 19th century: the transformation from a speculative philosophical enterprise to a scientific enterprise, arguably the greatest disciplinary change possible. The two main 20th-century changes in psychology, from the structuralist–functionalist to the behavioristic approach, and from the behavioristic to the cognitive approach, were merely fine tunings compared with the fundamental change that took place during the 19th century.

Within a quarter of a century of the introduction of Fechnerian–Wundtian psychology to the United States by Charles Peirce in 1869, the Fechnerian–Wundtian model became the accepted model for psychology at those American institutions that became research and PhD oriented (this institutional reorientation took place essentially during the same quarter century). In that quarter-century, psychology became widely recognized as a science and as an independent discipline, as witnessed by the fact that PhDs were increasingly granted in psychology as such and by the fact that a professional society, the American Psychological Association, had been established. And within another decade, psychologists were admitted to the National Academy of Sciences. The change from a philosophical to a scientific discipline was as rapid as it was remarkable.

It is not surprising that the individual who sought and received the world's first PhD in psychology, founded the nation's first productive (but institutionally "antisanctioned") psychology laboratory, and founded the first scientifically oriented psychology journal was the founder of the APA. G. Stanley Hall did not leave the intellectual legacy that William James did, but Hall left an organizational legacy matched by no other psychologist.

During the 20th century, the field of psychology would grow and expand to an extent that perhaps not even Hall (and certainly not James) could foresee. However, much that was to come was clearly seen by Hall. It was Hall, after all, who would bring Freud and Jung to the United States for Clark University's vigesimal celebration in 1909 and who founded the *Journal of Applied Psychology* in 1917. But one wonders whether even Hall could have foreseen the growth of the APA from the 26 original members to today's more than 100,000 members and affiliates.

REFERENCES

American Physiological Society. (1987). Appendix 1: Members of Council, 1887–1987. In J. R. Brobeck, O. E. Reynolds, & T. A. Appel (Eds.), *History of the American Physiological Society: The first century, 1887–1987* (pp. 499–507). Bethesda, MD: American Physiological Society.

Appel, T. A. (1987). Founding. In J. R. Brobeck, O. E. Reynolds, & T. A. Appel (Eds.), *History of the American Physiological Society: The first century, 1887–1987* (pp. 11–29). Bethesda, MD: American Physiological Society.

Baldwin, J. M. (1930). James Mark Baldwin. In C. Murchison (Ed.), *History of psychology in autobiography* (Vol. 1, pp. 1–30). Worcester, MA: Clark University Press.

Benjamin, L. T., Jr. (1975). Psychology at the University of Nebraska, 1889–1930. *Nebraska History, 56,* 375–387.

Benjamin, L. T., Jr., & Bertelson, A. (1975). The early Nebraska Psychology Laboratory, 1889–1930: Nursery for presidents of the American Psychological Association. *Journal of the History of the Behavioral Sciences, 11,* 142–148.

Boring, E. G. (1950). *A history of experimental psychology* (2nd ed.). New York: Appleton-Century-Crofts.

Bryson, G. (1932). The comparable interests of the old moral philosophy and the modern social sciences. *Social Forces, 10,* 20–21.

Cadwallader, T. C. (1974). Charles S. Peirce (1839–1914): The first American experimental psychologist. *Journal of the History of the Behavioral Sciences, 10,* 291–298.

Cadwallader, T. C. (1975). Peirce as an experimental psychologist. *Transactions of the Charles S. Peirce Society, 11,* 167–186.

Cadwallader, T. C. (1987). The origins and accomplishments of Joseph Jastrow's 1888-founded chair of comparative psychology at the University of Wisconsin. *Journal of Comparative Psychology, 101,* 321–326.

Cadwallader, T. C., Noonan, D. F., & Wetmore, K. E. (1981, August). *On the "founding" of psychology laboratories.* Paper presented at the 89th Annual Convention of the American Psychological Association, Los Angeles.

Cantor, J. H. (Ed.). (1991). *Psychology at Iowa: Centennial essays.* Hillsdale, NJ: Erlbaum.

Cattell, J. M. (1928). Early psychological laboratories. *Science, 67,* 543–548.

Cattell, J. M. (1943). The founding of the [American Psychological] Association and of the Hopkins and Clark Laboratories. *Psychological Review, 50,* 61–64.

Chamberlin, T. C. (1988). Biennial report of the president of the University of Wisconsin. In *Biennial report of the board of regents of the University of Wisconsin for the two fiscal years ending September 30, 1988* (pp. 35–58).

Cope, J. I. (1951). William James's correspondence with Daniel Coit Gilman, 1877–1881. *Journal of the History of Ideas, 12,* 609–627.

Cowles, E. (1888). Insistent and fixed ideas. *American Journal of Psychology, 1,* 222–270.

Delabarre, E. B. (1889a). On the seat of optical after-images. *American Journal of Psychology, 2,* 326–328.

Delabarre, E. B. (1889b). Colored shadows. *American Journal of Psychology, 2,* 636–643.

Donaldson, H. H. (1885). On the temperature sense. *Mind, 10,* 399–416.

Ebbinghaus, H. (1913). *Memory: A contribution to experimental psychology* (H. A. Ruger & C. E. Bussenius, Trans.) New York: Teachers College, Columbia University. (Original work published 1885)

Eells, W. C. (1963). *Degrees in higher education.* Washington, DC: Center for Applied Research in Education.

Ellis, J. (1973). *The New England mind in transition: Samuel Johnson of Connecticut, 1696–1772.* New Haven, CT: Yale University Press.

Evans, R. B. (1984). The origins of American academic psychology. In J. Brozek (Ed.), *Explorations in the history of psychology in the United States* (pp. 17–60). Lewisburg, PA: Bucknell University Press.

Evans, R. B., & Cohen, J. B. (1987). *The American Journal of Psychology:* A retrospective. *American Journal of Psychology, 100,* 321–362.

Fay, J. W. (1966). *American psychology before William James.* New York: Octagon. (Original work published 1939)

Fechner, G. T. (1860). *Elemente der Psychophysik* (2 vols.). Leipzig: Breitkopf & Härtel. (Vol. 1 was translated by H. E. Adler and edited by E. G. Boring and D. H. Howes as *Elements of psychophysics.* New York: Holt, Rinehart, & Winston, 1966)

Fisch, M. H. (1964). Was there a Metaphysical Club in Cambridge? In E. C. Moore & R. S. Robin (Eds.), *Studies in the philosophy of Charles Peirce* (2nd series, pp. 3–32). Amherst: University of Massachusetts Press.

Fisch, M. H., & Cope, J. I. (1952). Peirce at the Johns Hopkins University. In P. P. Wiener & F. H. Young (Eds.), *Studies in the philosophy of Charles Peirce* (pp. 277–311, 355–360, 363–374). Cambridge, MA: Harvard University Press.

Garvey, C. R. (1929). List of American psychology laboratories. *Psychological Bulletin, 21*, 652–660.

Genzmer, G. H. (1937). Smith, Benjamin Eli. *Dictionary of American biography.* New York: Scribners.

Haddock, W. J. (1889). Report of the secretary. *Report of the State University of Iowa* [Regents's Reports, 1887–1889], pp. 29–43.

Hall, G. S. (1895). Editorial. *American Journal of Psychology, 7*, 3–4.

Hall, G. S. (1923). *Life and confessions of a psychologist.* New York: Appleton.

Hall, G. S., & Hartwell, E. M. (1884). Bilateral asymmetry of function. *Mind, 9*, 93–109.

Harper, R. S. (1949). The laboratory of William James. *Harvard Alumni Bulletin, 51*, 169–173.

Harper, R. S. (1950). The first psychological laboratory. *Isis, 41*, 158–161.

Haskell, D. C. (Comp.). (1953). *The Nation, Volumes 1–105, New York, 1865–1917: Vol. 2. Index of contributors.* New York: New York Public Library.

Haskell, T. L. (1977). *The emergence of professional social science: The American Social Science Association and the nineteenth-century crisis of authority.* Urbana: University of Illinois Press.

Hawkins, H. (1960). *Pioneer: A history of the Johns Hopkins University.* Ithaca, NY: Cornell University Press.

Hearst, E., & Capshew, J. H. (Eds). (1988). *Psychology at Indiana University: A centennial review and compendium.* Bloomington, IN: Indiana University Department of Psychology.

Hickok, L. P. (1848). *Rational psychology: Or, the subjective idea and the objective law of all intelligence.* Auburn, NY: Derby, Miller.

Hickok, L. P. (1854). *Empirical psychology; or, the human mind as given in consciousness: For the use of colleges and academies.* Schenectady, NY: Van Deborgert.

James, W. (1868). Moral medication. *The Nation, 7*, 50–52. (Unsigned. James is identified as the author in D. C. Haskell [1953, p. 258]. Reprinted in James [1987].)

James, W. (1869, March 10). [Unsigned review of *Planchette: Or, the despair of science*]. *Boston Daily Advertiser.* (James is identified as the author in McDermott [1967, p. 813]. Reprinted in James [1986].)

James, W. (1872). [Unsigned review of *De l'intelligence*]. *The Nation, 15*, 139–141. (James is identified as the author in McDermott [1967, p. 815]. Reprinted in James [1987].)

James, W. (1873). [Unsigned review of *Contributions to mental pathology*]. *Atlantic Monthly, 31*, 748–750. (James is identified as the author in McDermott [1967, p. 813]. Reprinted in James [1987].)

James, W. (1874). [Unsigned review of *An Essay on the Principles of Mental Hygiene,*

Responsibility in Mental Disease, and *Principles of Mental Physiology*]. *The Nation*, *19*, 43. (James is identified as the author in McDermott [1967, p. 813]. Reprinted in James [1987].)

James, W. (1875a). [Unsigned note concerning Professors W. Wundt & E. Hitzig]. *The Nation*, *20*, 377–378. (James is identified as the author in Haskell [1953, p. 258]. Reprinted in James [1987].)

James, W. (1875b). [Unsigned review of *Grundzüge der physiologischen Psychologie*]. *North American Review*, *121*, 195–201. (James is identified as the author in McDermott [1967, p. 815]. Reprinted in James [1987].)

James, W. (1876). The teaching of philosophy in our colleges [Unsigned]. *The Nation*, *23*, 178–179. (James is identified as the author in Haskell [1953, p. 258]. Reprinted in James [1978].)

James, W. (1878). Brute and human intellect. *Journal of Speculative Philosophy*, *12*, 236–276. (Reprinted in James [1983].)

James, W. (1879a). Are we automata? *Mind*, *4*, 1–22. (Reprinted in James [1983].)

James, W. (1879b). The spatial quale. *Journal of Speculative Philosophy*, *13*, 65–87. (Reprinted in James [1983].)

James, W. (1882). The sense of dizziness in deaf-mutes. *American Journal of Otology*, *4*, 239–254. (Reprinted in James [1983].)

James, W. (1890). *Principles of psychology* (2 vols.). New York: Holt. (A three-volume edition has been published [1981] by Harvard University Press in the series The Works of William James, under the imprint of the Committee on Scholarly Editions of the Modern Language Association.)

James, W. (1892). *Psychology* ("Briefer Course"). New York: Holt. (Republished 1984 by Harvard University Press in the series The Works of William James.)

James, W. (1978). *The works of William James: Essays in philosophy* (F. B. Burkhardt, Gen. Ed.). Cambridge, MA: Harvard University Press.

James, W. (1983). *The works of William James: Essays in psychology* (F. B. Burkhardt, Gen. Ed.). Cambridge, MA: Harvard University Press.

James, W. (1986). *The works of William James: Essays in psychical research* (F. B. Burkhardt, Gen. Ed.). Cambridge, MA: Harvard University Press.

James, W. (1987). *The works of William James: Essays, comments, and reviews*. (F. B. Burkhardt, Gen. Ed.). Cambridge, MA: Harvard University Press.

Jastrow, J. (1890). Studies from the Laboratory of Experimental Psychology of the University of Wisconsin. *The American Journal of Psychology*, *3*, 43–58.

Jastrow, J. (1930). Joseph Jastrow. In C. Murchison (Ed.), *History of psychology in autobiography* (Vol. 1, pp. 135–162). Worcester, MA: Clark University Press.

Ketner, K., & Cook, J. E. (Comps. & Annots.). (1975). Charles Sanders Peirce: Contributions to *The Nation*, Part One: 1869–1893. *Graduate Studies Texas Tech University*, No. 10.

Koelsch, W. (1987). *Clark University, 1887–1987*. Worcester, MA: Clark University Press.

Kuhn, T. S. (1970). *The structure of scientific revolutions* (2nd ed.). Chicago: University of Chicago Press.

Ladd, G. T. (1887). *Elements of physiological psychology.* New York: Scribners.

Locke, J. (1690). *Essay concerning human understanding.* London: Holt.

Lynchburg College. (1989). *Lynchburg College chartering ceremonies for Psi Chi.* Lynchburg, VA: Lynchburg College, Department of Psychology. (I thank my graduate student Pamela Jones for providing a copy of this document.)

Madden, E. H. (1963). *Chauncey Wright and the foundations of pragmatism.* Seattle: University of Washington Press.

McCosh, J. (1882). The Scottish philosophy as contrasted with the German. *Princeton Review, 10,* 326–344.

McDermott, J. J. (Ed.). (1967). *The writings of William James.* New York: Modern Library.

National Academy of Sciences. (1889). [Grants awarded]. *Proceedings,* o.s., *1,* Part III, p. 317.

Patrick, G. T. W. (1932). Founding the Psychological Laboratory at the State University of Iowa. *Iowa Journal of History and Politics, 30,* 404–416.

Pauly, P. J. (1986). G. Stanley Hall and his successors: A history of the first half-century of psychology at Johns Hopkins. In S. H. Hulse & B. E. Green (Eds.), *One hundred years of psychological research in America: G. Stanley Hall and the Johns Hopkins tradition* (pp. 21–51). Baltimore: Johns Hopkins University Press.

Peirce, C. S. (1869a). Professor Porter's "Human Intellect." *The Nation, 8,* 211–213. (Reprinted in Peirce [1984] and Ketner & Cook [1975].)

Peirce, C. S. (1869b). The English doctrine of ideas [Review of *Analysis of the Phenomena of the Human Mind*]. *The Nation, 1,* 461–462. (Reprinted in Peirce [1984] and Ketner & Cook [1975].)

Peirce, C. S. (1880). On the algebra of logic. *American Journal of Mathematics, 2,* 15–57. (Reprinted in Peirce [1986].)

Peirce, C. S. (1984). *Writings of Charles S. Peirce: A chronological edition* (Vol. 2, 1867–1871; E. C. Moore, Ed.). Bloomington: Indiana University Press.

Peirce, C. S. (1986). *Writings of Charles S. Peirce: A chronological edition* (Vol. 4, 1879–1884; C. J. W. Kloesel, Ed.). Bloomington: Indiana University Press.

Peirce, C. S. (in press). *Writings of Charles S. Peirce: A chronological edition* (Vol. 5, 1884–1886; C. J. W. Kloesel, Ed.). Bloomington: Indiana University Press.

Peirce, C. S., & Jastrow, J. (1884). On small differences of sensation. *Memoirs of the National Academy of Sciences, 3,* 73–83. (Reprinted in Peirce [in press].)

Perry, R. B. (1935). *The thought and character of William James* (2 vols.). Boston: Little, Brown.

Princeton University. (1908). *General catalogue of Princeton University: 1746–1906.* Princeton, NJ: Author.

Rauch, F. A. (1840). *Psychology; or, a view of the human soul, including anthropology.* New York: Dodd.

Reid, T. (1785). *Essays on the intellectual powers of man.* Edinburgh, Scotland: Bell.

Reid, T. (1788). *Essays on the active powers of the human mind.* Edinburgh, Scotland: Bell.

Richardson, D. N., Burrell, H. A., & Rich, J. W. (1889). Report of the Board of Regents. *Report of the State University of Iowa, 1887–1889,* pp. 3–11.

Robin, R. S. (1967). *Annotated catalogue of the papers of Charles S. Peirce.* Amherst: University of Massachusetts Press.

Rosenberg, R. P. (1961). The first American Doctor of Philosophy degree: A centennial salute to Yale, 1861–1961. *Journal of Higher Education, 31,* 387–394.

Ross, D. (1972). *G. Stanley Hall: The psychologist as prophet.* Chicago: University of Chicago Press.

Ryan, W. C. (1939). *Studies in early graduate education: The Johns Hopkins, Clark University, The University of Chicago.* New York: Carnegie Foundation for the Advancement of Teaching.

Schaeffer, C. A. (1893). President's report, 1891–93. *Report of the State University of Iowa, 1891–1893,* pp. 19–50.

Snow, L. F. (1907). *The college curriculum in the United States.* New York: Teachers College, Columbia University.

Sokal, M. M. (1972). Psychology at Victorian Cambridge: The unofficial laboratory of 1887–1888. *Proceedings of the American Philosophical Society, 116,* 145–147.

Sokal, M. M. (1981). *An education in psychology: James McKeen Cattell's journal and letters from Germany and England, 1880–1888.* Cambridge, MA: MIT Press.

Spencer, H. (1855). *Principles of psychology.* London: Longman, Brown, Green, & Longmans.

Stewart, D. (1854). *Elements of the philosophy of the human mind: Revised and abridged, with critical and explanatory notes, for the use of colleges and schools* (Francis Bowen, Ed.). Boston: Munroe.

Taine, H. A. (1871). *On intelligence* (T. D. Haye, Trans., Revised with additions by the author). London: Reeve. (Original work published 1870)

Tewksberry, D. G. (1932). *The founding of American colleges and universities before the civil war.* New York: Teachers College Press.

Thorndike, E. L. (1943). James' influence on the psychology of perception and thought. *Psychological Review, 50,* 87–94.

Upham, T. C. (1826). *Elements of intellectual philosophy.* Brunswick, ME: Griffin.

Upham, T. C. (1831). *Elements of mental philosophy.* Brunswick, ME: Griffin.

Vande Kempe, H. (1983). A note on the term "psychology" in English titles: Predecessors of Rauch. *Journal of the History of the Behavioral Sciences, 19,* 185.

Veysey, L. R. (1965). *The emergence of the American university.* Chicago: University of Chicago Press.

Wenley, R. M. (1917). *The life and works of George Sylvester Morris*. New York: Macmillan.

Wiener, P. P. (1949). *Evolution and the founders of pragmatism*. Cambridge, MA: Harvard University Press.

Wilson, L. N. (1920). List of degrees granted at Clark University and Clark College, 1889–1920. *Clark University Library Publications, 6*(3).

Woodburn, J. A. (1940). *History of Indiana University: Vol. I, 1820–1902*. Bloomington: Indiana University.

Wundt, W. (1874). *Grundzüge der physiologischen Psychologie* [Principles of physiological psychology]. Leipzig, Germany: Engelmann.

2

ORIGINS AND EARLY YEARS OF THE AMERICAN PSYCHOLOGICAL ASSOCIATION: 1890 TO 1906

MICHAEL M. SOKAL

The American Psychological Association (APA) emerged at a particular time, in a unique social and institutional environment, and as the result of actions of specific individuals. Like any organism suddenly appearing in a given environment, it had to adapt to its ecological setting and find itself an ecological niche in which it could thrive, or at least survive. The course of events surrounding its establishment reflected America in the late Gilded Age, its emerging university system, the organizational precedents set by other American scientists of the period, and the personal interplay between G. Stanley Hall and his contemporaries. These factors did more to shape the course of events surrounding its establishment—and its character during its earliest years—than did any of the intellectual and scientific issues to which psychologists devoted their attention during that period.

From the start, the APA was explicitly the *American* Psychological Association; although its membership always included Canadians, its character has always reflected its U.S. base. In particular, through the Gilded Age, the nation's intellectual life gradually coalesced around America's newly emerging universities. As the institutional builders of the period looked to Europe and adopted (in large part) the German research ideal as the basis for new universities in Ithaca, New York (Cornell, founded in 1865); Baltimore (Johns Hopkins, 1876); Worcester, Massachusetts (Clark, 1887); Chicago, Illinois (University of Chicago, 1891); and Palo Alto, California (Stanford, 1892), the older colleges—which an earlier society had charged with instilling discipline and piety in its professional leaders—began converting into universities that emphasized graduate education. (In short, they adapted, and even mutated, in response to changes in their immediate environment; see Veysey, 1965.) So, too, did many state universities; by 1890, those in California, Indiana, Michigan, and Wisconsin, for example, had more in common with the private universities than with most other public universities. In all of these institutions, the educational magnates adopted the principle of division of labor that their industrial counterparts had found so successful; thus, highly specialized departments thrived. These usually focused on one of the research-based academic disciplines that had emerged in the 19th-century German universities. Johns Hopkins and others, for example, bragged regularly about their seminar-based instruction in classical philology (Hawkins, 1960). Physics, too, emerged from natural philosophy, as for the first time large numbers of Americans began to call themselves scientists and practice research (Kevles, 1978).

Meanwhile, through the 1880s, research-oriented scientists based in universities and in federal scientific agencies grew dissatisfied with the older scientific organizations, such as the American Association for the Advancement of Science (AAAS), founded in 1848. The AAAS opened its membership to all who paid its dues, published only summary proceedings of its peripatetic summer meetings, and comprised only two general sections, which limited program time for any one discipline. In 1882, responding to the interests of researchers, the AAAS adapted itself by establishing nine slightly more specialized sections, each of which could hold its own scientific programs. But this halfway move did little to satisfy these special interests and led instead to further adaptation by promoting further discussion that led to the formation of disciplinary societies with restricted membership (Appel, 1988).

In 1883, biologists and geologists founded the Society of Naturalists of the Eastern United States (soon renamed the American Society of Naturalists) that "encouraged the formation of disciplinary societies"—including, eventually, the APA—"and enabled them to survive their early years when there were still few prospective members with the desired training and attainment" (Appel, 1988, p. 90). In many ways, it represented a transitional form between the AAAS and the highly specialized and limited-membership organizations of research scientists that soon emerged. The earliest of these, the American Physiological Society, appeared in 1887 and restricted its membership to those who had "conducted and published an original research" (Appel, p. 94) in physiology. When its organizers invited only 28 researchers to join as charter members, they deliberately excluded many who taught physiology at American medical schools and all whose interests were solely clinical. Within the decade, other specialists founded the Association of American Anatomists (also in 1887; renamed the American Association of Anatomists in 1909), the Geological Society of America (1888), the American Morphological Society (1890; renamed the American Zoological Society in 1902), and the Botanical Society of America (1892). Through the 1890s and even afterward, the American Society of Naturalists provided an infrastructure that provided a nurturing environment for these new societies. As the "Affiliated Societies," they usually met together for three days between Christmas and New Year's Day. The American Society of Naturalists scheduled only a presidential address and a symposium, with speakers from all of the organizations present, on a topic of general interest. Its secretary took charge of all local arrangements, including reduced-rate rail fares and an extensive social program. Then as now, the societies' members all enjoyed and often profited more from these less structured sessions and informal discussions in the halls than they did from any formal presentations, and these meetings did much to promote the growth of research-oriented science in late 19th-century America (Appel).

PSYCHOLOGY SLOWLY EMERGES

In many ways, however, philosophy and its subdiscipline, psychology, lagged behind their cohort. Through the 1880s, conventional mental and moral philosophy, rooted in the Scottish realism of the late 18th century, continued to serve the needs of many colleges, which saw no reason to change. The new universities, however, often sought to move beyond this tradition and establish research-based philosophy departments alongside those in the sciences. But their founders often found German Idealism uncongenial, or at least they projected their own concerns on their institutions' trustees. By the mid-1880s, then, at least some of them began considering the newly emerging discipline of experimental psychology as a substitute (Ross, 1972). After all, psychology had always been a part of philosophy, and even those who taught mental philosophy in American colleges had long since begun to bring German physiological psychology into their texts and classes.

By 1892, American universities had established about 20 psychological laboratories, and at some of them, psychology dominated philosophy (Garvey, 1929; Murray & Rowe, 1979). These laboratories taught a science that had already begun to adapt to the new environment in which its practitioners found themselves. Their psychology moved away from Germany's, with its focus on the working of the normal, healthy, adult male mind in laboratory conditions; American psychologists began quite early to assimilate evolutionary, primarily Darwinian, principles into their science. American psychology also retained from its mid 19th-century phrenological tradition, and to some degree from the earlier Scottish realism, an interest in life in the real world. From the start, then, this science was functionally oriented and deeply concerned with development—especially with individual differences (i.e., the variation that made natural selection possible). Americans were also more interested in the latent practicality of their science; therefore, although little pre-1900 psychology focused directly on applied problems, much was at least potentially applicable, as it often dealt with the "real world" outside the laboratory (O'Donnell, 1985).

The new science had also begun to adapt to its professional environment and develop its own infrastructure, as G. Stanley Hall established the *American Journal of Psychology* in 1887 (Dallenbach, 1937; Hall, 1923; Ross, 1972). Like most late 19th-century American scientific periodicals, it was privately owned, and despite its title, it played for Clark University the house-organ role played by Wilhelm Wundt's *Philosophische Studien* for Leipzig students. Although it drew submissions from around the country, it often had more in common with Columbia's *Contributions to Philosophy and Psychology*, Harvard's *Psychological Studies*, Iowa's *Studies in Psychology*, the *Publications of the University of Pennsylvania*, and other locally oriented and sporadically issued university series, many of which were later subsumed in *Psychological Monographs*. No wonder, then, that in 1889, when European psychologists organizing the first International Congress of Psychology (in conjunction with the Paris Universal Exposition) tried to identify a national organization of psychologists in North America, they could find only the American Society for Psychical Research (ASPR; Wetmore, 1992). The two Americans attending the international congress, William James and Joseph Jastrow, knew the ASPR's limitations. Despite its name, it was as locally oriented as the different university publication series, and the Europeans even wrote of it as the "Boston Society." Although some evidence suggests that the ASPR sought to move beyond the narrow focus its name implied (Mauskopf, 1989), Jastrow strongly opposed any attempt to link psychical research to the new psychology and could argue, at least, that most American psychologists disparaged the organization and its interests. Thus, later international congresses ignored the ASPR. On their return to America, James and Jastrow probably reported these events to their colleagues, including G. Stanley Hall, who earned his Harvard PhD with James in 1878 and who directed Jastrow's Johns Hopkins dissertation in 1886.

Although these developments shaped the environment and formed the context within which the APA emerged, its particular form and initial character derived largely from the temperament of one individual, G. Stanley Hall. Unfortunately for the APA—which Hall founded in 1892—his disposition prevented all of the institutions he led from thriving under his leadership. Fortunately, however, within 18 months, the Association established an identity of its own, and by the mid-1890s Hall had little to say about the course of APA affairs.

THE AMBITIOUS G. S. HALL

Hall was strongly ambitious, and the opportunities for personal advancement he saw in the new psychology attracted him as much as any of the intellectual questions its practitioners asked (Koelsch, 1987). In 1884, he gained Johns Hopkins professorship in competition with two of America's leading philosophers, largely because Daniel Coit Gilman, the university's president, found him fittest for the environment of Baltimore. Gilman preferred Hall's laboratory-based psychology to George Sylvester Morris's Idealism and Charles Sanders Peirce's marital uncertainties (Ross, 1972). He also appreciated Hall's interest in child study and pedagogy, in part because he could cite its implied practicality, and (especially) Hall's status as an ordained Congregational minister, to defend the university against charges of religious irregularity. But the negative aspects of Hall's temperament emerged even before he assumed his professorship, and in 1883 he went out of his way to rid the university of those who might challenge his intellectual leadership (Ross, 1972; Sokal, 1981). Throughout his career, Hall often seemed to deal loosely with the truth. For example, in 1887, he obtained funds to start the *American Journal of Psychology* from Robert Pearsall Smith, a spiritualist active in the ASPR, who had expected the new journal to share his interests. As Hall's biographer (Ross, 1972) concluded, "to what extent Hall tacitly encouraged that assumption is unknown" (p. 170; cf. Dallenbach, 1937; Hall, 1923). Later that year, he became founding president of Clark University in Worcester, Massachusetts, and through the next half-decade continually misled the institution's principal benefactor, Jonas Clark, as to his educational policies and goals. Once Clark realized just how seriously Hall had deceived him, he withdrew his support from the university, and Hall, in turn, blamed this action for all of the trouble that followed. In building Clark University, Hall gathered a world-renown faculty with "extravagant promises" (Koelsch, p. 35) he could never fulfill and, in the years that followed, dealt with its members as he had dealt with Smith and Clark. By January 1892, these scholars and scientists had grown tired of Hall's "arbitrary ways, his double-dealing, and his constant attempts to blame either the trustees or Jonas Clark" (Koelsch, p. 35) for his own troubles (see also Ross, 1972). Finally, in April 1892, William Rainey Harper, president of the new University of Chicago (which would open the following fall) came to Worcester and hired most of Clark's faculty for his institution. Hall's colleagues in psychology, notably Edmund C. Sanford, stuck by him, but his hopes for Clark had collapsed.

Defeat rarely daunted Hall. During the previous summer (1891) he had renewed ties with the National Educational Association (NEA)—which had not yet evolved into a labor union—whose members had continually called for a more "scientific pedagogy." In response, Hall founded the *Pedagogical Seminary* (which after 1925 became the *Journal of Genetic Psychology*), and at the NEA's annual summer meeting in Toronto, Hall's informal discussions of "The Study of Children" attracted more attendees than did most official programs. In July 1892, Hall held a two-week summer school at Clark on "the higher pedagogy and psychology" that attracted dozens of school teachers, principals, and superintendents. The NEA's conservative leadership, however, fearing both Hall's innovations and his approach to others, put off pressures to establish an NEA child study department. (One finally emerged in 1894, with Hall as its first president; see Ross, 1972.) In the meantime, Joseph Jastrow, by then professor of psychology at the University of Wisconsin, began organizing a section of psychology for the World Columbian Exposition, planned for Chicago for the summer of 1893, and told Hall of his plans to visit eastern colleagues. Hall likely saw Jastrow's eastern trip as an opportunity to reassert himself. His Clark colleagues had deserted him, and the NEA's leadership proved unresponsive to his wiles, but he knew the specialized biological societies organized under the aegis of the American Society of Naturalists; he was a charter member of the American Physiological Society. Hall thus refocused his attention on his colleagues in psychology.

THE APA's "PRELIMINARY MEETING": JULY 1892

Sometime late in the spring of 1892, Hall invited many of these colleagues to join in forming an American psychological association, and on July 8, 1892, he gathered in his Worcester study a small group for that explicit purpose (see Cattell, 1917, 1929, 1943; Jastrow, 1943). A report on this "preliminary meeting" published only six weeks later emphasized an otherwise unspecified "general expression of opinion as to the form of the organization" ("The American Psychological Association," 1892, p. 104) and the decision to refer details to a seven-member committee, charged to organize the association's first annual meeting, "to report a plan of organization," and "to act as Council" (p. 104). Despite decades of speculation, no precise roll exists (Dennis & Boring, 1952; Fernberger, 1932, 1943); however, those attending heard papers by Clark professors, instructors, and alumni, and "Professor Jastrow asked the cooperation of all members for the section of psychology at the World's Fair, and invited correspondence upon the matter" (Cattell, 1894b, pp. 1–2). Most notably, the group learned that 26 men (including those present) had accepted membership in the new organization and had agreed to elect to membership 5 others, including 2 whom Hall had neglected to invite and 3 recent Leipzig PhDs—Hugo Münsterberg, Edward A. Pace, and Edward B. Titchener— who were about to assume professorships at Harvard, Catholic, and Cornell Universities, respectively, and had not yet arrived in (or returned to) America.

Although 6 of the 31 taught at Clark (and another 4 had earned their PhDs with Hall in Worcester or in Baltimore), they formed a diverse lot. By including several Canadians, at least 2 identifiable Jews (Jastrow and Münsterberg, although the latter had earlier converted to Lutheranism; see Hale, 1980), and a Roman Catholic priest (Pace; see Sexton, 1980), the early APA showed a greater openness than did many organizations of that time. Hall had always opened Clark to "outsiders," and this "patronage" contributed much to his academic success (Sokal, 1990). The professional interests in psychology of the charter members also varied greatly, and the group included psychiatrists (Edward Cowles and William Noyes of the McLean Hospital outside Boston), philosophers (e.g., John Dewey of Michigan, George S. Fullerton of Pennsylvania, James H. Hyslop of Columbia, and Josiah Royce of Harvard), pedagogists (e.g., William H. Burnham and Benjamin I. Gilman of Clark), as well as Leipzig- (or Clark- or Johns Hopkins-) trained experimentalists. Indeed, of late 19th-century approaches to psychology, Hall omitted only psychical research. To be sure, Hyslop and William James shared an interest in the subject, and James (at least) could not have been omitted. But if Hall had included ASPR activist Richard Hodgson among the initial members, many others—such as Jastrow (1900) and Columbia University's James McKeen Cattell (1893a)—would likely have declined membership.

In their diversity, however, these 31 men shared at least two other significant traits (besides their sex). First, they were all quite young. Aside from Cowles (aged 54), James and George T. Ladd of Yale (both 50) were the oldest, and Hall himself was only 48. At least 6 were in their 20s, and their average age was about 35. Like most of the university-based research-oriented fields of the late 19th century, psychology was a young man's science. And like most young men, its practitioners shared an enthusiasm for their science that infused their work. For its first few years, then, the American Psychological Association reflected an enthusiasm that did much to shape its character.

THE APA's FIRST ANNUAL MEETING: DECEMBER 1892

The enthusiasm and breadth of interest of its first members emerged clearly at the Association's first regular meeting, held at the University of Pennsylvania the following December (Cattell, 1894b). Of the 31 members, 18 attended the meeting and heard a dozen papers, many illustrating ways in which American psychology had evolved beyond the narrowly focused experimental tradition in which many of its members had been trained. For example, Jastrow's paper, "Experimental Psychology at the World's Fair," emphasized the kinds of anthropometric tests he planned to give the following summer to visitors to the section of psychology; William L. Bryan (1892) of Indiana University reported on his "Psychological Tests in the Schools of Springfield;" and Lightner Witmer of the University of Pennsylvania described the "Chronoscopic Measurement of Simple Reactions on All Classes of Persons." Even Cattell's detailed report of his massive reevaluation of classical psychophysical methods (Cattell, 1893b; Fullerton & Cattell, 1892) served primarily—or so one observer (O'Donnell, 1985) later claimed—"to demolish one of the cornerstones of traditional physiological psychology" (p. 144). In the program's final paper, Münsterberg attacked his colleagues' work as "rich in decimals but poor in ideas" (Cattell, 1894b, p. 11) and called for closer ties with philosophy (see also Münsterberg, 1898b). As the events of this first annual meeting illustrate, psychologists have never shied away from intellectual controversy.

In their enthusiasm for their new science, the psychologists worked together effectively to reach important professional goals. For example, they considered calls for cooperation from anthropologists, philosophers, and educators organizing symposia in connection with the Chicago World's Fair, but declined all of these invitations in order to "leave the members free to place their allegiance where they thought best" (Cattell, 1894b, p. 13).

Their new association gave other scholars the point of contact with psychology that they had sought and thus helped them claim their place in the late 19th-century scientific community. They elected Hall as president; heard his presidential address, "History and Prospects of Experimental Psychology in America;" and made plans to publish the proceedings of the meeting in his *American Journal of Psychology*. The first Council did not propose a constitution, but recommended the adoption of several "regulations . . . to be regarded as in effect in so far as the continuance of the Association depended upon them" (Cattell, 1894b, p. 13). Annual dues were set at $3, but unlike other organizations at the time, the APA did not spell out membership criteria. The regulations assigned "the right of nomination for membership [to] the Council," but stipulated that "the election [was] to be made by the Association." (Cattell, 1894b, p. 13). During the APA's first years, members applied their relatively loose standard rather strictly; although two recent Clark PhDs presented papers at this first annual meeting, they were not elected to membership. The Association did elect (on Council nomination) 11 new members. Significantly, none had been trained in experimental psychology, and although most worked at the intersection of psychology and traditional philosophy, at least two— Nicholas Murray Butler of Columbia and Jacob Gould Schurman of Cornell—were philosophers, with little real interest in psychology as such. The new Association thus reaffirmed its commitment to inclusiveness and worked to extend its influence more broadly. Cowles and Noyes—the psychiatrists who had accepted election the previous summer—did not attend and never participated actively in the Association's affairs; however, within six months of its founding, the APA could boast of 42 members and recognition from other learned societies.

Unfortunately, tensions within the psychological community soon diluted the good feelings that pervaded this meeting. As usual, most derived from Hall's behavior and the "personal and professional antagonism [he] aroused," (Ross, 1972, p. 235), which soon focused on his dictatorial editorship of the *American Journal of Psychology* (which, to be sure, he owned). American psychologists came to distrust his "capricious taste" and never knew what criteria he used in accepting or rejecting submissions. Dissatisfaction grew through 1892, and Hall's biographer (Ross, 1972) has speculated that support emerging at an informal gathering at the December 1892 APA meeting led Cattell and James Mark Baldwin of Princeton to approach Hall with several schemes to help make the *Journal* more responsive to them and the colleagues they represented. Negotiations led nowhere, however, and by late 1893, Baldwin and Cattell had made plans to establish the *Psychological Review* (*Review*), which first appeared in January 1894.

Hall did not attend the APA's second annual meeting, held in December 1893 at Columbia, and the Association dropped its plan to publish its proceedings in his journal.

LEADERSHIP CHANGES

Hall's detractors assumed leading roles in the Association; George T. Ladd served as president at the meeting, James was elected president for the following year, and Cattell was elected secretary (Cattell, 1894a). As host, Cattell had begun acting as secretary in the months before the meeting (Cattell, 1893–1894), arranging the program (he invited Hall to speak as former president and expressed regret when Hall decided not to attend), and dealing with local arrangements. He did so well that James (1893) praised his "tact, good humor, and flexibility of intellect." Through December 1893, Cattell also collected names of potential new members. He nominated for membership Mary Whiton Calkins of Wellesley College and Christine Ladd-Franklin of Baltimore, both of whom had already published extensively in the *American Journal of Psychology* and other journals. His letters on the subject argued that "we psychologists ought not to draw a sex-line" (Cattell, 1893–1894, pp. 5–7), and his colleagues agreed. Aside from several anthropological groups, which recognized that women could do kinds of fieldwork that no man could do, no other society had women members earlier in its development (Rossiter, 1982). Other experimentally trained psychologists, such as James R. Angell of Minnesota and Howard C. Warren of Princeton, also became members. However, as in 1892, at least four new members were more interested in philosophy than psychology, and several papers—such as "A Note on Anaximander" by Butler (Cattell, 1894a, p. 21) and "The Case of John Bunyan" by Royce (Cattell, 1894a, pp. 17–18)—seemed out of place to many. But philosophers at late-19th-century American universities lacked their own learned society to turn to, and through its first decade the APA served philosophy as much as it did psychology, a fact that had many implications for the Association.

In many ways, through the mid-1890s, and even afterward, the APA's development and adaptation to its changing environment articulated many of the patterns its members established during the first two years. As secretary, Cattell edited and published (in an edition of 300) the proceedings of the first meetings (Cattell, 1894a). From 1894 on, however, the Association published its annual proceedings in the *Psychological Review*, and at the annual meeting in 1894, the Association finally adopted its first formal constitution. It emphasized "the object of the Association [as] the advancement of Psychology as a science" and that "those are eligible for membership who are engaged in this work" (Cattell, 1895, p. 150). The constitution kept the Council's authority to nominate new members, but reaffirmed procedures that called for a vote of the membership on all new members. Through the next decade, successive Councils interpreted these newly stringent criteria rather loosely, and the 1906 Council explicitly noted that its predecessors had "historically and consistently recognized two sorts of qualifications: professional occupation in psychology and research" (Davis, 1907, p. 203). Despite attempts to tighten the nomination process, which called for nominators to list the publications of those who they proposed, the Association's membership policies remained inclusive through about 1905, when Councils openly began interpreting these criteria much more strictly. Membership reached 101 in 1898 and 127 in 1900 (Cattell, 1929).

CONNECTIONS WITH OTHER ORGANIZATIONS

From 1895, the APA met regularly with the other "Affiliated Societies" promoted by the American Society of Naturalists. Doing so had many practical benefits, as (like the other societies) the Association profited from the larger group's local arrangements ("Scientific Notes and News," 1895). Meeting formally and informally with other scientists and participating in the Society's annual symposium helped psychologists gain status for their science. In 1896, for example, William James represented the Association effectively in a symposium that focused on "The Inheritance of Acquired Characteristics" (Farrand, 1897). Through these early years the Association's annual programs included many philosophical papers, but many others illustrated American psychology's functional, developmental, and differential concerns. Many psychologists seemed to cluster around what was gradually becoming known as mental testing, and the collection of mental and physical statistics of large numbers of individuals. Scientifically, this concern for individual differences derived from an interest in the variation that made natural selection possible, and as Jastrow's plans for the World Columbian Exposition exemplified this tradition, the Association had promoted work along these lines from the start (Sokal, 1987). As noted earlier, even at the first annual meeting, others presented results of similar kinds of studies, and through the mid-1890s, Arthur MacDonald of the U.S. Bureau of Education regularly presented "Neuro–Social Data" of, for example, the "Sensibility to Pain by Pressure in the Hands of Individuals of Different Classes, Sexes, and Nationalities." More notably, in 1895, Livingston Farrand of Columbia described the "Series of Physical and Mental

Tests on the Students of Columbia College" (see Cattell & Farrand, 1896) that he and Cattell had undertaken "to obtain a record for comparative purposes of certain mental and physical characteristics of the students at different times during a period of rather active intellectual growth and at the same time to furnish material for a statistical study of the particular points examined" (Farrand, 1896, p. 124). This presentation stimulated excited discussion that led the Association, on Baldwin's motion, to establish a committee "to consider the feasibility of cooperation among the various psychological laboratories in the collection of mental and physical statistics" (Sanford, 1896b, p. 122). This committee was the APA's first venture beyond the sponsorship of meetings, and its activities deserve further attention.

THE APA COMMITTEE ON PHYSICAL AND MENTAL TESTS

In gathering what soon became known as the APA Committee on Physical and Mental Tests, the Association's leadership—President Cattell, Secretary–Treasurer Sanford, and Council members Baldwin, Dewey, Fullerton, James, and G. Ladd—sought both to ensure their control of the group and to involve those APA members who had experience with this type of work. Ignoring MacDonald, who had a well-deserved reputation as a crank (Gilbert, 1977), they named three of their own—Baldwin, Sanford, and Cattell (as chair)—to the committee, illustrating the centrality of the issue for the Association. Both Cattell and Sanford had sponsored testing programs in their laboratories, as had Jastrow and Witmer, the other two members of the committee, and Witmer soon began using these tests in an informal psychological clinic at the University of Pennsylvania. The testing programs concerned themselves primarily with sensory and motor capacities—for example, most measured different kinds of reaction times under varying conditions—and none reflected any overarching view of "the mind," or human ability or function. Despite the name the committee assumed and the goals of later tests, committee members were primarily concerned with the collection of mental and physical statistics. This interest had its roots in physical anthropometry, especially as practiced in England by Francis Galton, who had earlier done much to shape both Cattell's and Jastrow's scientific agendas and views on human variation (Sokal, 1987). Throughout the 1890s, the growing physical education movement reinforced this tradition, and the committee's work reflected its members' experience (e.g., Hartwell, 1893–1894).

Through 1896, the committee did most of its work through correspondence, which peaked only a month before the December meeting. Its preliminary report, presented at the meeting, listed "a series of physical and mental tests . . . especially appropriate for college students . . . the general public and, with . . . modifications, school children . . . which seemed most likely to reveal individual differences and development" (Baldwin, Cattell, Jastrow, Sanford, & Witmer, 1897, p. 132). It urged the Association's members to use a "variety" of such tests on students at their home institutions "so that the best ones may be determined." But it offered no criteria for "best" and never established a goal beyond the collection of statistics. Unfortunately, a crowded agenda prevented the Association at large from discussing the issues that were raised, and even in their letters to each other, its members seemed unsure about how they should proceed.

At the 1897 APA meeting, however, members began to address these issues, even as Jastrow (for example) emphasized the measurement of "the normal capacity of simple and typical sensory, motor and intellectual endowments" (Baldwin, Cattell, & Jastrow, 1898, p. 172). He also mentioned interests in "the distribution of such powers, their development in child growth, their relation to practical and daily pursuits, and their correlation with one another" (p. 172; i.e., just the kinds of issues to which functional psychologists of the late 19th and early 20th centuries devoted themselves). But these were clearly subsidiary to his (and the colleagues') primary goals, and although he reviewed "the selection of the capacities to be tested" (p. 172) and spoke of "(a) the senses, (b) the motor capacities, and (c) the more complex mental processes" (p. 173), his remarks focused on the first two and slighted the third. For his part, Cattell argued that tests should be easy to administer and emphasized the constraints that testers faced. Only Baldwin, whose concurrent studies of *Mental Development in the Child and the Race* (1895) helped set an agenda for 20th-century developmental psychology (Cahan, 1984), claimed that tests should be given "as psychological a character as possible" (Baldwin et al., p. 175). Thus, Baldwin disparaged many of the procedures suggested by his colleagues and even cited contemporaneous work by Alfred Binet on tests of memory. In reply, committee chair Cattell noted that the concerns Baldwin recommended "seem . . . rather a subject for research than for anthropometric tests" and admitted that "the tests most interesting to the psychologist are those most difficult to make in three minutes." (Baldwin et al., p. 176). He thus confirmed the committee's limited view of testing, which dominated its activities until it passed out of existence sometime in the late 1890s. However, in 1897, the Association appropriated $100 for the committee's use—its first expenditure for anything beyond administrative expenses—which its members used to purchase apparatus and have test forms printed.

Three years later, in 1900, MacDonald asked the Association (and others) to endorse his call for "the establishment in the Department of the Interior of the Psycho–Physical Laboratory [for] . . . the collection of sociological, anthropological, abnormal and pathological data [for] the study of criminal, pauper and defective classes" (cited in Gilbert, 1977, p. 183). But MacDonald's contentiousness had grown since 1895—one APA member called him "too disgusting a person for self-respecting people to have anything to do with" (Franklin, 1900)—and again the Association did nothing (Farrand, 1901). Even in the short run, the Committee on Physical and Mental Tests had no real impact on psychology's evolution. Most significant developments emerged elsewhere—notably at what were then known as "schools for the feebleminded"—without the APA's support or imprimatur. In 1906, the Association again discussed "the question of Organized Cooperation in Standardizing Psychologists Tests" (Davis, 1907, p. 202), and although many members doubted the propriety of organizing it at all, the Council appointed a Committee on Measurements. But like its predecessor it did little and had negligible influence on the practice of psychology. In many ways, then, the Association's first efforts to shape its members' science proved unsuccessful.

The APA proved equally uninfluential in other areas of concern. For example, in 1898, at Baldwin's instigation, it organized a Standing Committee on Psychological and Philosophical Terminology, charged it broadly to deal with "new terms" in these fields in both English and other languages, and urged its members to collaborate actively with psychologists from other countries. But aside from Baldwin's brief remarks in 1900, the committee never reported (Farrand, 1899, 1901). In 1897, Cattell urged the APA to hold an informal meeting that August in conjunction with the American Association for the Advancement of Science's (AAAS's) annual meeting, then being planned for Boston (Farrand, 1898). In July, *Science* even announced the time of the meeting ("Scientific notes and news," 1898), but the following September, *Psychological Review* noted that the "summer meeting . . . was given up owing to the small number of papers offered" ("Notes," 1898). In a similar action in 1900, the APA voted to allow members to organize "local sections" of the Association and immediately authorized "branches" in Cambridge, Massachusetts; Chicago; and New York (Farrand, 1901). In New York, the branch grew out of earlier meetings sponsored by the section for anthropology and psychology of the New York Academy of Sciences and met regularly through 1935, eventually leading to the formation of the Eastern Psychological Association in the 1930s (Benjamin, 1991). The branch centered in Chicago—known at various times as the Western Branch, the Northwestern Branch, and the North Central Branch—

sponsored and reported on several meetings through 1908 (Gore, 1905a, 1905b; "Notes," 1902, 1903; "Notes and News," 1904). But it then passed into oblivion, and direct antecedents of what emerged in 1928 as the Midwestern Psychological Association did not appear until 1926 (Benjamin, 1979).

PUBLICATION POSSIBILITIES CONSIDERED AND ABANDONED

Another potentially useful initiative emerged in 1900, when James H. Leuba, a Hall PhD who had taught at Bryn Mawr since 1898 (McBride, 1947), asked the Association "for financial support in publishing his catalogue of psychological literature" (Farrand, 1901, p. 159), a bibliography and card index of older and more recent publications in the field. Since 1894, however, the *Psychological Review* had annually issued a *Psychological Index*, a bibliography of current work in the field, so many members believed that Leuba's work was redundant, at least in part. But many members also shared Leuba's interests in earlier psychological literature (Leuba, 1900; Sanford, 1902a, 1902b), and one or two, perhaps, may have seen in his request an opportunity to challenge Baldwin's and Cattell's prominent positions within the field. As a result, the Association created a Committee on Bibliography "to take the whole matter under consideration." Its first report was tabled in 1901 (Farrand, 1902), but the following year the committee urged the Association to purchase "Prof. Leuba's collection belonging to the years prior to January 1, 1894" (Farrand, 1903, p. 151), to charge it with expanding the card index, and to begin plans to publish the bibliography. After a long discussion of the detailed report, the Association accepted this recommendation, but in 1903 the committee went further and urged the APA to hire an "executive agent who could carry on the correspondence necessary to secure the cooperation in this undertaking of the members of the association, and others" (Farrand, 1904, p. 35) and to assume general charge of the project. This recommendation would have had the APA employ its first staff member and spend more in one year than it had in the previous five years. The Association's "accumulated fund" could have supported this expenditure, and many members saw great value in the project. But many did not, and the Council urged its tabling. The committee still endorsed the plan at the Association's next two meetings, presenting detailed budgets that demonstrated how the APA could afford it. But consensus eluded continued discussion until the middle of the decade, when the Association at large learned that Benjamin Rand, a librarian working at Harvard, would publish a 1,200-page, two-volume

Bibliography of Philosophy, Psychology, and Cognate Subjects (Rand, 1905a, 1905b) as part of the *Dictionary of Philosophy and Psychology* that Baldwin (1901–1905) was editing. In 1906, the committee concluded, with some embarrassment, that "after an examination of the bibliography of Dr. Rand, it was regarded as injudicious that anything further be done in the matter" (Davis, 1907, p. 203).

Leuba's bibliography was not the only publication opportunity that the APA managed to avoid, and indeed, it never embarked on any publications program in its early years. In 1893, one option Baldwin and Cattell offered Hall in their attempts to broaden the *American Journal of Psychology* was to have it become—although still privately owned—the Association's official journal (Ross, 1972). Other societies benefited from similar contracts with other journals, as they guaranteed an outlet for reports of their meetings and the journals' owners could be sure of larger circulations. Some made large profits from such arrangements, even when the societies paid them less for each subscription than nonmembers paid, as wider distribution allowed them to sell additional advertising at higher rates. For example, Cattell did quite well financially when *Science* (which he owned and edited) became in 1900 the official journal of the AAAS (Sokal, 1980). Even earlier, the American Society of Naturalists adopted the *American Naturalist*, founded privately in 1867, as its official journal (Nyhart, 1979), and Baldwin and Cattell probably cited this example in their talks with Hall. But Hall proved intransigent; the Association issued its first volume of *Proceedings* in 1894 (at a cost of $55.93), and later that year it "resolved that the minutes should be printed in such journals as were prepared to print them in full" (Cattell, 1895, p. 151). Through the 1890s, most scientific periodicals had to spend more time soliciting submissions than screening them, and from 1895 Baldwin and Cattell's *Psychological Review* regularly published each meeting's full proceedings, thus serving the Association and its members well throughout the decade.

PSYCHOLOGICAL REVIEW EDITORS SPLIT

Later in 1895, Cattell urged the Council to arrange for APA members to have their $3 annual dues credited toward annual subscriptions to his and Baldwin's *Review* (which then cost $4) or Hall's *Journal* (then $5). The journals' owners would have then had to provide subscriptions at effective rates of $1 and $2, respectively, but would have benefited from the increased circulation that Cattell projected. The Council, however, declined his proposal, as Sanford (representing Hall and by then, himself, an editor of the *Journal*) spoke against it (Sanford, 1896a). Unlike the *Review*—which regularly ran advertisements for typewriters and bicycles, as well as books and graduate programs—the *Journal* refused to carry such notices, in order (so it claimed) to keep its reviews "more impartial" (Hall, 1895, p. 5). Hall, thus, would have earned less from this arrangement than would Baldwin and Cattell. In any event, the Association again refrained from taking the initiative, and the *Psychological Review* continued to publish detailed reports on APA meetings through 1904. During these years, the relations between the *Review*'s two owner–editors grew progressively worse, and they soon began alternating (rather than sharing) editorial control, with Baldwin having responsibility for odd-numbered years ("Notes," 1896). By April 1904, their differences had become irreconcilable, and Cattell suggested (perhaps as a ploy) that the APA take charge of the *Review*, the *Psychological Index*, and the series of *Psychological Review Monographs* that had appeared during the preceding decade. But the Association's leaders again avoided taking action, and late that year, after a bitter and divisive public debate,[1] Cattell sold his share of the *Review* to Baldwin (1926, Vol. 1).

In 1905, as Baldwin continued the *Review*, he established the *Psychological Bulletin*, which began that year to carry the Association's proceedings. Cattell meanwhile had founded the *Journal of Philosophy, Psychology and Scientific Methods*, whose control he soon yielded to his philosopher colleagues at Columbia, and which in 1920 dropped the final four words of its title. In the early 1910s, soon after a sex scandal forced Baldwin from Johns Hopkins, he had to yield control of the *Psychological Bulletin, Index, Monographs,* and *Review* to his junior colleague, Howard C. Warren, of Princeton. Warren retained private ownership through the mid-1920s, when he sold them to the Association at prices far below their assessed values (Fernberger, 1932).

The Association's sluggish response to initiatives and its seeming inability to capitalize on opportunities did not stem from any financial constraints. After all, the first Council had set annual dues at $3 in 1892—a level confirmed in the first constitution of 1894—and an inclusive membership policy combined with a lack of serious expenses led to an unchecked growth for the Association's "accumulated fund." It opened at $50.30 in 1892, reached $800.88 in 1898, jumped to $1,585.78 at the Association's 10th meeting in 1901, and reached $2,770.17 5 years later (Buchner, 1903; Davis, 1906). (During the APA's first decade, the Consumer Price Index remained at just about one quarter of its 1967 level; through the 1890s,

---

[1]Historians have yet to publish an account of this episode, which the papers of those who were actively involved richly document (e.g., see Cattell, 1904a, 1904b; Judd, 1904; Münsterberg, 1904).

nonfarm employees earned, on the average, $455 annually; and Cattell's $5,000 salary in 1905 probably made him one of the highest paid APA members [U.S. Bureau of the Census, 1975]). The Association did make several grants to support its members' research—most notably, that for the Committee on Physical and Mental Tests (Farrand, 1898, 1899; "Notes," 1898)—but for the most part its only expenses were secretarial. In 1895, the Council discussed reducing annual dues to $1, but Cattell's argument against the move—that "it would be very difficult to raise them if they were once put down" (Sanford, 1896a)—prevailed. Seven years later, the Council first formally recommended a constitutional amendment that would have decreased dues, but the Association at large tabled the motion (Farrand 1905). The rapidly growing accumulated fund, however, led to renewed calls for decreases. In 1904, the Council recommended a decrease in dues, to $1 annually, and a remission of two thirds of the dues paid for the previous year. As the constitution required, the 1905 annual meeting re-affirmed the dues decrease and instructed the Council "to consider the whole question of the guardianship and utilization of the Association's accumulated fund, and to report upon the same at the next annual meeting" (Davis, 1906, p. 39). In doing so, the Council realized the rashness of its act and attempted to double dues to $2, a proposal that the Association at large quickly stifled (see Davis, 1907). (Dues again reached $2 only in 1919 [see Fernberger, 1932]). With its final report on the accumulated fund, which finally appeared in 1907, the Council reaffirmed the early APA's apparent inability to act. It found "at present no special activity of the association which requires the expenditure of any money which might be properly drawn from this fund" and thus urged its preservation "till such time as the association shall formulate special work which will require its use in whole or in part" (Woodworth, 1908, p. 35).

Ironically, in its early years the Association achieved perhaps its greatest success by promoting the development of philosophy, its parent discipline, in a way that encouraged it to be professional and grow through the early 20th century as other disciplines had done in the late 19th century. In doing so, the APA alienated many of those psychologists who had campaigned most strongly for psychology's independence from philosophy, a group of experimentalists that included both those with functional concerns and those whose work continued the traditional research fostered since the late 1870s by German psychological laboratories. In several ways, this second group seemed to many to be the APA's natural constituency. After all, the physiologists and others had founded their scientific societies to promote basic research, and the membership criteria their societies adopted decried the kinds of practical issues that interested many American psychologists. But just about all up-to-date life science after Darwin, whether physiological or psychological, was functional, and "functional" in psychology typically implied a concern for life in the real world, not necessarily implied by "functional" in physiology. As John O'Donnell (1985) has shown, functional concerns led American psychology to evolve toward behavioristic perspectives typically unsympathetic with traditional experimental psychology. Those APA members with these concerns felt slighted on two accounts: by the Association's support for philosophy and by their psychological colleagues' interest in practicable problems. As early as 1896, an *American Journal of Psychology* comment—almost surely written by Titchener, who (with Sanford) had joined Hall as editor the previous year—complained about "the retirement of the experimentalists" from the Association. Although Titchener overstated the case, he did emphasize another reason for his dissatisfaction (i.e., the form of presentation demanded by the format of the Association's annual meeting). He thus claimed that

> unless the meetings are allowed to take the form of a conversazione, the apparatus employed shown in their working, and the results made to speak for themselves in charts and diagrams near the apparatus, it would seem that the drift of the Association must continue in the nonexperimental direction. ("The American Psychological Association," 1896, p. 448)

In 1904, Titchener self-assuredly invited both kinds of experimentalists to meet and focus on just these kinds of presentations, which APA meetings continued to ignore. This group soon took on a life of its own, evolving eventually into the Society of Experimental Psychologists. It has its own history, which others have dealt with effectively (Boring, 1938; Goodwin, 1985). But as these historians have made clear, few of its members, besides Titchener, ever felt the need to withdraw from the APA. Psychologists can thus learn much by tracing the course of the APA's inclusive policy as an adaptive response to developments in its intellectual and professional environment and by following its influence on the Association's development.

GRADUAL INDEPENDENCE FOR PHILOSOPHY

Although the APA's early support for philosophy may seem out of place to at least some late 20th-century psychologists, through the century's first half decade, at least, psychology's position as a newly scientific offspring of philosophy made ties between the disciplines seem quite appropriate. Even as it complained about the retirement of the experimentalists and decried the format of APA annual meetings, the *American Journal of Psychology* noted that "the plan and restrictions of the meetings are of a kind to favor" the philosophers, and admitted that "it is not that the systematic psychologists are forcing their way unduly to the front" ("The American Psychological Association," 1896, p. 448). Other more general factors also shaped these developments, as many late-19th-century philosophers tried to help their discipline evolve in its new intellectual environment. In particular, as they worked to adapt their field for the new universities' hierarchy, they sought to follow their specialized siblings, and inasmuch as they lacked their own national society, they flocked to the APA (Veysey, 1979; Wilson, 1979). At times their presentations seemed to dominate the Association's meetings, as interpretations of "The Freedom of the Will" (Chrysostom, 1895) and similar topics provoked much discussion. An early 20th-century statistical analysis concluded that only about 12% of the papers presented at annual meetings during the APA's first decade focused on philosophical issues (Buchner, 1903). Only one other subject, experimental psychology, commanded more attention, and at several meetings—notably those of 1896 at Harvard, under the presidency of Mary W. Calkins, and 1898 at Columbia—APA members actually heard more philosophical papers than papers on any other single topic. Furthermore, as soon became clear, Titchener was not the only psychologist who found this trend displeasing.

As a result, in 1895, "the question of the formation of a philosophical society or a philosophical section within the present Association was . . . referred to the Council with full power to act" (Sanford, 1896b, p. 122). Thus, at the 1896 meeting most of the large cluster of "papers of a distinctly philosophical character" were scheduled on one morning (Farrand, 1897, p. 107). But this action did not satisfy all psychologists, and some seemed particularly disturbed that many newly elected members had stronger credentials in philosophy than psychology. Witmer thus proposed formally (a) that the APA "select only such papers and contributions to the program of the annual meeting as are psychological in subject matter"; (b) that the Council begin to "plan for the formation of an American Philosophical or Metaphysical Association" as one of the "present Affiliated Societies"; and, going still further, (c) that the Council post, for all nominees for membership, "a statement of the[ir] contribution or contributions to psychology" (cited in Farrand, 1897, p. 109). Although many APA members shared some of Witmer's concerns, they knew him as one of the Association's most contentious members, and few wanted to restrict membership. But in 1897, the Council did ask nominators to list the publications of the new members they proposed, and for the first time, the Association held parallel sessions,

"Section A . . . for the discussion of physical and mental tests, and Section B . . . for the reading of psychological papers" (Farrand, 1898, p. 145).

Despite this compromise, many psychologists still perceived problems with the philosophers' large presence, and at the 1898 meeting—when philosophical papers again dominated the program—they took action. Led this time by Sanford, one of the APA's best-liked members, the Association resolved to instruct the Council to consider and report on "the organization of the Association with reference to a possible philosophical section," to poll its members on their opinion about this matter, and to arrange "the programme for the next meeting to gather philosophical papers . . . into . . . one session" (Farrand, 1899, pp. 147–148). During the following 12 months, psychologists debated the issue, notes on it appeared in the *Psychological Review* and elsewhere (e.g., Bliss, 1899), and at the 1899 meeting, although the parallel sessions appeared to "work satisfactorily, . . . many members would have been glad to have been present in both sections at the same time" ("Notes and News," 1900, p. 280). In an editorial note written, perhaps, by Sanford, the *American Journal of Psychology* thus claimed that "there seemed little desire to take any action that might lead to an actual division of the Association" ("Notes and News," 1900, p. 280). But others disagreed, and psychologists and philosophers both continued working toward that end.

Only two days after the end of the 1899 APA meeting, philosophers meeting in Kansas City on January 1, 1900, organized the Western Philosophical Association, "to stimulate an interest in philosophy in all its branches and to encourage original investigation" ("Notes," 1900, p. 104). Two of the five members of its first Executive Committee, including its president, Frank Thilly of the University of Missouri, were active APA members, and the organizers clearly profited from the APA's example and, indeed, from that set by the other "Affiliated Societies." About 20 months later, philosophers in the East, led by Cornell professor J. E. Creighton (who had served on the APA Council from 1898), followed the lead of their western colleagues and founded an American Philosophical Association ("Notes," 1902; cf. Creighton, 1902; Gardiner, 1926). These organizers were again among the many who had spoken at APA meetings as members during the preceding half decade, and the first president of the American Philosophical Association after Creighton was A. T. Ormond of Princeton, who had been a charter member of the APA. As these new organizations appeared, fewer individuals sought APA membership. But all three societies grew through the early 1900s, and the APA met jointly with the Western Philosophical Association in 1902 and 1907, and with the American Philosophical Association in 1904, 1905, and 1906 (see "The

American Philosophical Society," 1902). These philosophical societies thrived and finally amalgamated in the late 1910s. Today's American Philosophical Association comprises three divisions: Eastern, Central, and Pacific.

CONSOLIDATING CHANGE

By 1905, the APA could put aside its fears of being dominated by philosophers and resume its growth, which had been slowed only by the withdrawal of philosophers from the Association in 1902. American universities boomed through the 20th century's first decade, and psychology grew along with its host campuses. Perhaps more importantly, other institutions, such as psychiatric hospitals and schools for the feebleminded, began hiring psychologists, and this development had many longer term implications for psychology's evolution (Napoli, 1981). During the APA's first decade, these universities and other institutions established 30 new psychological laboratories, and by 1910 about 70 U.S. institutions supported such facilities (Garvey, 1929). In 1906, the Association elected 19 new members, bringing its membership to about 181. The Council announced plans to tighten its application of the membership criteria—"engage[ment] in the advancement of Psychology as a science" (Davis, 1907, p. 203)—that had been in effect since 1894. As noted earlier, it explicitly recognized that its predecessors had "historically and consistently recognized two sorts of qualifications: professional occupation in psychology and research" (Davis, 1907, p. 203). With continued growth of psychology, however, the Council decided that it would strictly interpret the first of these criteria, "so that, in the absence of research, positions held in related branches, such as philosophy and education, or temporary positions, such as assistantships in psychology, are not regarded as qualifying a candidate for membership" (p. 203). It even went so far as to propose a constitutional amendment that would have allowed the Council, by unanimous vote, to "drop any member of the Association who has not been engaged in the advancement of Psychology for a period of five or more years" (Davis, 1907, p. 203). The Association at large, however, referred this amendment back to the Council, which tabled it the following year. The APA may have decided to adopt a more exclusive membership policy, but it was not about to dismiss its long-term members (Woodworth, 1908).

But why did psychologists continue to join the American Psychological Association through its early years, even as failed in its attempts to develop a range of programs in support of its members' research and other professional interests? More particularly, why did experimentalists retain their APA membership, even as from 1904 they annually met together separately to discuss their scientific research?

An early *American Journal of Psychology* editorial (Hall, 1895), which inflated Hall's role in the origins of American psychology, emphasized the Association's role in encouraging cooperation among the country's psychological laboratories and in promoting a psychological "esprit de corps." Through its first years, the Association did foster enthusiasm and good feeling that meant much to those who had previously worked in isolation. But this good feeling began to break down by end of the decade, when several members stopped attending APA meetings lest they run into those with whom they felt antipathy (Münsterberg, 1898a; Scripture, 1899). More seriously, the Association's record after 1895 belies any claim that it actually promoted psychological cooperation. A deeper answer to these questions lies in recognizing the ecological niche that the Association filled for its members in the scientific environment of early 20th-century America. On one level, it supplemented the journals that published their research by fostering, through its annual meetings, the rapid exchange of ideas and information. The experimentalists, of course, found this function of lesser importance than did most other psychologists of the period. But even they found in the APA an informal forum in which they could discuss their professional concerns and through which they could follow their colleagues' gossip. Then, as now, the passing hallway conversations and spontaneous discussions over meals that these meetings fostered often meant more to those attending than did any formal sessions.

On another, more significant level, the APA gave its members a conduit that allowed them to communicate with the larger American scientific community and, even more important, one through which others could recognize their discipline. After all, in establishing a new science, psychologists of a century ago faced (or believed they faced) much opposition (or at least ignorance) from their scientific contemporaries. The Association's continued ties with the American Society of Naturalists thus meant much to the APA's first members, and a 1902 invitation to affiliate with the AAAS and send a delegate to the AAAS council meant even more (Farrand, 1903). From the following year, the APA met regularly with the AAAS and took part in the Convocation Week programs that the larger association, following the naturalists' lead, organized annually from 1903 on, during the week between Christmas and New Year's Day. To be sure, some psychologists took greater pride that the National Academy of Science elected several of their colleagues to membership, recognizing Cattell in 1901, James in 1903, and Royce in 1906 (Cattell, 1929). But such recognition was beyond most psychologists, and they looked instead to the American Psychological Association for a sense of legitimacy.

By 1906, then, the American Psychological Association had established itself as an important feature in the environment in which psychology in America thrived. If it could not point to an unblemished record of success during the preceding dozen years, neither could any other contemporaneous scientific organization. More important, during its early years, the APA's members established a firm foundation on which their successors could build a highly effective institution. This achievement, then, was the APA's first real success.

REFERENCES

The American Philosophical Society and the American Philosophical Association. (1902). *Popular Science Monthly, 61,* 91–92.

The American Psychological Association. (1892). *Science, 20* (old series), 104.

The American Psychological Association. (1896). *American Journal of Psychology, 7,* 448–449.

Appel, T. A. (1988). Organizing biology: The American Society of Naturalists and its "Affiliated Societies," 1883–1923. In R. Rainger, K. R. Benson, & J. Maienschein (Eds.), *The American development of biology* (pp. 87–120). Philadelphia: University of Pennsylvania Press.

Baldwin, J. M. (1895). *Mental development in the child and the race: Methods and processes.* New York: Macmillan.

Baldwin, J. M. (Ed.). (1901–1905). *Dictionary of philosophy and psychology* (3 vols. in 4 books). New York: Macmillan.

Baldwin, J. M. (1926). *Between two wars (1861–1921).* (Vol. 1). Boston: Stratford.

Baldwin, J. M., Cattell, J. M., & Jastrow, J. (1898). Physical and mental tests. *Psychological Review, 5,* 172–179.

Baldwin, J. M., Cattell, J. M., Jastrow, J., Sanford, E. C., & Witmer, L. (1897). Preliminary report of the Committee on Physical and Mental Tests. *Psychological Review, 4,* 132–138.

Benjamin, L. T., Jr. (1979). The Midwestern Psychological Association: A history of the organization and its antecedents. *American Psychologist, 34,* 201–213.

Benjamin, L. T., Jr. (1991). A history of the New York Branch of the American Psychological Association, 1903–1935. *American Psychologist, 46,* 1003–1011.

Bliss, C. B. (1899). Proposed changes in the American Psychological Association. *Psychological Review, 6,* 237–238.

Boring, E. G. (1938). The Society of Experimental Psychologists: 1904–1938. *American Journal of Psychology, 51,* 410–423.

Bryan, W. L. (1892). On the development of voluntary motor ability. *American Journal of Psychology, 5*, 125–204.

Buchner, E. F. (1903). Ten years of American Psychology: 1892–1902. *Science, 18*, 193–204, 233–241.

Cahan, E. D. (1984). The genetic psychologies of James Mark Baldwin and Jean Piaget. *Developmental Psychology, 20*, 128–135.

Cattell, J. M. (1893a). Esoteric psychology. *The Independent, 45*, 316–317.

Cattell, J. M. (1893b). On errors of observation. *American Journal of Psychology, 5*, 285–293.

Cattell, J. M. (1893–1894). [Unpublished letter book] In J. M. Cattell papers, Library of Congress, Washington, DC.

Cattell, J. M. (1894a). The American Psychological Association. *Psychological Review, 1*, 214–215.

Cattell, J. M. (Ed.). (1894b). *Proceedings of the American Psychological Association.* New York: Macmillan.

Cattell, J. M. (1895). Report of the secretary and treasurer for 1894. *Psychological Review, 2*, 149–152.

Cattell, J. M. (1904a, April 16). Letter to H. Münsterberg. H. Münsterberg papers, Boston Public Library, Boston, MA.

Cattell, J. M. (1904b, May 9). Letter to H. Münsterberg. H. Münsterberg papers, Boston Public Library, Boston, MA.

Cattell, J. M. (1917). Our psychological association and research. *Science, 45*, 275–284.

Cattell, J. M. (1929). Psychology in America. *Science, 70*, 335–347.

Cattell, J. M. (1943). The founding of the association and the Hopkins and Clark laboratories. *Psychological Review, 50*, 61–64.

Cattell, J. M., & Farrand, L. (1896). Physical and mental measurements of students of Columbia University. *Psychological Review, 3*, 618–648.

Chrysostom, B. (1895). The freedom of the will. *Psychological Review, 2*, 157–158.

Creighton, J. E. (1902). The purposes of a philosophical association. *Philosophical Review, 11*, 219–237.

Dallenbach, K. M. (1937). The American Journal of Psychology: 1887–1937. *American Journal of Psychology, 50*, 489–506.

Davis, W. H. (1906). Report of the secretary for 1905. *Psychological Bulletin, 3*, 37–41.

Davis, W. H. (1907). Report of the secretary for 1906. *Psychological Bulletin, 4*, 201–205.

Dennis, W., & Boring, E. G. (1952). The founding of the APA. *American Psychologist, 7*, 95–97.

Farrand, L. (1896). Series of physical and mental tests on the students of Columbia College. *Psychological Review, 3*, 124.

Farrand, L. (1897). Report of the secretary and treasurer for 1896. *Psychological Review, 4*, 107–110.

Farrand, L. (1898). Report of the secretary and treasurer for 1897. *Psychological Review, 5*, 145–147.

Farrand, L. (1899). Report of the secretary for 1898. *Psychological Review, 6*, 146–148.

Farrand, L. (1901). Report of the secretary for 1900. *Psychological Review, 8*, 158–160.

Farrand, L. (1902). Report of the secretary for 1901. *Psychological Review, 9*, 134–136.

Farrand, L. (1903). Report of the secretary for 1902. *Psychological Review, 10*, 150–153.

Farrand, L. (1904). Report of the secretary for 1903. *Psychological Bulletin, 1*, 33–36.

Farrand, L. (1905). Report of the secretary for 1904. *Psychological Bulletin, 2*, 37–38.

Fernberger, S. W. (1932). The American Psychological Association: A historical summary, 1892–1930. *Psychological Bulletin, 29*, 1–89.

Fernberger, S. W. (1943). The American Psychological Association, 1892–1942. *Psychological Review, 50*, 33–60.

Franklin, C. L. (1900, December 21). Letter to J. M. Cattell. J. M. Cattell papers, Library of Congress, Washington, DC.

Fullerton, G. S., & Cattell, J. M. (1892). On the perception of small differences, with special reference of the extent, force, and time of movement. *Publications of the University of Pennsylvania* (Philosophical Series No. 2).

Gardiner, H. N. (1926). The first twenty-five years of the American Philosophical Association. *Philosophical Review, 35*, 145–158

Garvey, C. R. (1929). List of American psychological laboratories. *Psychological Bulletin, 26*, 652–660.

Gilbert, J. B. (1977). Anthropometrics in the U.S. Bureau of Education: The case of Arthur MacDonald's "laboratory." *History of Education Quarterly, 17*, 169–195.

Goodwin, C. J. (1985). On the origins of Titchener's experimentalists. *Journal of the History of the Behavioral Sciences, 21*, 383–389.

Gore, W. G. (1905a). Meeting of the north central section of the American Psychological Association. *Psychological Bulletin, 2*, 6–10.

Gore, W. G. (1905b). Proceedings of the meeting of the north central section of the American Psychological Association. *Psychological Bulletin, 2*, 200–203.

Hale, M., Jr. (1980). *Human science and social order: Hugo Münsterberg and the origins of applied psychology.* Philadelphia, PA: Temple University Press.

Hall, G. S. (1895). Editorial. *American Journal of Psychology, 7*, 3–8.

Hall, G. S. (1923). *Life and confessions of a psychologist.* New York: Appleton.

Hartwell, E. M. (1893–1894). Interrelation of mental, moral, and physical training. In *Report of the Commissioner of Education* (pp. 458–459). Washington, DC: U.S. Government Printing Office.

Hawkins, H. (1960). *Pioneer: A history of the Johns Hopkins University, 1874–1889.* Ithaca, NY: Cornell University Press.

James, W. (1893, December 30). Letter to J. M. Cattell. J. M. Cattell papers, Library of Congress, Washington, DC.

Jastrow, J. (1900). The modern occult. *Popular Science Monthly, 57,* 449–472.

Jastrow, J. (1943). American psychology in the '80's and '90's. *Psychological Review, 50,* 65–67.

Judd, C. H. (1904, March 29). Letter to H. Münsterberg. H. Münsterberg papers, Boston Public Library, Boston, MA.

Kevles, D. J. (1978). *The physicists: The history of a scientific community in modern America.* New York: Knopf.

Koelsch, W. A. (1987). *Clark University, 1887–1987: A narrative history.* Worcester, MA: Clark University Press.

Leuba, J. H. (1900, May 23). Letter to J. M. Cattell. J. M. Cattell papers, Library of Congress, Washington, DC.

MacDonald, A. (1900, July 6). Letter to J. M. Cattell. J. M. Cattell papers, Library of Congress, Washington, DC.

Mauskopf, S. H. (1989). The history of the American Society for Psychical Research: An interpretation. *Journal of the American Society for Psychical Research, 83,* 7–29.

McBride, K. E. (1947). James H. Leuba: 1867–1946. *American Journal of Psychology, 60,* 645–646.

Münsterberg, H. (1898a). Letter to J. M. Cattell. J. M. Cattell papers, Library of Congress, Washington, DC.

Münsterberg, H. (1898b). The danger from experimental psychology. *Atlantic Monthly, 81,* 159–167.

Münsterberg, H. (1904, May 28). Letter to J. M. Cattell. H. Münsterberg papers, Boston Public Library, Boston, MA.

Murray, F. S., & Rowe, F. B. (1979). Psychology laboratories in the United States prior to 1900. *Teaching of Psychology, 6,* 19–21.

Napoli, D. S. (1981). *Architects of adjustment: The history of the psychological profession in the United States.* Port Washington, NY: Kennikat Press.

Notes. (1896). *Psychological Review, 3,* 705.

Notes. (1898). *Psychological Review, 5,* 344–346, 554, 677.

Notes. (1900). *Psychological Review, 7,* 104, 323–324.

Notes. (1902). *Psychological Review, 9,* 103, 216, 327–328, 431–432.

Notes. (1903). *Psychological Review, 10,* 223–224.

Notes and news. (1900). *American Journal of Psychology, 11,* 280–281.

Notes and news. (1904). *Psychological Bulletin, 1,* 45, 133–135, 291–292.

Nyhart, L. K. (1979). *The American Naturalist, 1867–1886: A case study of the relationship between amateur and professional naturalists in nineteenth-century America* (Senior thesis), Princeton University.

O'Donnell, J. M. (1985). *The origins of behaviorism: American psychology, 1870–1920*. New York: New York University Press.

Rand, B. (1905a). *Bibliography of philosophy, psychology, and cognate subjects* (Vol. 1). New York: Macmillan.

Rand, B. (1905b). *Bibliography of philosophy, psychology, and cognate subjects* (Vol. 2). New York: Macmillan.

Ross, D. (1972). *G. Stanley Hall: The psychologist as prophet*. Chicago: University of Chicago Press.

Rossiter, M. W. (1982). *Women scientists in America: Struggles and strategies to 1940*. Baltimore: Johns Hopkins University Press.

Sanford, E. C. (1896a, January 10). Letter to E. B. Titchener. E. B. Titchener papers, Cornell University Archives, Ithaca, NY.

Sanford, E. C. (1896b). Report of the secretary and treasurer for 1895. *Psychological Review, 3,* 121–123.

Sanford, E. C. (1902a, May 24). Letter to J. M. Cattell. J. M. Cattell papers, Library of Congress, Washington, DC.

Sanford, E. C. (1902b, December 1). Letter to J. M. Cattell. J. M. Cattell papers, Library of Congress, Washington, DC.

Scientific notes and news. (1895). *Science, 2,* 803.

Scientific notes and news. (1898). *Science, 8,* 73.

Scripture, E. W. (1899, November 29). Letter to J. M. Cattell. J. M. Cattell papers, Library of Congress, Washington, DC.

Sexton, V. S. (1980). Edward Aloysius Pace. *Psychological Research, 42,* 39–47.

Sokal, M. M. (Ed.). (1981). *An education in psychology: James McKeen Cattell's journal and letters from Germany and England, 1880–1888*. Cambridge, MA: MIT Press.

Sokal, M. M. (1987). James McKeen Cattell and mental anthropometry: Nineteenth-century science and reform and the origins of psychological testing. In M. Sokal (Ed.), *Psychological testing and American society, 1890–1930* (pp. 21–45). New Brunswick, NJ: Rutgers University Press.

Sokal, M. M. (1990). G. Stanley Hall and the institutional character of psychology at Clark, 1889–1920. *Journal of the History of the Behavioral Sciences, 26,* 114–124.

U.S. Bureau of the Census. (1975). *Historical statistics of the United States: Colonial times to 1970* (Vol. 1). Washington, DC: U.S. Government Printing Office.

Veysey, L. (1965). *The emergence of the American university*. Chicago: University of Chicago Press.

Veysey, L. (1979). The plural organized worlds of the humanities. In A. Oleson & J. Voss (Eds.), *The organization of knowledge in modern America, 1860–1920* (pp. 51–106). Baltimore: Johns Hopkins University Press.

Wetmore, K. (1992). *A note on the founding of the American Psychological Association.* Unpublished manuscript, Harvard Medical School.

Wilson, D. J. (1979). Professionalization and organized discussion in the American Philosophical Association, 1900–1902. *Journal of the History of Philosophy, 17,* 53–69.

Woodworth, R. S. (1908). Report of the secretary for 1907. *Psychological Bulletin, 5,* 33–37.

3

GROWING PAINS: THE AMERICAN PSYCHOLOGICAL ASSOCIATION FROM 1903 TO 1920

RAND B. EVANS

The first decade of the American Psychological Association, as we have seen from Chapter 2, was one in which the commonality of interests among members was emphasized over their differences. The APA's early membership was made up of experimental psychologists of various systematic stripes and of philosophical psychologists, alienists, metaphysicians, and even an architect, just to name a few. By the end of the decade, however, the mood of the Association had become more exclusionary. The second and third decades of the APA considered in this chapter saw a continuation of this tendency toward exclusivity. This exclusionary attitude was a natural reflection of the professionalization of psychology in America in the early 20th century. It was an attempt to define psychology apart from the disciplines and subject matters from which it developed in the 19th century. Whether the Association, in its attempts at professionalization, was trying to define itself in relationship to the realities of contemporary psychology or was trying to define contemporary psychology in reference to itself is a deeper question. Both motivations appear at work during the period under consideration here. The new Association would ultimately fail at both, but it was not for lack of trying. The definition of a discipline almost requires a certain pause in development, a period of time in which change has slowed sufficiently to allow for the development of perspective, but psychology in the first two decades of this century changed at a rate almost without equal before or since (see Watson & Evans, 1991).

The major change in the American psychological scene in the first two decades of this century was not the advent of John B. Watson's behaviorism, as one might think. In fact, the rise of behaviorism had only a minor influence on the American psychological scene before World War I (Samelson, 1981). The major change was a general trend of American psychological thought toward utilitarianism. Watsonian behaviorism can be seen, more than anything else, as merely a part of this utilitarian trend in psychological work, with the accompanying rise of applied psychologies both inside and outside the academy. E. B. Titchener remarked on this trend as early as 1909:

> If, then, one were asked to sum up, in a sentence, the trend of psychology during the past ten years, one's reply would be: Psychology has leaned, very definitely, towards application. And if the questioner were thereupon to look for proof of this statement, he would find it confirmed not only by the range and variety of current practical work, but also and more particularly by the incursion into the field of practice of men whose training and previous interests might naturally have held them aloof. (Titchener, 1910, p. 406)

At the same time that the membership and officers of the APA were proclaiming psychology as a science and attempting to separate it from philosophy and other subject matters, the scientific enterprise was being overtaken almost imperceptibly by application. The failure of American psychologists as represented by the APA to come to grips with the fact that psychology was becoming not a single, scientific, academic discipline but a mixed discipline with multiple goals would lead the Association to repeated failures in its attempts to standardize and define psychology. Although most of the APA's initiatives during the approximately 20 years under discussion here must be categorized as failures, the attempts themselves and the organization required to launch them helped to establish the Association as the primary body representing whatever psychology, in fact, was.

GOVERNANCE

It is sometimes difficult to know just what is meant by "the Association" in reference to the American Psychological Association during these early years. There was no central office of the APA. The only presence that could be identified as the APA outside of the business meetings of the annual convention was the president, the Council of Directors, the secretary, and a few committees with particular mandates. Resolutions were voted on at the annual meetings, but only a portion of the membership attended the meetings, and only a portion of those attended the business meeting.

By and large, the APA appears to have been controlled by the Council. Fernberger[1] (1932, p. 37) wrote that the president had no more power than any other member of the Council. The secretary was nothing like an executive officer in those days: His primary duties centered around arranging details of the annual convention, preparing the annual report of the organization, and carrying out some correspondence at the behest of the Council or president.

By the beginning of the second decade of its existence, the APA was no longer G. Stanley Hall's creature. Control of the organization had quickly been taken over by a group that nominally revolved around the figure of William James (Evans & Cohen, 1987). These individuals did not always act in James's interests, but often in his name. It was this general group that made up G. Stanley Hall's original Council of Directors: James Mark Baldwin, then at Toronto, later at Johns Hopkins; James McKeen Cattell, then of the University of Pennsylvania, later at Columbia; G. S. Fullerton of the University of Pennsylvania, Cattell's close associate; William James of Harvard; George T. Ladd of Yale; and J. J. Schurman of Cornell. Although these individuals would go on and off the Council over the years, most continued to have immense influence on the development of the Association (Camfield, 1973, p. 67). By the end of the APA's first decade of existence, G. Stanley Hall, effectively powerless in his own organization, had largely deserted it, rarely attending meetings during the remainder of his life.

The Council had exceptional powers, particularly before 1912. Not only did it propose the slate of officers to the membership at the annual meeting, it nominated not only the president and secretary but also all new members. The Council also nominated new members for itself, which resulted in the perpetuation of the interests and viewpoint of the original Council. The membership of the Association at the annual meetings rarely, if ever, went against the nominations of the Council in those days.

In 1912, the procedure was changed and a committee was established

---

[1] I am indebted to Samuel Fernberger's "The American Psychological Association: A Historical Summary, 1892–1930" (1932). His work was invaluable in the preparation of this chapter.

to nominate the president and two members of the Council; this committee was nominated from the floor at the annual convention. The first such Nominating Committee was made up of James R. Angell of Chicago as chair and John B. Watson of Johns Hopkins and Edward L. Thorndike of Columbia as members (Fernberger, 1932, p. 35). The experiment was tried for 3 years, but this procedure was hardly more democratic than the earlier nomination by the Council. In 1916, the Nominating Committee was restructured to consist of the retiring president and the two most recent presidents of the APA; nomination was initiated from the membership at large and counted by the Nominating Committee. The slate was then voted on by secret ballot by all members. This was certainly more democratic, but if the intent of the change was to bring new blood into the presidency, it did not succeed, at least through the 1920s. During the first decade of the APA's existence, virtually all of the presidents of the organization were drawn from its Council (the only exception was Hugo Münsterberg [1898] of Harvard). During the next two decades, the tendency persisted, with only Mary Calkins (1905) of Wellesley, John B. Watson (1915) of Johns Hopkins, and Walter Dill Scott (1919) of Northwestern not being members of the Council prior to their election as president.

The nomination and election of the members of Council were also carried out through this method until 1922. In that year, the policy was changed again in regard to the nomination of the members of Council, with the Council again assuming nomination powers for itself. The Council remained self-perpetuating until the reorganization of the APA in the 1940s and the creation of a divisional structure.

MEMBERSHIP

The changes in policies concerning membership demonstrate perhaps better than anything else the movement from inclusiveness to exclusiveness in the APA. Membership in the APA had grown steadily from the 31 original members in 1892 to approximately 125 in 1899; by 1920, membership was approximately 450 (Fernberger, 1932, p. 5). During its first decade, the APA had no real requirements for membership except that the individual be nominated by the Council of the Association and voted on by the membership at the meeting. No records exist as to the criteria, if any, that were actually used by the Council for the nomination of members, except for a statement made in 1906: The Council announced that it had interpreted the APA Constitution's statement that its membership should be reserved for those engaged in "the advancement of Psychology as Science" to mean professional occupation in psychology and research in psychology ("Proceedings," 1907, p. 203). How far back these two criteria had actually been used and what exactly was meant by "professional occupation" is unclear, and there is no indication that individuals had actually been rejected for lack of such qualifications.

In 1900, the number of proposed new members fell to four, an all-time low. Whatever the cause, it was short-lived because the number of new members rose sharply the following five years to 22 in 1905. Fernberger (1932, p. 9) wrote that it was this large number of new members that led the Council to define membership qualifications more stringently in 1906. That year, the Council announced that it was adhering more closely to the requirement for publications. The Council stated that "in the absence of research, positions held in related branches, such as philosophy and education, or temporary positions such as assistantships in psychology, are not regarded as qualifying a candidate for membership" ("Proceedings," 1907, p. 203).

The result was a drop in new members over the following five years, down to half the 1905 figure by 1909. By 1911, however, the rate of new members had rebounded to a new high, again leading the Council to upgrade its entry requirements. This time, it was required that prospective new members supply their membership forms to the secretary at least a month before the time of election" and that these recommendations be accompanied by a statement of the candidates' professional position and by copies of his published researches" ("Proceedings," 1912, p. 44). This change may have resulted from the fact that the Council no longer knew most of the new members personally and needed objective information on them and the time to review such information.

The Council continued to tighten requirements for membership during the period before the outbreak of World War I. For instance, in 1915, Charles H. Judd urged that instructors be considered as holding "temporary positions," thus eliminating such individuals from consideration for membership unless they had publications "of a psychological character" ("Proceedings," 1916, p. 48). In 1916, a list of academic degrees, including institutions and dates, were added to the list of information on the membership application form. Also in 1916, applications that had been unfavorably passed on were no longer carried over for another year, presumably so that individuals who were refused would have a year to meet the requirements without having to go through the entire application process again ("Proceedings," 1916, p. 48).

Although these actions may have prevented a precipitous increase in membership, the rise was still very fast, at least in the eyes of the Council. Fernberger (1932) saw these attempts to limit membership as failures.

After World War I, however, a committee was established that made a definite statement on membership. Chaired by E. G. Boring, then at Clark University, the committee included Knight Dunlap of Johns Hopkins University and Lewis Terman of Stanford. The committee reported back in 1921, recommending

> that the [membership] qualifications should be formulated in accordance with the object of the Association, "the advancement of psychology as a science" as stated in the Constitution; and they [the committee] believe that this end will be most readily secured by placing emphasis upon scientific publication. They believe further that the time has come to abandon professional position or title as a basis for election on account of the reason that the multiplication of special positions, especially in non-academic fields of psychology, makes the interpretation of the significance of position impracticable. (Fernberger, 1932, p. 11)

The result of this report was the establishment of the following requirements for membership: "(1) acceptable published research of a psychological character and (2) of the degree of Doctor of Philosophy, based in part on a psychological dissertation. . . . (3) it is also expected that the Council shall assure itself that the nominee is actively engaged in psychological work at the time of the nomination" (Fernberger, 1932, p. 12).

It is instructive to dwell on these machinations concerning membership because they indicate some of the forces at work within the Association, both exclusionary and inclusionary. The exclusionary tendency that predominated the first two decades of the 20th century was to eliminate from membership individuals who were not directly involved in psychological pursuits. The definition of *psychology* officially hinged on the terminology of the Association's Constitution as "the advancement of psychology as a science," which was primarily that of academic psychologists involved in research, primarily experimental research. In general, it was the individuals on the periphery of psychology who were eliminated, those with a nonprofessional, amateur's interest in the field and those primarily involved in philosophy.

Chapter 2 discussed the primary group that was excluded, the philosophers. By the end of the first decade of the American Psychological Association, the philosophical complement of the APA had separated and formed the American Philosophical Association; this was certainly beneficial for the professionalization of philosophers in America. Although the two associations maintained some informal ties during the first years of the

20th century, those ties loosened and finally dissolved by the end of World War I. The APA and the American Philosophical Association met together in convention after the breakup, but it was typically in deference to the host of a particular meeting, such as William James, who, although revered by the psychological community, was clearly more closely associated with philosophers than with psychologists.

The divorce of the psychologists and the philosophers came when it did perhaps because the American Psychological Association could afford to do it. The membership had risen precipitously, from 31 members at the first formal meeting in 1892 to approximately 125 members in 1902. The Association was becoming too large and impersonal in the view of some, but to others, the departure of the philosophers was a simple act of purification, making room on the program for more papers on modern psychological research topics, as opposed to discussion of philosophical issues. This latter goal was achieved: The percentage of papers delivered at APA meetings devoted to philosophical and historical topics peaked at over 50% in the period from 1897 to 1901 but dropped to approximately 20% by 1916. Of that 20%, most were historical (Cattell, 1917).

The inclusionary process of the first two decades of the 20th century was that of a gradual extension of the definition of scientific psychology to include not only academic, experimental psychology, but also applied psychology, whether inside or outside of the academic setting. James McKeen Cattell, in his address to the Association on the occasion of its 25th anniversary in 1917, presented figures on papers delivered at the meetings of the APA over its first 25 years. Although the percentage of experimental psychological papers remained relatively constant over this period (at about 30%), papers on applied psychology rose from none in the 1892–1896 period to approximately 30% by the 1916 meeting (Cattell, 1917).

The recognition of this reality was perhaps the stimulus for the recommendation by Boring's committee in 1921 to define membership in terms of activity rather than in terms of the area of the activity. Although Boring and his committee paid lip service to scientific psychology, it is clear that their view of the proper work of a psychologist was much broader than the way it was used prior to World War I. They emphasized "scientific publication" and the holding of a doctorate as the primary requirements for membership, not one's institutional placement or title. The reality of applied psychology and nonacademic roles for psychologists led to an implicit redefinition of the terms *psychological* and *scientific*. It is clear that Boring's committee fully intended to broaden the base of the APA beyond that of theoretical, academic psychology and, in doing so, to include the sizable number of applied psychologists who had taken positions outside of colleges and universities after World War I. It would take some time for the effect of this change in membership requirements to be felt, but it is clear that the high-water mark of the APA as a community of academic, experimental psychologists was reached in the early 1920s. The 1920s would also see the creation of associate membership status, which would bring an even broader class of individuals into the APA. The struggle over the control of the Association between academic experimentalists and applied or professional psychologists really began in the 1920s and has not abated since.

THE REVOLT OF THE EXPERIMENTALISTS

The exclusion of the philosophers from the APA was a matter of "too little, too late" for some, like E. B. Titchener. Titchener was perhaps America's most effusive proponent of psychology as an academic, laboratory discipline; he saw as a primary goal for psychology its complete separation from philosophy. Titchener's view of psychology, although considerably more extreme than that of the ruling body of the APA, reflected many of their concerns. Titchener was convinced that the APA meetings, rather than providing a sounding board for the professionalization of a scientific, experimental psychology, had become merely a place to be seen. As early as 1898, G. Stanley Hall, ever ready to play the role of founder, proposed to Titchener some sort of organization that would provide a forum for experimentalists (Goodwin, 1985). Titchener made no response to Hall's notion, but the idea may have germinated in Titchener years later.

In 1904, Titchener founded his own organization. He had hoped to call it "the Fechner Club" (after G. T. Fechner, the founder of psychophysics), but the name never took; instead, the group was simply called "The Experimentalists." Titchener's stated purpose for the new organization was not to compete with the APA, but to provide an alternative for experimental psychologists who were serious about discussing research. The group was small, and it intended to represent the cream of experimentalists. The meetings of the group were held in the spring, rather than around New Year's, as were APA's. Titchener argued that he did not want to do anything that would negatively affect the APA, and, in fact, the founding of Titchener's Experimentalists had little effect on the APA: those who were invited to the Experimentalists' meetings also attended the APA. It was, however, the first real or imagined revolt of experimental psychologists from the Association (Boring, 1939, 1967).

THE STANDARDIZATION OF PSYCHOLOGY

Camfield (1973) wrote that because psychologists

> sought establishment as a scientific profession, they became increasingly concerned with their reputation as a science. Their desire for scientific stature was, however, to be largely frustrated in the years before 1917. The principal source of this frustration was the persistence of widespread and fundamental differences among the psychologists. They were unable to reach agreement among themselves as to the definition of their field and its phenomena, or with regard to proper methods of investigation. Consequently, they laid themselves open to the criticism and ridicule of the more established sciences. (p. 73)

Camfield's contention is supported quite clearly by the operations of the American Psychological Association during this period. However, the APA made several attempts to define and standardize several aspects of the field. The definition of the professional psychologist apart from other professionals, at least in terms of membership as discussed above, was one of these attempts.

Methodological Standards

As we have seen in Chapter 2, as early as 1895, a committee chaired by James McKeen Cattell and including James M. Baldwin, Joseph Jastrow, Edmund C. Sanford, and Lightner Witmer was formed, calling itself the Committee on Physical and Mental Tests. They reported to the Association the following year with a series of tests that they "considered appropriate for college students tested in a psychological laboratory" (Fernberger, 1932, p. 43). The purpose of this list of tests was apparently to standardize measurement procedures in laboratories across the country. Fernberger (1932) counted the actions of this committee as the APA's first venture into clinical psychology. After an initial report the following year, the committee seems to have largely dissipated.

The APA's next major venture into standardization was the establishment of the Committee on the Standardizing of Procedure in Experimental Tests in 1906, chaired by James R. Angell, who seems to have chaired a large number of committees in those days. Members appointed to the committee were Charles H. Judd, Walter Pillsbury, Robert S. Woodworth, and Edmund C. Sanford. Sanford, who had served on the committee of a decade before and who apparently considered it all a waste of effort, refused to serve again and was replaced by Carl Seashore (Fernberger, 1932, p. 44). The Committee was charged with coming up with standardized tests for groups and for individuals, of an applied nature and of a technical nature, and for humans and for animals. It is not surprising that the Committee was unable to do all that it was appointed to do, but it is amazing that they did as much as they did.

James R. Angell was a very efficient administrator, and he parceled out projects to members of the Committee and to others in the field with the intent of publishing their results. It was as though the APA was underwriting a methodological handbook on an encyclopedic scale, but the result was far less than that.

R. S. Woodworth collaborated with F. L. Wells and formulated what would become the Woodworth-Wells Association Tests (Woodworth & Wells, 1911). This appears to have been the only really applied project produced through the Committee; the others were more experimentally oriented. For example, W. B. Pillsbury of the University of Michigan put together a monograph on "Methods for the Determination of the Intensity of Sound" (1911).

Carl Seashore published on the measurement of pitch discrimination (1911). Seashore explained that his report was called for by the APA "in the belief that the systematic criticism and trial of current methods and means, and the statement of the essential implications, would economize effort for future workers and further the prospects of practical applications of the test." Seashore admitted that "the measurement may be made by so many different kinds of apparatus of various degrees of worth, by so many methods of procedure more or less adequate, under so many hypotheses more or less specious, for so many purposes more or less legitimate, that the situation is very complicated" (Seashore, 1911, p. 21).

James R. Angell (1911) published on "Methods for the Determination of Mental Imagery" as his contribution to the effort. Angell also approached Robert M. Yerkes in 1906 with the request that he carry out a project for the Committee. The result was Yerkes's important monograph in collaboration with John B. Watson, "Methods of Studying Vision in Animals" (Yerkes & Watson, 1911).

In 1911, the committee was given the job of reporting on the relative merit of different forms of experimental apparatus, but nothing seems to have come of it. In fact, most of the projects begun by the Committee were apparently never completed, at least not under the designation of the Committee. Fernberger (1932) wrote that at the 1916 meeting of the APA, there was a question raised on the floor on the whole matter of such standardization (p. 45). Shepard Ivory Franz moved that the Committee be disbanded, but the motion was defeated. Even so, the work of the

Committee appears to have bogged down: No progress was reported in 1917 or in 1918, and the committee was disbanded in 1919.

The committee was a failure in terms of not doing all it was intended to do, but its efforts appear to have stimulated others in the field to do their own standardization work. In 1910, G. E. Whipple produced his classic *Manual of Mental and Physical Tests* (1910; revised and expanded in 1914–1915), which did for the testing field the very thing that Angell's committee had apparently been set up to do and that Titchener's four-volume *Experimental Psychology* (1901–1905) had already done for sensation, perception, emotion, and action. Along the same lines as Whipple's work, but in a somewhat different field, was William Healy and Grace Fernald's "Tests for Practical Mental Classification," published in 1911.

The lapsing of the Committee was perhaps due in part to the realization that procedural standardization was a gradual and continual process and not the purview of a single committee.

Standardization of Psychological Terminology

The terminology of a field is a key to its professionalization. Psychology has always been plagued by the fact that much of its terminology is commonsense in nature, which promoted and continues to promote the notion that psychological theories are themselves commonsense. As early as 1898, the APA appointed a Committee on Psychological and Philosophical Terminology at James M. Baldwin's behest (Fernberger, 1932, p. 82). Baldwin chaired the Committee, whose members included Hugo Münsterberg and Josiah Royce of Harvard, James McKeen Cattell of Columbia, Edmund C. Sanford of Clark, and J. E. Creighton of Cornell, among others. The duties of the committee were to recommend new terms in psychology and philosophy, a choice of alternative terms, and translations of words into and out of English (Fernberger, 1932). Although the committee reported only once, in 1900, it appears that the work of the Committee formed the basis of James M. Baldwin's classic *Dictionary of Philosophy and Psychology* (1901).

In 1915, Knight Dunlap of Johns Hopkins urged the appointment of a committee to "consider the matter of uniformity in the usage of psychological terms" ("Proceedings," 1916). The committee was established, with Howard C. Warren as chair. It developed a survey that was sent to APA members around the country, attempting to determine the commonality of the usage of psychological terms by American psychologists. The result was initially disappointing, with only a couple of brief reports published in the *Psychological Bulletin* in 1917 and 1921. The work of the group bore fruit somewhat later, however, when Howard C. Warren, like Baldwin before him, used material from this committee to develop his *Dictionary of Psychology* (1934). The advisory board listed in Warren's book was basically the same as that of the APA Committee.

These were only a few of many such attempts to standardize psychology. In 1908, for instance, the Committee on Methods of Teaching Psychology and Teaching Experiments was established, chaired by Carl E. Seashore and including as members James R. Angell, Mary Calkins of Wellesley College, Edmund C. Sanford, and G. M. Whipple, to "gather materials for a discussion . . . on the topic: 'Methods of Teaching Psychology'" (Fernberger, 1932, p. 80). The Committee sent out questionnaires to normal schools, colleges without laboratories, and colleges with psychological laboratories. The report of the findings was presented the following year and was published in the *Psychological Monographs* (Seashore, 1909). The Committee continued to collect information and reported findings in 1914 and 1916, but there is no record of any additional published material.

Although such study committees continued to operate, it was evident by 1919 that the standardization of terminology, of research or teaching methodology, or of contents of course syllabi in psychology was either untenable or too enormous a task for a volunteer committee with little or no funding. Still, many of these reports provide revealing glimpses into the attitudes of psychologists of that period and a rich source of information into the ways in which American psychology functioned in those days.

Educational Standards

Oddly enough, of all of the areas in which one might expect standardization, the educational preparation of psychologists was one that received very little attention. Although membership standards emphasized the PhD in psychology, just what constituted that degree was not addressed.

A committee *was* established in 1913 on the Academic Status of Psychology, however. Howard C. Warren of Princeton chaired the group, with John Dewey of Columbia, C. H. Judd of Chicago, Bird Baldwin of Swarthmore College, and Margaret Washburn of Vassar as members. This committee made a study of, among other things, introductory courses and advanced courses in psychology. The purpose was not to standardize the curriculum, however, but to urge that "the Association adopt the principle that the undergraduate psychological curriculum in every college and university, great or small, should be planned from the standpoint of psychology and in accordance with psychological ideals, rather than to fit the need and meet the demands of some other branch of learning" (Fernberger, 1932, p. 81). The purpose of this resolution was to curb the trend of psychology programs to design their undergraduate programs primarily to serve the interests of education and other external programs, rather than for the benefit of psychology majors. The APA passed the resolution, but that was the extent of its influence.

The Committee on the Academic Status of Psychology provided a number of studies that give an interesting if uneven picture of the status of psychology in colleges and universities ("Committee," 1914) and normal schools ("Committee," 1915). Bird Baldwin took the chair of the Committee in 1916 and issued reports on a survey on "Differentiations Between Psychological Experiments and Mental Tests" ("Committee," 1916) and on a survey of the status of general and experimental psychology, child psychology, and applied psychology in American colleges and universities ("Committee," 1919). These reports were valuable because they related the variety of views concerning these topics. There is no indication, however, that the Committee recommended any action that chose one view or method over another.

The only significant attempt to standardize psychological education during this period was instigated by Whipple in 1915 regarding individuals giving psychological tests. His resolution, which was accepted at that year's APA meeting, stated as follows:

> Whereas: Psychological diagnosis requires thorough technical training in all phases of mental testing, thorough acquaintance with the facts of mental development and with various degrees of mental retardation. And whereas: There is evident a tendency to appoint for this work persons whose training in clinical psychology is inadequate; Be it resolved; That this Association discourages the use of mental tests for practical psychological diagnosis by individuals psychologically unqualified for this work. ("Proceedings," 1916, p. 49)

This resolution led to the creation in 1917 of a committee of the APA "on the qualifications for psychological examiners and other psychological experts" (Fernberger, 1932, p. 46). This committee was chaired by M. E. Haggerty of the University of Minnesota and had among its members Grace Fernald, Leta Hollingworth, Lewis Terman, and G. M. Whipple. The result of the committee's report (published in 1918) was the establishment of a committee in 1919 "to consider methods of procedure for certifying Consulting Psychologists" (Fernberger, 1932, p. 46). This new committee was chaired by Bird Baldwin and included as members W. F. Dearborn and Leta Hollingworth. Its report the following year favored certification for mental testers and had a provision for removing the certificate for cause. The proposal was accepted, but without the provision for removing certification. A standing committee was formed on the certification of consulting psychologists, with F. L. Wells as chair.

The APA's first attempt at certification would end in disappointment in the 1920s (as Chapter 5 will show), but it was a significant early attempt by the APA to take the lead in regulating the professional activities of psychologists (Fernberger, 1932, p. 47). Moreover, much of the work of the committees of the American Psychological Association came to a halt during World War I, when large numbers of psychologists were drawn into military service (see Chapter 4 for further details of the participation of the APA in the war effort).

THE APA AND THE INTERNATIONAL CONGRESS OF PSYCHOLOGY

One of the purposes of the national organization of a learned society is to gain recognition for the discipline it represents. In the early part of this century, such recognition was enhanced by hosting an international congress. No such congress had ever met in the Americas, and after the turn of the century, several American psychologists came to the belief that America was ready to be recognized on an equal standing with the national psychologies of Europe. As early as 1905, at the Fifth International Congress of Psychology in Rome, James M. Baldwin of Johns Hopkins and others urged the organizing body of the congress to hold a future meeting in the United States. In 1909, a formal petition was presented and was accepted for a meeting in 1913. The American Psychological Association was not initially involved in the matter, but virtually all of the organizers were, then or formerly, officers of the APA. The story of why the international congress did not meet in America in 1913 has been told in detail elsewhere (Evans & Scott, 1978).

Briefly, the organization of the congress bogged down because of interpersonal maneuvering and bickering. It largely came down to a battle between the nominal followers of G. Stanley Hall, headed by E. B. Titchener, and the nominal followers of William James, headed by James McKeen Cattell. The maneuvers, beside which any present-day professional intrigues pale in comparison, were described by William James as an "inconceivable paltriness of spirit that seems to have shown its head for the 1st time in our American psychological world" (Evans & Scott, 1978, p. 718). It was not really the "first time," of course, and James was largely unaware of the degree to which he had been manipulated by his friends.

James was the nominal president of the congress. With his death in

1910, matters only became more complicated. Cattell drew the APA into the matter by proposing that all of the past presidents of the APA, as well as Titchener, who was not currently a member, serve as vice presidents of the congress. This would supposedly eliminate the problem of leadership, although all it did was to leave the presidency unfilled and undefined. Cattell clearly intended to be *de facto* president, a role he had been playing through James for some time, much to the consternation of his detractors. At the 1910 meeting of the APA, Cattell arranged to have his plan accepted by the membership at the business meeting.

Titchener's supporters urged him to come back to the APA. The likelihood was that the president of the APA elected at the Christmas, 1912, meeting would be the president of the congress, and Titchener's followers felt that his election would be assured. Titchener acquiesced and rejoined the APA in 1910. He was made a member of the Congress Arrangements Committee, which included John B. Watson, who was secretary of the congress; Walter Bingham, who was the new secretary of the APA; Edmund C. Sanford; Hugo Münsterberg; and James McKeen Cattell. Aside from the two *ex officio* members, who were largely nonaligned, the old James–Hall split was evenly represented on the Committee, with Münsterberg and Cattell preserving the Jamesean side and Sanford and Titchener that of Hall. As some had expected, Cattell unilaterally took over the role of organizer and, apparently knowing of the possibility of Titchener rising to the presidency of the APA and thus to preeminence at the Congress, worked assiduously to prevent it. "I do not think it follows that he [Titchener] will be elected president of the Association that year," Cattell wrote to Hugo Münsterberg.

> I should myself prefer a young man. In any case the President of the Association will not necessarily preside, but perhaps a senior vice-president, who would be Hall or Ladd. We decided to have a memorial meeting in honor of James and I presume that the functions of any presiding officer would be reduced to a minimum and might be filled by different persons. (Evans & Scott, 1978, p. 720)

Cattell clearly did not intend that for Titchener to be president of the congress. If it appeared that he might be, Cattell would work to minimize the role of the presidency.

In all of the maneuvering on the matter of organization, however, the parties involved failed to carry out the second part of their task, to investigate the desirability of the congress. Münsterberg, on his visit to Germany in 1911, polled the leaders in European psychology and found that there was very little interest in attending an international congress in the United States. His assessment was that such a congress would be a disaster, and he communicated this to the leaders of the proposed congress.

At the 1911 meeting of the APA, the advisability of holding the congress was discussed. There was considerable sentiment to drop the congress for fear of embarrassment if none of the Europeans came. Cattell was not ready to give up, however, and on his motion, the APA secretary, Walter Bingham, was instructed to secure by mail from the members of the APA and the other two societies that were to meet with the congress, the Southern Society and the North Central Association, "an informal expression of opinion regarding the desirability of having the congress in America" ("Proceedings," 1912, pp. 43–44). Before such a vote could be taken, however, Titchener wrote to the members of the Congress Arrangements Committee stating his reasons for asking that the plan for the 1913 congress be abandoned. Cattell was outvoted, and the congress was finally abandoned.

Those who criticize the sometime Byzantine proceedings of present-day APA councils may take some comfort in the knowledge that such things are not new to the APA and, in fact, are perhaps now less problematic than they were in earlier days.

Although the APA Board was again unsuccessful in its attempt to mediate a squabble in the name of a national psychology, all of this at least demonstrated that the APA, then less than 20 years old, was acting like the representative of American psychology it was meant to be.

It has been possible in this chapter to touch on only a few of the initiatives and activities of the American Psychological Association during the first two decades of this century. In many ways, this period encapsulates some of the issues and problems that have continued to hound the Association and its members up to the present day: What is a psychologist as distinguished from the professional/practitioner in other fields? What is the appropriate training for a psychologist? What, if any, is the role of standardization in procedures used by individuals calling themselves psychologists? That these questions were not answered should not surprise us: We have yet to fully answer them.

When the war was over, the atmosphere of American psychology was somehow different. The experience of so many psychologists in applied psychological work in the military radically changed the American psychological scene. The experiences gained in the war probably accelerated the rise of utilitarianism in psychology by a decade, although the place of academic and of applied psychology in the APA would only be resolved after the second world war a generation later.

REFERENCES

Angell, J. R. (1911). Methods for the determination of mental imagery. *Psychological Monographs*, No. 53, 61–111.

Baldwin, J. M. (1901). *Dictionary of psychology and philosophy*. New York: Macmillan.

Boring, E. G. (1939). The Society of Experimental Psychologists: 1904–1938. American Journal of Psychology, *51*, 410–424.

Boring, E. G. (1967). Titchener's experimentalists. *Journal of the History of the Behavioral Sciences*, *3*, 316.

Camfield, T. M. (1973). The professionalization of American psychology, 1870–1917. *Journal of the History of the Behavioral Sciences*, *9*, 66–75.

Cattell, J. M. (1917). Our psychological association and research. *Science*, *45*, 275–284.

Committee on the Academic Status of Psychology. (1914). *Report of the Committee on the Academic Status of Psychology: The academic status of psychology in colleges and universities*. Privately published.

Committee on the Academic Status of Psychology. (1915). *Report of the Committee on the Academic Status of Psychology: The academic status of psychology in the normal schools*. Princeton, NJ: Privately published.

Committee on the Academic Status of Psychology. (1916). *Report of the Committee on the Academic Status of Psychology: A survey of psychological investigations with reference to differentiations between psychological experiments and mental tests*. Swarthmore, PA: Privately published.

Committee on the Academic Status of Psychology. (1919). *Report of the Committee on the Academic Status of Psychology: A survey of I. general and experimental psychology, II. child psychology, and III. applied psychology*. Iowa City, IA: Privately published.

Evans, R. B., & Cohen, J. B. (1987). The American Journal of Psychology: A retrospective. *American Journal of Psychology*, *100*, 321–362.

Evans, R. B., & Scott, F. J. D. (1978). The 1913 International Congress of Psychology: The American congress that wasn't. *American Psychologist*, *33*, 711–723.

Fernberger, S. W. (1932). The American Psychological Association: A historical summary, 1892–1930. *Psychological Bulletin*, *29*, 1–89.

Goodwin, C. J. (1985). On the origins of Titchener's experimentalists. *Journal of the History of the Behavioral Sciences*, *21*, 383–389.

Healy, W., & Fernald, G. (1911). Tests for practical mental classification. *Psychological Monographs*, *13*(Whole No. 54).

Pillsbury, W. B. (1911). Methods for the determination of the intensity of sound. *Psychological Monographs*, *13*(Whole No. 53).

Proceedings of the fifteenth annual meeting of the American Psychological Association. (1907). *Psychological Bulletin*, *4*, 201–221.

Proceedings of the twentieth annual meeting of the American Psychological Association. (1912). *Psychological Bulletin, 9,* 41–92.

Proceedings of the twenty-fourth annual meeting of the American Psychological Association. (1916). *Psychological Bulletin, 13,* 41–100.

Samelson, F. (1981). The struggle for scientific authority: The reception of Watson's behaviorism 1913–1920. *Journal of the History of the Behavioral Sciences, 17,* 399–425.

Seashore, C. (1909). General report on the teaching of the elementary course in psychology: Recommendations. *Psychological Monographs, 12*(Whole No. 5).

Seashore, C. (1911). The measurement of pitch discrimination. *Psychological Monographs, 13*(Whole No. 53).

Titchener, E. B. (1901–1905). *Experimental psychology: A manual of laboratory practice* (4 vols.). New York: Macmillan.

Titchener, E. B. (1910). The past decade in experimental psychology. *American Journal of Psychology. 21,* 404–421.

Warren, H. C. (1934). *Dictionary of psychology.* Boston: Houghton Mifflin.

Watson, R. I., & Evans, R. B. (1991). *The great psychologists: A history of psychological thought* (5th ed.). New York: Harper/Collins.

Whipple, G. M. (1910). *Manual of mental and physical tests.* Baltimore: Warwick & York.

Woodworth, R. S., & Wells, F. L. (1911). Association tests. *Psychological Monographs, 13*(Whole No. 57).

Yerkes, R. M., & Watson, J. B. (1911). Methods of studying vision in animals. *Behavior Monographs, 1,* 1–90.

4

THE AMERICAN PSYCHOLOGICAL ASSOCIATION AND WORLD WAR I: 1914 to 1919

THOMAS M. CAMFIELD

World War I presented the scientists of the United States unprecedented opportunities for advancing the cause of science in the context of national service. Prominent American scientists were convinced that the scientific community could render the nation valuable, if not in fact essential, assistance with the conduct of the war. They were, furthermore,

This chapter draws extensively upon my doctoral dissertation, *Psychologists at War: The History of American Psychology and the First World War* (The University of Texas at Austin, 1969). What is presented here is a substantial abridgment of the dissertation, approached from a slightly different perspective to highlight the history of the American Psychological Association. As indicated in several references, I have here just touched upon some topics which are much more fully developed in the dissertation. On virtually all points, the documentation to be found in the dissertation is considerably more extensive.

The dissertation was supported in part by grants from the National Science Foundation (GS 1142) and the National Institute of General Medical Sciences (1-FL-GM-33, 360–01).

I wish to acknowledge the kind and generous assistance I received from my wife, Sharon, in the preparation of this manuscript. Two colleagues, Gregg Cantrell and Gary Bell, rendered much appreciated assistance. I would also like to thank Janice Goldblum, an archivist at the National Academy of Sciences, for her generous assistance with the revision of my references to materials located there.

quick to recognize the novel opportunities the national crisis offered for improving the whole scientific establishment: opportunities to secure greater public and private endowments for scientific research and to obtain greater recognition of the values of science to American society by means of demonstrably valuable service. With a patriotic opportunism not altogether different from that of bankers and munitions manufacturers, the nation's scientists moved to exploit the extraordinary circumstances of the war crisis in behalf of civilization and American science.

In common with anthropologists and astronomers, botanists, chemists, geologists and mathematicians, pathologists, physiologists, physicists, and even zoologists, psychologists were confident that science, and their discipline in particular, could render important services to the nation. By 1917, American psychologists had attained a level of scientific development from which they could advance claims to specialized knowledge and techniques capable of practical application. On the other hand, because their science lacked maturity and their social establishment fell short of the autonomy and stature they desired, they viewed national service in the war crisis as a possible means of accelerating both their scientific and professional progress. Virtually all fields of applied psychology stood to benefit directly from any substantive program of service supported by the government or the military. American psychologists could, moreover, expect that the "pure" as well as the "applied" aspects of their science would, at least in the long run, benefit from a general improvement in the discipline's professional reputation.

It was the extent of their success at professional development, not the shortcomings of it, which was to enable American psychologists to take advantage of the war crisis. Of critical importance was the existence of an effective, established, national organization representing the discipline. The American Psychological Association, inasmuch as it had become *the* national professional organization of American psychologists, was to serve as the essential instrument through which they would obtain opportunities for service and through which they would mobilize their laboratories and scientists. Professional affiliations with the American Association for the Advancement of Science (AAAS) and the National Academy of Sciences (NAS) placed American psychologists in a position to benefit from the efforts of these organizations to further the general interests of science in the United States. The APA had accepted an invitation to affiliate with the AAAS in 1902, and had thereafter participated in its activities through a designated representative and by means of coordinated annual meetings. Six members of the APA, moreover, had been elected to membership in the NAS (Walter B. Cannon, James McKeen Cattell, John Dewey,

G. Stanley Hall, William James, and Josiah Royce; Edward L. Thorndike was elected in 1917). In both organizations, psychologists became actively involved with representatives of other disciplines in the promotion of science in America (for additional background information, see Rand Evans's preceding chapter; see also Camfield, 1969, 1973).

In the years before the outbreak of the war in Europe, a small group of scientists with memberships in both the AAAS and the NAS had begun to coordinate their efforts to champion American science. Among these were such men as George Hale (astronomy), Robert Millikan (physics), A. A. Noyes (chemistry), Edwin G. Conklin (zoology), Charles B. Davenport (biology and zoology), Robert S. Woodward (geography and geology), and James McKeen Cattell (psychology). These men had initiated efforts to reform and revitalize the NAS as early as 1910 (Dupree, 1957, pp. 302–325; Millikan, 1950, pp. 124–156). Disappointment with their progress within the NAS led them to turn to the AAAS, through which they established the Committee of One Hundred on Scientific Research by action of the Association at its meeting in December 1913. When the Committee was organized the following April, among the initial members were three representatives of the American Psychological Association: James McKeen Cattell, E. B. Titchener, and James R. Angell. Cattell's involvement, as secretary of the Committee and as a member of its Executive Committee, along with his membership on the Policy Committee of the AAAS, was extensive (AAAS, 1914).

PREPARING FOR WAR: 1915–1916

Prompted by the widespread and indignant American reaction to the May 1915 German submarine sinking of the liner *Lusitania* and by the subsequent diplomatic negotiations with Germany regarding submarine warfare, President Woodrow Wilson determined, in July of 1915, to undertake a program of United States military preparedness. His decision presented the promoters of American science a situation of great potential. Although they recognized that the quasi-official basis of the National Academy of Sciences made it the organization most suitable for use in the situation, Hale and his colleagues nonetheless continued to work through both the NAS and the AAAS, because they could not at first be sure they would be able to bring the National Academy into vigorous action (Dupree, 1957, pp. 308–309). Early in 1916, the group determined to expand the activities of the Committee of One Hundred by creating subcommittees representing the various branches of science (AAAS, 1917, pp. 57–58). The course of the European war soon provided an occasion for them to press the matter. The renewal of German submarine warfare, culminating with the sinking of the liner *Sussex*, led to a German–American diplomatic crisis in March and April. Hale and his colleagues successfully utilized the crisis to secure approval from both the NAS and President Wilson of a plan for national scientific preparedness (Dupree, 1957, pp. 308–310; Hale, 1916; Millikan, 1950, pp. 124–125). Once the NAS and the president had given their sanction to the creation of what was to become the National Research Council (NRC), Hale and his colleagues concentrated on the thorough development of this Council. With Hale as the Council's chairman, they set out to construct a permanent, government-supported, broadly representative organization with purposes and functions reaching far beyond the immediate mobilization of the nation's scientific resources for preparedness or war. In this context, they determined that the NRC's structure should include committees representing all of the various branches of science, "to be selected in consultation with the president of the corresponding society" (NAS, 1916, p. 607; see also NAS, 1917a, p. 228).

Through the fall of 1916, the AAAS Committee of One Hundred and the newly established National Research Council functioned as separate entities, working to organize the nation's scientific community while, at the same time, they endeavored to coordinate their activities. The AAAS, for example, proceeded to organize 13 subcommittees of various scientific specialties. Among them was a Psychology Subcommittee, chaired by Cattell, with E. L. Thorndike, Carl Seashore, John B. Watson, and Robert M. Yerkes as its members. All except Yerkes were former presidents of the APA; Yerkes had just been elected to the office (AAAS, 1917, pp. 57–58). When the Executive Committee of the NRC voted, in mid-November 1916, to organize several scientific research committees, there were also to be 13, and among them was to be a committee representing the science of psychology. The two organizations also proceeded to wrestle with and finally to work out an agreement whereby the NRC research committees would essentially incorporate and replace those established through the Committee of One Hundred. The agreement, arrived at by action of the AAAS at its annual meeting, and by the Executive Committee of the NRC, in December 1916, provided that the AAAS, the national associations of the branches of science, and the NRC would appoint approximately equal numbers of members to the science committees to be established by the NRC (NAS, 1917a, p. 228).

By the end of 1916, then, leaders of the American scientific community had successfully used President Wilson's preparedness campaign to establish an agency and a framework for mobilizing the nation's scientific resources for public service in the looming war crisis and beyond. Members of the American Psychological Association had participated in these activities as members of the NAS and the AAAS and its Committee of One Hundred. They had, moreover, managed to see that a Psychology Committee (whose membership would be largely determined by the APA) would be among the committees to be created by the NRC to represent the branches of science. American psychologists, through the agency of their national association, were positioned to take advantage of such opportunities as the developing crisis situation presented them.

YERKES TRIES TO MOBILIZE PSYCHOLOGISTS

Neither the APA nor those of its members who were active in the scientific preparedness movement seem to have pressed forward with the matter of professional service in January and February of 1917. Indeed, there is no evidence of an effort to establish a Psychology Committee of the NRC until after the United States declaration of war in early April. Robert Yerkes, the newly elected president of the APA, did, in a January 23, 1917, personal letter to President Wilson, indicate his approval of the president's foreign policies and offer his services to the government (Yerkes, 1917a). By the last week of March, Yerkes had become convinced that the United States would soon be in the war and that psychologists could, and should, perform a variety of valuable wartime services (Yerkes, 1917b). Thereafter, as president of the APA, he assumed the self-appointed task of mobilizing his profession for patriotic service.

Undoubtedly, Wilson's April 2 request for a declaration of war and the Senate's April 4 passage of the declaration led Yerkes to make use of a unique opportunity to sound out his colleagues and to muster support among them on the matter of professional service in the forthcoming war effort. It happened that the annual meeting of E. B. Titchener's Society of Experimentalists had gathered at Harvard University, with Yerkes and (APA Secretary) Herbert Langfeld as hosts, on April 6, the day of the final passage of the congressional declaration of war. With Titchener's approval, Yerkes and Langfeld hastily arranged a session that evening for "discussion of the relations of psychology to the national defense." Seven psychologists and, by special invitation, an army captain who taught military science and tactics at Harvard addressed the meeting of some 40 psychologists, suggesting various relations of psychology to military affairs and the possible ways in which psychological knowledge and techniques could be made applicable to the war effort. In the discussion that followed, "many other suggestions were made by individuals," and the meeting concluded with the appointment of Yerkes, Walter Bingham, and Raymond Dodge as "a committee from this mass meeting to gather information concerning the possible relations of psychological procedures to military problems" (Yerkes, 1918a, pp. 85–86).

Yerkes's next move was to invoke the support of the larger body of professional psychologists. He was well aware that divisive tendencies were characteristic of the profession and, more immediately, that many psychologists regarded the Society of Experimentalists unfavorably, if not contemptuously (Dunlap, 1917; Watson, 1916). Yerkes, in consultation with former APA president Raymond Dodge and former APA secretary R. M. Odgen, determined a strategy that would attempt simultaneously to mobilize the entire profession behind Yerkes's leadership and to forestall criticism. After conferring on the evening of April 6, the trio decided that Yerkes should take steps as president of the APA to bring that organization into action as the organ for mobilizing psychologists and coordinating their planning and activities. This move, as Yerkes explained it to APA Council member Walter Bingham, "seemed a way to escape the risk of action by such a small and special group as met. . ." (Yerkes, 1917c). The same night, Yerkes addressed a letter to the members of the Association's Council (Yerkes, 1918a, pp. 86–87). Except for a reference to "consultation with a number of members of the association," Yerkes's letter gave no indication of the Experimentalists' discussion or their creation of a committee to consider applications of psychology to military affairs. It was, rather, a letter from the Association's president requesting the Council's support of actions that would use the association to "unite us as a professional group in a nation-wide effort to render our professional training serviceable" (p. 87). Yerkes laid his appeal before the Council strictly on a basis of patriotic service to the nation in its time of crisis:

> Gentlemen: In the present situation, it is obviously desirable that the psychologists of the country act unitedly in the interests of defense. Our knowledge and our methods are of importance to the military service of our country, and it is our duty to cooperate to the fullest extent and immediately toward the increased efficiency of our Army and Navy. Formalities are not in order. We should act at once as a professional group as well as individually. (p. 86)

The letter called on the Council to give Yerkes authority to proceed with the appointment of committees from among the Association's membership, as well as with efforts to secure the application of psychological methods to military problems, and urged the Council members to give the matter their immediate attention so that he might have their replies as soon as possible.

Yerkes pressed forward during the next several days with efforts to prepare psychologists for national service. To explore the accommodation of psychological knowledge to military needs and to accumulate information that would help psychologists secure an opportunity to serve, Yerkes solicited bibliographical materials on the relations of feeblemindedness to military problems (Doll, 1917) and, more importantly, arranged a promised trip to consult with the Canadian Military Hospitals Commission (Yerkes, 1917b). The day before leaving for Canada, Yerkes undertook to solidify his mobilization efforts and to prepare the way for psychologists to render professional service. In a skillfully crafted letter (Yerkes, 1917d) to George E. Hale, chairman of the NRC, he endeavored to obtain that organization's support.

His appeal to Hale emphasized three matters: American psychologists had obvious and important services to render in the crisis; under the leadership of the officers of the APA, they were seeking to mobilize; and the psychologists were anxious to cooperate fully with the work of the NRC. Already developing a rationale with which to argue the case for employment of professional psychologists, Yerkes approached Hale with the view that it was "evident that the human factor is quite as important in the war as the non-human. . . ." Expert "psychological examiners can at once aid materially," he noted, in such areas as the selection of recruits, of non-commissioned officers, and of individuals with special abilities, and in the reeducation of soldiers returned with physical or mental disabilities. Enclosing a copy of his April 6 letter to the APA Council, Yerkes informed Hale that "if authorized by the Council, I shall, as President of that Association, proceed to organize the psychologists of the country in the interests of defense. I am told," he went on to say, "that your National Research Council contemplates the selection of a psychologist to serve on your Board. . . . If you have not made a selection, will you not do so at the earliest possible moment, so that the person who serves on your Board may also be appointed on our chief committee? We naturally wish to cooperate with you to the fullest extent." Yerkes concluded his letter by suggesting that those nations already at war recognized the value to the war effort of the science of psychology: "I may leave at any time for Ottawa, whence I have been summoned for conference with representatives of the Military Hospitals Commission. Their psychological workers desire my advice concerning methods of dealing with the returned soldiers . . . While in Canada I propose to gather information, so far as possible, concerning the use of psychological knowledge and methods in Europe" (Yerkes, 1917d).

Yerkes's letter elicited an immediate reply by telegram from Hale, who requested that Yerkes confer with him in Philadelphia on April 14th (Yerkes, 1917e). Hale's use of the interim between his April 10 telegram and the April 14 conference suggests that Yerkes's letter had proved effective. On the 11th, Hale secured authorization from the NRC's Executive Committee for the creation of a Committee on Psychology. Hale was to name the chairman, who was to become a member of the NRC (NAS, 1917b, p. 531). Evidently considering the possibility of naming Yerkes to the committee chairmanship, Hale sought the advice of Walter B. Cannon, a Harvard physiologist and APA member, who knew Yerkes and who was known and respected by Hale. Cannon wired a response: "Yerkes vessitile [sic] ingenious imaginative industrious / expert in tests of mental ability / he tends to work independently rather than in cooperation / position as president of the psychological association may offset his tendency to follow only his own councils [sic]" (Cannon, 1917).

No doubt Cannon's qualified recommendation, together with the fact that Yerkes could not yet report with finality on the response of the Association's Council to his April 6 request, led Hale to maintain a tentative position in his April 14 conference with Yerkes. Apparently Hale went no further than to say that the NRC was considering the creation of a Psychology Committee and that, should they determine to do so, Yerkes, as president of the APA, might be called upon to undertake the chairmanship of the committee. In any event, Hale asked that Yerkes compile and send to him (drawing upon the Canadian consultations) information and suggestions relative to the possible applications of psychology to military affairs, and that Yerkes attend the forthcoming meeting of the NRC in Washington on April 19. Hale indicated that the decision to organize a Psychology Committee of the NRC would be withheld pending Yerkes's determination of the support of his association's Council and his appearance before the NRC (Yerkes, 1917f).

The APA Council Divided on Mobilization

Upon his return to Cambridge on April 15th, Yerkes discovered that the members of the Association's Council had responded to his request of the 6th with less unanimity and enthusiasm than he had anticipated. Of the five who had replied, one, H. L. Hollingworth (1917), expressed opposition to the whole idea of mobilizing psychologists. The other four—representing a majority of the six-man Council—approved of the proposal in general, but the responses of two of them indicated that Yerkes could not safely proceed independently. Walter Bingham's reply represented an apparent attempt to preempt Yerkes's leadership by detailing a program of service (complete to the point of specifying projects, committees, and personnel) and sending it out not only to Yerkes but also to several other leading psychologists (Franz, 1917; Watson, 1917; Yerkes, 1917g). Roswell P. Angier of Yale University, a close personal friend of Yerkes, suggested that whatever action the Association took would be of such great importance that "we ought to have a special meeting of the Council to consider the personnel of such committee or committees as well as the general plan under which they are to work." Such a meeting, he further noted, "would put the full authority of the Council behind you so that you would not have to bear the responsibility of action alone" (Angier, 1917). Confronted with these responses, and perhaps heeding Angier's good advice, Yerkes determined that a meeting of the Association's Council would be essential.

By this point Yerkes could, nonetheless, feel relatively assured that he would affect mobilization of the nation's psychologists and that they would have representation in the NRC (Yerkes, 1917h). What remained was to formalize the Association's program and the matter of Research Council representation. With indications of support from the majority of the Association's Council, Yerkes could (and did) proceed to work with Hale on suggested lines of psychological services and arguments presentable to governmental and military authorities in behalf of such services—on the assumption that the organization of a Research Council Psychology Committee was a formality soon to be completed (Yerkes, 1917f). Similarly, the matter of securing the backing of the APA posed only the problem of getting the Council members to agree to a centralization of organization and planning under the auspices of the Association. To get this agreement, Yerkes had but to emphasize that this was the only possible route to NRC recognition and that professional unity and cooperation would be essential if opportunities for service were to be secured.

Although formalization of the arrangements was not complete until the end of April, Yerkes seems to have had no further significant difficulties. He appeared before the meeting of the NRC on the 19th (NAS, 1917b, pp. 580–582). While in Washington, he conferred with Hale and obtained definite approval for the organization of a Research Council Psychology Committee as soon as the Association's Council had met and approved the proposal. Apparently, Yerkes and Hale even discussed and tentatively agreed on the personnel who would be appointed to the Psychology Committee (Hale, 1917a; Yerkes, 1917p).

The APA Council, at the special meeting in Philadelphia called for April 21 and 22, provided its approval. Because the four Council members who had already indicated their support were the only ones in attendance,

Yerkes and the Council had little difficulty deciding to throw the machinery of the Association behind mobilization for national service and in mapping out a rather thorough program designed to implement this decision. The Council voted "that the President be instructed to appoint committees from the membership of the American Psychological Association to render to the Government of the United States all possible assistance in the psychological problems arising from the present military emergency" (Yerkes, 1918a, p. 91). It nominated three members to represent the Association on the National Research Council and voted to allot a thousand dollars from the Association's funds for war service activities and to set up a special finance committee to raise and disburse additional funds for war service needs (pp. 91–93).

The APA War Service Committees Formed

The Council created and selected chairmen for 12 committees of the Association to carry forward an extensive program of proposed services. A "committee on psychological literature relating to military affairs," chaired by Madison Bentley, was to prepare a bibliography of pertinent literature and provide references and digests of important literature to the other committees. A "committee on the psychological examination of recruits," chaired by Yerkes himself, was to prepare a plan and devise methods for tests that would eliminate the "mentally unfit" from among the ranks of recruits. As initially conceived, this plan called for the adaptation and use of general intelligence examinations in conjunction with a variety of tests of special mental functions (such as memory, suggestibility, and rapidity of learning) for the rapid detection of recruits with intellectual deficiencies, psychopathic tendencies, nervous instability, and inadequate self-control.

E. L. Thorndike would chair a third committee on "the selection of men for tasks requiring special aptitude." This committee was to develop techniques to identify the special psychological requirements of men assigned to duties in the artillery service and the signal corps and, subsequently, to devise tests to detect the required aptitudes. The task assigned to the "committee on psychological problems of aviation," chaired by H. E. Burtt, was basically no different from that of the committee on tasks requiring special skill; separate committee status simply acknowledged the unique and complex nature of the skills requirements of aviators (Yerkes, 1918a, pp. 91–97, 105–110).

Two committees, chaired respectively by S. I. Franz and John B. Watson, one on "psychological problems of incapacity, including those of shell shock, re-education, etc." and one on "psychological problems of vocational characteristics and vocational advice," aimed at bringing a variety of psychological knowledge and techniques to bear upon the study, diagnosis, treatment, and reeducation of the American troops returned with mental and physical disabilities. As envisioned in April of 1917, the activities of these committees would engage the efforts of specialists in such fields as psychological testing and physiological, vocational, and educational psychology (Yerkes, 1918a, pp. 91–92, 110).

Neither the general nor the specific activities of four other committees established by the Association's Council were effectively clarified. A "committee on recreation in the army and navy," chaired by George A. Coe, seemed to have no immediately defined functions, except, in some vague way, to promote morale and morality among the troops by devising ways to determine the adequacy of recreational facilities and activities and ways to improve on them (Coe, 1917; Yerkes, 1917i). The functions of Charles H. Judd's "committee on the pedagogical and psychological problems of military training and discipline" the Council apparently considered self-evident. Educational psychologists would channel their knowledge and techniques toward problems of military drill and training, with a view to improving existing methods (Yerkes, 1917j). Similarly, the Council seems to have considered the work of Walter Dill Scott's "committee on problems of motivation in connection with military activities" and Robert S. Woodworth's committee on "problems of emotional characteristics, self-control, etc., in relation to military demands" either self-evident or subject to ready definition by the committees themselves. Scott had pioneered in the field of the psychology of advertising, and presumably his committee's activities were to be aimed at applying psychological principles of advertising to military problems: motivation of enlistments, production of propaganda to stimulate civilian and military morale, and so forth (Bentley, 1917; Tufts, 1917; Yerkes, 1917k; Yerkes, 1918a, pp. 105–108). The unspecified tasks of the committee on problems of emotional characteristics apparently were to encompass such matters as the investigation of the effects of fatigue and other war conditions on the imagination, with a view to finding explanations of such phenomena as cowardice, fear, panic, and heroism, and the development of psychological tests that would reveal basic emotional characteristics (Franz, 1917; Woodworth, 1917; Yerkes, 1917g, 1918a, p. 110).

Finally, two other committees, chaired respectively by Carl Seashore and Raymond Dodge, would use the knowledge and techniques of two special fields to deal with "acoustic problems . . . in relation to military service" and "problems of vision which have military significance." The Association's Council anticipated that the activities of these committees would include determining the auditory and visual acuity requirements of specific military tasks (like those of lookouts, forward observers, and naval gunners) and testing recruits for these special positions, as well as devising training devices for them. The activities of these committees would, furthermore, involve studies of such problems as the localization of sound and "the possibility of developing ability to discriminate different projectiles by their sound" (Yerkes, 1918b, pp. 111–112; see also Seashore, 1917; Troland, 1917).

Convincing Others of Psychology's Usefulness

In support of this formidable array of proposed contributions to the nation's war effort, the psychologists constructed an impressive justifying rationale. Yerkes had, from the beginning, recognized the need to formulate a program that would recommend itself to governmental and military authorities and to buttress the program with practical arguments attractive to these authorities. The presentation of a convincing program, he realized, would be crucially important to the success of the whole endeavor (Yerkes, 1917d). If the psychologists were to render patriotic service and to reap the benefits of scientific and professional advancement that such service would make possible, they would have to create opportunities for themselves. Yerkes explained the situation quite succinctly to a colleague: "We need good avenues of approach to the military authorities. They naturally know next to nothing about psychological problems or our ability to solve them, and we can hope for no opportunities of service except as we discover them for ourselves and make known our ability and willingness to develop them" (Yerkes, 1917l).

Yerkes and his colleagues were able to come up with several seemingly telling arguments with which to approach the authorities. As the mainstay of their rationale they exploited the commonsense appeal and ostensibly indisputable validity of two basic premises: (a) the human factor was as important in warfare as the material and (b) psychologists, as the scientific experts on matters of human behavior, had vital contributions to make to the war effort. Yerkes's repeated use of these premises in defense of the psychologists' general claims of utility in the crisis established them as the foundations of the entire rationale (Camfield, 1969, p. 119, Note 16).

Responsibility for presentation of the case for the psychologists' proposed wartime services fell largely to Yerkes. In the weeks following the United States declaration of war, he pressed the case before George Hale again and again—both to improve the psychologists' prospects of securing NRC recognition and to provide material for Hale to use "in connection with getting the subject before the proper Washington authorities in a convincing way" (Yerkes, 1917m).

Yerkes's consultations in Canada enabled him to underscore his arguments with specific references to the experiences of an American ally. Indeed, his most thorough presentation of the psychologists' case came in the form of a letter to Hale (1917n) summarizing his findings while in Canada:

> With the thought that a brief statement concerning the relations of psychology to military affairs, as indicated by the study of Canadian conditions, may be of service to you, I am submitting the following, the substance of which is approved by various officials of the Military Hospitals Commission of Canada and doubtless would similarly commend itself to other military authorities. . . .

Investing the Canadian officials with his own basic premises, Yerkes opened his report with the following statement:

> There exists in military and political circles in the Dominion of Canada the opinion that since the human factor in war is so obviously important, psychology, since it is an attempt to deal scientifically with all aspects of conscious behavior, should be of extreme practical service. Canadian military statistics indicate the urgent need of methods of psychological examining. . . . Obviously, it is as important to eliminate in the process of recruiting the mentally unfit as it is the physically unfit. Canadian reports indicate that somewhere between two and five per cent of enlisted men are included in the following categories: (a) feeble-minded; (b) insane or psychopathic; (c) affectively peculiar, delinquent, incorrigible. Nearly all of these individuals should be detected by psychological examination and the Government thus saved from needless risk of disaster, expense, and later, liability. (Yerkes, 1917n)

Yerkes pointed out in his report that approximately 10% of the soldiers returned to Canada as incapacitated were classified as "nervous and mental cases." "These," he asserted, "obviously demand psychological study and treatment. Canadian officials recognize the need, but . . . have been unable to meet it adequately because of the lack of competent psychological experts." In defense of yet another of the proposed services of American psychologists, Yerkes concluded his account with a reference to official opinion in Canada concerning the problems of reeducation:

> One of the most conspicuous and socially important of the problems created by the great war is that of re-education. Thousands of soldiers return maimed physically and mentally. They must be fitted to return to society as effective members. The varied problems of re-education present many important psychological aspects, and the expert in the

study and control of human behavior should be invaluable. Today Canadian officials are seeking, not only at home, but in France, England, and the United States for expert advice, information, and other forms of aid in matters psychological. (Yerkes, 1917n)

"I went to Canada," Yerkes summed up his appeal, "with the opinion that psychology might be made to serve in various military situations; I returned, after conference with the administrative staff of the Military Hospitals Commission, with the conviction that the aid of this science is in great demand and that it is the duty of the United States to avail itself immediately of its great psychological resources" (Yerkes, 1917n; see also Camfield, 1969, p. 113).

Just as Yerkes considered the elimination of the mentally unfit in the process of recruiting to be of obvious importance, so, too, assistance with the selection of men for tasks requiring special skills and with the selection of officers and noncommissioned officers did not seem to require supporting arguments beyond the most cursory suggestion as to their value. Yerkes did emphasize, more than once, that these were areas in which psychologists could immediately apply their methods to military problems (Yerkes, 1917m, 1917n). Furthermore, he forwarded with one of his many letters to Hale a letter from Walter Dill Scott, Professor of Applied Psychology at the Carnegie Institute of Technology, that served to corroborate his contentions about psychologists' serviceability in these three areas. With reference to the psychological examination of recruits, Scott suggested that "there would be no difficulty in securing a system more or less competent" for determining and testing for the "minimum intellectual standing for efficiency in the army. . . ." Scott went on to note that the principle behind a system for selecting men for positions of responsibility—a system being devised by Carnegie Tech psychologists and "being used with very great satisfaction by large corporations"—could be "immediately applied to selecting for any position of responsibility in the army." Singling out the development of "special tests to determine fitness" for positions requiring special skills as yet another service psychologists could render, Scott urged that "a concentration of energy here . . . might result . . . in very great service to the army at once" (Scott, 1917).

Scott's letter did more to strengthen the psychologists' rationale than simply supplement Yerkes's proposals with additional arguments. It managed to convey a sense of the magnitude and urgency of the nation's wartime crisis, and, at the same time, to present the psychologists' proposal of professional assistance in a self-confident and reassuring manner. Scott's letter enabled Yerkes to confirm yet another, distinct element in the rationale: the significant argument, heretofore only alluded to without substantiating evidence, that Yerkes's professional colleagues shared his convictions as to the value and feasibility of applications of their science to military affairs. Yerkes specifically sought to use the letter in this manner; he made special note of the fact that it was a "spontaneous" statement from a prominent psychologist and emphasized, "I am especially pleased by his enthusiasm and his definite recognition of the importance of psychology in this crisis" (Yerkes, 1917n).

As if to solidify his case, Yerkes added one final twist to the psychologists' rationale, a variation on the learn-from-the-experience-of-nations-already-at-war line of reasoning. "A significant argument in favor of prompt action by the United States," he wrote to Hale, was the fact that the vast majority of literature dealing with mental problems and war was German. "Germany is undeniably a most efficient nation in the present conflict," he went on to argue. "The probability is that she is making more effective use of psychological methods than is any other country" (Yerkes, 1917n).

The NRC Establishes a Psychology Committee

Following the special meeting of the Association's Council, Yerkes hastened a letter to Hale: "The Psychological Council is enthusiastically in favor of the organization of a committee, and unless some unforeseen difficulty arises, I see no reason why . . . the National Research Council should not proceed with appointment. I am naturally anxious to have this matter settled at the earliest possible moment and a chairman appointed so that our work may go forward" (Yerkes, 1917o). After conferring with Cattell, who represented the AAAS in accordance with the NRC committee selection process (Cattell, 1917; Yerkes, 1917p), Yerkes submitted to Hale for appointment to the committee the names of nine psychologists. Seven had served as presidents of the APA (Yerkes, Cattell, Dodge, Seashore, Thorndike, Watson, and Hall); the other two (Franz and G. M. Whipple) were former APA councilmen.

Hale officially designated Yerkes chairman of the NRC Psychology Committee on April 30, 1917 (Hutchinson, 1917; Walcott, 1917). Formal letters of appointment to the other members of the Committee followed 10 days later (Hale, 1917b). In the meantime, Yerkes proceeded to activate the committees established by the Association's Council (Yerkes, 1917q), while H. S. Langfeld, the Association's secretary, moved forward with mobilization of the entire profession by means of an April 28th communication to the Association membership informing them of the Council's action, requesting their advice and suggestions, and soliciting indications of willingness to serve and to make laboratory facilities available (Langfeld, 1917).

THE APA READY FOR ACTIVE WAR ASSISTANCE

By the end of April 1917, the nation's psychologists gave every evidence of being poised and ready to answer the nation's call to arms. Mobilization of the profession through its national association was well under way. Incorporation into the NRC—the agency designated by President Wilson to organize the nation's scientific resources for use in the war effort—had been secured. The officers and members of the APA had formulated, given organizational structure to, and begun work on an extensive program of proposed contributions to the war effort. And they had armed themselves with arguments and information in defense of the practicality and importance of their proposed services that governmental and military authorities could not readily dismiss. The efforts of the officers and members of the APA had placed American psychologists in a position that would give them maximum opportunities to pursue professional assignments in the war effort.

By this point, the APA, as an organizational entity, had rendered its most extensive and most important contributions to what were to develop into the national service programs of the psychological profession. The Psychology Committee of the NRC, beginning in May of 1917, became the clearing house for coordinating and directing the war service activities of the profession, and, although chaired by the current president of the APA and composed of former presidents and council members of the Association, the Committee functioned as an agency of the NRC. As self-conscious representatives of their scientific profession, the members of the Psychology Committee continued throughout the war to be concerned with the advancement of their science and the reputation and status of their profession. To that extent, they were, in effect, continuing to represent the purposes of the APA.

Psychologists Not Immediately Accepted

The transformation of opportunities to pursue professional service into actual programs of service was neither easily nor readily achieved. Several realities of the situation became clear rather quickly: (a) Skeptics within and outside of the profession had serious doubts about the ability of the young science and its practitioners. (b) Medical doctors in general, and psychiatrists in particular, were prepared to obstruct efforts by psychologists to encroach on their areas of expertise. (c) Military officials, characteristically resistant to innovations, to interference with ordinary routine, and to additional paperwork, stood opposed to all proposals for improving the nation's armed services except for those of demonstrable value and immediate applicability. (With no knowledge of the science of psychology, or at best a little knowledge laced with gross misconceptions, military officers could hardly have been expected to respond positively to proposals whose reliability, value, and applicability were questioned by respected members of the profession itself, as well as by representatives of the more established sciences.) (d) For the NRC as a whole, there was no government financing except in cases where specific projects were undertaken at the request of specific governmental agencies. (For a thorough treatment of these points, see Camfield, 1969, pp. 121–181.)

Toward the end of May, in a letter to Yerkes, Hale bluntly summarized the conditions imposed by these realities:

> In the case of psychology, it is obvious that the first thing to do is to prove conclusively that the psychologists can perform service of unquestioned value to the government. . . . It is of fundamental importance that no tests be adopted which are not absolutely conclusive, because if they were, the science of psychology would suffer an injury from which it would not recover for many years. (Hale, 1917c)

In point of fact, Yerkes and his colleagues had been overconfident with respect to the scientific development of their discipline. Psychologists were technically unprepared to perform most of the services they proposed; they offered the nation potential assistance, not immediate applications. In the field of applied psychology, even the most advanced techniques were open to criticism and would require adaptation to meet military needs. Also, the psychologists had greatly underestimated the obstacles in the path to authorized programs of service. For all of their enthusiastic preparations of April 1917, more than three months passed before they secured any significant opportunity even to demonstrate their capacity to assist the nation in its crisis. Four months more elapsed before they managed to transform these "trials" into officially approved services (Camfield, 1969, pp. 121–181).

Although the Association's role diminished after April 1917, it did not altogether cease to function with regard to the pursuit of national service. Through May, June, and July of 1917, the Psychology Committee worked with and through the APA in a variety of ways as psychologists struggled feverishly to secure military consideration and trial of a few of their more promising proposals. Yerkes, for example, regularly identified himself in his correspondence with public officials, as well as with private citizens and organizations, as the president of the American Psychological Association and chairman of the Psychology Committee of the National Research Council (see, for example, Yerkes, 1917r, 1917s, 1917t, 1917u). He even used APA letterhead stationery in a mid-June 1917 "Dear Professor ___" letter to the Association's membership seeking the names of psychologists willing to enter public service as examiners (Yerkes, 1917u). The dozens of replies to this letter and to a follow-up "Dear Colleague" letter in July (Yerkes, 1917v), as well as to Langfeld's earlier April 28th circular to the Association's members, amounted to Association contributions to the NRC's Psychology Committee. At the first meeting of the Psychology Committee, held at Columbia University on May 18, 1917, the actions of the Association were reported, along with reports given by or for the 12 committees that the APA's Council had created a month earlier. In the absence of funding through the NRC, the Psychology Committee voted to approach the APA for a thousand dollars to help finance the Committee's war service efforts (NRC, 1917).

At its second meeting, on June 28th, the Psychology Committee took up the question of the status of the 12 APA committees. Hale, speaking for the NRC, had expressed to Yerkes his view that these should become subcommittees of the Psychology Committee only as the progress of their work made it seem desirable. While they complied with the essence of Hale's position by formally seeking to have only five of the APA committees designated as subcommittees in their subsequent report to the NRC, the records indicate that Yerkes and the members of the Psychology Committee followed their own inclination and treated the APA committees—at least those that continued to function outside of a base in the military and that showed any promise of useful results—as subcommittees of their NRC Committee (NRC, 1917; see also Yerkes, 1917w).

War Service Programs Initiated

After psychologists began to make their way into military service in August of 1917, the Association's role vis-à-vis the profession's developing programs of war service was essentially at an end. The December 1917 annual meeting may be said to have offered a forum for reporting on, and arousing further support for, the profession's war work (APA, 1917). (The profession's still privately owned journals, especially the *Psychological Bulletin*, served in a similar capacity throughout the war.) Also, the Association's members voted to compensate their officers for expenses incurred during their efforts early in the war to mobilize the profession for national service (APA, 1917). Otherwise, from August of 1917 on, the profession's war service activities must be properly regarded as official activities of the NRC's Psychology Committee and of the various branches of military service under which they became established.

By the end of December 1917, psychologists had established for themselves a distinctive professional role in the nation's war effort. This role was a substantial one as well, for they had transformed official "trials" of potential services into duration-of-the-war authorizations for large-scale programs under the direction of the adjutant general (the Committee on Classification of Personnel), the surgeon general (the Psychological Examination of Recruits) and the Signal Corps (representation on the Aviation Examining Boards and research activities). (For details, see Camfield, 1969, pp. 121–181.) The achievement was of monumental importance for the science and the profession of psychology. It conveyed stature to the science and prestige to the profession, and it paved the way toward even greater enhancement of the discipline's status. The psychologists had won a major professional victory with the military endorsement of their science and authorizations for its application. For the moment, they were elated to be marching lockstep with members of the military, medical, and other scientific professions in Woodrow Wilson's great crusade.

The 1917 annual meeting of the Association provided an occasion to celebrate this achievement. "It is my agreeable duty as President of the American Psychological Association," Yerkes told his colleagues, "to present to you in outline the history of the organizing of psychological military service. . . . Our profession has brought to the front the desirability and the possibility of dealing scientifically and efficiently with the principal human factors in military organization and activity," he asserted; "the demand for psychologists and psychological service promises, or threatens, to be overwhelmingly great" (Yerkes, 1918a, p. 85). Services already authorized, he noted, would require more than 300 trained psychologists. With obvious pride, he related to his colleagues that

> In Europe, psychologists have served conspicuously in the great war but psychology has done little. In this country, for the first time in the history of our science, a general organization in the interests of certain ideal and practical aims has been affected. Today American psychology is placing a highly trained and eager personnel at the service of our military organizations. We are acting not individually but collectively on the basis of common training and common faith in the practical value of our work. (p. 85)

PSYCHOLOGICAL SERVICES PERFORMED

From substantive bases within the military establishment, psychologists were able to expand both the scope and the extent of their professional services to the nation during the course of 1918. By the time of the Armistice, well over 400 psychologists had participated in a professional capacity in the nation's war effort (NRC, 1920). The range of their activities, moreover, had been surprisingly broad, and their assistance had extended to no less than half a dozen agencies of the War Department, as well as to the Navy Department.

Psychologists developed many lines of service within the Surgeon General's Department of the Army. The largest in scale and significance was their conduct of the intelligence examining of 42,238 officers and 1,684,723 recruits (and anyone else available for testing, including camp followers). They also performed extensive services as members of the Medical Examining and the Disability Boards, as educational and training advisors to the commanders of the Development Battalions, and as caseworkers and consultants in the Reconstruction Hospitals (for a detailed treatment, see Camfield, 1969, pp. 183–217).

Extensive as they were, the psychologists' activities under the surgeon general did not equal in magnitude or contribution to the nation the massive program developed by the Adjutant General's Committee on Classification of Personnel in the Army. Under the direction of Walter Dill Scott, this committee devised and developed a thorough system for the occupational classification and assignment of the Army's personnel. This "enormous and glorified employment agency," as one of the Committee members described it (Thorndike, 1919, p. 56), interviewed and classified almost three and a half million recruits during the course of the war. It filled Staff Corps requisitions for nearly 600,000 specialists in addition to selecting nearly one million men for assignments to such technical units as engineering, aviation, and ordnance. Within the overall scheme of the personnel system established by Scott's Committee, the actual science of psychology figured only slightly—principally in relation to developing reliable tests of trade proficiency. The Committee's contribution to the war effort did not hinge upon applications of psychological knowledge or techniques nearly so much as upon applications of the principles of scientific management. Even so, applied psychologists had initiated, developed, and directed the whole program, and it proved of unquestionable value in handling one of the nation's crucial wartime problems—the rapid mobilization of a large, effective fighting force. The field of applied psychology achieved a major boost in public esteem as a direct consequence (for details, see Camfield, 1969, pp. 218–226).

In the Signal Corps, psychologists under the direction of John B. Watson were called upon to develop a system for the selection, classification, and assignment of men similar to that of Scott's Committee but specifically for use by the Corps's Aviation Section. Watson established, and psychologists served on, the Aviation Examining Boards. Along with other scientists, psychologists conducted a wide range of investigations (as, for example, on problems of oxygen deficiency and on nystagmus) to determine and develop tests to assess the various special skills required for success as an aviator. They even studied and helped train homing pigeons (Camfield, 1969, pp. 226–230).

Among still other areas of professional service during the war, psychologists became actively involved in the development of a troop morale program at the request of the chief of staff's director of training (Camfield, 1977). For the Military Intelligence Branch of the General Staff, psychologists developed a brief training course in the psychology of observation and report and devised training exercises and tests for observers and scouts. For the Committee on Education and Special Training, psychologists assisted with the overall development of the Student Army Training Corps (SATC) program. They developed intelligence examining procedures for the selection of SATC recruits and prepared a course in military psychology to be included in the curriculum of the program. A request to the NRC from the Chemical Warfare Service for help with visual problems of gas masks led to the assignment of Raymond Dodge and Knight Dunlap to conduct studies of gas mask design; significant improvements in the overall design of the masks in regard to comfort and utility resulted. (For additional details on these services, see Camfield, 1969, pp. 240–248.)

Psychological assistance to the Navy began with another project undertaken by Raymond Dodge—development of a training device for naval gunners. Ultimately, Dodge and a number of psychologists contributed to the development of devices and techniques for the selection and training of other specialists needed by the Navy—listeners, lookouts, members of the fire control squads, and radio and telegraph operators (Camfield, 1969, pp. 248–257).

Altogether, by the end of the war American psychologists could point with pride to a truly impressive array of programs and services indicative of their success in demonstrating to hard-nosed and hard-pressed military and governmental officials the practical utility of their science. The program of the Association's December 1918 annual meeting stands as a tribute to the profession's achievements. Twenty-one of the 22 papers presented were summary reports of the extensive programs developed and the varieties of services rendered in the war effort (APA, 1918).

PSYCHOLOGY AND THE APA DISRUPTED

The program of the 1918 annual meeting reflected something else with respect to the Association and the Great War—namely, the war's disruptive impact on the profession and the Association representing it. That one, lonely "other" paper signified that the profession's ordinary scientific investigations had, during the war period, virtually ceased. Large numbers of psychology professors had abandoned their classrooms and laboratories for uniformed national service, where the only research in demand was applied research and where there was neither time nor money for, nor much interest in, basic research. The adverse effect of the war on basic psychological research had been noticeable at the end of 1917, when, at the Association's 26th annual meeting, only 31 papers had been presented, less than half the customary number (APA, 1917). Yet other signs of the war's disruption of scientific progress included the Psychological Review Company's suspension of publication of its *Journal of Experimental Psychology* for lack of material and the inability of the Society of Experimentalists to hold their spring meeting in 1918, because of the military service obligations of most of its members (Titchener, 1919).

The war affected the affairs of the APA in still other ways. Attendance at both the 1917 and 1918 annual meetings was down. The 1918 meeting was almost cancelled, and would have been had the war continued; the November 11th Armistice enabled the Association's Council to rescind an earlier decision to abandon plans for a meeting that year (Yerkes, 1918b). Association committees, which had in the prewar years regularly conducted inquiries and investigations and reported on them, ceased to function during the war. Three such committees had nothing to report at either the 1917 or the 1918 meetings; they had suspended work on their assignments as a consequence of the demands of war service (APA, 1917, 1918). This two-year interruption of their work was to lead to a major house cleaning at the 28th annual meeting in 1919, when the Association's members voted simply to discharge all these old committees (APA, 1919).

One committee of the Association was active during the war. It was, in fact, a product of the war. This was a Committee on the Qualifications of Psychological Examiners and Other Psychological Experts, established at the 1917 meeting (APA, 1917). The officers and members of the Association, as a result of their experiences in the pursuit of war service, had come to recognize the necessity of establishing standards and qualifications to protect the profession from the damage of quackery as the demand for practical applications of its knowledge rose. Another committee, also established at the 1917 meeting, was to survey and report to the Association on the general quality of publications in the field of applied psychology (APA, 1917). This, too, reflected concern for protecting the profession's reputation through an effort to identify and denounce pseudoscientific publications. The Association considered the report of its Committee on Qualifications presented at the 1918 meeting to be of sufficient importance to justify expenditure of Association funds for its publication and distribution. Indeed, as the holding of a symposium on "The Future of Pure and Applied Psychology" at the 1918 meeting also verified, the nation's psychologists clearly realized their war service had greatly accelerated their profession's entry into the world of practical applications and professional practitioners (APA, 1918).

APPLIED PSYCHOLOGY FLOURISHES

The remarkable developments in the field of applied psychology prompted by the demands, and made possible by the opportunities, of the war, and the popularity and recognition achieved by the profession as a result of its war service, more than made up for the war's interruption of basic psychological research and its disruption of the Association's activities. In the brief span of the war period, the cooperative and concerted effort of American psychologists to adapt the accumulated knowledge and techniques of their science to practical uses easily exceeded the entirety of the profession's applied research during the years preceding the war. The applied research of the war period hastened the refinement of such existing techniques as intelligence, aptitude, and rating tests. It also prompted investigations leading to the development of such new applied techniques as tests of acquired abilities and tests of emotional stability (Camfield, 1969, pp. 272–275).

By the end of the war, the field of applied psychology had acquired respectability within the psychological profession. "Applied psychology . . . is scientific work," asserted Edward Thorndike in 1919. "Making psychology for business or industry or the army is harder than making psychology for other psychologists, and intrinsically requires higher talents" (Thorndike, 1919, p. 60). For the psychologists themselves, other scientists, military personnel, and the general public, the psychologists' war work had affirmed the essential validity of psychological testing techniques. Psychological testing became something of a fad in the nation's business and industrial world following the war; the wartime selection and classification activities had kindled visions of happy and efficient workers in the minds of the nation's corporate managers. Interest in the potential uses of intelligence tests for educational purposes similarly grew to fad-like proportions in the postwar years. Within five years, some 50 group point-scale tests, patterned after the Army Alpha examination, had been developed for applications ranging from the kindergarten through the university level, and there was a heavy demand for all of them. (For details, see Camfield, 1969, pp. 276–281, 283–285.)

The growth and development of the American psychological profession and improvements in the academic standing of psychology during the decade following the war further reflected the overall impact of the war on American psychology. There was a wholesale improvement in the academic standing of the discipline following the war. For the first time in the profession's history, it found itself with an abundance of students, jobs, and funds. New departments, departments separated from affiliations with education and philosophy, new buildings to house departments and laboratories, larger appropriations to provide for new faculty, salary increments for existing faculty, and better equipped laboratories—all catalogued the new status of psychology in the academic world. The number of psychologists in the United States increased rapidly. Membership in the APA more than tripled, increasing from 336 in 1917 to 1,101 by 1930. (For details, see Camfield, 1969, pp. 285–288.)

The APA mirrored the influence of the war on the profession in several other ways as well. The Association honored Walter Dill Scott for the distinction he had helped bring to the profession through his war service by electing him to the presidency of the Association in 1919 (APA, 1919). Lewis M. Terman, who had distinguished himself with his work on the Army's intelligence examining program, was recognized by election to the Council the same year. Also at the 1919 annual meeting, the Association established a special Section on Clinical Psychology. This was to forestall a splintering of the Association as a result of the organization during the war of a new group, the American Association of Clinical Psychologists (APA, 1919; see also American Association of Clinical Psychologists, 1918).

At the same time, the Association replaced its wartime Committee on Qualifications of Psychological Examiners and Other Psychological Experts with a new committee, this one charged with inquiring into methods for the certification of consulting psychologists. Thus did the APA commence to wrestle with the many and difficult problems associated with the great public market for applications of psychology in the postwar decade and beyond.

REFERENCES

American Association for the Advancement of Science. (1914). Report of the Committee of One Hundred on scientific research of the AAAS. *Science, 39,* 680–682.

American Association for the Advancement of Science. (1917). Report of the Committee of One Hundred on scientific research of the AAAS. *Science, 45,* 57–58.

American Association of Clinical Psychologists. (1918). Proposed constitution and minutes of the second annual meeting, 28 December 1918. National Academy of Sciences Archives [hereafter NAS Archives]: NAS–NRC Central File: Institutions, Associations, Individuals: American Association of Clinical Psychologists.

American Psychological Association. (1917). Proceedings of the 26th annual meeting, 27–29 December 1917. *Psychological Bulletin, 15,* 25–56.

American Psychological Association. (1918). Proceedings of the 27th annual meeting, 27–28 December 1918. *Psychological Bulletin, 16,* 33–61.

American Psychological Association. (1919). Proceedings of the 28th annual meeting, 29–31 December 1919. *Psychological Bulletin, 17,* 33–82.

Angier, P. (1917). Letter to R. M. Yerkes, 10 April 1917. NAS Archives: NAS–NRC Central File: Institutions, Associations, Individuals [hereafter Institutions]: American Psychological Association [APA]: General.

Bentley, M. (1917). Letter to R. M. Yerkes, 3 May 1917. NAS Archives: NAS–NRC Central File: Institutions: APA: Committee on Psychological Literature.

Camfield, T. M. (1969). Psychologists at war: The history of American psychology and the first world war. *Dissertation Abstracts International, 30,* 5370A. (University Microfilms No. 70–10,766)

Camfield, T. M. (1973). The professionalization of American psychology, 1870–1917. *Journal of the History of the Behavioral Sciences, 9,* 66–75.

Camfield, T. M. (1977). Will to win: The United States Army troop morale program of World War I. *Military Affairs, 41,* 125–128.

Cannon, W. B. (1917). Telegram to G. E. Hale, 12 April 1917. NAS Archives: NAS–NRC Central File: Executive Committee: Committee on Psychology: General.

Cattell, J. M. (1917). Letter to R. M. Yerkes, 24 April 1917. NAS Archives: NAS–NRC Central File: Executive Committee: Committee on Psychology: General.

Coe, G. A. (1917). Letter to R. M. Yerkes, 23 May 1917. NAS Archives: NAS–NRC Central File: Institutions: APA: Committee on Recreation in Army and Navy (May–November, 1917).

Doll, E. A. (1917). Letter to R. M. Yerkes, 10 April 1917. Robert M. Yerkes Papers, Historical Library of the Medical Library of Yale University, New Haven, CT [hereafter Yerkes Papers].

Dunlap, K. (1917). Letters to R. M. Yerkes, 22 March and 6 April 1917. Yerkes Papers.

Dupree, A. H. (1957). *Science in the Federal Government: A history of policies and activities to 1940.* Cambridge, MA: Harvard University Press.

Franz, S. I. (1917). Letter to R. M. Yerkes, 17 April 1917. NAS Archives: NAS–NRC Central File: Institutions: APA: General.

Hale, G. E. (1916). National Research Council, preliminary report of the organizational committee to the president of the Academy. *Proceedings of the National Academy of Sciences, 2,* 507–508.

Hale, G. E. (1917a). Letter to R. M. Yerkes, 25 April 1917. NAS Archives: NAS–NRC Central File: Executive Committee: Committee on Psychology: General.

Hale, G. E. (1917b). Letters to R. M. Yerkes, G. M. Cattell, G. S. Hall, G. M. Whipple, E. L. Thorndike, R. Dodge, S. I. Franz, J. B. Watson, and C. E. Seashore, 10 May 1917. NAS Archives: NAS–NRC Central File: Executive Committee: Committee on Psychology: General.

Hale, G. E. (1917c). Letter to R. M. Yerkes, 23 May 1917. NAS Archives: NAS–NRC Central File: Executive Committee: Committee on Psychology: General.

Hollingworth, H. L. (1917). Letter to R. M. Yerkes, 8 April 1917. NAS Archives: NAS–NRC Central File: Institutions: APA: General.

Hutchinson, C. T. (1917). Letter to R.M. Yerkes, 30 April 1917. Subject file: NRC, Yerkes Papers.

Langfeld, H. S. (1917). Letter to R. M. Yerkes (and others), 28 April 1917. NAS Archives: NAS–NRC Central File: Institutions: APA: General.

Millikan, R. A. (1950). *Autobiography.* New York: Prentice Hall.

National Academy of Sciences. (1916). Reports of the meetings of the executive committee of the NRC. *Proceedings of the NAS, 2,* 605–608, 738–740.

National Academy of Sciences. (1917a). Reports of the meetings of the executive committee of the NRC. *Proceedings of the NAS, 3,* 227–230, 438–443, 530–536.

National Academy of Sciences. (1917b). Minutes of the meeting of the NRC on Thursday, April 19, 1917. *Proceedings of the NAS, 3,* 580–582.

National Research Council. (1917). Record of the meeting of the psychology committee of the NRC, 18 May 1917. NAS Archives: NAS–NRC Central File: Executive Committee: Committee on Psychology: Meetings: Minutes.

National Research Council. (1920). War service record of psychologists compiled by the NRC, 24 December 1919, and supplementary war service record of psychologists compiled by the NRC, 21 February 1920. NAS Archives: Anthropology and Psychology Series: Projects: War Service Records of Psychologists.

Scott, W. D. (1917). Letter to R. M. Yerkes, 14 April 1917 (enclosed with R. M. Yerkes's letters of 16 April to G. E. Hale). NAS Archives: NAS–NRC Central File: Executive Committee: Committee on Psychology: General.

Seashore, C. E. (1917). Letter to R. M. Yerkes, 9 May 1917. NAS Archives: NAS–NRC Central File: Institutions: APA: Committee on Acoustic Problems of Military Importance (April–November, 1917).

Thorndike, E. L. (1919). Scientific personnel work in the army. *Science*, n.s., *49*, 53–61.

Titchener, E. B. (1919). Letter to R. S. Woodworth, 15 March 1919. Box 3, Edward Bradford Titchener Papers, Cornell University Collection of Regional History and University Archives, Cornell University, Ithaca, NY.

Troland, L. T. (1917). Letter to R. M. Yerkes, 4 May 1917. NAS Archives: NAS–NRC Central File: Institutions: APA: General.

Tufts, J. H. (1917). Letter to W. D. Scott, 2 May 1917. Walter Dill Scott Papers, University Archives, Northwestern University, Evanston, IL [hereafter Scott Papers].

Walcott, C. D. (1917). Letter to R. M. Yerkes, 30 April 1917. Subject file: NRC, Yerkes Papers.

Watson, J. B. (1916). Letter to H. C. Warren, 14 April 1916. Yerkes Papers.

Watson, J. B. (1917). Letter to R. M. Yerkes, 19 April 1917. Yerkes Papers.

Woodworth, R. S. (1917). Letter to R. M. Yerkes, 19 April 1917. NAS Archives: NAS–NRC Central File: Institutions: APA: General.

Yerkes, R. M. (1917a). Letter to President Woodrow Wilson, 23 January 1917. Yerkes Papers.

Yerkes, R. M. (1917b). Letter to C. C. Brigham, 28 March 1917. Yerkes Papers.

Yerkes, R. M. (1917c). Letter to W. V. Bingham, 6 April 1917. Box 1, Walter Van Dyke Bingham Papers, Hunt Library, Carnegie Institute of Technology, Pittsburgh, PA.

Yerkes, R. M. (1917d). Letter to G. E. Hale, 9 April 1917. NAS Archives: NAS–NRC Central File: Executive Committee: Committee on Psychology: General.

Yerkes, R. M. (1917e). Telegram to G. E. Hale, 10 April 1917. NAS Archives: NAS–NRC Central File: Executive Committee: Committee on Psychology: General.

Yerkes, R. M. (1917f). Two letters, both with enclosures, to G. E. Hale, 16 April 1917. NAS Archives: NAS–NRC Central File: Executive Committee: Committee on Psychology: General.

Yerkes, R. M. (1917g). Letter to S. I. Franz, 23 April 1917. Yerkes Papers.

Yerkes, R. M. (1917h). Letter to W. D. Scott, 17 April 1917. Scott Papers.

Yerkes, R. M. (1917i). Letter to G. A. Coe, 5 May 1917. NAS Archives: NAS–NRC Central File: Institutions: APA: Committee on Recreation in Army and Navy (May–November, 1917).

Yerkes, R. M. (1917j). Letter to C. H. Judd, 5 May 1917. NAS Archives: NAS–NRC Central File: Institutions: APA: Committee on Pedagogical and Psychological Aspects of Military Training and Discipline (April–September, 1917).

Yerkes, R. M. (1917k). Letter to W. D. Scott, 15 June 1917. Scott Papers.

Yerkes, R. M. (1917l). Letter to E. L. Thorndike, 7 May 1917. NAS Archives: NAS–NRC Central File: Institutions: APA: General.

Yerkes, R. M. (1917m). Letter to G. E. Hale (opening with "I have found opportunity . . ."), 16 April 1917. NAS Archives: NAS–NRC Central File: Executive Committee: Committee on Psychology: General.

Yerkes, R. M. (1917n). Letter to G. E. Hale (opening with "I have decided to send . . ."), 16 April 1917. NAS Archives: NAS–NRC Central File: Executive Committee: Committee on Psychology: General.

Yerkes, R. M. (1917o). Letter to G. E. Hale, 23 April 1917. NAS Archives: NAS–NRC Central File: Executive Committee: Committee on Psychology: General.

Yerkes, R. M. (1917p). Letter to J. M. Cattell, 23 April 1917. NAS Archives: NAS–NRC Central File: Executive Committee: Committee on Psychology: General.

Yerkes, R. M. (1917q). Letter to (chairmen of the committees), 27 April 1917. NAS Archives: NAS–NRC Central File: Institutions: APA: General.

Yerkes, R. M. (1917r). Letter to J. P. Byers, 4 May 1917. NAS Archives: NAS–NRC Central File: Institutions: APA: Committee on Psychological Examination of Recruits.

Yerkes, R. M. (1917s). Letter to F. B. Brandt, 4 May 1917. NAS Archives: NAS–NRC Central File: Institutions: APA: Committee on Psychological Examination of Recruits.

Yerkes, R. M. (1917t). Letter to Surgeon General Braisted, Department of the Navy, 5 May 1917. NAS Archives: NAS–NRC Central File: Institutions: APA: Committee on Psychological Examination of Recruits.

Yerkes, R. M. (1917u). Letter to Dear Professor____, 13 June 1917. NAS Archives: NAS–NRC Central File: Institutions: APA: Committee on Psychological Examination of Recruits.

Yerkes, R. M. (1917v). Letter to Dear Colleague, 21 July 1917. NAS Archives: NAS–NRC Central File: Institutions: APA: Committee on Psychological Examination of Recruits.

Yerkes, R. M. (1917w). Letter to Members of the Psychology Committee of the NRC, 14 June 1917. NAS Archives: NAS–NRC Central File: Executive Committee: Committee on Psychology: General.

Yerkes, R. M. (1918a). Psychology in relation to the war. *Psychological Review*, *25*, 85–115.

Yerkes, R. M. (1918b). Letter to H. S. Langfeld, 16 November 1918. NAS Archives: NAS–NRC Central File: Institutions: APA: General.

5

THE APA BETWEEN THE WORLD WARS: 1918 to 1941

FRANZ SAMELSON

Keep the science pure but not . . . too pure. (G. S. Hall)[1]

Historical periodization is a problematic game. The period discussed here, however, does have both a clear beginning and a well-marked end, together with a fairly pronounced halfway point at which the mostly sunny climate of the prosperous twenties changed to the turbulent lows of the thirties, to end in the great storm of World War II. The developments in American psychology or affecting it and its organizations in these years were many. Most of them have already been treated by a number of authors.[2]

This chapter is based in part on a paper presented at the 20th meeting of Cheiron at Princeton University, Princeton, New Jersey, June 1988. It is part of a larger project supported by NSF Grants SOC78/12165 and SES-8510477, which are gratefully acknowledged. I would also like to thank the Archives of the History of American Psychology at Akron, Ohio; the Carnegie Mellon, Cornell, and Harvard University Archives; and, last but not least, the Manuscript Division of the Library of Congress for their assistance.

[1]Cited in Langfeld, 1919, p. 34.
[2]Benjamin (1977), Capshew (1986), Finison (1976, 1978), Harris, Unger, and Stagner (1986), Hilgard (1987), Morawski (1986), Napoli (1981), O'Donnell (1979), Samelson (1977), and Sokal (1984), to name some of them. This chapter makes no pretense to be either complete or original; too many authors have already trod this path to even acknowledge all of the secondary sources.

What follows is a selective account of some of the important actions and events related to the American Psychological Association.

GROWING UP IN THE ROARING TWENTIES

Halfway through the interwar decades, Samuel W. Fernberger, unofficial historian of the APA, wrote his classic history of the Association from its founding to 1930. To do so seemed worthwhile to him because "the character of the Association has changed from that of a very modest organization into that of a 'big business,' or at least so it appears to the eyes of an academic psychologist" (1932a, p. 1). By the end of the interwar period, this description must have appeared doubly appropriate. From some 360 members on Armistice Day, APA membership had grown to approach 3,000 by the time of the Battle of Britain.[3] The record of the 1918 business meeting had taken all of three pages in the *Psychological Bulletin*. By 1940, the transactions, including reports of the various committees, covered over 40 printed pages; the treasurer's report alone required more space than the whole 1918 record. Income was up tenfold from a paltry $900 in 1919, as were expenses. Yet the balance on hand had grown to over $40,000 in 1940; the Association, incorporated in January 1925 "in the District of Columbia without a special act of Congress" (Anderson, 1925, p. 82; 1926, p. 123) at the cost of $25.12, had discovered the need for a Committee on Investment (Olson, 1938, p. 591). The most ominous symbol of the changes, however, may have been the decision, in 1928, to abandon the conviviality of the annual banquet at the Association's year-end meeting and to schedule a formal evening session for the presidential address in its stead (Fernberger, 1929, p. 128).

Two things the Association had accomplished in these years were, according to Fernberger, (a) to maintain higher and higher standards for membership, which made it an honor as well as a professional necessity to be elected to membership, and which gave its members a "group self-consciousness which . . . has done more toward defining psychology in this country . . . " than anything else (1932a, p. 88); and (b) to acquire and maintain a group of journals covering the field of psychology. On the other hand, the Association had, in his opinion, utterly failed in every attempt, from small matters of scientific terminology to the major issue of the certification of consulting psychologists, to exercise control over psychology

---

[3]"Number of Members and Associates in the APA Since 1916" (table). Box I-3, Records of the APA, Library of Congress, Washington, DC.

or psychologists—a poignant comment considering that in this period Watson's phrase of psychology as "the prediction and control of behavior" had become part of the standard rhetoric. Yet "psychology in America," Fernberger concluded, "could not possibly have gained the position it now holds in the academic and professional world without the effect of the Association, defining the field and bringing the psychologists together for concerted action" (p. 89). These reflections by a pillar of the APA highlight the major issues of the interwar years: expansion, the growth of applied work, and the maintenance of "scientific" standards; the acquisition and development of professional journals; and attempts to control the nature of psychology while maintaining unity in the face of increasingly more powerful centrifugal forces.

The Legacy of the War

The successful participation of psychologists in World War I, largely under the guidance of the APA (as described in Chapter 4), had produced a number of far-reaching effects. It had, as James McKeen Cattell's graphic phrase went, "put psychology on the map of the United States" (cited in Samelson, 1979, p. 106). The general public had been, and was continuing to be, exposed to a good deal of publicity, especially about the Army testing program and its alleged achievements (Samelson, 1979, pp. 104–108). Mental testing was proposed as the solution to major problems, in business and industry, in education, in immigration control, and so forth. Soon the "IQ craze" was sweeping the country (see Napoli, 1981; Samelson, 1977; and Chapter 4 above).

A second, corollary effect was the impact of this success story on the interests of younger psychologists and especially on the recruitment of aspiring practitioners in the various applied fields, quickly leading to a massive influx of graduate students. A third development, pointing in another direction, involved the willingness of hard-science academics to accept psychology as, at least in part, a respectable natural science. This rise in status was brought about as well as symbolized by the inclusion of psychology in the new National Research Council (NRC), the establishment of an NRC Division of Psychology (jointly with anthropology), and the selection of one psychologist (James R. Angell) as president of the NRC and another (Robert M. Yerkes) as director of its Research Information Service. The inclusion of psychologists among recipients of NRC research grants, the support by the NRC of the APA's efforts to start an abstract journal, and the participation of psychologists in pathbreaking NRC committees (e.g., for research on problems of sex) soon followed.

A different consequence, a bit less obvious in its effects, grew out of the close personal contact among psychologists thrown together by the war. It resulted in the formation of relationships, closer than usual for academics, among the future influentials of the discipline and which created some longlasting personal bonds, as well as some antipathies. The most important of these networks was probably the one linking E. G. Boring, Robert M. Yerkes, Lewis M. Terman, and Richard M. Elliott, all important psychologists in their own right as well as influential players in the APA,[4] located at strategic places in the academic landscape: Harvard, Yale, Stanford, and Minnesota.

One more result of the war might be surmised: its contribution to the decrease in influence of Edward B. Titchener and his brand of psychology on the United States. When the country entered the war in April 1917, Titchener's Experimentalists, then meeting in Cambridge, quickly started to organize for their war efforts under the aegis of the APA (see Chapter 4). Titchener himself considered his presence as a British subject improper in this American affair and withdrew from this first meeting. As he later claimed, he kept waiting in vain for a long time afterward to be asked to participate in the war work. Yerkes (and probably others) had taken, or so he claimed, Titchener's withdrawal as symbolizing the rejection of applied and unscientific activities, an attitude Titchener had expressed forcefully on earlier occasions (Titchener, 1919). It appears plausible that this exclusion, inadvertent or not, of Titchener from the war effort aggravated the other factors leading to the gradual demise of his influence in the United States. Incidentally, he was also to resign twice before his death from the APA, once in 1922 and, having withdrawn the resignation upon the urging of his friends, once more in 1926 (Fernberger, 1927, p.139), in protest against the dues increase to $5 (Titchener, 1924).

The Certification Struggle: Failure for Whom?

The first postwar APA meeting in Baltimore, "very well attended, especially by men in the service" (Langfeld, 1919, p. 33), summed up the war developments and hinted at things to come. It elected the psychologist with the highest Army rank, Colonel Walter D. Scott, as new APA president and listened to paper sessions almost exclusively dealing with war work. In addition, the program had arranged for a symposium on the "Future of Pure and Applied Psychology." As Edward L. Thorndike saw this future (fairly accurately, as it turned out), there would be as many "doing" psy-

---

[4]Correspondence 1919–1969, E. G. Boring Papers, Harvard University Archives, Cambridge, MA.

chology in 20 years as would be teaching it—although both groups needed to remain scientific. Major Yerkes proposed to confine training in applied psychology to certain institutions with specialized programs. And APA founder G. Stanley Hall agreed that psychology needed to remain a science, pure but not too pure, and that the impetus received by applied psychology from the war was all to the good. In his final comment, he saw "the future of the world depend[ing] in a peculiar sense upon American psychologists" (Langfeld, 1919, pp. 34, 49), a prediction overshooting, for better or worse, the mark by a wide margin.

In addition to this symposium, but not mentioned in the Proceedings, it appears that Letha S. Hollingsworth presented a report on the organization and constitution of an independent American Association of Consulting Psychologists, initiated at the previous APA meeting. The plan provoked an extended discussion leading, because of strong opposition to this sepa-ratist move, to the decision to postpone the formation of the new splinter group until the following year. At least this is the account of the events given by J. E. Wallace Wallin (1960, p. 302), one of the protagonists on the clinicians' side, who complained about the omission of these and similar occurrences from the published Proceedings of APA meetings.[5] In any case, the published record of the next APA meeting, in 1919, shows that a conference committee, chaired by APA Council member Bird T. Baldwin, recommended the creation of an APA section of Clinical Psychology (Lang-feld, 1920, p. 37). Following initial silence, a preemptive move by the APA leadership had succeeded in stopping the rebellion this time; it had not, however, solved the underlying problems, which would crop up again and again. In fact, less than 2 years later, an independent New York State Association of Consulting Psychologists was formed to promote "high stand-ards of professional qualifications" and to stimulate "research [on] . . . psychological analysis and evaluation" ("Notes and News," 1921, p.439). In contrast with APA criteria, 2 years of graduate work in psychology were sufficient for membership. It was this group that would spearhead the suc-cessful organizing drive of applied psychologists in the thirties.

There were perhaps two or three main issues underlying this protracted struggle. First was the basic question of the nature of psychology and of the APA. From its inception, the APA had inscribed the "advancement of psychology as a science" on its banners. Even though clinical and other applied interests had been represented from the start, they were only tol-erated, whereas the dominant center of the APA insisted on promoting an

---

[5]The occurrence of such omissions raises a serious problem for histories of the APA, which by and large rely on the official versions contained in printed proceedings and committee reports.

academic, pure-science perspective. Second, and deriving from this fundamental and exclusionist principle, was the other, pragmatic issue of the control of practitioners. Keeping them out of the Association would either leave them free to do whatever they wanted in an open marketplace or hand over control to others, most likely state legislatures, who might create rules affecting everybody, including APA members; educating the public and lobbying legislators would be the APA's only weapons. On the other hand, the admission of the bulk of practitioners into the organization would lower its standards and weaken its main claim to scientific status. It would also give their potentially large number a say in the policies of the association and would create practical and legal problems of specification and enforcement of rules for psychological practice. Neither of the alternatives looked very attractive. In the background, there may also have been a third issue: the desire uniting the core of the APA, itself not really homogeneous in interests or unanimous in philosophy, to avoid sharing power with a flock of outsiders.

It is not possible to spell out all of the moves and countermoves in this protracted struggle, only present its outlines. In addition to the new Clinical Section, the 1919 APA meeting set up a committee to consider procedures for certification, taking current attempts at related legislation into account. In the years to follow, a succession of committees recommended dropping plans for the licensure of non-APA members; certifying APA members through election to a new section of "Consulting Psychologists," because "Clinical" was an inappropriate description of the range of activities to be certified; and organizing Educational and Industrial sections as conduits in the certification process. The latter proposals for additional sections were eventually rejected or tabled. In the end, only 25 members were certified as Consulting Psychologists. It had become obvious in the meantime that the high standards required for election to the section (a PhD degree and a rather loosely defined competence in consulting practice), or perhaps the payment of a $35 fee, kept most practitioners from applying. John B. Watson was probably not alone when he replied to Frederic L. Wells's invitation to join the section that he felt honored by the suggestion but could not "see the use of such a fee" (Watson, 1922).

On the other hand, those who did become certified, like Terman and Wells, did not really need certification. Thus, in 1927 the policy of certifying Consulting Psychologists was voted out of existence on the recommendation of the Committee on Certification Policy, according to Fernberger (1932a, p. 51), the relevant sections of the bylaws were stricken, and the $35 fee was returned. The Standing Committee on Certification had already anticipated such an outcome: Its 1926 report, apparently written by Wells, had diagnosed the personality traits of the APA scientists as the obstacle, stating that "scientific men are predominantly schizoid, and while commonly energetic and at times heroic in the pursuit of personal aims and ideals, seldom exhibit the capacity for resolute common action which is observable in professional and more markedly in industrial groups" (Fernberger, 1927, p. 149).

However, the culprit may not have been the schizoid character of APA scientists. As at the start of this episode, it turns out that the official record of the ending needed amplification. This time, Fernberger (1932b) himself published a correction on the basis of information from Margaret F. Washburn, who had chaired the Committee on Certification Policy. According to her, a mail vote had produced a "very clear result" in favor of continuing certification, which was thereupon recommended by her committee. Instead, however, the APA Council of Directors discharged the committee with thanks and unanimously recommended the very opposite action to the annual meeting: to eliminate certification. After extended discussion and several attempts from the floor to save certification, the Council's move carried the day (Fernberger, 1928, p. 131). Apart from the significance of this outcome, which created the basis for the splinter organizations of the thirties, the report and the correction give us a rare glimpse into the inner workings of the APA, although it is obviously problematical to generalize from this one instance.

Two Successes: Journals and Associates for the APA

Discounting the failed attempt to set up a workable certification program, started by a minority (and ending in a victory for the Council, at least temporarily), the major APA projects of the twenties turned out to be big successes. One of these projects, like the others initiated or supported by the Council, was the acquisition of scientific journals. The opening move was made in 1919, when a committee was appointed to cooperate with the NRC Division of Anthropology and Psychology in the establishment of a psychological abstract journal (Langfeld, 1920, p. 38). The project was an ambitious and expensive one, taking a good deal of time and effort to work out the financing arrangements. Fortunately, the Laura Spelman Rockefeller Memorial, under Beardsley Ruml, a Chicago psychology PhD, had started to fund major psychology projects, and in 1926 agreed to provide a 10-year grant of $76,500 (Fernberger, 1927, p. 149). Combining this assistance with a dues increase of $3 for both Members and the new group of Associates, the APA began publication of the *Psychological Abstracts*, its new international abstract journal, in January 1927.

Important as the *Abstracts* were, the major coup was the purchase in 1925 of the Psychological Review Company's journals (*Psychological Review, Psychological Bulletin, Psychological Index, Psychological Monographs*, and *Journal of Experimental Psychology*) for the very reasonable price of $5,500 (plus interest), almost half of which was eventually waived by its former owner— a few months before the crash, as chance would have it. Howard C. Warren, psychology professor at Princeton and a former president of the APA, had acquired most of these journals from J. Mark Baldwin in 1911, after the latter had left the country. In 1916, Warren had added the new *Journal of Experimental Psychology* to his holdings. Even though the *American Journal of Psychology* had been the first American psychology journal, Warren's journals had come to play an important role for psychology and for the APA, which regularly published its proceedings in the *Bulletin* after its inception in 1904. By a stroke of luck, the Association was able to round out its set of publications when it received another journal as a gift one year after the purchase of Warren's journals: In 1926, Morton Prince presented the deed to his *Journal of Abnormal and Social Psychology* to the APA.

The second major project of the twenties was the attempt to absorb the quickly increasing number of psychologists into the APA while maintaining control and even strengthening its standards (and finances). Although in the early days "almost any respectable person who desired membership" was elected to the APA (Fernberger, 1932a, p. 9), once the Association had achieved a critical mass it began to progressively tighten membership requirements. When the number of new admissions shot up after the war to a new high, a committee to revise membership requirements was appointed in 1920 upon Council recommendation. At the next meeting, this committee, chaired by Boring, proposed, instead of any changes, a more explicit definition and a strict enforcement of the rules, bearing in mind the "advancement of psychology as a science" in accordance with the Association's constitutional mandate. Spelling out these rules, the committee put a new emphasis on scientific publications in contrast with the older criterion of professional titles or positions, because these seemed to proliferate in a confusing fashion. On this basis, "acceptable published research of a psychological character" was added to the PhD dissertation as a prerequisite, together with being "actively engaged in psychological work" (Boring, 1922b, p. 75). This stiffened entrance requirement was approved by the meeting, but the committee's further proposal to create, by the election of 100 APA Fellows, a new class of members with more advanced scientific standing was tabled.

Two years later, the Council initiated a look at another new membership category, this time in the form of a lower class of "Associates."

The committee appointed for this task, again chaired by Boring, presented its report the following year. The "growth of the science of psychology" had, in addition to raising the qualifications of full APA members, created a distinct group of persons doing scientific work at less advanced levels, work not involving research. It appeared "expedient" to admit such persons as Associates of the APA if they either were engaged in primarily psychological work or held a PhD in psychology. The new Associates would not have the right to vote or hold office, but they would be permitted to take the floor at annual meetings. Concluding its recommendation, the committee pointed out that if the APA required more money for its new journals, it could "make subscription to an abstract journal mandatory [for] Associates" (Anderson, 1925, p. 83). Fernberger's comment (1932a, p. 15) that the creation of the Associate status "cannot entirely be divorced from the Association's acquisition of a group of . . . journals . . ." was not based on sheer guesswork.

The Associates' privilege to hold the convention floor, recommended by Boring's committee, was stripped away in the final vote, whereas their dues were raised by $3, presumably needed for the new journals (Anderson, 1925, pp. 75, 78). The change in bylaws became effective the following year. Applicants for the new Associate status appeared quickly, especially after graduate study beyond the first year was declared acceptable for the Associates' "psychological work" requirement (Fernberger, 1928, p. 133), whereas the hurdle for Member status had been raised once more by specifying published research "beyond the doctoral dissertation" (Fernberger, 1927, p. 153). Within 5 years, the number of Associates equaled that of APA Members, and by 1940 would outstrip it 3 to 1.

The introduction of the Associate class changed the APA's character from that of a self-proclaimed scientific elite group in the direction of that of a mass organization, although not quite like some populist social science societies, which were open even to interested amateurs. The efforts of the pure scientists at the APA's core had paid off. At least for the time being, the Association and its leaders had successfully harnessed the expanding population of professional psychologists and its resources, even though (or perhaps because) they still kept out large numbers of technicians and semiprofessionals, and they had done so without making too many concessions to threaten the APA's scientific standards. For some, however, this was not enough. In 1928, Knight Dunlap and others founded an exclusive National Institute of Psychology, which lasted until at least 1938 without leaving much of a record of its existence, not to mention any accomplishments. About the same time, the scientific elite reorganized, after Titchener's death, his old group of Experimentalists into a formal "Society of Experimental Psychologists" or "SEP" (Boring, 1938).

Another Success: The International Congress

Soon after the Associate issue had been settled, the APA embarked in earnest on a third project to crown the earlier successes: to bring the International Congress of Psychology to America for the first time. There had been a number of false starts before, including the debacle of 1913 (see Chapter 3). In 1923, a special committee chaired by Cattell had recommended that an invitation be issued for 1926. After the Council had taken a close look at the organizational problems of such an intercontinental affair, it had announced its unanimous opposition to this date. By 1926, however, the Council proposed to begin the planning process, whereupon the members at that year's meeting, going the Council one better, voted to extend the invitation to a 1929 date (Fernberger, 1927, p. 145). Although the Congress was nominally managed by an independent National Committee, it was organized by the APA, which elected the committee's officers and 15 members (Fernberger, 1928, p. 132); by coincidence, all of them turned out to be former APA Presidents or Council members, except for William McDougall of Duke, who had not managed, or not tried, to become an insider after coming to this country.

In early September 1929, the Ninth International Congress of Psychology was held in New Haven, Connecticut, followed by a meeting of the APA Council, which had cancelled the regular year-end APA convention. The Congress heard over 400 papers, about one fourth of them presented by foreign, mostly European, visitors. Some major figures addressed the assembled psychologists: Claparede, Koehler, Michotte, Pieron, Stern, and Thorndike. J. McKeen Cattell shocked the assembly with an attack on McDougall, although nobody seems to have been able to recall exactly what he had said (Sokal, 1984, p. 296). Karl Lashley gave the APA president's address, and Watson had to miss his hero Pavlov's lecture because he had booked passage to Europe before learning of Pavlov's visit (Watson, 1929). All in all, it was a rousing success. It was also a good investment for the APA, which more than doubled the $1,000 it had advanced to the National Committee (Woodworth, 1930, p. 566).

Running an Organization

During the interwar years, the APA was, directly or indirectly, involved in a variety of other activities and issues. In 1925, for instance, a suggestion came from the NRC Division to consider publication of a Psychology Handbook as a reference source. Gradually, a plan emerged to produce a series of 16 smaller handbook volumes covering the various areas of scientific psychology, from the "History of Experimental Psychology" all the way to "Animal Psychology" (Fernberger, 1927, p. 151), the latter tacked on almost as an afterthought. Eventually, the project died when the Council's recommendation to begin raising money for the work was defeated in a confusing succession of votes (Fernberger, 1929, p. 126). This outcome was, incidentally, one of the rare times a Council recommendation was voted down by the members present at the business meeting, who usually supported the Council's lead. Even when the Council reversed its own position as it did in 1923 and 1924, the membership vote followed the Council both times, first to decline an invitation to join the newly organized Social Science Research Council (SSRC) in 1923, and in the next year to accept it (Anderson, 1924, p. 74; 1925, p. 72). The published record contains no hint of the reasons for the initial rejection and subsequent reversal (cf. Samelson, 1981).

Boring was to claim later (1947) that in his time the governance of the APA had been very democratic. Yet in the conspicuous case described earlier, the Council had turned around, at the annual meeting, the clear-cut results of an (unreported) mail vote on certification. In many other instances, the Council's recommendations in effect set policy. One of the obvious questions about this process concerns the attendance at the business meetings and the size and composition of the votes taken, but this information was reported only rarely. Apparently, the procedures usually involved voice votes rather than actual counts. Specific figures were reported in a 1925 vote of 12 to 40 (Anderson, 1926, p. 120), one in 1927 of 73 to 20 (Fernberger, 1928, p. 131), and one in 1928 of 43 to 40 (Fernberger, 1929, p. 126), indicating what one might expect: that the number of members present and voting at such meetings was only some fraction of the total membership—roughly one fifth in these recorded cases. One might combine this fact with Fernberger's (1932a, p. 35) claim that the Council, with its control of the nominating process, was by and large a "self-perpetuating" body. His statement, cited earlier, about the APA's role in defining the field of psychology in America and bringing about concerted action would then carry added meaning; it was the inner circle of the APA that had been the moving force behind the psychologists' "concerted action" much of the time. As we have seen, this force was directed generally toward controlled expansion and selective strengthening of the discipline and the upholding of academic standards. It attempted to reestablish the primacy of a pure or scientific and largely experimental psychology, after the war and its aftermath had shifted the balance in the direction of applied work (cf. O'Donnell, 1979; Samelson, 1980). When new interest groups tried to move APA policy in different directions, as in the certification attempts of that decade and the varied causes of the decade to come, the Council tried to absorb their impact and maintain a steady course instead, "shunning the floodlight of 'social significance,'" as Bruner and Allport put it in their review of past trends (1940, p. 774).

Up to here, this chapter has been silent about the *content* of this scientific psychology so vigorously promoted, about its theoretical debates and empirical achievements. However, the present organizational history does not have enough room for a full report, complex as it would have to be. The period had started with Watson's first exposition of his behaviorist system in 1919. In the mid-twenties, it saw a heated debate about behaviorism that ended in a draw (Samelson, 1985b). Titchener's system had ceased to grow in influence, whereas the German Gestalters were gaining some prominence (Sokal, 1984). The infatuation with testing and the flirtation of some psychologists with matters of race, eugenics, and immigration restriction was abating by 1925 (Samelson, 1978). Toward the end of the decade, the translation of Pavlov's book (1927) planted the seeds of neobehaviorist experimentalism. Added to these developments was the growth of various branches of applied psychology (cf. Napoli, 1981). The maturing science of psychology was going through a turbulent period of fading old certainties, new starts, and proliferating systems. As Bruner and Allport (1940, p. 773) characterized it, "The impression [of this decade] is one of diversity and vigor. Psychology had mounted the steed of prosperity and had dashed off in all directions at once. It was the predepression era, and the universe . . . was endlessly expanding." But 7 weeks after the farewells at the International Congress, the stock market crashed. The problems of the country were about to change dramatically, and with it the role of psychology, even if one has to look hard to find explicit references to the crash or to the ensuing Depression in the psychological literature.

THE 1930s: CONTAINING CENTRIFUGAL FORCES

If the twenties had been a period of interregnum and transition for the discipline, the next decade saw the beginnings of some major theoretical–methodological developments that would dominate American psychology long beyond the mid-century mark. The APA, on the other hand, had successfully strengthened its position in the earlier period and laid the organizational groundwork for the expansion to come, if unity could be maintained. The thirties, in contrast, found the Association acting mostly in response to problems intruding from the outside rather than initiating any major new projects. The main issues—(a) maintaining the APA's leading role in the face of proliferating new organizations and (b) coping with novel demands arising, beyond sheer growth, from the dramatic economic and political events of the period—seem to have kept it busy enough.

External Success and Internal Disarray

By 1930, American psychology had come a long way. It had just staged a successful International Congress, symbolizing its full-fledged academic status as an independent discipline. One of the last holdovers, Harvard, was finally getting ready to establish a Department of Psychology separated from philosophy. Earlier in the decade, intelligence testing, behaviorism, and "Freudism" had made psychology a household word. Although battles on the boundary would continue, esoteric knowledge production was increasingly marking the line between an academic discipline and pop psychology, charlatans, and other outsiders. Private foundations were contributing large sums of money to various projects, and even the hard-science NRC, joined by the "softer" Social Science Research Council, had accepted psychology and begun to provide funds for selected research problems and for fellowships to train the next generation of scientists. In short, psychology had achieved the trappings of independence: an autonomous disciplinary structure demarcated from other fields and from outsiders, control over training, some extramural financing, and a strong professional organization with a flourishing journal network.

But all was not well with the growing discipline. Psychology had "oversold itself" in the past decade and was providing no help to the country in the present crisis, wrote one-time Titchenerian Grace Adams (1934), by then a disenchanted outsider, in the *Atlantic Monthly*. Insiders, too, were troubled. In public, Clark L. Hull (1935) deplored the chaotic state of psychological theory in his presidential address, listing a dozen systems competing with each other. And in private, Boring lamented to his friend Fernberger in 1930 that "psychologists simply do not agree . . . [instead they display] a perfectly incomprehensible diversity of opinion" (Boring, 1930). Even the usually sanguine James McKeen Cattell was pessimistic about finding psychologists of any stature when he called for nominations to the National Academy of Science (Cattell, 1933).

Although the claim to scientific status had united mainstream psychologists from the beginning, the direction that would lead to scientific progress of the discipline was unclear. Watson had added some useful slogans, but had not been much help with specifics, and he had abandoned the field; Titchener was dead, in body and in spirit; and new psychological systems, some of them foreign imports, were proliferating without gaining more than local allegiance. There was neither a shared paradigm, nor a consensus on evaluative criteria, nor even a common language. The center of the science was in disarray, and the insistence of the APA leadership on maintaining the high level of formal credentials for membership may have been an inverted reflection of this condition.

What was needed was an effort to solidify the scientific core, which was fragmented into a gaggle of "contemporary schools." Struggling with the unseemly and distasteful problem of disagreement and controversy in what claimed to be an objective, rational science, an issue Boring (1929) had discussed in his presidential address, he teamed up with Langfeld and Weld to take stock of what was solid in psychology. Eschewing the profusion of theories and theorists, they produced *Psychology: A Factual Textbook* (Boring, Langfeld, & Weld, 1935; emphasis added). Beyond this retreat to facts, Boring found in the newly labeled notion of *operationism* the path to the roots of disagreement and from there, he hoped, to the reestablishment of consensus. His sights set higher than Boring's, Hull (1935) was beginning his crusade for "a way out" of the squabbles and confusion. Fashioning himself after Newton, he proceeded to elaborate an intricate model for truly scientific psychological theory, illustrated in his "Mathematical Theory of Rote Learning." Along the way, he proselytized the young Experimentalists where he could, gave battle to competing formulations wherever he found them, and succeeded at least in setting the terms of the debate on theory construction (Krech, 1974, pp. 233–234; Samelson, 1985a; Smith, 1986).

Organizational Housekeeping

In the meantime, the APA's concerns dealt initially with various housekeeping chores such as membership requirements, election rules, and committee work on divers topics. Gradually and unenthusiastically, the Association turned to consider the direct impact of the Depression on the employment opportunities of psychologists. Eventually, it had to confront the repercussions of the economical and political developments at home and abroad, on the one hand, and of the explosive growth of applied fields of psychology, on the other.

The decade began with a break in an old tradition. On the basis of the precedent of the successful September meeting of the International Congress, the date of the APA annual meeting was shifted from year-end to the fall. Apparently, the issue affected enough members directly to energize a 3-to-1 vote to override the Council, which had recommended to wait for the result of a membership poll by mail (Brigham, 1931, p. 188). On other matters, the membership was less united. As the election committee reported, nominations for president were extremely scattered, with 300 ballots spread over more than 30 different nominees, according to an earlier report (Boring, 1923, p. 68). The leading candidates in 1929 and 1930 had received all of 9% and 15 % of the nominations, respectively. Although disturbed by the possibility that agreements among a few individuals might win nomination and eventual election for the candidate of a small minority, the committee itself could not agree on the best solution for this problem (Brigham, 1931, p. 192)—a persistent one that provided the justification for the Council's guiding if not manipulative hand.

The 1930 meeting saw the start of a little-known project. Apparently upon a request from the recently formed National Advisory Council on Radio in Education, an advisory Committee on Psychology was appointed. Chaired by Walter V. Bingham, the Committee soon organized the participation of psychologists in a novel, large-scale experiment in educational broadcasting. Between October 1931 and April 1932, a series of weekly 15-minute lectures on psychological topics, preceded by talks on economics, were broadcast by a number of stations across the nation. Subsequently, the set of lectures appeared in print under the title *Psychology Today* (Bingham, 1932). Besides publishing the book, the University of Chicago, which played a major role in the project, distributed listener notebooks before the broadcasts, together with a request for audience feedback (Lumley, 1932, p. 753). It is interesting to note that among the 30 prominent psychologists presenting lectures was none other than John B. Watson, who spoke on "How to Grow a Personality." Despite his diatribes against academic psychology after his abrupt departure from academia in 1920, Watson had maintained membership in the APA longer than is commonly realized. He had also continued to play an active role on editorial boards of APA publications, among other things. As for the radio committee, it continued to report plans for further broadcasts, but apparently lacked the funds to ever go on the air again after the Depression began to bite.

Another public issue moved the Association to respond without hesitation. For several years, an APA Committee on Precautions in Animal Experimentation had distributed a code for laboratory procedures, together with warnings to avoid the use of language potentially objectionable to humane societies. But in 1931, legislation was introduced to prohibit the use of dogs in medical experimentation in the District of Columbia. A unanimous APA Council quickly joined the AAAS in a protest resolution, copies of which were sent to all House members (Brigham, 1931, p. 661). In subsequent years, efforts to lobby national and state legislators in defense of animal experimentation were made repeatedly. This ready action stood in contrast to the strong resistance put up by the traditionally conservative and WASPish Association against efforts to involve it in other political issues. One of these, a Council proposal in 1933 to inquire into racial discrimination against psychologists in Nazi Germany, was tabled permanently (Paterson, 1933, p. 638). When some of the victims of this discrimination sought refuge in the U.S., the APA waited until 1938 to acknowledge the problem of displaced foreign psychologists by the appointment of a committee to "survey" it (Olson, 1939, p. 761), allocating all of $50 for this work. Fortunately, individual psychologists and other organizations, including the regional psychology associations, were more generous. In 1940, the Burks Committee, as it had come to be called, after its indefatigable chairperson Barbara Burks, urgently requested more adequate support of its work with the appeal that the "only way now open to us to fight for our professional integrity is to strengthen our efforts in behalf of psychologists who [took] refuge here from tyranny abroad" (Olson, 1940b, p. 718). The APA budgeted $200 for the next year.

Dealing With the Depression

Of course, hesitation to assist the refugees was in part due to the shortage of jobs even for indigenous psychologists. Although the Depression did not seem to threaten seriously the positions of most established academics[6] or the recruitment of new disciples, money was getting tighter and finding jobs for one's students became increasingly harder. Instructed to study the question of the "over-production of psychologists" (W. S. Hunter, cited in Finison, 1976, p. 748), a high-powered APA committee organized a survey of academic job prospects. Rejecting what the committee termed overly optimistic expectations by some major departments, it produced a rather dismal prognosis (Paterson, 1933, pp. 653, 655). Yet the APA establishment first reaffirmed its credo that "training in experimental psychology is fundamental and required for all psychologists" (APA Committee on the Ph.D. Degree, 1934, p. 71). Subsequent discussion of ways to deal with the job shortages included comments about supply and demand, raising PhD standards, and redirecting graduate training. But the committee failed to reach a consensus, Boring resigned from what he thought was a futile task, and the remaining committee personnel had to be reshuffled. The

---

[6]It seems remarkable how rarely the Depression is mentioned in the journals or in private letters.

new chair, Albert T. Poffenberger, decided that little could be done about redirecting graduate training. Even the NRC pamphlet on "Careers in Psychology," which promoted academic research careers, could not be revised to reflect the new realities, because of a lack of funds. In any case, it did not seem useful to tamper too much with the "laws of supply and demand" (Paterson, 1934, p. 664).

Continuing pressures from below and from the outside led to the establishment of an APA Committee on the Social Utilization of Unemployed Psychologists. Its survey discovered that many of the 200 unemployed psychologists it found had had only limited training; furthermore, almost half of them lived in New York City, making unemployment largely a local problem and, in addition, "only in part a product of the depression" (Paterson, 1936b, p. 702). Furthermore, any attempt to find Work Project Administration (WPA) jobs would be bound to fail because such jobs were open only to persons on relief, and few of the unemployed psychologists were poor enough to qualify. Nonetheless, the Committee urged the APA to accept responsibility for the cultivation of new fields for practical psychological service. Eventually, a committee to increase opportunities for psychological service was set up jointly by the recently organized, leftist Psychologists League, the Association of Consulting Psychologists, and a reluctant APA pushed into cooperation with more active separatist groups (Paterson, 1936b, p. 687; cf. Finison, 1976, 1978). However, perhaps because of the Association's reluctance, it took the APA a year to appoint its representatives to the committee, and the records fail to report any substantial achievements.

Yet one success was indirectly related to this committee's efforts: a WPA project to construct a comprehensive index for the discontinued *Psychological Index*, directed by Poffenberger, Brown, Wetmore, Ansbacher, and Miller (1939) and providing jobs for a number of psychologists. Another was the establishment of yet another committee, the Committee on Psychology and the Public Service, which did provide assistance to a number of psychologists in obtaining government jobs (Olson, 1939, p. 759). But these were rather limited results; although the Depression had not yet ended, the issues of concern to the APA and the Psychologists League were beginning to shift. Several converging factors had militated against the APA's energetic involvement in the plight of unemployed psychologists, just as the parent discipline had shown surprisingly little interest in studying the Depression, unemployment, and their psychological ramifications, or in offering advice on how to cure these ills. As a survey of publications on the psychological effects of unemployment, which could find only a fraction of its sources in American psychology journals, concluded, "some of the most important problems [of this topic] have been left untouched in the years since the depression" (Eisenberg & Lazarsfeld, 1938, p. 385). Another psychologist gave the following critical but not unfair summary:

> When the United States entered the first World War, psychologists, as a . . . group, volunteered their professional services. Their contribution was considerable. . . . When the United States entered the big world depression, psychologists did nothing and, as a group, have so far done nothing. For nearly 10 years we have suffered through a national social and economic crisis; yet from [journals and meeting programs] one might conclude that psychologists were oblivious to the fact that our social institutions are rattling about our ears. (Gundlach, 1940, p. 613)

It appears, however, that oblivion operated in two directions. There is no indication that Roosevelt and the New Dealers ever called on psychologists or their organizations for professional advice on the problems shaking the country (cf. Karl, 1963; Poffenberger, 1936, p. 12). Nor has this issue ever been noticed, let alone explained, by historians of psychology (as far as I know).

PSYCHOLOGY'S "IMPENDING DISMEMBERMENT" AND MIRACULOUS RESCUE

In an address prepared for the 1938 meeting of the National Institute of Psychology, Knight Dunlap, former APA president and member of its inner circle, warned that the discipline was being torn apart by powerful, divisive forces. Indeed, in the 1930s American psychology struggled with some internal tensions that led Dunlap to predict the "impending dismemberment of psychology" (Dunlap, 1938). Yet by 1945, this grave danger had been averted. A reorganized and reinvigorated APA entered the postwar world with high hopes and reborn aspirations.

The Rise of Separatist Movements

In the past, women, Jews, and others labeled "weak sisters" had had to find employment outside of the academic departments, in applied work. Yet by the thirties, an ever-increasing number of psychologists had been following their own interests or the labor market into positions outside of the universities and colleges. One third of the APA membership was employed outside of academia, up from 6% in 1917 (Cattell, 1917; Finch, 1938), as was a sizable but undetermined number of nonmembers. After the earlier attempts to establish industrial and educational sections and certification for consulting psychologists inside the APA had failed, independent organizations representing the interests of the new professionals began to emerge. The spearhead of the movement was the New York Association of Consulting Psychologists, organized in 1921 (v.s.). After reorganization as the Association of Consulting Psychologists in 1930, it began to attract a nationwide membership and in 1937 started its own *Journal of Consulting Psychology*. Dozens of other local and regional groups of applied psychologists, more or less formally organized, sprang up in this period.

In 1937 these groups, joined by the disbanding Clinical Section of the APA, merged into the new American Association for Applied Psychology (AAAP), protesting meanwhile that this action "does not and should not mean antagonism toward nor competition with the APA" (Paterson, 1940, p. 9). In fact, most of its leaders and a large part of its membership were APA members. Furthermore, the admission standards for the new association were even higher than those of the APA. Still unbending, the "APA [remained] faithful to its objective as a scientific society" (Olson, 1940a). As ex-APA secretary and second president of the AAAP Donald G. Paterson put it, "The inability of the American Psychological Association to meet the needs of applied psychology [was] an historical fact" (1940, p. 9). However, given the large representation of APA Members among its leadership, it came as no surprise that the new AAAP requested affiliation with the APA in one of its first moves. The linkup became effective in 1938, together with the APA affiliation of the Western and Midwestern Psychological Associations (Olson, 1938, p. 591).

On the political left, meanwhile, a revolt had been brewing against the APA, which was politically conservative like its hard-science models (Kevles, 1987, pp. 261–266). Responding to the social problems of the Depression and the rise of fascism, concerned psychologists were joining together in a movement to apply their expertise to vital and controversial issues, ready to abandon neutral science and the illusion of objectivity to become relevant. Ranging from the radical left to "Mild Pinkism" (Estabrooks, 1936), this group's sizable membership was ambivalent about involvement in social action (cf. Finison, 1976). Warned by some "APA elders" about damage to its scientific program by attempts "merely to agitate for a revolutionary change in our social-economic institutions" (Paterson, 1936a), the group was organized independently at first because "formal affiliation might very well prove to be embarrassing to both parties" (Krechevsky, 1936). Eventually, the desire to maintain scientific legitimacy won out and a Society for the Psychological *Study* of Social Issues (SPSSI; italics added) affiliated itself with the APA in 1937. A year later, it joined other regional associations in spearheading the APA protest, over the dissent of the Psychometric Society, against holding the next International Congress in Nazi-fied Vienna (Olson, 1938, p. 591; cf. Harris, Unger, & Stagner, 1986). The Psychologists League, prodding the APA from a position farther to the left, remained unaffiliated until it faded away during the war, by which time a different disaffected group organized itself as the National Council of Women Psychologists (cf. Napoli, 1981, Chap. 4).

Holding on to the Reins

The emergence of separatist and activist organizations confronted the mainstream APA with the problem of regaining control over the centrifugal forces threatening to pull the discipline apart, while avoiding the appearance of providing radicals with "camouflage under [its] protective skirts" (Estabrooks, 1936). The new mechanism of affiliation succeeded in maintaining formal links and preventing open warfare between the groups. An attempt to create a substantive consensus from the bottom up saw an APA committee struggle throughout the decade to develop a shared set of examination items for the Elementary Psychology course. When last heard from, the committee complained that it had to sift through a huge pool of ambiguous and therefore useless questions; almost all of the remaining items were limited to testing only rote memory for bits of facts or definitions (Olson, 1942, pp. 731–32). What is surprising now is not the outcome of this attempt, but rather the naïveté of its conception. Today, nobody would even think of undertaking this task. But in the thirties, psychologists were, as this episode reminds us, still a relatively small if not unanimous community whose aspirations toward unity had been long since abandoned. One half of the new PhDs still came from the leading six universities, and almost three fourths of their total number from no more than a dozen institutions (Fernberger, 1940, p. 315).

While such efforts to fashion a shared credo out of doctrinal struggles were under way, the establishment was trying to maintain organizational control over the discipline. Although the APA had been growing steadily, the creation of the Associate membership in 1925, together with the tightening of requirements for full membership, had produced a two- if not three-tier organization. In the decade before World War II, the number of full Members had risen by only 88 (in contrast with 1,340 new Associates) and made up less than one fourth of the APA roster of some 2,800 psychologists; furthermore, two thirds of this minority had received their PhDs before 1925 (APA, 1939; Fernberger, 1940, p. 314). In spite of increasing expenses, APA coffers had been getting fuller and fuller since 1925, mainly because of the growing number of Associates (Fernberger, 1943, pp. 37, 43, Figs. 3, 5). Yet when the annual meeting became too crowded, the program committee put in writing what may have been unwritten policy before: Members' abstracts (if properly formatted) were automatically put on the program because their authors' APA standing was "presumptive evidence [of being] worthy of acceptance." But for Associates, whose status was taken to indicate "little more than a professional interest in Psychology," acceptance was restricted to only those submissions "most suitable for the Program" (Olson, 1940b, p. 713). Of course, the Associates could not protest, because they had been disenfranchised as well as silenced (v.s.). The requirement of "publications beyond the dissertation," difficult to meet for young professionals outside of the elite research-oriented departments, was allowing only a trickle of new blood into the ranks of the voting constituency. And an informal survey of "older active members," reported at the same meeting, showed a majority for maintenance of the status quo concerning membership requirements (Olson, 1940b, p. 722).

Yet the influence of even the aging Member in-group seems to have been limited compared with that of the inner circle around the Council of Directors. Election to the Council—the APA's governing board, which was for the first 20 years an autonomous and self-perpetuating body, according to Fernberger—had been opened up in 1914 by permitting members to add nominations of their own to those made by the Council; this crack in the door was closed again, in a somewhat roundabout way, in 1934 (Paterson, 1934, pp. 654, 655). As Fernberger (1932a, pp. 35, 37) commented, the democratization had been more apparent than real. The statistics seem to confirm this view: For over 20 years since the fluke of Watson's election in 1915 (Samelson, 1981), all APA presidents had at some time before their election served a term on the Council—the same Council that made up the nomination ballots for president and new Council members, although with spaces for write-ins. Furthermore, since 1925, not only had all of the Council members who had moved up to the presidency been self-designated experimentalists or a variant thereof,[7] but all except one (Thurstone) were also members of that elite group, the Society of Experimental Psychologists (SEP).

It is not easy to solve the riddle of this uniform outcome of the Council's selection process, which was given some maneuvering room by the wide dispersion of nominating votes. The accessible record is not very illuminating, only providing a clue in this rare comment: ". . . destroy this letter and regard your memories of it as highly confidential" (Boring, 1922a). A plausible inference is, however, that a small group of aging experimentalists were trying to run the Association according to their own beliefs as

---

[7]As shown by their primary research interest listed in the 1939 APA directory.

best they could, although not in complete control. In the process, the "ins" attempted to restrain the "outs" with a Council resolution condemning "organized blocks, electioneering, or caucusing [as] inappropriate in a scientific organization such as the APA" (Olson, 1941, p. 830).

Broadening the Base

As pressures grew, establishment control began to slip and new voices were heard. Some Young Turks adopted the label "experiment*ing* psychologists" in thinly veiled criticism of the exclusive "Society of [older] Experiment*al* Psychologists" (Benjamin, 1977). Attempting to contain the centrifugal forces, the power structure became more flexible. In 1938, Gordon W. Allport, a nonexperimentalist and (in Boring's terms) "sociotrope" (rather than "biotrope") SPSSI founder, over 10 years younger than the presidents preceding him, was elected even before his term on the Council had expired, a unique occurrence. Of course, his recent appointment as chairman at Harvard had probably helped. At the same time, the Association created a new Committee on Scientific and Professional Ethics (Olson, 1938, p. 590). Undoubtedly, this action was related to a shift of APA members' interests in the previous 20 years from "theoretical and academic problems to clinical and practical problems," as Fernberger (1938, p. 281) reported.

In addition to the applied interests, the social–political ones were also beginning to get their due. There was the vote, mentioned earlier, to move the International Congress away from Hitler's Vienna; the appearance of another Fernberger (1939) report on the academic career difficulties of women psychologists; and finally, in the same year, the adoption of a resolution in support of academic freedom generally, and Dr. Krechevsky (Krech) in his conflict with the University of Colorado in particular, together with a call to study those aspects of America "safeguarding . . . our fundamental liberties" (Olson, 1939, p. 754). The storm was rising: Several months earlier, a meeting of the NRC Division had already begun to discuss the possible contributions of psychology to the national government in an emergency (p. 773; see also Chapter 6, this volume).

Two years later, the discriminatory policy concerning the program at the Annual Meeting was dropped: Members' abstracts were to receive the same critical scrutiny as those of Associates. The restrictive membership requirement of "acceptable published research" was changed, on the basis of a mail vote, to a much broader and amorphous "evidence of acceptable contribution to psychology" (Olson, 1941, pp. 831, 835). In the face of complaints "that a clique tends to control nominations," the nominating procedures for and by the Council were, after a lengthy public justification of past practices, made more explicit as well as open to input by the membership (pp. 830, 845). But an attempt to change the core provision of the APA constitution still met a brick wall. For 50 years, the "advancement of Psychology as a *science*" had been the Association's purpose. When a committee recommended to the Council to add advancement "as a profession" as a second objective, this radical proposal was not accepted. Apparently, it was not even voted on (pp. 866, 832). Traditions and power are not given up easily.

A Miraculous Rescue

However, as President Stone wrote to Secretary Olson, "We certainly must keep the leadership in psychological matters in the hands of the APA as far as possible" (Stone, 1942). In a sudden turnabout, as G. W. Allport wrote confidentially to SPSSI members 6 months after Pearl Harbor, a "new and in some ways revolutionary activity" emerged from Yerkes' Survey & Planning (S&P) Subcommittee, established by the Emergency Committee to chart the future of psychology: "Since it explicitly considers not only the advancement of psychology as a science, but its professionalization and its possibilities for public service . . . , its future promises rich returns" (Allport, 1942). Indeed, the committee report (Boring et al., 1942) used the phrase "Psychology as Science and as Profession," rejected the year before, as its title. In the same year, another SPSSI leader (and ESP researcher rather than SEP member), Gardner Murphy, came to head the wartime APA, although the refusal of a security clearance denied him his seat on the NRC Emergency Committee.[8]

It is useless to speculate about "what might have been" without World War II and the forces it generated. But they obviously aided, enormously and fortuitously, the centripetal dynamics that led, with surprising speed and against remarkably little opposition, to the reconstitution of a united APA. Initiated, without a clear mandate, by some old friends and acquaintances from World War I (Boring, Edgar A. Doll, R. M. Elliott, and Yerkes), and joined by younger blood (primarily E. R. Hilgard), the effort succeeded in reintegrating most of the breakaway organizations. (For the details of this development, see Chapter 6, in this volume.) The reborn Association's objective had indeed been broadened to the "advancement of psychology as a science, as a profession, and as a means of promoting human welfare." At least on paper, this tripartite formula united the three

---

[8]See, among others, Allport, 1944.

main factions of the thirties—the traditional experimental scientists, the rapidly growing numbers of applied (i.e., clinical, consulting, and industrial) practitioners, and the social–political activists—even though the union may not have been based on love. Brought together by their novel wartime activities and unified, for a time, by patriotic purposes, the different groups had discovered a convergence of their long-term interests even in the absence of substantive consensus. The writing on the wall was clear: "Present-day trends appear to make it inevitable that an increasing share of long-range scientific research will be sponsored and supported by governmental bodies, either directly or through grants to research organizations," a confidential report from the S&P Subcommittee stated. There would be projects for everybody, from sensory discrimination to gerontology and highway safety to the psychological relationship of the individual to his government ("Psychological Research," n.d.).

The symbolic as well as pragmatic expression of this new commonality of interest appears in a resolution passed at the first postwar meeting of the new APA's Board of Directors: to establish a permanent Central Office in Washington, giving "large weight to the importance of a location near to agencies of government already established and those contemplated in an expansion of research with government support. The post-war establishment will continue to use a substantial number of psychologists" (Olson, 1945, p. 710). Just 4 years earlier, a poll had shown a massive preference for a midwestern location for a permanent APA secretariat; Washington had been named by only 5% (Olson, 1941, pp. 853–854). The new vote in favor of selecting Washington was followed by messages to the SSRC and the American Association for the Advancement of Science and a telegram to President Truman, urging the inclusion of the social sciences in the proposed National Science Foundation (Olson, 1945, p. 713). In its early years, psychology had been concerned with its acceptability to academia; World War I had brought psychology to the attention of the public and of private foundations. Now the focus had shifted once more, to government as the new client. Obtaining leverage in the postwar welfare state required professional unity, which was achieved by this reunification—although eventually, after another shift in funding sources made group interests diverge again, the centrifugal forces were to get the upper hand once more.

REFERENCES

Adams, G. (1934, January). The rise and fall of psychology. *Atlantic Monthly*, pp. 82–92.

Allport, G. W. (1942). Letter to members of the SPSSI, 25 August 1942. Box F-3, APA Records, Library of Congress, Washington, DC.

Allport, G. W. (1944). Letter to L. Carmichael, 29 August 1944. Fl. SPSSI Misc. 1944–45, Correspondence 1930–1945, Gordon W. Allport Papers, Harvard University Archives, Cambridge, MA.

American Psychological Association. (1939). *APA Yearbook 1939*. Washington, DC: Author.

Anderson, J. E. (1924). Proceedings of the thirty-second annual meeting of the American Psychological Association. *Psychological Bulletin, 21*, 69–82.

Anderson, J. E. (1925). Proceedings of the thirty-third annual meeting of the American Psychological Association. *Psychological Bulletin, 22*, 69–85.

Anderson, J. E. (1926). Proceedings of the thirty-fourth annual meeting of the American Psychological Association. *Psychological Bulletin, 23*, 113–126.

APA Committee on the Ph.D. Degree in Psychology. (1934). Standards for the Ph.D. degree in psychology. *Psychological Bulletin, 31*, 67–72.

Benjamin, L. (1977). The psychological Round Table: Revolution in 1936. *American Psychologist, 32*, 542–549.

Bingham, W. V. (Ed.). (1932). *Psychology today*. Chicago: University of Chicago Press.

Boring, E. G. (1922a). Letter to K. Dallenbach, 21 February 1922. Correspondence 1919–1969, Boring Papers, Harvard University Archives, Cambridge, MA.

Boring, E. G. (1922b). Proceedings of the thirtieth annual meeting of the American Psychological Association. *Psychological Bulletin, 19*, 65–76.

Boring, E. G. (1923). Proceedings of the thirty-first annual meeting of the American Psychological Association. *Psychological Bulletin, 20*, 61–74.

Boring, E. G. (1929). The psychology of controversy. *Psychological Review, 36*, 97–121.

Boring, E. G. (1930). Letters to S. W. Fernberger, 14 November 1930, and to K. Dallenbach, 1 November 1934. Correspondence 1919–1969, Boring Papers, Harvard University Archives, Cambridge, MA.

Boring, E. G. (1938). The Society of Experimental Psychologists: 1904–1938. *American Journal of Psychology, 51*, 410–423.

Boring, E. G. (1947). Letter to E. R. Hilgard, 9 December 1947. Correspondence 1919–1969, Boring Papers, Harvard University Archives, Cambridge, MA.

Boring, E. G., Bryan, A. I., Doll, E. A., Elliott, R. M., Hilgard, E. R., Stone, C. P., & Yerkes, R. M. (1942). Psychology as science and profession. *Psychological Bulletin, 39*, 761–772.

Boring, E. G., Langfeld, H. S., & Weld, H. P. (1935). *Psychology: A factual textbook*. New York: Wiley.

Brigham, C. C. (1931). Proceedings of the thirty-eighth annual meeting of the American Psychological Association. *Psychological Bulletin, 28*, 181–198.

Bruner, J. S., & Allport, G. W. (1940). Fifty years of change in American psychology. *Psychological Bulletin, 37*, 757–776.

Capshew, J. H. (1986). *Psychology on the march: American psychologists and World War II*. Unpublished doctoral dissertation, University of Pennsylvania.

Cattell, J. M. (1917). Our psychological association and research. *Science, 45*, 275–284.

Cattell, J. M. (1933). Confidential memorandum for the psychologists of the National Academy, 14 November 1933. M 1109, Walter R. Miles Papers, Archives of the History of American Psychology, Akron, OH.

Dunlap, K. (1938). *The impending dismemberment of psychology*. Manuscript of address to the National Institute of Psychology, Columbus, OH, 7 September 1938. M 565, Knight Dunlap Papers, Archives of the History of American Psychology, Akron, OH.

Eisenberg, P., & Lazarsfeld, P. F. (1938). The psychological effects of unemployment. *Psychological Bulletin, 35*, 358–390.

Estabrooks, G. H. (1936). Letter to D. Krechevsky, 10 April 1936. Box I-12, APA Records, Library of Congress, Washington, DC.

Fernberger, S. W. (1927). Proceedings of the thirty-fifth annual meeting of the American Psychological Association. *Psychological Bulletin, 24*, 137–158.

Fernberger, S. W. (1928) Proceedings of the thirty-sixth annual meeting of the American Psychological Association. *Psychological Bulletin, 25*, 125–139.

Fernberger, S. W. (1929) Proceedings of the thirty-seventh annual meeting of the American Psychological Association. *Psychological Bulletin, 26*, 121–132.

Fernberger, S. W. (1932a). The American Psychological Association: A historical summary, 1892–1930. *Psychological Bulletin, 29*, 1–89.

Fernberger, S. W. (1932b). Correction. *Psychological Bulletin, 29*, 307.

Fernberger, S. W. (1938). The scientific interests and scientific publications of members of the American Psychological Association, Inc. *Psychological Bulletin, 35*, 261–281.

Fernberger, S. W. (1939). Academic psychology as a career for women. *Psychological Bulletin, 36*, 390–394.

Fernberger, S. W. (1940). On election to membership in the American Psychological Association. *Psychological Bulletin, 37*, 312–318.

Fernberger, S. W. (1943). The American Psychological Association, 1892–1942. *Psychological Review, 50*, 33–60.

Finch, F. H. (1938). Employment trends in applied psychology [abstract]. *Psychological Bulletin, 35*, 677.

Finison, L. J. (1976). Unemployment, politics, and the history of organized psychology. *American Psychologist, 31*, 747–755.

Finison, L. J. (1978). Unemployment, politics, and the history of organized psychology, II. *American Psychologist, 33*, 471–477.

Gundlach, R. H. (1940). Psychologists' understanding of social issues. *Psychological Bulletin, 37*, 613–620

Harris, B., Unger, R. K., & Stagner, R. (Eds). (1986). Fifty years of psychology and social issues. *Journal of Social Issues, 42*, No. 1.

Hilgard, E. R. (1987). *Psychology in America: A historical survey.* San Diego, CA: Harcourt Brace Jovanovich.

Hull, C. L. (1935). The conflicting psychologies of learning: A way out. *Psychological Review, 42,* 491–516.

Karl, B. (1963). *Executive Reorganization and reform in the New Deal.* Cambridge, MA: Harvard University Press.

Kevles, D. J. (1987). *The physicists.* Cambridge, MA: Harvard University Press.

Krech, D. (1974). David Krech. In G. Lindzey (Ed.), *A history of psychology in autobiography* (Vol. 6). Englewood Cliffs, NJ: Prentice-Hall.

Krechevsky, D. (1936). Letter to D. G. Paterson, 14 April 1936. Box I-12, APA Records, Library of Congress, Washington, DC.

Langfeld, H. S. (1919). Proceedings of the twenty-seventh annual meeting of the American Psychological Association. *Psychological Bulletin, 16,* 33–36.

Langfeld, H. S. (1920). Proceedings of the twenty-eighth annual meeting of the American Psychological Association. *Psychological Bulletin, 17,* 33–38.

Lumley, F. H. (1932). An evaluation of fifteen radio talks in psychology by means of listener's reports. *Psychological Bulletin, 29,* 753–764.

Morawski, J. G. (1986). Organizing knowledge and behavior at Yale's Institute of Human Relations. *Isis, 77,* 219–242.

Napoli, D. S. (1981). *Architects of adjustment.* Port Washington, NY: Kennikat Press.

Notes and news. (1921). *Psychological Bulletin, 18,* 439.

O'Donnell, J. M. (1979). The crisis of experimentalism in the 1920s: E. G. Boring and his uses of history. *American Psychologist, 34,* 289–295.

Olson, W. C. (1938). Proceedings of the forty-sixth annual meeting of the American Psychological Association. *Psychological Bulletin, 35,* 579–621.

Olson, W. C. (1939). Proceedings of the forty-seventh annual meeting of the American Psychological Association. *Psychological Bulletin, 36,* 740–783.

Olson, W. C. (1940a). Letter to S. Habbe, 9 July 1940. Box I-2, APA Records, Library of Congress, Washington, DC.

Olson, W. C. (1940b). Proceedings of the forty-eighth annual meeting of the American Psychological Association. *Psychological Bulletin, 37,* 699–733.

Olson, W. C. (1941). Proceedings of the forty-ninth annual meeting of the American Psychological Association. *Psychological Bulletin, 38,* 819–885.

Olson, W. C. (1942). Proceedings of the fiftieth annual meeting of the American Psychological Association. *Psychological Bulletin, 39,* 713–758.

Olson, W. C. (1945). Proceedings of the fifty-third annual meeting of the American Psychological Association. *Psychological Bulletin, 42,* 695–747.

Paterson, D. G. (1933). Proceedings of the forty-first annual meeting of the American Psychological Association. *Psychological Bulletin, 30,* 631–655.

Paterson, D. G. (1934). Proceedings of the forty-second annual meeting of the American Psychological Association. *Psychological Bulletin, 31,* 647–667.

Paterson, D. G. (1936a). Letter to D. Krechevsky, 21 April 1936. Box I-12, APA Records, Library of Congress, Washington, DC.

Paterson, D. G. (1936b). Proceedings of the forty-fourth annual meeting of the American Psychological Association. *Psychological Bulletin, 33*, 677–720.

Paterson, D. G. (1940). Applied psychology comes of age. *Journal of Consulting Psychology, 4*, 1–9.

Pavlov, I. P. (1927). *Conditioned reflexes* (G. V. Anrep, Trans.). London: Oxford University Press.

Poffenberger, A. T. (1936). Psychology and life. *Psychological Review, 43*, 9–31.

Poffenberger, A. T., Brown, H. C., Wetmore, R. G., Ansbacher, H., & Miller, S. C. (1939). Indexing the *Psychological Index. Psychological Bulletin, 36*, 477–487.

Psychological research appropriate to government sponsorship. (n.d.). ["Confidential"]. Prepared for the Emergency Committee in Psychology, NRC, by the Subcommittee on Survey & Planning. Box I-8, APA Records, Library of Congress, Washington, DC.

Samelson, F. (1977). World War I intelligence testing and the development of psychology. *Journal of the History of the Behavioral Sciences, 13*, 274–282.

Samelson, F. (1978). From "Race Psychology" to "Studies in Prejudice." *Journal of the History of the Behavioral Sciences, 14*, 265–278.

Samelson, F. (1979). Putting psychology on the map: Ideology and technology in intelligence testing. In A. R. Buss (Ed.), *Psychology in social context* (pp. 103–168). New York: Irvington.

Samelson, F. (1980). E. G. Boring and his *History of Experimental Psychology. American Psychologist, 35*, 467–470.

Samelson, F. (1981). Struggle for scientific authority. *Journal of the History of the Behavioral Sciences, 17*, 399–425.

Samelson, F. (1985a). *On behaviorism and its competitors, 1930–1950: The case of the conflict model.* Paper presented at the annual meeting of Cheiron, the University of Pennsylvania, Philadelphia, PA.

Samelson, F. (1985b). Organizing for the kingdom of behavior. *Journal of the History of the Behavioral Sciences, 21*, 399–425.

Smith, L. D. (1986). *Behaviorism and logical positivism.* Stanford, CA: Stanford University Press.

Sokal, M. M. (1984). James McKeen Cattell and American psychology in the 1920s. In J. Brozek (Ed.), *Explorations in the history of psychology in the United States* (pp. 273–323). Lewisburg, PA: Bucknell University Press.

Stone, C. P. (1942). Letter to W. C. Olson, 3 July 1942. Box I-9, APA Records, Library of Congress, Washington, DC.

Titchener, E. B. (1919). Letter to R. M. Yerkes, 17 March 1919, and subsequent exchange. Correspondence Files, Robert M. Yerkes Papers, Yale University Archives, New Haven, CT.

Titchener, E. B. (1924). Letter to E. C. Sanford, 6 October 1924. Box 5, Titchener Papers, Cornell University Archives, Ithaca, NY.

Wallin, J. E. W. (1960). History of the struggles within the APA to attain membership requirements, test standardization, certification of psychological practitioners, and professionalization. *Journal of General Psychology, 63*, 287–308.

Watson, J. B. (1922). Letter to F. L. Wells, 26 October 1922. Box D-8, APA Records, Library of Congress, Washington, DC.

Watson, J. B. (1929). Letter to W. V. Bingham, 26 August 1929. Box 9, Walter V. Bingham Papers, Carnegie Mellon University Archives, Pittsburg, PA.

Woodworth, R. S. (1930). Ninth International Congress of Psychology: Report of the treasurer. *Psychological Bulletin, 27*, 565–566.

6

THE POWER OF SERVICE: WORLD WAR II AND PROFESSIONAL REFORM IN THE AMERICAN PSYCHOLOGICAL ASSOCIATION

JAMES H. CAPSHEW AND ERNEST R. HILGARD

World War II marked a significant turning point in the history of the American Psychological Association. Before the war, the APA functioned as a disciplinary society that did little more than publish a few scientific journals and host an annual meeting. Afterward, it grew into an activist association with a large central office that represented and served the professional interests of its members. The rise of the APA into the large, complex, and powerful institution we know today can be traced to the circumstances of the Second World War, when the organization redefined its role in the profession through a set of far-reaching internal reforms.

The wartime reformation of the APA led to tremendous postwar growth (see Figure 1). Membership increased from 2,739 in 1940 to over 70,000 by 1990. Perhaps even more striking is the growth in per capita terms: In 1920 there were approximately 3.7 APA members per million U.S. inhabitants, in 1950 about 48 per million, and in 1980 nearly 221 per million

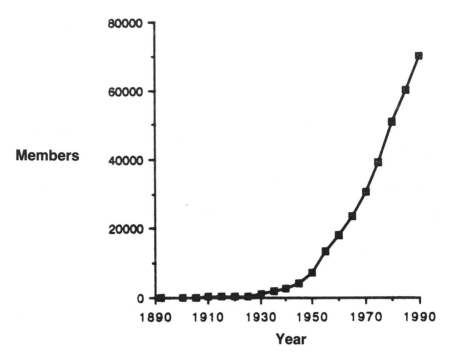

Figure 1: American Psychological Association membership, 1892–1990.

(Hilgard, 1987). The causes of this growth are to be found in the blend of science and practice that American psychologists pursued so successfully in the post-World War II context.

To those who have joined the APA since 1945, it is hard to imagine how simply it operated in the prewar years. There was no central office whatever, and the administrative structure depended largely on the generosity of the universities in which the most active officers happened to be located. Likewise, the annual meetings were usually hosted by a university. Because the APA president served a 1-year term, much of the organizational continuity was provided by the secretary and the treasurer, who remained in office for longer periods. These officers were joined in administrative tasks by a six-person Council, whose members served terms of 3 years, with two members being elected each year.

THE APA AND WAR MOBILIZATION

As World War II approached, the American Psychological Association became involved in efforts to mobilize psychologists for the national emergency.[1] Like their fellow citizens, APA members were aware of Hitler's war aims, which he had declared as early as 1937, and knew about the German military offensives that led to the formation of the Allied coalition. The first formal moves to involve psychologists in the nascent U.S. war effort came in April 1939, when the Division of Anthropology and Psychology of the National Research Council (NRC) voted to establish a Committee on Public Service in the event of war. The psychologist members of the Division were appointed by the APA, and represented the interests of its members as well as of psychology in general. The Committee was soon renamed the Committee on the Selection and Training of Military Personnel, reflecting what psychologists had done in the First World War, and was headed by John G. Jenkins, chair of the University of Maryland psychology department.

The next move to involve psychologists was made at the annual meeting of the APA hosted jointly by Stanford University and the University of California, Berkeley. The meeting convened on September 4, 1939, coincidentally the day after England and France declared war against Germany following Hitler's invasion of Poland. Program chair Walter R. Miles felt compelled to recognize the war declaration despite the lack of a scheduled place on the program, and in an impromptu speech during the opening session, he acknowledged the widespread concern over the international situation. A concrete invitation for service was presented by Dean Brimhall, a psychologist who was research director of the Civil Aeronautics Authority. He announced that nearly $6 million had been appropriated for the training of approximately 15,000 civilian pilots, with a portion of the funds slated for research, including psychological studies relating to the selection and training of pilots.

Further meetings under the aegis of the NRC Division of Anthropology and Psychology took place, and soon the APA organized its own Emergency Committee. Likewise, the American Association for Applied Psychology (AAAP), formed in 1937 to advance psychology outside of academe, created a similar group. As it became apparent that the United States would eventually join the Allied war effort, the NRC sponsored a Conference on Psychology and Government Service in August 1940. Representatives from the APA and the AAAP were invited, as well as psychologists involved in other national societies. Discussion at the conference led to a unanimous agreement to establish a central coordinating group, which was christened the Emergency Committee in Psychology (Dallenbach, 1946).

---

[1]The mobilization of American psychologists for the Second World War is treated in detail by Capshew (1986/1987).

The Emergency Committee in Psychology was administered under the wing of the NRC, located in Washington, DC, at the center of efforts to mobilize science on behalf of national defense. The Committee became a virtual "war cabinet" for psychology (Carmichael, 1943) and sponsored and coordinated the varied activities of psychologists in the military services, government agencies, and volunteer organizations. Among its most significant activities was its support of the Office of Psychological Personnel, an employment clearinghouse set up in early 1942 to match potential employers with psychologists seeking to be involved in war-related programs. Not surprisingly, the Emergency Committee counted many APA leaders among its most active members, including former APA presidents Robert Yerkes, Walter Miles, Walter Hunter, and Leonard Carmichael, as well as a host of others who would distinguish themselves both during and after the war.

Although the APA and its members were actively involved in the war effort, the mobilization of psychology revealed that the organization was facing a major challenge to its position as the country's leading organization of psychologists. A variety of special groups, such as the American Association for Applied Psychology, the Society for the Psychological Study of Social Issues, and the Psychometric Society, had arisen during the 1930s, in part because the APA remained in the mold of a traditional learned society. Although each group had a membership that largely overlapped that of the APA, they represented different intellectual and professional interests in psychology, and their existence threatened to fragment even further an already diverse discipline.

Wartime mobilization also created new sources of institutional power in psychology. The APA was only one of an entire spectrum of organizations involved in the war effort under the umbrella of the Emergency Committee in Psychology sponsored by the NRC. Because of its inclusiveness, the Emergency Committee came to serve not only as a central office for mobilization, but also as a forum for debating professional issues. The proper social role of psychology became the principal issue as academic purists and applied practitioners alike were drawn into wartime programs. Psychologists' new occupational roles, undertaken in an atmosphere of patriotism and public service, encouraged the efforts of those interested in promoting psychology as an applied discipline as well as a source of basic scientific knowledge.

Seeking to place the temporary wartime alliance between psychological science and national service on a permanent footing, Robert M. Yerkes emerged as a leading advocate for professional reform. Working through the structure of the Emergency Committee, he carved out a semiautonomous base for his activities—the Subcommittee on Survey and Planning—and recruited a group of powerful allies. Their agenda was to yoke the academic and applied wings of the discipline together in a common professional enterprise. They sought to enroll the psychology community in their project by reforming one of its oldest and most powerful institutions, the American Psychological Association. Capitalizing on long-term demographic trends, the Survey and Planning Subcommittee took advantage of unique wartime circumstances to engineer consent for the reforms. In a relatively straight-forward manner, the diverse interest groups in psychology were organizationally united by the end of the war in a thoroughly revamped APA.

THE SUBCOMMITTEE ON SURVEY AND PLANNING

Perhaps more than any other American psychologist, Robert Yerkes (1876–1956) was aware of the professional opportunities that war provided. The First World War had transformed his own career and increased his determination to apply "psychobiological" science to contemporary social problems. Part of his aim was to heighten psychology's scientific and professional standing, and he spent 5 years after the war working for the National Research Council trying to achieve that goal (Haraway, 1989; Reed, 1987). At the start of World War II, Yerkes attempted to gain official recognition for psychology in the military and civilian defense establishments. He failed, however, to convince government authorities that psychologists needed to be systematically mobilized. Instead, the task of organizing wartime work fell largely to entrepreneurs and leaders in the profession, and mobilization proceeded in an ad hoc and piecemeal fashion, in contrast with the centralized administration characteristic of other fields (Capshew, 1986/1987).

These disparate efforts were coordinated through the Emergency Committee in Psychology, which was established in 1940 as a central organizing group. The Committee was composed of representatives from six national organizations: the American Psychological Association, the American Association for Applied Psychology, the Society for the Psychological Study of Social Issues, the Society of Experimental Psychologists, the Psychometric Society, and Section I (Psychology) of the American Association for the Advancement of Science. Within 6 months after the Japanese attack on Pearl Harbor in December 1941, Yerkes was seeking ways to increase the effectiveness of the group, which was headed by Cornell psychologist Karl Dallenbach. A faithful scientific disciple of his teacher E. B. Titchener, Dallenbach had chosen to interpret the Emergency Committee's mandate narrowly: He believed that the group should play a strictly advisory role and respond only to official requests for assistance rather than initiate projects of its own. Yerkes, in contrast, was inclined to capitalize on the ambiguity of professional authority caused by the war. He saw the disruption of psychology's normal routines as an opportunity for innovation and chafed under Dallenbach's conservative leadership.

Yerkes had been a member of the Emergency Committee since its formation in 1940, and served on a variety of its subcommittees. In the spring of 1942, Yerkes was asked to investigate the feasibility of holding a conference for long-range planning in psychology. The idea had been suggested earlier by the recent president of the AAAP, Edgar Doll of the Vineland Training School in New Jersey, who offered to host the meeting. Yerkes recommended that the Emergency Committee sponsor such a conference, and he was authorized to select a group "to prepare a report on long-range as well as emergency problems" (Dallenbach, 1946, p. 530).

Exercising his characteristic sagacity, Yerkes chose the following seven psychologists to serve as conferees: Richard M. Elliott, Edwin G. Boring, Edgar A. Doll, Calvin P. Stone, Alice I. Bryan, Ernest R. Hilgard, and Carl R. Rogers. He was careful to pick influential individuals from both applied and academic psychology who represented a range of interests in the discipline and who were sympathetic to his cause. His choices were partly constrained by the logistics involved in balancing regional representation against proximity to the East Coast corridor and by the availability of psychologists who were not already too busy with war work.

Among the most senior members of the group was Richard M. Elliott (1887–1969), longtime chair of the University of Minnesota psychology department and one of Yerkes's oldest professional friends. As a Harvard graduate student, Elliott had studied psychopathology under Yerkes, receiving his PhD with Hugo Münsterberg in 1913. He taught at Harvard for a year and then at Yale until 1918, when he was commissioned into the Army as a psychological examiner. After the war, he assisted Yerkes in preparing reports on the wartime accomplishments of psychologists for the Surgeon General's Office and the NRC. Yerkes, who had been appointed head of the Minnesota psychology department in 1917 *in absentia*, decided to remain with the NRC and recommended Elliott in his place. Elliott demonstrated a flair for administration and helped build Minnesota into a major center of applied as well as experimental psychology (Elliott, 1952).

The relationship between Yerkes and prominent Harvard psychologist Edwin G. Boring (1886–1968) also extended back to the First World War, when Boring helped him produce the massive National Academy of Sciences report on psychological examining in the U.S. Army (Boring, 1952). A former APA president (1928), Boring was a vigorous proponent of experimental psychology, although his reputation was based primarily on his achievements as an expositor and historian. His well-known A *History of Experimental Psychology* was published in 1929 and was the inaugural volume in the Century Psychology Series under the editorship of Richard Elliott. Boring's negative view of nonexperimental psychology was being reshaped by the exigencies of war, and his writing skills and extensive network of professional contacts were valuable resources for the committee's work (Capshew, 1986/1987).

Edgar A. Doll (1889–1968) was a mental tester who specialized in mental deficiency. Director of research at Vineland Training School in New Jersey, Doll was a protégé of Henry Goddard and a veteran of the World War I psychology program. Active in the affairs of the AAAP, he served as its president in 1940–41. Doll had raised issues of long-range planning in the Emergency Committee, which provided support for Yerkes's efforts, and his offer to host the conference at Vineland ensured a congenial environment for the meeting.

At the time of his appointment, Stanford experimental psychologist Calvin P. Stone (1892–1954) was serving as president of the APA. Like Doll, he had been involved in Yerkes's psychology program in the First World War as a predoctoral student. Although he was best known for his extensive research on animal behavior, Stone's interests spanned a wide range, including abnormal psychology and Freudian theory. He and the influential mental tester Lewis Terman formed the core of the Stanford psychology faculty.

The only female member of the group was Alice I. Bryan (b. 1902). A Columbia PhD and professor, Bryan was secretary of the AAAP and was active in the New York Association for Applied Psychology. Career contingencies had led her into an unusual area of practical psychology: research and consulting on reading and library use. As one of the chief organizers of the National Council of Women Psychologists in late 1941, she was gaining professional visibility for her wartime work (Bryan, 1983; Capshew & Laszlo, 1986).

After receiving his PhD from Yale in 1930, Ernest R. Hilgard (b. 1904) taught there for 3 years. He spent the summer of 1931 at the Yale Laboratories of Primate Biology becoming acquainted with Robert Yerkes and comparative psychology. Through a variety of professional contacts, he was invited to Stanford in 1933 by Lewis Terman, head of the psychology department. Advancing quickly, he became a full professor in 1938. He was an active experimental researcher in the psychology of learning, who maintained a strong interest in social issues. He was a member of the SPSSI (and became its president for 1944–45) and served on the APA Council in 1942–44. After spending a sabbatical year at Chicago in 1940–41, Hilgard became involved in war work with Rensis Likert in the U.S. Department of Agriculture Division of Program Surveys (Hilgard, 1974, 1986).

Carl R. Rogers (1902–1987) was later added to the original group. Holding a PhD from Columbia Teachers College, he was a clinical psychologist at Ohio State University, a leading center of applied psychology. Like Hilgard, he had been active in the social gospel movement as a young man. A member of the AAAP, he was beginning to receive recognition for his work on client-centered therapy. During the war, he was involved in training survey researchers in nondirective interviewing techniques (Rogers, 1966).

As these brief sketches indicate, the conference group contained representatives of nearly all the major interests—experimental psychology, mental testing, applied psychology, and social psychology—in some form. It was heavily weighted toward major academic departments: Yale, Harvard, Stanford, Minnesota, and Columbia. Of the eight members, only three had obtained their PhDs before 1919, but all of the male members, except for Hilgard and Rogers, had been involved in the World War I psychology programs. Each member of the group had been highly active in professional organizations, in particular the APA, the AAAP, and, to a lesser extent, the SPSSI.

Yerkes had assembled a hard-working and harmonious group of psychologists, dedicated to professional progress yet sensitive to the power of existing interest groups. They gathered at the secluded but easily accessible campus of the Vineland Training School in southern New Jersey for the first time in June 1942 (see Photo 19). Meeting for an entire week, the group produced a wide-ranging series of recommendations. The overall thrust of their report emphasized increased planning for psychology, both in wartime and for the postwar period. To that end, they recommended the establishment by the NRC of a general planning board independent of the Emergency Committee. Dallenbach, perceiving a threat to the primacy of the Emergency Committee, vetoed the idea and formed the Yerkes group into a Subcommittee on Survey and Planning instead.

The most revolutionary idea proposed by the Yerkes group was that a "central American institute of psychology" should be established "to provide professional services of personnel, placement, public relations, publicity, and publication" (Yerkes et al., 1942a, p. 629). The group viewed the wartime Office of Psychological Personnel as a prototype of such an organization, and sought to expand its functions and place them on a more permanent footing. Following this major proposal was a whole set of related recommendations, including provision for an intersociety convention to discuss the plan. The Emergency Committee approved the proposal for consideration and arranged for its dissemination to the governing boards of national psychological societies and its publication in the *Psychological Bulletin* (Dallenbach, 1946).

The Survey and Planning Subcommittee's main task was postwar planning. In envisioning the postwar role of psychology, the group wrote the following:

> Psychology as the science of behavior and experience and as major basis for mental engineering undoubtedly will play an increasingly important role in human affairs. . . . In the new world order its knowledge and skills should be professionalized steadily and wisely so that its applications may keep pace with emerging human needs and demands for personal and social guidance. Foremost among the conditions necessary for the sound and socially profitable maturation of the science and of its technology are: unity of spirit and action; optimal provision for the effective training of psychologists as teachers, practitioners, and investigators; and the creation of such occupational specialties within applied psychology as will satisfy individual and group demands for help in living. (Yerkes et al., 1942a, pp. 623–624)

Although the convictions expressed in this paragraph were endorsed by the entire committee, the phrasing was pure Yerkes. His agenda was now attached to a potentially successful instrument, and the process of enrolling the rest of the community had begun.

PREPARING FOR REORGANIZATION

As the initial proposal for a central institute was being circulated among the profession, the Survey and Planning Subcommittee suggested that an intersociety convention be held to discuss ideas for a central institute. The Emergency Committee threw its weight behind the plan by voting "to endorse in principle the development of a permanent service organization for psychology" at its September 1942 meeting. The convention was tentatively scheduled for the spring of 1943, and each of the six societies represented in the Emergency Committee was invited to send five delegates apiece. The recently formed National Council of Women Psychologists, of which Alice Bryan was a prime mover, successfully petitioned for representation of their 200-member group. Somehow, an obscure, inactive organization called the National Institute of Psychology, founded in 1929 and composed of prominent experimentalists, was resurrected and managed to obtain an invitation.[2] In addition to these two groups, the Department of Psychology of the American Teachers Association, an Af-

---

[2]Incorporated in Washington, DC, in 1929, the National Institute of Psychology had a membership limit of 50, composed of active researchers under 60 years of age. Apparently, the group's only activity was the election of new members, who were generally well-known experimental psychologists.

rican–American organization, was also invited to send a delegate (Dallenbach, 1946, p. 565).

In preparing publicity for the convention, the modifier "constitutional" mysteriously slipped into the deliberations of the Emergency Committee, and the meeting became known as the "Intersociety Constitutional Convention." Neatly echoing the title of the convention that organized the United States of America, the phrase resonated with psychologists' patriotic sentiments and probably contributed to the sense that a basic restructuring of the profession was appropriate ("Preparation," 1943).[3]

The number of delegates from each society was first set at five apiece, until the organizers realized the advantages of proportional representation based on membership size. Some, but not all, of the small groups voluntarily decreased their number of delegates. Thus, the Psychometric Society had five representatives, as many as the APA and the AAAP, whereas the remainder had three or fewer. Each society was free to choose its delegates to the Intersociety Constitutional Convention in its own way. The APA conducted an elaborate election for its representatives. From a long list of nominations, a slate of 18 candidates was drawn up; APA members were instructed to vote for their choices by ranking them. Only 359 ballots were returned from over 700 eligible voters, indicating something less than enthusiastic interest. Five delegates (all former APA presidents) and four alternates were thus elected. In contrast, AAAP president C. M. Louttit was authorized to select representatives from that organization. Survey and Planning Subcommittee member Ernest Hilgard was an unsuccessful candidate for SPSSI and for APA representative but managed to become a delegate from the obscure National Institute of Psychology (Hilgard, 1974). The SPSSI chose three delegates, the National Council of Women Psychologists and the AAAS Psychology Section picked two each, and the Department of Psychology of the American Teachers Association had one.[4]

---

[3]Karl Dallenbach, chair of the Emergency Committee, was perturbed about the implications of the new label, and exaggerated its influence on the subsequent proceedings (Dallenbach, 1946, pp. 565–566).

[4]Delegates and alternates to the Intersociety Constitutional Convention:
American Psychological Association (5). Delegates: J. E. Anderson, L. Carmichael, C. P. Stone, R. M. Yerkes, C. L. Hull. Alternates: S. H. Britt, E. R. Hilgard, H. Woodrow, W. C. Olson.
American Association for Applied Psychology (5). Delegates: P. S. Achilles, S. H. Britt, A. I. Bryan, E. A. Doll, C. M. Louttit. Alternates: S. L. Pressey, A. W. Kornhauser, C. R. Rogers, R. A. Brotemarkle, W. C. Trow.
Society for the Psychological Study of Social Issues (3). Delegates: G. W. Allport, G. Murphy, T. M. Newcomb. Alternates: E. R. Hilgard, O. Klineberg, G. Watson.
Psychometric Society (5). Delegates: J. W. Dunlap, H. A. Edgarton, A. P. Horst, I. Lorge, M. W. Richardson. Alternates: P. J. Rulon, B. D. Wood.
Society of Experimental Psychologists (2). Delegates: E. G. Boring. R. S. Woodworth. Alternates: W. S. Hunter, S. W. Fernberger, D. G. Marquis.
National Council of Women Psychologists (2). Delegates: F. L. Goodenough, G. C. Schwesinger. Alternates: T. M. Abel, M. A. Bills.
American Association for the Advancement of Science, Section I (2). Delegates: H. E. Garrett, E. Heidbredder.

Yerkes and his committee members planned carefully for the Intersociety Constitutional Convention. Between March and June of 1943, Yerkes sent six letters to the delegates, outlining possible organizational structures and explaining procedures for the meeting. The Subcommittee prepared an elaborate 46-page *Handbook and Agenda* for the meeting. It contained a statement of the convention's purposes, a discussion of the professional needs of psychologists, and data concerning the Office of Psychological Personnel (OPP) and existing societies and journals. Its centerpiece was the presentation of three alternative structures for a national association: a federation of existing societies, the creation of an ideal new society, and the modification of the APA. Projected budgets and finances for the various alternative plans were included, along with a suggested timetable for implementing the decisions arising from the convention (Intersociety Constitutional Convention, 1943b; Yerkes et al., 1942b).

The handbook made explicit reference to the American Constitutional Convention of 1787 in discussing the tension between organizational centralization and decentralization in psychology. In seeking to provide the delegates with useful models of other scientific organizations, the document cited the broad scientific and professional purposes of the American Chemical Society as nearly ideal, needing only the substitution of "psychology" for "chemistry" and "mental engineering" for "industry" (Intersociety Constitutional Convention, 1943b, pp. 14, 18).

The handbook also contained some revealing statistics on the organizational affiliations of American psychologists. The figures documented both the expansion of interest groups and the continuing dominance of the APA, which was by far the largest and most inclusive society (Table 1). Of the three major groups founded in the 1930s—the American Association for Applied Psychology, the Society for the Psychological Study of Social Issues, and the Psychometric Society—only the last drew a significant portion of its members from outside of the APA's orbit. Although the AAAP was only a fifth of the size of the APA in 1942, over one fourth of the APA's voting members also belonged to the AAAP. The multiple cross-memberships of American psychologists testified to their shared and overlapping interests (Figure 2). But what of those professional psychologists who chose not to belong to these organizations? The APA had long assumed that its membership was practically coextensive with the entire body of the

National Institute of Psychology (1). Delegate: E. R. Hilgard. Alternates: G. R. Wendt, A. T. Poffenberger.

American Teachers Association, Department of Psychology (1). Delegate: H. G. Canady.

Source: American Psychological Association Papers (I-6/ICC 1943), Library of Congress Manuscript Division, Washington, DC.

TABLE 1

Membership in American Psychology Societies, 1937–1944

Society	1937	1938	1939	1940	1941	1942	1943	1944
American Psychological Association	2,138	2,318	2,527	2,739	2,937	3,231	3,476	3,806
Society of Experimental Psychologists	50	50	50	50	50	50	50	—
National Institute of Psychology	—	—	—	—	43	41	—	—
Department of Psychology, American Teachers Association	—	10	15	25	26	29	32	—
Psychometric Society	158	221	240	236	245	232	—	—
SPSSI	—	374	349	327	291	294	242	273
AAAP	—	—	411	564	608	638	659	—
National Council of Women Psychologists	—	—	—	—	—	253	261	258

Note: SPSSI = Society for the Psychological Study of Social Issues. AAAP = American Association for Applied Psychology. Sources: Intersociety Constitutional Convention, 1943b; Portenier, 1967.

nation's psychologists. Without alternative measures, it was difficult to challenge this assumption. However, the OPP, by gathering data on psychologists regardless of organizational affiliation, provided unprecedented statistics on the profession, and by early 1943 its records revealed a potentially disturbing fact: At least 761 psychologists who were qualified for APA membership were not members (Britt, 1943).

ORGANIZING THE INTERESTS

The Intersociety Constitutional Convention (ICC) was called to order on Saturday morning, May 29, 1943, by Robert Yerkes, chair pro tempore. Attended by 26 delegates from nine national psychological societies, the meeting was held in the Hotel Pennsylvania in New York City. Yerkes opened the convention by comparing psychology with the physical sciences and engineering:

> Recent decades have witnessed the rapid transformation of our physical environment by discovery, invention, and the development of engineering skills. The time is ripe for equally innovational changes in human nature, its controls, and expressions. Physical conditions are such that this revolution *can* happen now. Furthermore, there are signs that it *may* happen, whatever the attitude of our profession. It is fitting for us to resolve that it *shall* happen, facilitated to the utmost by our directive energies, and our specialized knowledge, wisdom, and skills.

He expressed hope that existing forms of human engineering would be

Cross-Memberships with APA

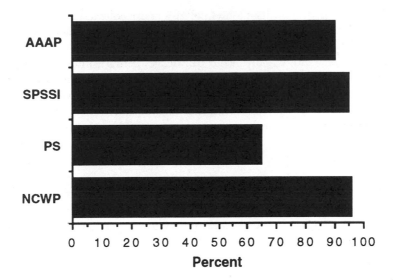

Cross-Memberships with AAAP

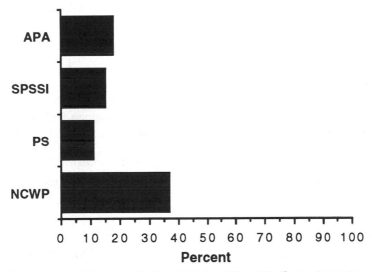

Figure 2: Membership overlap among national psychology societies, 1943. (Source: Intersociety Constitutional Convention, 1943b. AAAP = American Association for Applied Psychology; NCWP = National Council of Women Psychologists; PS = Psychometric Society; SPSSI = Society for the Psychological Study of Social Issues.)

augmented by further attempts "to assure and to increase life's values through services of guidance, direction, counseling and enlightenment" (ICC, 1943a, pp. 1–2).

Like Moses leading the chosen people to the Promised Land, Yerkes painted a utopian vision of the future:

> The world crisis, with its clash of cultures and ideologies, has created for us psychologists unique opportunity for promotive endeavor. What may be achieved through wisely-planned and well-directed professional activity will be limited only by our knowledge, faith, disinterestedness, and prophetic foresight. It is for us, primarily, to prepare the way for scientific advances and the development of welfare services which from birth to death shall guide and minister to the development and social usefulness of the individual. For beyond even our wildest dreams, knowledge of human nature may now be made to serve human needs and to multiply and increase the satisfactions of living. (ICC, 1943a, p. 2)

Yerkes concluded his evangelistic address with a benediction: "With you, my fellow psychologists, I pray that from this, the first Intersociety Constitutional Convention of our profession, wisdom may flow like a mighty river of enlightenment and good will" (ICC, 1943a, p. 2).

Yerkes presided over the unopposed election of permanent officers, who were Edwin Boring (chair), Ernest Hilgard (vice-chair), Alice Bryan (secretary), and Edna Heidbredder (vice-secretary). All except Heidbredder had been members of the Survey and Planning Subcommittee.

In his opening statement, Boring dramatized the mission of the convention:

> Our problem is the problem of federalization vs. states' rights. . . . Our dilemma concerns the question as to how far certain privileges of interest-groups should be delegated to central authority, and how far they should be retained by these groups where competence and interest are maximal. . . . Hence our task is to find the optimal point between the pole of federalization and the pole of states' rights. (ICC, 1943a, p. 3)

By extending the rhetoric of the constitutional convention leading to the United States of America, Boring tried to reinforce the perception of the convention as a new beginning for psychology, an opportunity to recast the foundations of professional activity.

The delegates agreed to follow the tentative agenda set before the meeting. They spent the morning discussing the topic "should the scientific and technological aspects of psychology be developed together or separately?" and describing their aspirations for the convention. After lunch, Boring summarized the morning's discussion under four major points. All agreed that pure and applied work (science and technology) were "inextricably related," but that a "professional attitude" separated applied from academic psychologists. As a consequence, professional psychologists were more concerned with public relations and ethical issues of practice. It was felt that training should encompass both scientific and professional aspects of psychology. Finally, there were questions concerning the definition of the scope of the field. As Boring put it, "broadening the scope of psychology brings with it both advantages and disadvantages" (ICC, 1943a, p. 4).

Following some discussion of the general characteristics desired in a central organization, Leonard Carmichael suggested that three committees be appointed to consider the alternative plans. The first was to explore the modification of the APA's by-laws so that it might "function as a stronger and more inclusive central national psychological organization." The second was to draw up a plan for an ideal new association, without regard to existing organizations. The third was to formulate a way to federate existing societies to accomplish common objectives. Boring accepted Carmichael's suggestion and appointed the committees.[5]

The committees met in the evening and prepared their reports; the ICC reconvened the next morning and heard the committee plans. The federation committee, chaired by APA delegate Calvin Stone, recommended that psychology be organized along the lines of the American Institute of Physics, which provided general services to an array of specialized societies in the physical sciences. Federation, the committee argued, would insure maximum autonomy for existing groups to set high standards and would encourage interdisciplinary relationships. It would be less likely for small groups to be dominated by larger ones, avoiding the danger of a "top-heavy" organization. The pluralism of federation was seen by some as a way of maintaining grass-roots participation, whereas others (for instance, Hilgard) expressed concern that it would result in an ill-defined "hodge-podge" (ICC, 1943a, pp. 7–8).

Next, SPSSI representative Gardner Murphy presented the report of the committee on an ideal society. A poll of the delegates regarding the functions of a new organization indicated overwhelming concern with personnel services, including placement, and with professional training, followed by planning, public relations, and interdisciplinary activities. Referring to a tentative plan included in the ICC agenda handbook that called for a central secretariat and sections for interest groups, Murphy advanced various suggestions, including the provision for public relations and overall planning within the secretariat. He argued for a strong emphasis on interest-group sections and noted six areas of activity: clinical, educational, business (i.e., the AAAP), social issues (i.e., the SPSSI), tests and measurements (i.e., the Psychometric Society), and "psychobiology" (i.e., experimental psychology). To overcome "rationalizations or psychological resistances"

---

[5]The committee members were as follows: To revise APA by-laws: Anderson (chair), Carmichael, Doll, Hilgard, Richardson; to plan an ideal society: Murphy (chair), Britt, Canady, Heidbredder, Louttit; to plan a federation: Stone (chair), Achilles, Goodenough, Kornhauser, Newcomb (ICC, 1943a, p. 6).

against creating a new organization, the committee suggested that the APA's structure could be modified to serve the functions of an ideal society (ICC, 1943a, pp. 8–9).

The committee to consider revision of APA by-laws was chaired by John Anderson, the current APA president. Noting that APA articles and by-laws of incorporation allowed for "drastic changes," the committee proposed a systematic reorganization. The first change recognized the expanded purpose of the APA: the advancement of psychology as a "profession" as well as a "science." Suggesting general and section membership classes, the committee held that members could belong to any number of sections for which they were eligible, in addition to a primary affiliation. A council of representatives would be elected with section representation according to size and with at-large and regional representatives. A full-time secretary–treasurer would be elected, as well as a president-elect. Responsibility for publications and meeting programs would be divided between the council and the sections (ICC, 1943a, pp. 10–12).

Of the three committee reports, the APA reorganization plan generated by far the most interest among the delegates. Federation appeared to be an ambiguous and vague solution, and the ideas for an ideal society could be easily incorporated into plans to reorganize the APA. By remaking the structure of the APA, psychologists could have their cake and eat it too: the prestige of an important and venerable society, as well as the efficiency of a revamped organization. There was little reason or incentive to destroy the APA: American psychologists continued to look to it for leadership and to rely on it for scientific legitimation. Its 50th anniversary celebration in 1942 had brought in its wake a series of articles and reminiscences that lauded psychology's rich heritage and emphasized its continuing relevance to the present (see Boring, 1943a). The dislocations of war underscored the sense that an era was passing and that members of an earlier, pioneering generation were passing the torch to their descendents working in a different set of historical circumstances. The presence of septuagenarian Robert S. Woodworth at the convention as a delegate from the Society of Experimental Psychologists can be understood in this context. As the embodiment of the catholic "Columbia style," he was a vital link to the early days of American psychology. Among the few surviving members of his generation, he was nearly alone in remaining professionally active.

The Second Day

When the ICC reconvened Sunday afternoon, the conferees began to discuss the proposal to reorganize the APA. Each society representative was given the opportunity to react to the proposal and to bring up any grievances against the APA. Widespread dissatisfaction was expressed over the lack of voting privileges for APA associate members and the consequently restricted chances for participation by younger psychologists. Gladys Schwesinger, speaking for the National Council of Women Psychologists, felt that female psychologists had also had inadequate opportunities for participation in APA affairs. In a similar vein, Herman Canady, representative of the Black American Teachers' Association, criticized the neglect of African American institutions in psychology by the APA.[6] Former APA president Clark Hull added a note of caution to the proceedings, saying, "I want to register my belief that railroading does sometimes occur in the APA especially when controversial issues are presented as unanimously approved without discussion" (ICC, 1943a, pp. 12–14).

In addition to the general problems of representation in the APA, special interest group delegates registered specific complaints. Psychometric Society members Phillip Rulon and Marion Richardson complained that their joint annual meeting programs with the APA had suffered because of poor planning by APA organizers.[7] SPSSI secretary Theodore Newcomb, supported by Gordon Allport, felt that the APA had not been active enough in protecting the political freedom of psychologists, citing the recent congressional investigation of Columbia psychologist Goodwin Watson (see Capshew, 1986/1987; Sargent & Harris, 1986). Edgar Doll stated the basic problem succinctly: "The essential failure of the APA to recognize emergent groups is the primary objection to the APA." He contended that if the APA would have been more responsive to the social and professional interests of psychologists, separate societies would never have been formed. Psychologists wanted to belong to a unified discipline, and the overlapping memberships between the APA and the other societies provided evidence of this desire (ICC, 1943a, p. 16).

Steuart Britt of the AAAP indicated that if the APA were to be restructured to include the functions of the AAAP and other groups, the AAAP would go along. Anderson, clearly in favor of restructuring the APA, candidly agreed with the complaints against the APA. Reminding the group of their unprecedented authority, he said; "Any recommendations which come from such a group as this Convention will be virtually man-

---

[6]Canady represented the interests of Black psychologists in a manner similar to the position of the National Council of Women Psychologists, saying, "We are interested primarily in psychology. We don't think of ourselves as negro psychologists. We are simply psychologists who by accident happen to be negroes" (ICC, 1943a, p. 17).

[7]This complaint was made despite the fact that the Psychometric Society did not have enough papers to arrange a program for their 1941 meeting, and barely enough papers for the previous meeting (Dunlap, 1942).

datory since we represent different degrees, types, and shades of opinion with the organization" (ICC, 1943a, p. 15). APA leaders Carmichael and Boring threw their weight behind the reorganization plan; Boring summarized the discussion as follows:

> The Chair thinks it was said that the APA, while seeming to be continued in the proposed plan, would be so altered that it would be absorbed by the new organization; that the AAAP would be incorporated with its sections becoming Divisions of the new APA; that the SPSSI presumably would be made a Division; that Section I [Psychology, the AAAS] would be unaffected; that the other societies which have been mentioned [the Society of Experimental Psychologists; the National Institute of Psychology] would seem to be left outside insofar as they represent interest groups. Additional interest groups would grow up, and existing groups might go out of existence. (ICC, 1943a, p. 16)

As the afternoon session drew to a close, Yerkes tried to redirect the discussion back to the concrete details of revising the APA by-laws. Allport successfully proposed to extend further the APA's stated purpose of advancing psychology as a science and a profession by adding the phrase "and as a means of promoting human welfare" (ICC, 1943a, p. 17). In preparation for the final day of the convention, Boring appointed a committee on organization to draft a preliminary statement of the group's recommendations. Carmichael chaired the group, which met that evening.[8]

The Third Day

The report prepared by Carmichael's committee was distributed to each delegate, and outlined the basic structure of the new society as follows. The certificate of incorporation was to be reworded to say that: "the object of this society shall be to advance psychology as a science, as a profession, and as a means of promoting human welfare." Two classes of membership were proposed: Fellow (equivalent to APA Member) and Member (equivalent to APA Associate). In addition, divisions could have similar separate categories for nonmembers if they desired. Divisions, organized around interest groups, required a minimum of 50 members and would be the basis for representation on the Council. The initial divisions would be General Psychology, Clinical, Educational, Business and Industrial, Consulting, the Psychometric Society, and the SPSSI. New divisions could be started with a petition by at least 50 members, and old ones disbanded because of low membership or lack of interest. Geographical branches, such as the regional

---

[8]Other members were Achilles, Allport, Anderson, Britt, Doll, Edgerton, Goodenough, Hilgard, and Murphy (ICC, 1943a, p. 12).

psychological associations, and other societies would be considered for affiliation with the APA. The Council of Representatives was to be the major governing body, with proportionate representation from each division and with members-at-large elected by the entire association. Provision was made for a representative of African American universities and colleges. Two new offices were added: a president-elect and a full-time executive secretary. The Board of Directors would consist of the executive officers (president, president-elect, recording secretary, and treasurer) and five members of the Council. The creation of a Policy and Planning Board to provide overall direction was suggested. A central office would continue to handle APA publications, as well as those of other groups if they wished (ICC, 1943a, p. 25).

Carmichael, Doll, and Allport drafted a motion to accept the report:

> [We] move that having given careful consideration to various proposals placed before us, this Convention record its decision that the objectives in view can most effectively and economically be achieved through a closer and more organic tie between the reconstituted present national psychological societies and their present affiliates, and that, in view of legal, material, and professional considerations, the name of this national organization should be the American Psychological Association. (ICC, 1943a, p. 20)

The motion was passed.

In the ensuing discussion, the delegates presented various minor amendments to the plan. Among the most important was Britt's suggestion to allow present AAAP Fellows to become Fellows of the new APA automatically. Yerkes offered a successful motion that allowed the executive secretary an indefinite term of office. Boring appointed a Continuation Committee, consisting of Hilgard (chair), Anderson, Bryan, and Doll (Allport and Boring were later elected as members also), to prepare a detailed reorganization plan that would incorporate the proceedings and discussions of the ICC. The plan would then be submitted for consideration to the constituent societies through their delegates. Near the close of the convention, Irving Lorge, a Psychometric Society representative, moved that the plan include a statement "that the reorganization shall go into effect when approved by both the APA and AAAP" (ICC, 1943a, p. 27). This was an important procedural move that created a mechanism for ratifying the changes by the large associations, which represented a majority of American psychologists.

In 3 days, 26 psychologists had reached an agreement on how to achieve their common professional goals. Now it remained to be seen whether the majority of their colleagues would be convinced to go along.

ENGINEERING CONSENT FOR REFORM

The ICC Continuation Committee was responsible for devising a workable and acceptable reorganization plan. Although Hilgard was chair of the committee, he leaned heavily on Boring, the senior member of the group. Boring, who was indefatigable once his interest was aroused, paid careful attention to the task, bossing everyone around and fussing endlessly over details. Soon after the convention ended, he told Bryan to circulate the minutes to the delegates and to prepare notices for the *Psychological Bulletin* and *Science*. He suggested that the notice emphasize the unification of psychology and gloss over the retention of the name of the American Psychological Association as "merely a convenient means." Bryan was more sensitive to the concerns of AAAP members and decided not to mention the new organization's proposed name in the public announcements (Boring, 1943b; Bryan, 1943).

Boring volunteered to draft an "introductory sales talk" for the plan that would try to calm AAAP fears about being "absorbed" by the APA while at the same time be pleasing to the APA (Boring, 1943c). Hilgard agreed that this was a good idea, but wanted to revise the plan itself first. Anderson felt that continued work on the by-laws was premature, and advocated holding a vote on principles first. Overriding this suggestion, Hilgard tried to balance thoroughness with speed in preparing a comprehensive plan in time for the annual society meetings in September (Hilgard, 1943a).

By the middle of July, a tentative draft of the plan was sent to the delegates and officers of the national psychology societies. The bulk of the 25-page document consisted of by-laws for the "reconstituted" APA. In a brief summary of the convention, the report emphasized the basic principles of organization: the functional autonomy of interest groups, and administrative centralization. Adroitly addressing the issue of sovereignty, the report claimed that organizational reform could be accomplished

> only by a reconstitution of the present structure of the American Psychological Association in such a way that it include within its expanded structure the functional interests and professional atmosphere of the American Association for Applied Psychology. The Convention recommends, therefore, a *de facto* amalgamation of these two societies under new forms and a *de jure* continuation of the old society, with its

appropriate name, its prestige and [its assets]. (Continuation Committee, 1943, pp. i-ii)

Preliminary Acceptance

At their September 1943 meetings, the APA and AAAP governing councils accepted the Continuation Committee's recommendations and appointed a joint committee to manage their implementation. Their action raised a technical point of order: Did APA and AAAP leaders have the authority to act without the formal approval of their memberships? This was a procedural question similar to the one raised about the Intersociety Constitutional Convention and its authority to act on behalf of all American psychologists. As before, the issue was glossed over as the reformers continued to rely on the tacit approval of the psychology community. Hilgard, Bryan, and Anderson continued as members of the new committee, and Hilgard retained his chairmanship (Hilgard, 1943b). The joint committee called for an advisory mail vote by AAAP and APA members, then a final revision of the by-laws, followed by a formal ratification vote. This schedule would permit formal adoption of the reorganization plan by September 1944 and allow time to elect new officers and to make the organization fully operational by the following year. These recommendations were widely publicized, along with commentary (E. E. Anderson, 1944; J. E. Anderson, 1944; ICC, 1943c; Valentine & Anderson, 1944).

A Minor Rebellion

The rumble of discontent expressed by AAAP Board of Affiliates chair Harriet O'Shea before the ICC turned into a minor rebellion after the AAAP and the APA adopted its tentative plan. In March 1944, O'Shea circulated a list of 11 reasons against merging the APA and the AAAP. Under the pretense of providing equal time for the opposing view, O'Shea sent the list, which was typed on AAAP letterhead, to officers and representatives of the 10 state applied psychology groups affiliated with the AAAP (O'Shea & Rich, 1944). Located primarily in the Midwest, the state societies had a combined membership of approximately 250; they were composed mainly of practitioners and were oriented toward occupational issues such as licensing. These societies were never a potent force in the AAAP, and the reorganization threatened to marginalize them further. Because most of the members of these groups worked in institutions such as child guidance clinics and hospitals through war mobilization and did not get caught up in the excitement of psychology projects in Washington and elsewhere, it was easy for them to feel out of the mainstream.

O'Shea's compilation of complaints expressed the concern that the interests of applied psychologists had not received proper consideration. Naturally, they viewed applied psychology in terms of practice, in contrast with AAAP leaders, who were inclined to include its academic and research aspects as well. After carving out a niche for themselves in the AAAP, the practitioners were understandably fearful of losing even this modicum of professional recognition. The list also questioned the timing of the merger, suggesting that applied psychology was "not yet securely enough established or clearly enough defined to be ready to merge its identity with that of the whole field of psychology" (O'Shea & Rich, 1944). A related point advised that the merger ratification be delayed until after the war in order to allow psychologists in the military to return to their civilian positions and study the plan carefully.

O'Shea's list prompted a swift reaction from the former director of the Office of Psychological Personnel, Steuart Britt. He thought that O'Shea was on a personal crusade, and criticized her use of AAAP letterhead, which implied official endorsement. She reacted by implicating him as part of the "pressure group" in the East that was pushing the reorganization (O'Shea, 1944). A more formal public response was made by AAAP executive secretary Alice Bryan, a member of the Survey and Planning Committee. In an open letter to O'Shea, Bryan (1944) addressed the issues. Pointing out that the reorganization was not a "merger" of the APA and the AAAP, she drew attention to the fact that the plan had been thoroughly discussed at each successive stage by representatives of each society, including the AAAP. The interests of applied psychologists were well served, she argued: Of the 19 charter divisions proposed, 13 dealt with applied psychology. Furthermore, the new APA's divisional structure itself was a logical extension of the divisional structure of the AAAP. With the support of the AAAP president, Albert Poffenberger of Columbia, Bryan's letter was widely circulated and eventually published in the *Journal of Consulting Psychology* (Poffenberger & Bryan, 1944). Proponents of the reorganization applauded Bryan's assertive response in private, hoping that the episode was finished (Britt, 1944; Louttit, 1944; Marquis, 1944; Yerkes, 1944).

Ratification

The dissent expressed by O'Shea was effectively squelched by these tactics, and the ratification process continued. Two mail votes were taken in 1944 regarding the proposal; both indicated strong approval. One ballot canvassed the opinions of APA and AAAP members, whereas the other was sent to all American psychologists on the rolls of the OPP (Hilgard, 1945a; Olson, 1944). The APA and the AAAP officially approved the proposal in September 1944 and set September 1945 as the date for the new organization to begin. To plan for the transition, two important committees were formed. The Division Organization Committee, chaired by Hilgard, named temporary chairs and secretaries for each of the new APA's charter divisions. The Committee on the Constitution, also chaired by Hilgard, worked out details of organizational representation (Hilgard, 1945b). The new APA was inaugurated on September 6, 1945, a month after the end of the war.

Within a few months, Dael Wolfle was installed as the first APA executive secretary. Before joining the staff of the Applied Psychology Panel of the wartime Office of Scientific Research and Development in 1944, he had been on the University of Chicago faculty. During the war he had also served on the Emergency Committee in Psychology (representing the Psychometric Society) and had gained recognition for his administrative talents. As head of the central office, Wolfle played a key role in managing APA affairs and helped to make the society a powerful center of influence.

OUTWARD VISION, INWARD GLANCE

The new APA embodied the lessons of World War II. The psychology community's wartime alliance with the military establishment signaled the start of a new social contract; psychologists sought to broaden their base of social support by marketing their expertise more widely. They had learned to submerge their narrow specialty interests in favor of a broad consensus on the great practical value of their discipline. They agreed with Allport that "the promotion of human welfare" was a desirable goal, and placed it alongside the more prosaic purposes of advancing psychology as a science and profession in the new APA constitution.

As psychologists looked outward to society for legitimacy, they spent relatively little time thinking about the institutional arrangements to accomplish their goals. As this chapter has shown, the APA was adopted as a convenient vehicle to pursue new disciplinary priorities. The Subcommittee on Survey and Planning shaped the agenda for professional reform and managed to channel it into organizational restructuring. The new APA put a unified public front on what continued to be an extremely diverse field. However, even that public front was not complete. The Psychometric Society declined an invitation to become a charter division, despite the fact that its representatives had been involved in the reorganization planning (Kurtz et al., 1945).

Potentially more serious than the Psychometric Society's lack of participation was the failure of psychologists to consider the larger consequences of unification. Aside from the complaints of a disaffected few, no attempt was made to gauge the long-term effects of reorganization. It seemed as if everyone chose to believe in the rosy future predicted by Robert Yerkes. That optimistic vision proved to be compelling under wartime circumstances, and the reformation of the APA came to be seen as an inevitable step in the professional evolution of psychology.

After a few years of postwar growth, one of the chief architects of the new APA reminded his colleagues about the tensions inherent in the wartime reorganization. Edwin Boring (1949) noted that

> whatever happens to us, APA is going to remain a huge organism with two heads, a professional and a scientific. That is what we wanted from the start and what we now have. Let us not forget the advantages it has given us. The two heads are on the same end of the animal, and, if either of them thinks the other is aiming in the wrong direction, let it look around to see where its tail had come from in 1945. (p. 532)

Between 1945 and 1956, the year Yerkes died, the APA added nearly 1,000 new members every year, growing from 4,000 to 14,000 in the immediate postwar decade. Psychology was well on its way to becoming a large and influential scientific profession in the United States. By the early 1960s, it was clear that growth was concentrated in applied areas, particularly clinical psychology, and the strains between the scientific and professional wings of the discipline became more noticeable (see Hughes, 1952; Tryon, 1963). APA membership continued to increase through the 1980s, and the number of divisions representing special interest groups proliferated until there were more than 45. In 1988, after coexisting for more than four decades, the two heads of the APA organism began to part company, and the American Psychological Society was organized as a way to refocus attention on the scientific dimensions of psychology. Interestingly, the rhetoric surrounding its formation seemed to echo themes of professional unity and disciplinary cooperation that were common around the time of the Second World War.

REFERENCES

Anderson, E. E. (1944). A note on the proposed by-laws for a reconstituted APA. *Psychological Bulletin, 41,* 230–234.

Anderson, J. E. (1944). A note on the meeting of the Joint Constitutional Committee of the APA and AAAP. *Psychological Bulletin, 41,* 235–236.

Boring, E. G. (1929). *A history of experimental psychology.* New York: Century.

Boring, E. G. (1943a). The celebrations of the American Psychological Association. *Psychological Review, 50,* 1–4.

Boring, E. G. (1943b). Letter to A. I. Bryan, 9 June 1943. Edwin G. Boring Papers (Bryan 1942–43), Harvard University Archives, Cambridge, MA.

Boring, E. G. (1943c). Letter to E. R. Hilgard, 2 June 1943. Edwin G. Boring Papers (He-Hi 1942–43), Harvard University Archives, Cambridge, MA.

Boring, E. G. (1949). Policy and plans of the APA: V. Basic principles. *American Psychologist, 4,* 531–532.

Boring, E. G. (1952). Autobiography. In E. G. Boring (Ed.), *A history of psychology in autobiography* (Vol. 4, pp. 27–52). Worcester, MA: Clark University Press.

Britt, S. H. (1943). Letter to W. C. Olson, 13 May 1943. American Psychological Association Papers (K-8/AAAP), Library of Congress Manuscript Division, Washington, DC.

Britt, S. H. (1944). Letter to A. I. Bryan, 27 April 1944. American Psychological Association Papers (K-7/D-13), Library of Congress Manuscript Division, Washington, DC.

Bryan, A. I. (1943). Letter to E. G. Boring, 9 June 1943. Edwin G. Boring Papers (Bryan 1942–43), Harvard University Archives, Cambridge, MA.

Bryan, A. I. (1944). Letter to H. O'Shea, 18 April 1944. American Psychological Association Papers (I-6/AAAP 1944–46), Library of Congress Manuscript Division, Washington, DC.

Bryan, A. I. (1983). Autobiography. In A. N. O'Connell & N. F. Russo (Eds.), *Models of achievement: Reflections of eminent women in psychology* (pp. 69–86). New York: Columbia University Press.

Capshew, J. H. (1986/1987). Psychology on the march: American psychologists and World War II (Doctoral dissertation, University of Pennsylvania, 1986). *Dissertation Abstracts International, 47A*, 3858.

Capshew, J. H., & Laszlo, A. C. (1986). "We would not take no for an answer": Women psychologists and gender politics during World War II. *Journal of Social Issues, 42*(1), 157–180.

Carmichael, L. C. (1943). [Review of *Psychology for the fighting man*]. *Science, 98,* 242.

Continuation Committee. (1943). Report and recommendations of the Intersociety Constitutional Convention of psychologists to the societies represented. American Psychological Association Papers (I-5/ICC 1943), Library of Congress Manuscript Division, Washington, DC.

Dallenbach, K. M. (1946). The Emergency Committee in Psychology, National Research Council. *American Journal of Psychology, 59,* 496–582.

Dunlap, J. W. (1942). The Psychometric Society: Roots and powers. *Psychometrika, 7,* 1–8.

Elliott, R. M. (1952). Autobiography. In E. G. Boring (Ed.), *A history of psychology in autobiography* (Vol. 4, pp. 75–95). Worcester, MA: Clark University Press.

Haraway, D. J. (1989). A pilot plant for human engineering: Robert Yerkes and the Yale Laboratories of Primate Biology, 1924–42. In *Primate visions: Gender, race, and nature in the world of modern science* (pp. 59–83). London: Routledge.

Hilgard, E. R. (1943a). Letter to E. G. Boring, 12 June 1943. Edwin G. Boring Papers (He-Hi 1942–43), Harvard University Archives, Cambridge, MA.

Hilgard, E. R. (1943b). Letter to E. G. Boring, 5 September 1943. Edwin G. Boring Papers (He-Hi 1942–43), Harvard University Archives, Cambridge, MA.

Hilgard, E. R. (1945a). Psychologists' preferences for divisions under the proposed APA by-laws. *Psychological Bulletin, 42,* 20–26.

Hilgard, E. R. (1945b). Temporary chairmen and secretaries for proposed APA divisions. *Psychological Bulletin, 42,* 294–296.

Hilgard, E. R. (1974). Autobiography. In G. Lindzey (Ed.), *A history of psychology in autobiography* (Vol. 6, pp. 129–160). Englewood Cliffs, NJ: Prentice-Hall.

Hilgard, E. R. (1986). From the social gospel to the psychology of social issues: A reminiscence. *Journal of Social Issues, 42*(1), 107–110.

Hilgard, E. R. (1987). *Psychology in America: A historical survey.* San Diego, CA: Harcourt Brace Jovanovich.

Hughes, E. C. (1952). Psychology: Science and/or profession. *American Psychologist, 7,* 441–443.

Intersociety Constitutional Convention. (1943a). Condensed transcript, 29–31 May. American Psychological Association Papers (I-6/ICC 1943), Library of Congress Manuscript Division, Washington, DC.

Intersociety Constitutional Convention. (1943b). *Handbook and agenda.* American Psychological Association Papers (K-8/AAAP), Library of Congress Manuscript Division, Washington, DC.

Intersociety Constitutional Convention. (1943c). Recommendations of the Intersociety Constitutional Convention of psychologists: I. Statement of the Joint Constitutional Committee of the APA and AAAP. II. Statement by the Continuation Committee of the convention. III. By-laws appropriate to a reconstituted American Psychological Association. IV. Sample blank for survey of opinion on the proposed by-laws. *Psychological Bulletin, 40,* 621–647.

Kurtz, A. K., Flanagan, J. C., Lorge, I., Richardson, M. W., Rulon, P. J., & Thurstone, L. L. (1945). Report to the Psychometric Society by its Committee on Reorganization and Divisional Status. *Psychometrika, 10,* Appendix C, iii–v.

Louttit, C. M. (1944). Letter to A. I. Bryan, 22 April 1944. American Psychological Association Papers (K-7/D-13), Library of Congress Manuscript Division, Washington, DC.

Marquis, D. M. (1944). Letter to A. I. Bryan, 4 May 1944. American Psychological Association Papers (K-7/D-13), Library of Congress Manuscript Division, Washington, DC.

Olson, W. C. (1944). Proceedings of the fifty-second annual meeting of the American Psychological Association, Inc., Cleveland, Ohio, September 11 and 12, 1944. *Psychological Bulletin, 41*, 725–793.

O'Shea, H. (1944). Letter to S. H. Britt, 22 March 1944. American Psychological Association Papers (K-7/D-13), Library of Congress Manuscript Division, Washington, DC.

O'Shea, H., & Rich, G. J. (1944). Reasons against merging the AAAP and APA. American Psychological Association Papers (K-7/D-13), Library of Congress Manuscript Division, Washington, DC.

Poffenberger, A. T., & Bryan, A. I. (1944). Toward unification in psychology. *Journal of Consulting Psychology, 8*, 253–257.

Portenier, L. G. (Ed.). (1967). *The International Council of Psychologists, Inc.* Greeley, CO: International Council of Psychologists.

Preparation for the Intersociety Constitutional Convention. (1943). *Psychological Bulletin, 39*, 127–128.

Reed, J. (1987). Robert M. Yerkes and the mental testing movement. In M. M. Sokal (Ed.), *Psychological testing and American society, 1890–1930* (pp. 75–94). New Brunswick, NJ: Rutgers University Press.

Rogers, C. R. (1966). Autobiography. In E. G. Boring & G. Lindzey (Eds.), *A history of psychology in autobiography* (Vol. 5, pp. 341–384). New York: Appleton-Century-Crofts.

Sargent, S. S., & Harris, B. (1986). Academic freedom, civil liberties, and SPSSI. *Journal of Social Issues, 42*(1), 43–67.

Tryon, R. C. (1963). Psychology in flux: The academic–professional bipolarity. *American Psychologist, 18*, 134–143.

Valentine, W. L., & Anderson, J. E. (1944). Chart of the proposed APA reorganization. *Psychological Bulletin, 41*, 41.

Yerkes, R. M. (1944). Letter to A. I. Bryan, 6 May 1944. American Psychological Association Papers (K-7/D-13), Library of Congress Manuscript Division, Washington, DC.

Yerkes, R. M., Boring, E. G., Bryan, A. I., Doll, E. A., Elliott, R. M., Hilgard, E. R., & Stone, C. P. (1942a). First report of the Subcommittee on Survey and Planning for Psychology. *Psychological Bulletin, 39*, 619–630.

Yerkes, R. M., Boring, E. G., Bryan, A. I., Doll, E. A., Elliott, R. M., Hilgard, E. R., & Stone, C. P. (1942b). Psychology as science and profession. *Psychological Bulletin, 39*, 761–772.

7

RAPID GROWTH AND CHANGE AT THE AMERICAN PSYCHOLOGICAL ASSOCIATION: 1945 TO 1970

MEREDITH P. CRAWFORD

The quarter of a century extending from 1945 to 1970 constituted the formative years of the "new" American Psychological Association, created by the major reorganization discussed in the previous chapter. During this period, its membership climbed from 4,183 to 30,839, or 637%. The number of psychologists involved in the "governance structure" grew from 157 to 491, or 212%. Its operating budget grew from $110,000 to $5,147,000, or 45 times (while the Consumer Price Index about doubled). Its Central Office made successive moves from two rented rooms to the purchase of a former townhouse and then to the construction and operation of an eight-story building in downtown Washington, DC, beginning its occupancy of

During the time that this chapter was being prepared, Dael Wolfle's history of the American Association for the Advancement of Science (AAAS), covering this same time span, was published (Wolfle, 1989). Because Wolfle was the first executive secretary of the APA, before he took the same position with the AAAS, he exercised a profound influence on the parallel development of both associations. His volume provides a valuable commentary on the development of the several sciences over this quarter century.

the first two floors in September 1964. There, the Association continued its ever-expanding efforts to advance psychology through its publication and abstracting activities and the operation of its annual convention, attended by perhaps 2,000 in 1946, and by 8,043 in 1970.

This chapter is divided into three parts. The first and largest concerns the structure of the Association and traces its growth and differentiation between 1945 and 1970. The second comments on four important influences on psychology and the Association, especially during the first decade of the period: the heritage of World War II, the creation of the National Science Foundation, the very large increase in federal funding for psychology, and the "computer revolution." The third part concerns functions of the Association; two of them have been chosen for discussion: those undertaken in the promotion of psychology as a science and in its promotion as a profession.[1]

GROWTH AND DIFFERENTIATION OF THE ASSOCIATION

This section begins with a discussion of the formal structure of the APA and its membership. It moves into the evolution of the "governance structure" and of the Central Office.

Corporate Documents

The Certificate of Incorporation and the Bylaws set forth the legal basis for the corporate existence of the Association as a tax-exempt entity.

Certificate of Incorporation

Although founded in 1892, the APA's incorporation was not marked by a certificate until one was requested of the District of Columbia in 1925. It stated that "the object of this society shall be to advance psychology as a science." This was to be accomplished by holding meetings, issuing publications of a scientific nature, and performing other lawful acts in furtherance of its scientific mission. It also provided that, in the event of its dissolution, its assets would go to the American Association for the Advancement of Science (AAAS). The only amendment to the Certificate was made in 1939: It gave the Board of Directors the authority to dispose of the assets to some other organization should the AAAS lose its tax-exempt status.

---

[1]How the Association began to pursue its third objective, the advancement of psychology as a means of promoting human welfare, first codified in the new constitution of 1945, will be left to Chapters 11 and 12.

Bylaws

New charter. As recounted in Chapter 6, the new structure of the Association that emerged from the reorganization was documented by an extensive revision of the existing APA Bylaws. That revision was adopted by unanimous vote at the last business meeting of the membership in September 1944 and became effective in September 1945 (APA, 1946a). By this action, the membership stated what it wanted the reorganized Association to be, and delegated to the newly created Council of Representatives, specified in that document, certain powers and authorities with which to pursue the three objectives of the Association. It follows, therefore, that any amendment to the Bylaws can ony be effected by (mail) vote of the membership.

The 22 articles in these Bylaws can be grouped as follows: Article I stated the three objectives of the Association and Article II defined the membership classes and requirements, and the Association's sanctions against unethical conduct. A later section stated the dues required of each member. Six articles defined the elements of the governance structure, whereas another four pertained to the operation of the corporation ("Nominations and Elections," "Central Office," "Publications," and "Annual Convention"). One article made provision for affiliated groups and branches, whereas another listed organizations with which the APA was already affiliated. The remaining three displayed the corporate seal, provided for amending the Bylaws, and offered enabling legislation.

Revisions 1945–1970. A variety of amendments were made over the years that affected only some of the facets of Association operation or that were minor housekeeping acts. However, one of the most extensive general revisions was posed by the Policy and Planning Board in 1960 (APA, 1960a) after the Board's (and especially its chairman for 1958–59, C. W. Bray's) consultation with staff of the Central Office and legal counsel to explore "ways APA might accomplish its function more effectively" (p. 135). The Board made its study with two principles in mind: (a) "The Bylaws should incorporate only those features of APA organization and function over which the full membership should exercise control." Procedures and policies "not of great concern to the full membership should be determined by action of the Council" (p. 135). (b) The wording should be revised in several places in the document to allow for flexibility in the future as, for example, not specifying the exact size of boards and committees. As we shall see later, these principles led to the formulation of the Rules of Council (later called "Association Rules") some years later.

Some of the more extensive of these revisions should be mentioned.

Article I, "Objectives," was expanded by elaborating on the ways the Association promotes human welfare, "by encouragement of psychology in all its branches in the broadest and most liberal manner. . . ." Examples cited were research and the improvement of its methods and conditions, and improvements in the "qualifications and usefulness of psychologists through high standards by promotion of diffusion of psychological knowledge in various ways" (p. 136). Another specific change recommended including even more detail about the handling of ethics cases and defining the role of the Committee on Scientific and Professional Ethics as an investigatory and advisory one, while placing final decision authority with the Board of Directors rather than the Council.

Membership

When a group of people who have a common interest band together to form an organization to facilitate their enjoyment of that interest, the qualification for joining may be little more than an active interest in the subject. Additional criteria for membership depend on two kinds of considerations. The first is the level of knowledge and expertise in the area, which will set the level of oral and written communication among members. Such a requirement is the primary concern for a scientific society. The second consideration comes into play when members of the group begin to offer their services, particularly on an individual basis, to the public. This applies to a professional association whose members seek certification or licensure to protect the public and to establish markets for their services.

The first of these considerations was generally sufficient for the prewar APA, whose members were mostly engaged in teaching and research. Upon joining with the American Association for Applied Psychology (AAAP) in 1944, the second consideration became more relevant for the APA and has been of increasing significance ever since. Ethical behavior, of course, has always been a requirement for every member, whether teacher, scientist, or practitioner.

Development of Ethical Standards

Members of the APA have long used appropriate psychological research methods in the development of the policies and procedures of the Association. Nowhere is this better illustrated than in the development of ethical standards.

In 1935, when the membership totaled only some 2,300, a special committee was appointed to consider ethical matters and to resolve some complaints on an informal basis. In 1939, the committee recommended the appointment of a standing committee to consider complaints pertaining to the Association, to scientific colleagues and students, to research subjects, and to clients or nonpsychologists who seek psychological advice. This committee did not think the time was ripe to legislate a complete code.

After functioning for several years, in 1948 the committee recommended that work begin on the preparation of a formal code. A new Committee on Ethical Standards for Psychology was formed under the chairmanship of Nicholas Hobbs. Rather than enunciating a vague set of generalities, the Committee took an empirical approach. It first laid out 16 criteria that the code should meet (Hobbs, 1948); the following are a few examples:

The code should

- be an expression of the "best ethical practice in the field of psychology as judged by a large representative sample of members of the American Psychological Association" (p. 83).

- be an outgrowth of intensive research.

- be "empirically developed."

- involve wide participation by APA members in its formulation, which should help in implementation of the code.

Some of the other criteria called for a statement of the code in specific terms and for it to be adequate for psychologists working in different fields, enlightening to nonpsychologists, subject to revision by simple methods, and finally adopted, item by item, by the membership.

The Hobbs committee used a variant of the "critical incident technique" developed by John Flanagan (with whom Hobbs was associated in World War II). The Committee asked, by letter, each of the some 7,500 members of the Association "to describe a situation that they know of firsthand in which a psychologist made a decision having ethical implications, and to indicate what the correspondent perceived as being the ethical issue involved" (APA, 1953, p. vi). More than 1,000 replies were classified into six categories: public responsibility, clinical relationships, teaching, research, writing and publishing, and professional relationships. After much study by the Committee of the comments made by members to the publication of each draft section in the *American Psychologist*, its recommendations were adopted by the Council in 1952. In 1953, they were published as *Ethical Standards of Psychology* (APA, 1953). The 171 pages in this volume presented, under the six main headings, from three to six subareas, in each of which the problem was stated, followed by a collection of critical incidents relevant to it and a statement of a principle. These standards were adopted on a trial basis for 3 years, after which they were revised at intervals. During the 1960s, they were gradually distilled into 10 principles to be applied in many or all kinds of situations. Concurrent with the development of the code, revisions were made in Article II of the Bylaws, which laid down procedures for handling cases brought by the Committee to the Board of Directors for a decision.

Membership Classes

In prewar years, the leadership of the Association strongly favored the possession of a doctorate, based in part on a dissertation of a psychological nature, as the minimum requirement for full membership and the use of the title *psychologist*. This sentiment persisted after the war as the Policy and Planning Board struggled to formulate the proper standards for the various classes of membership. However, this board recognized the fact that many people, both in the Association and outside of it, were employed in full-time psychological work with less than doctoral training (APA Policy and Planning Board, 1957).

In 1954, the Council formally requested the Policy and Planning Board to study the standards for membership, which, at that time, were those set forth in Article II of the original (1946) Bylaws. These classes of membership were defined as follows:

- *Fellow.* Holder of doctoral degree based in part on a dissertation psychological in nature, prior membership as an Associate and acceptable, published research beyond the dissertation *or* four years of acceptable professional experience. The nomination was made by a Division to the Board of Directors, which, if approved, was recommended to the Council.

- *Associate.* Holder of a doctorate *or* completion of two years of graduate work in psychology, *or* completion of the year of graduate study and one year of professional experience; *or* that the individual be a distinguished person recommended by the Board of Directors.

- *Life Member.* A Fellow or an Associate for 25 years and attainment of age 65.

At the outset of its work, the Policy and Planning Board identified several of the considerations and problems involved in the determination of membership requirements. These included the following:

- Membership in the APA defines a person as a psychologist in the eyes of the public.

- The Membership Committee has a difficult time in assessing the qualifications of a candidate when he or she does not have the doctorate.

- The meaning of *Fellow* may have been degraded.

- Many subdoctoral psychologists need to be included in APA.

- The category of *Life Member* is meaningless beyond the waiver of dues.

As a result of its deliberations, the Policy and Planning Board recommended to the Board of Directors that the categories be revised. After some years of debate, the Council approved three classes of membership: *Fellow, Member*, and *Associate*. On approval by the membership, this change went into effect at the beginning of 1958. Standards for Fellow were strengthened by requiring the nominating division to furnish the Membership Committee with clear evidence of the candidate's unusual or outstanding accomplishment in psychology. The new category of Member required the doctorate, thus preserving the time-honored criterion. The class of Associate was continued for subdoctoral psychologists, but it was stipulated that when an Associate was awarded the doctorate, he or she would automatically be raised to Member. The Life Member category was dropped, but waiver of dues, when requested, for members over 65 years of age and with 25 years of membership was retained. Various types of *Affiliates*, such as *Student, Division*, and *Foreign* were recognized, but, as in 1945, they were not counted as members of the Association.

Growth of Membership

From 1945 to 1970, Association membership grew more rapidly than during any 25-year period before or since. The increase was 6.7-fold, as compared with 2.2-fold for the next 20 years following (see Appendix for membership figures by years). The figures for 1957 and 1958 illustrate the changes brought about when the Member category was introduced and the Life Member category was dropped. At that time, the bulk of the Associates had the doctorate and were shifted to the Member category.

Obligations and Benefits to the Individual Member

A definitive approach to the topic of member obligations and benefits would have come from a systematic investigation to find the reasons that a representative sample of psychologists would give for joining, renewing membership, or resigning from the Association. Respondents could report their evaluations of the relative importance of the obligations and benefits associated with membership. However, no such study seems to have been

TABLE 1
The Changing Dues Structure

Year	Associate	Member	Fellow
1946	$6.00	—	$10.00
1948	$12.00	—	$17.50
1956	$20.00	—	$20.00
1957		Prorated to income	
1958	—	$25.00	$25.00
1959	$17.00	$20.00	$25.00
1960	$20.00	$30.00	$30.00
1965	$30.00	$45.00	$45.00
1970	$30.00	$45.00	$45.00

done during the 25-year period under consideration, but a relevant event did occur: Ten prominent scientific members of the Association organized the Psychonomic Society in 1960. This action may be taken as an expression of their dissatisfaction with the mechanisms for rapid communication among psychologists "whose primary interest is in research and scholarship" (APA, 1960b, p. 281). But because the organizers stated that this did not represent a secession from the APA (and indeed, the organizers did remain members), the new society represented a way to increase the satisfaction of a segment of the membership without their leaving or altering the Association.

Obligations. The most general obligation of a member is one that, as noted above, has always existed but became comprehensively defined during the first decade of the new Association, following the publication of the *Ethical Standards of Psychologists*, which provided members with a guide to what constituted ethical behavior in various kinds of professional situations. This obligation has been clearly stated in the Preamble to the *Ethical Principles of Psychology* as follows: "Acceptance of membership in the American Psychological Association commits the member to adherence to these principles" (APA, 1989, p. xxviii).

The payment of dues is a very tangible obligation for each member, except for those excused for long membership or age. Dues for different classes of membership were stated in the Bylaws of 1945, but, in line with the clarifying and simplifying of the amendments, as discussed above, they came to be set, from time to time, by the Council. Changes in the dues structures over the 25-year period are shown in Table 1.

In response to concerns about how easily different groups of members could afford APA dues, a sliding scale, based on each member's income for the previous year, was adopted. However, the scheme caused great difficulty in budgeting and offended a substantial number of members, and it was abandoned after a trial in 1957. In addition to a one-dollar set-aside from each member's dues to one division, each division could assess its

TABLE 2
Exercise of the Franchise in 1953

Voters	Bylaw ballot	% voting presidential nomination	% voting presidential election	N
Fellows	26.3	52.1	46.7	1,760
Associates	18.4	37.1	35.1	4,233
All members	19.6	34.4	30.1	10,903

Note: From Dennis & Girden, 1955, p. 212.

members additional dues to meet the needs of that division. During the late 1960s, discussions began on charging differential dues in terms of the kinds of services that different groups of members received from the APA, but no changes were made until recently.

Although ethical behavior and the payment of dues are obligations on every member, enforced through the threat of loss of membership, there are other activities in which voluntary participation is expected when appropriate. One is participation in the governance structure. By some it has been regarded as a necessary chore, by others as opportunity to participate in Association corporate affairs, to gain visibility among one's colleagues, and to lend a hand in promoting one or more of the several branches of psychology. During the early 1950s, concern was expressed by the Board of Directors about the relatively small portion of members who served on boards and committees and the appearance of the same faces at various meetings. Calls went in the *American Psychologist* in 1951 and thereafter asking members in which activities they would be willing to participate. These efforts, along with the advent of jet air travel some years later, seemed to broaden member participation and improve geographical representation.

Another expected "obligation" has been the exercise of the franchise. Member response to the annual solicitation of nominations for president-elect and to the ballots that followed for election of the president-elect and division officers and for the approval of proposed amendments to the Bylaws was substantially less than unanimous. This has been the subject of frequent comment in the *American Psychologist*. Dael Wolfle lamented the low turnout in one of his "Across the Secretary's Desk" commentaries in the first volume of that publication (1946a). Ten years later, figures were published on participation in the elections of 1953 by Fellows and Associates (Table 2). Indifference to voting on the part of many members has been a persistent problem, but one that is not unique to the APA.

Benefits. Insofar as individual members are committed to one or more of the Association's objectives, progress toward each can be seen as a benefit to the individual as well as to the whole enterprise of psychology. Official advocacy of psychology by the APA may indirectly advance the career of the individual.

A more personal benefit accrues to each member by his or her listing in the *Directory*, a volume that identifies the person as a psychologist; notes, where appropriate, Diplomate status awarded by the American Board of Examiners in Psychology; and lists members by location and division membership—conveniences to all who use the volume.

One of the three major functions of the Central Office, when established in 1946, was the assumption of a placement service for psychologists that had been operated by psychologists under the auspices of the National Research Council during the war. The new APA Office continued the service of transmitting information between employers and job seekers, but not of evaluating candidates or making recommendations. The Office began the publication of the *Employment Bulletin* in the late 1940s and, from the beginning, arranged facilities for providing information and spaces for job interviewing at the APA annual convention and, soon thereafter, on request, at regional association meetings.

The annual convention itself has provided individual members with the opportunity to participate in programs, to be informed about new developments in his or her field, and to mingle with psychologists of old or recent acquaintance. For several years, members attended at no cost, but, since the late 1950s, a registration fee has been required, which has been less for members than for nonmembers. The Central Office, over the years, has found ways of reducing members' transportation and lodging costs.

This same history of financial savings to members has applied to the prices of APA publications. Through the late 1940s, each member received the *Psychological Bulletin*, the *Abstracts*, the *American Psychologist*, and the *Directory* with payment of dues. As Association costs have gone up, members have received the *American Psychologist* without extra charge and, beginning in 1970, the *Psychological Monitor*. Prices for members have always been less than for nonmembers.

Another benefit available to members needing it was the work of the Committee on Academic Freedom and Conditions of Employment during the 1950s and, during the 1960s, of the Committee on Equal Opportunity in Psychology. These committees investigated instances of alleged discrimination and curtailment of academic freedom in employment practices.

Of course, certain types of benefits have been secured for members that are not unique to the nature of the Association. Insurance coverage is one of these. In the late 1940s, on the recommendation of a special committee on insurance, the Council appointed members of the board of the APA Insurance Trust (APAIT), a corporation that has operated separately from the Association but that has reported directly to the Board of Directors and to the membership on an annual basis. In its early years, the APAIT offered life, health, and accident insurance to members at attractive rates and, over the years, it has added other coverages, including income protection and professional liability insurance.

Building Blocks

As shown in Chapter 6, the new Association was structured to provide for the expressions of members' interests in both the central core of psychology and a number of specialized areas. Some of these interests were represented by organizations that sent representatives to the Intersociety Constitutional Convention. From this conference there emerged two kinds of groups: One, divisions, furnished the original building blocks of the Association, whereas the other, state associations, soon thereafter began to furnish a different kind of structure.[2]

Divisions

Article VII of the new Constitution began with the statement, "The special interests that lie within the Association shall be represented by Divisions." It went on to specify that 50 Associates or Fellows would be the minimum number required to petition the Council for recognition. Criteria to be used in setting up new divisions included evidence that it represented "the emergence of an active and unitary interest of a group of members which falls within the scope of the Association." Other criteria specified that the membership not be limited to a single geographical area and that establishment "would not be inimical to the welfare of any existing Division." The Bylaws also stated that "a Division [should remain] autonomous in all matters within its field that are not reserved to the Association." APA membership was not required for division affiliation, but only APA members who were Associates or Fellows could be called members of the division or represent the division on the Council of Representatives. General principles were stated about how division bylaws and committee structures must conform to APA guidelines.

Association bylaw statements about divisions did not change much from 1946 to 1970. The minimum number of Association members required to petition for the recognition of a new division was changed from the fixed

---

[2]There have been a number of other psychological organizations, such as the regional associations, that have gained affiliate status with the APA. Although these associations have added strength and promoted some unity in American psychology, they were not an organic part of the Association and hence are not included in the "building blocks."

number of 50 to 1% of the APA membership. Authority was granted divisions to handle special funds (or delegate it to the Central Office) and to own or operate a journal (under the supervision of the APA Publications Board).

Almost as soon as the list of the 19 charter divisions was announced, vigorous concerns were expressed about the large number of them. Many members felt that the overall "unity" of psychology was being threatened in organizational terms, and they expressed the conviction that there does exist a fundamental set of core concepts in psychology that would be weakened. In his important paper that summarized the history of the formation of divisions, Doll presented a careful critique of the original 19 and suggested that "a possible reduction of Divisions to as few as eight [would be possible] by combining cluster interests with areas of application and types of employment" (Doll, 1946, p. 341). Such combinations would be in line with a principle that Doll enunciated: "The whole of psychology is more important than any of its Divisions but has a barren future independent of them" (p. 337). In 1950, Wolfle devoted most of his annual report as executive secretary to ways of reducing the number of divisions (Wolfle, 1950).

In 1954, Dorothy Adkins raised the feasibility of reducing the number by means of a factor analysis of the replies of 3,152 members to a survey of interests in the kinds of things psychologists do (laboratory experimentation, listening to people, etc.). Her results pointed to a possible reduction to seven divisions (Adkins, 1954). A year later, Fillmore Sanford, while executive secretary, characterized the struggles that the Policy and Planning Board had been having over divisional structure, and reported on a study made in the Central Office for that board. A survey was taken of the interests of a random sample of 2,000 members. On analysis, three factors emerged that led Sanford to group member interests into three categories: (a) "making neat and valid generalizations about things," (b) solving the real-life problems of individuals, and (c) dealing with personal matters on a somewhat nomothetic, rather than an ideographic, basis (Sanford, 1955). He could place most of the divisions in the framework of these three clusters.

During the late 1950s, the Council of Representatives debated vigorously each petition to form a new division. Some members of the Council resisted on the grounds of fragmentation and increasing complexity of the APA. Others felt that the health of psychology would be enhanced by letting divisions proliferate, so long as they met the criteria stated in the Bylaws. Thus, between 1945 and 1970, 2 of the charter divisions combined and 12 new ones were recognized (see Table 3).

A comparison of the membership of each of the 17 divisions that

TABLE 3
Division Recognition, 1944–1970

	Division	Year of recognition
20	Adult Development and Aging	1944
21	Applied Experimental and Engineering Psychology	1956
22	Rehabilitation Psychology	1958
23	Consumer Psychology	1960
24	Theoretical and Philosophical Psychology	1962
25	Experimental Analysis	1965
26	History of Psychology	1966

existed in 1950 and that of the 31 that existed in 1970 reveals that total division membership in 1950 represented only 69% of the APA membership of 7,272, whereas, by 1970, total division membership was 120% of the Association membership of 30,831. Apparently, more members began to join one or more divisions. In 1950, the divisions with the largest memberships were Clinical and Abnormal, Consulting and Guidance, and Personal and Social, in that order. Of the 29 divisions recognized in 1970, Personality and Social was the largest, followed by Clinical and Abnormal, and Educational. In 1970, the percentage of the members in each division who were Fellows ranged from 42% in Counseling, 41% in Military, and 37% in Experimental down to 1% in Psychotherapy, and none in Hypnosis or in State Association Affairs. As would be expected, the older divisions tended to have the largest proportion of Fellows. The 41% in Military reflected the fact that a large portion of available, well-trained psychologists were involved in World War II and continued their Division 19 membership although no longer active in Defense affairs.

Over the 25 years covered here, division interests were the leading determinant of the nature of the Association and the way it chose to pursue its three objectives. Divisions planned substantive programs for the annual convention within the time limits allotted to each. They also owned or managed journals and were responsible for certain occasional publications of the Association; by both of these types of publications, they have influenced the range of content in American psychological literature. Another practice that has promoted the unique nature of each division is the requirement that nominations for APA Fellow arise in a division and that the member be known as an "APA Fellow in [division name] Psychology."

State Associations

In 1935, an association of psychologists was formed in the District of Columbia. It set a pattern for the 8 state psychological associations that sprang up around the country in 1939, and for the 2 that followed in 1941.

These 11 organizations had no formal connection with the APA, although many APA members participated in their formation. Several of the 11 were affiliated with the AAAP.

The APA Bylaws published in 1946 recognized the existence of state associations and provided for their affiliation with the APA if 10 or more of their members belonged to the Association. Article XV of these Bylaws stated that "the state organization should be representative of *all* the kinds of interests in psychology in that state" (emphasis added). The Bylaws also created the Conference of State Psychological Associations, which was to be made up of one representative per 100 members of each state body. The Conference elected representatives to the APA Council.

Between 1946 and 1958, associations were established in 34 more states. In response, APA Bylaws were amended to provide for direct representation on the Council from each association (or a combination of two or more smaller associations) with 100 or more members who belonged to the APA. In apparent neglect of the objective stated in the bylaw for across-the-board representation of psychology, the primary interests of state psychological associations soon focused on professional practice and on the promotion of state laws to regulate it. The increased representation on the basis of state association membership moved the substantive balance of the Council toward the professional and practice side.

In the very early years of the new APA, an association committee was established to help in the formation of state associations. It provided, for example, suggestions for model association bylaws that were in harmony with those of the APA. A longtime member of the Central Office Staff, Jane Hildreth, was helpful to members involved in starting new state associations. This was but one of the many relatively new activities in the Central Office undertaken to provide support of professional psychology.

Governance Structure

In this section, I will follow the development of the organizational structure in which members have performed their volunteer service for the Association. This structure includes the officers, the Council of Representatives, and the several boards and committees that, collectively, have come to be called the "governance structure" of the APA. I will then follow with a section concerning the personnel and offices of the Central Office.

Officers of the Association

The president. The design of the new Association created the new office of president-elect. The president-elect was to serve for one year, somewhat in the role of vice president, and then to succeed to the presidency in the second year. Therefore, each year, members were given the opportunity to make nominations for this office and were later furnished ballots for the election. Members ranked the candidates, and the winner was determined by an iterative process known as the Hare system (which was not well understood by the membership at first). During the 1940s, and into the early 1960s, the candidates were usually fairly well known to the electorate through their writings or their presentations at meetings. In 1965, when the Association membership had reached some 24,000, the Council decided that brief biographical sketches of each candidate would accompany the ballot.

The duties and responsibilities of the president-elect and the president were spelled out in some detail in the 1946 Bylaws but only in summary form in the 1970 edition. This change resulted, in part at least, from the developed capabilities of the Central Office staff to handle the bulk of administrative and business matters. The 25 men who served as president during this period are listed in the Appendix. All of them were members of college or university faculties at the time of their presidencies. In terms of their major psychological interests, they may be roughly classified as follows: experimental, 7; social, 5; psychometrics, 4; personality, 4; clinical, 3; educational, 1; and developmental, 1. As Hilgard has pointed out, most of them had served during World War II in uniform or as civilians and had returned to academic life with increased confidence in the usefulness of psychology in practical affairs (Hilgard, 1978, p. 399). Most of them used their presidential addresses to integrate a major segment of their own research and scholarship. Reflecting broadening experiences during the war years, their presentations were concerned with larger projects than were those of prewar presidents. The presidents varied considerably in their interest in and involvement with the operational affairs of the Association, and in their tastes for roles as presiding officer of the Council or chairman of the Board of Directors.[3]

The recording secretary. The Bylaws of 1946 specified that this office be held by a Fellow nominated by the Board of Directors and elected by the Council for a term of 3 years, renewable once. The duties of the secretary were spelled out in some detail, and pertained to keeping the official records of the Association, including the preparation of annual reports of the proceedings of the Board of Directors and the Council. As was the case with the office of president, the 1970 edition of the Bylaws contained much less

---

[3]It should be noted that the APA Oral History Project is currently gathering transcripts of interviews with as many former presidents as possible.

detail about the secretary. Also, the requirement that the holder of this office, and of that of the treasurer, be a Fellow was deleted because of the changes in the requirements for Member and Fellow made in 1958 (as noted earlier). Members of the Central Office staff, particularly Jane Hildreth, provided increasingly valuable service in assisting the secretary at Board and Council meetings and throughout the year as the affairs of the Association grew in volume and complexity.[4]

The treasurer. This office was also defined in the 1946 Bylaws. Like the secretary, the treasurer was to be elected by the Council on nomination by the Board of Directors. Unlike the secretary, he or she was to serve a term of 5 years, renewable once. Again, the duties of this chief financial officer of the Association were spelled out in much more detail in the 1946 edition than in the 1970 edition of the Bylaws. The principal duty of the treasurer was to chair the Finance Committee and, in that capacity, to prepare the annual budget and to present and defend it before the Board of Directors and the Council. Because the publications operation has always been the largest single financial operation of the Association, the treasurer is, ex officio, a member of the Publications Board. As will be related in a later section, the employment of a well-trained specialist in financial matters, and the development of his business staff, gave the psychologist treasurers excellent support and relieved each of a great deal of detail.[5]

The Council of Representatives

The Council was created to be the legislative body of the Association, acting for the membership as a whole at the annual business meetings. The Bylaws of 1946 stated that it "shall have full power and authority over the affairs of the Association, within the limits of these Bylaws." Although these Bylaws authorized the Council to "adopt and publish rules and codes for the transaction of its business, provided they do not conflict with these Bylaws," the Rules of Council were not promulgated until 1960, as will be noted below.

The Council that met in Philadelphia in 1946 was made up of 10 officers and members of the Board of Directors, 9 representatives from geographical regions, 52 from divisions, 2 from the Conference of State Psychological Associations, and 1 Special Representative from an affiliated educational group. These totaled 74 regular members. (At that time, the

---

[4]Those who served as secretary during this quarter century were Donald Marquis, 1946; Helen Peak, 1947–1949; Dorothy Adkins, 1950–1952; Ann Anastasi, 1953–1955; Launor Carter, 1956–1961; Edwin Newman, 1962–1964; and Wilbert McKeachie, 1965–1971.

[5]Those who served as treasurer during the period were Willard Valentine, 1946–1947; Calvin Shartle, 1948–1957; Meredith Crawford, 1958–1967; and William McGeehe, 1968–1974.

presidents and secretaries of the divisions were allowed to attend, which could bring the total attendance up to 113.) Twenty-five years later, in 1970, Council membership totaled 139, made up of the 10 officers and members of the Board of Directors and 96 division and 33 state association representatives.

Ever since the Council began to function, continuing efforts have been made to keep it representative of the entire membership and at a size that would allow for an orderly exchange of views and efficient conduct of business. Representativeness in terms of scientific and professional interests was to be achieved by seating delegates from the divisions. At first, geographical representativeness was sought by including one representative from each of nine rather arbitrarily drawn geographical districts and, to a lesser extent, by representation from the Council of State Psychological Associations. Later, it was achieved by direct representation from each qualified state association.

To control the size of the Council as the APA membership grew, the number of representatives allowed from each division was changed from a fixed fraction of division membership to a percentage of APA members who belonged to a division. State associations whose membership included 100 or more APA members continued to have one representative each.

In 1966–67, representativeness was considered from another angle by a commission headed by George Albee (who was later president of the Association). Because many members belonged to more than one division and some belonged to none, it was proposed that the strength of representation from each division be based on the predominant interests of members of the Association, regardless of their divisional memberships. The commission designed a ballot to be sent to each member. On it, he or she could distribute a total of 10 votes to one or more of the divisions or state associations, the interests of which the member wished to support. The results of such a vote were to determine the portion of a fixed number of seats on Council that would be allotted to each division or state association. After a trial period, this procedure was adopted, to become effective in 1970.

As the work load of the Council increased over the years, a number of steps were taken to provide for a thorough but more efficient conduct of business. In 1965, the Council decided to add a 2-day winter meeting in Washington to the traditional pair of meetings just before and during the annual convention in August or September. In the mid-1960s, presidents began the practice of appointing a parliamentarian to assist in procedural matters; Edwin Newman was the first to serve (in those days, the meetings proceeded under Robert's Rules of Order).

Preparation by the Central Office staff of agenda items for Board or Council use became more formal with the adoption of a rather standardized format, which presented a statement of the issue, its background, and usually a recommendation transmitting the views of the relevant board or committee. Because the Board of Directors had always reviewed each item before its consideration by the Council, the practice was adopted by the Council in 1956 of having the Board star each item it thought should be given explicit attention by the Council. The understanding was that those items not starred would be automatically, unanimously approved unless a Council member raised a specific question. (The 1946 Bylaws set the requirement, still in effect, that any petition submitted by 100 or more Association members, or by a vote of a Division, would be received by the secretary and placed on the agenda of the Board and Council at their next meetings.)

As noted earlier, the Policy and Planning Board proposed an extensive revision of the Bylaws in 1960. Its object was to remove much detail not of direct concern to the membership. The adoption of this revision was the occasion for the preparation of the first set of "Rules of Council," which later evolved into the present "Association Rules." The Rules "detailed the operational and managerial authority needed to conduct the affairs of the Association under the Bylaws" (APA Policy and Planning Board, 1960). These Rules have been subject to continuous updating and revision and have served well in guiding the work of the Council and, in turn, of subordinate boards and committees.

Finally, another improvement in Council operations was made in the early 1950s. It had to do with the preparation of archival records of the proceedings of the Council, the Board, and some committees, which always appeared in the November or December issue of the *American Psychologist*. Because a particular item was usually discussed at the meetings of the Council and the Board at different times during the year, the report of the matter was consolidated into a single item in the year's Proceedings. This change was made while the recording secretary was Launor Carter, who also began the use of a standardized, but somewhat flexible, set of categories for reporting these actions. This system has been used, with some modifications, by succeeding secretaries, which has made it fairly easy to follow the development of a topic over the years.

Boards and Committees

The Board of Directors. The 1946 Bylaws created the Board of Directors as "the administrative agent of the Council of Representatives [with] general supervision over the affairs of the Association." The Bylaws went on to spell out its normal and emergency powers. The Board has always been composed of the Association officers and six persons elected by the Council from its own membership for terms of 3 years. No important changes in the Bylaws statement about the Board appeared in the revision of 1970. The executive officer was added as a nonvoting member (he had always attended meetings), and provision was made for an increase in the number of meetings per year.

However, a somewhat subtle change in wording had significance for the conduct of everyday business. The earlier version stated that the Board should supervise the work of the executive secretary and "other employees of the Association." The quoted phrase did not appear in the 1970 version. The change reflected a possible conflict of relationships that sometimes caused trouble. Because members of the Central Office staff were assigned by the executive officer to support a board or committee, they sometimes made or implied commitments to these groups before first clearing them with the executive officer. Key staff members have usually been invited to sit with the Board, except when in executive session, to supply information. Because all matters going to the Council or coming from it go through the Board of Directors, it has indeed always been the "nerve center" of the Association.

Neal Miller made an interesting comment about the Board of Directors, on which he served a 3-year term in the late 1950s, and the 3 years that surrounded his presidency in 1961. During an interview done as part of the current President's Oral History Project, he said,

> With respect to the Board of Directors as a whole, I was greatly impressed that everyone behaved in a statesman-like manner once they got on the Board. Instead of representing a specific area like experimental psychology, or clinical, or an aspect of applied, they were all working together for the benefit of psychology as a whole. (Miller, 1986, p. 1)

The Policy and Planning Board. The only other board created by the 1946 Bylaws was the Policy and Planning Board, whose nine members were to be elected by the Council, but not necessarily from its own membership. Board members were elected for 3-year terms but were not to serve more than two consecutive terms. The membership of this Board was to represent, insofar as possible, "all the active interests of the Association." The mission of the Board was stated to be "the consideration of current and long-range policy." Its power was limited to the making of recommendations to the membership, the Council, and the Board of Directors, although it could make informal suggestions to a board or committee. Annual reports were required and have been published in the *American Psychologist* each year.

The Bylaws stated that this board was to consider, at 5-year intervals, the "structure and function of the Association as a whole." The composition or mission of this board has not changed significantly over the years. Some of the topics considered by the Board during its first 25 years suggest the range of its concerns: criteria for membership, the certification and licensing of psychologists, the establishment of an accreditation program, nondoctoral training, and the question of what the responsibilities of the Association should be for promoting training in the practical application of social and educational psychology and experimental methodology in real-life situations. Through the years, this board has attempted to stay ahead of the APA ship, helping to chart its course and to instigate repairs when necessary. Its annual reports provide a good record of creative thinking about the APA and provide portents of events to come. As the years went by, its influence became somewhat less as the Board of Directors got more and more into long-range policy. Association presidents who served during these 25 years varied a good deal in how valuable they thought the Board's advice to be.

Other boards, committees, task forces, and special assignments. In addition to the Council and the two boards just discussed, members served on a number of other committees and task forces as representatives to other organizations, as well as on other boards that were created after 1946. In 1946, when the APA membership stood at 4,427, some 84 members (or 1.897% of the membership) served, whereas in 1970, when Association membership totaled 30,839, about 374 (or 1.213%) were involved. Over these years, APA membership increased by a factor of 7, and board and committee membership by a factor of 4.5. Speaking more broadly, as the Association grew, each person serving in the governance structure "represented" a larger number of members.

Of the "standing committees" created by the Bylaws of 1946, three continue with about the same number of members and the same mission. They are the Committees on Finance, Ethics, and Elections, three functions that must be performed in almost any association. The Committee on Publications evolved into the Publications Board, as did the Convention Program Committee into the Board of Convention Affairs. The Committee on Committees, one of the original "standing committees," did not last, but some of its functions were taken over later by a new Committee on the Structure and Function of Council. The Committee on State Psychological Associations was no longer needed after the state associations gained direct representation on Council. The Committee on Public Relations somewhat lost its identity for a while. The responsibility of dealing with the public was spread more widely in the governance structure, and it became more focused in the staff assignments of the Central Office. Interests of the 1946 [Bylaw] Committee on Student Affiliates, together with those of three "special committees" formed in 1946 (the Committee of Departmental Chairmen, the Committee on Audio–Visual Aids, and the Committee on Graduate and Professional Training), melded into the formation of the Education and Training Board. Special Committees on Standards for Psychological Service Centers and on Clinical Psychology were the first two of several special committees that came to report through the Board of Professional Affairs. Similarly, the Committee on Precautions in Animal Experimentation joined other committees formed to report through the Board of Scientific Affairs.

It is apparent that the small number of boards and committees in 1946 did not represent much differentiation in areas of scientific or professional interest, nor, as we shall see, was there a great deal of corresponding differentiation in the staff of the Central Office. However, as the Association grew over the next 25 years, the five new boards referred to above were created by the Council. They were instituted to serve two purposes: (a) to relieve the Board of Directors of supervision of an increasing number of committees, task forces, and representatives to other organizations, and (b) to provide substantive leadership and integration to the efforts of related committees. In 1970, in line with new developments in the budgeting and financial management of the Association, as discussed below, the Council decided to give each board more responsibility for "effective allocation of funds" by allocating funds "to Boards and not to specific committees or activities of Boards" (McKeachie, 1971, p. 48).

By 1970, a matrix of boards and committees had been formed that represented the major thrusts of the Association. They are depicted in Table 4, which shows each board and the subgroups that reported through and were overseen by each. The number of members shown for each group provides a rough index of the relative magnitude of the APA's commitment of volunteer membership time and effort to different areas. As shown, Professional Affairs claimed 109 members, Education and Training 62, and Scientific Affairs 57.[6]

Central Office

As indicated in Chapter 6, it was apparent to the drafters of the new Constitution that the expanded Association would not be able to operate

---

[6]Similar allocations of resources will be shown later in the section on financial management. Some indication of the substantive contributions of these elements of the governance structure will be traced in the third part of this chapter, which deals with the ways the APA pursued two of its main objectives.

TABLE 4
Boards, Committees, Task Forces, and Representatives to Other Organizations, 1970–1971

Board	Other boards (M)	Standing committees		Continuing committees		Ad hoc committees		Task forces		Representatives to other organizations		Total M
		N	M	N	M	N	M	N	M	N	M	
Directors	12	4	20	4	32	4	13	1	7	2	3	87
Convention	7		—	4	15		—		—		—	22
Publications	11		—	1	16		—		—	1	1	28
Education & Training	10		—	3	20	3	17	2	11	3	4	62
Professional	9	7	40	7	40	1	4	6	50	6	6	109
Scientific	9		—	3	15	2	10	1	4	5	19	57
Policy & Planning	9		—		—		—		—		—	9
Totals	67	4	20	22	138	10	44	10	72	17	33	374

Note: N = Number; M = Total Memberships.

on volunteer effort alone, no matter how devoted or diligent the efforts of members like Secretary Willard Olson or Treasurer Willard Valantine. Therefore, Article XVIII of the revised Bylaws opened with the following statement: "The Association shall maintain a Central Office for the promotion of the objectives of the Association and its Divisions." The functions specified included handling the administrative details of the Association, issuing a *Yearbook*, facilitating the member placement service (already begun under the wartime auspices of the National Research Council), promoting public relations, "and such other general and specific services as allocated to it by the Council of Representatives or the Board of Directors." The divisions could procure services from the Central Office if they were consistent with the Bylaws and arranged through the Board of Directors. Paragraph 2 of the Article stated that the Central Office should be located and equipped as directed by the Council. Three other paragraphs provided for the position, and stated the general duties, of the principal employee, the executive secretary, and another specified that a budget for the office was to be submitted by the Finance Committee to the Council (to include an estimate of the expenses of members traveling on Association business). This Article made clear that the principal financial operation of the Association was the journal publication program.

Twenty-five years later, the single paragraph of the Bylaw Article on the Central Office preserved the essence of the original Article without specifying functions, but it added that the Office would provide services to the state associations much as it had been doing for divisions. It is interesting to observe how the phrase in the 1970 Bylaws, "objectives of the Association, *its* Divisions and *the* State Associations" (italics added) highlights the historic difference between the Association's relation to divisions and to state associations.

The Executive Secretary/Officer

In establishing the position of executive secretary of the newly constituted Association, its founders created what has become perhaps the most important position in organized psychology in the country, if not the world. The new Constitution (Article XVIII, p. 37) stated that

> the Association shall employ an Executive Secretary as the administrative agent of the Association and managing director of the Central Office, to work under the supervision of the Board of Directors. He shall be available to the officers and committees for professional consultation in connection with the affairs of the Association.

Nominated by the Board of Directors, the executive secretary was to be elected by a two-thirds majority of the members at a meeting of the Council. The term of office was 5 years, renewable once. The executive secretary's annual report was to concern nonfinancial matters, these being left to the treasurer.

The 1970 edition of the Bylaws reflected the change in the importance and authority of the position that occurred over the years. The title was changed from *secretary* to *officer* and the position was included among the officers of the Association. The incumbent was made a member of the Board of Directors, but without a vote, and his or her annual report could include both financial and nonfinancial matters. No limitation was put on the number of terms that the executive officer might serve. These changes were in response to the increasing load of responsibilities of the position, driven by an expanding and increasingly diverse membership and an ever-growing staff.[7]

In many ways, the most important holder of this office was Dael Wolfle because he was the leader who guided the new organization through its early years. He built an understanding of and confidence in the new arrangement among the membership by his cogent essays in the new house organ, the *American Psychologist*, of which he, like his successors, was editor. In addition to building the first staff of the Central Office, he pioneered in dealing with the federal government on many issues affecting psychology and science in general. He consolidated the journal publication operation and became involved in the preparation of annual budgets of the Association. He brought to the position substantial university classroom experience, wartime service in developing military technical training, and service in the Office of Scientific Research and Development. After some 5 years of service to the APA, Wolfle moved on to direct the first national study of trends in the supply, demand, and education of the nation's "educated professionals." Thereafter, he served as the executive officer of the AAAS until 1970, when he returned to his alma mater, the University of Washington.

Under circumstances somewhat different from those surrounding his successors, Wolfle began his term when the governance structure was small and involved people that he had known well. His era has been characterized as one of hope and challenge. In his first annual report, he wrote that "psychology came out of the war with an excellent reputation as a scientific discipline and as an art which could contribute to the solution of many

---

[7]Six men held this office during this 25-year span. They were Dael Wolfle, 1946–1950; Fillmore Sanford, 1950–1956; Roger Russell, 1956–1960; John G. Darley, 1960–1963; Arthur W. Brayfield, 1963–1969; and Kenneth B. Little, 1969–1975. Space does not allow for an account of the stewardship of each or for detailed backgrounds the expertise that each brought to the position.

human problems" (Wolfle, 1946b, p. 538). Wolfle built effectively on that foundation.

Wolfle's successors tried, in ways appropriate to their times, to serve psychology as broadly and as effectively as he had. Fillmore Sanford knew relatively little about the workings of the APA when he left Haverford College to succeed Wolfle, but he learned rapidly and brought a good-humored approach to his work, to his reports, and to the problem of divisional structure.

Roger Russell was persuaded by then president-elect Lee Cronbach to leave his position in the Spearman Chair of Psychology at the University of London to return to the States to succeed Sanford. Russell brought an international point of view to the Association and stimulated an increasing number of psychological contacts abroad.

John (Jack) Darley had been a veteran of early Association affairs when he took leave from the University of Minnesota to serve for over 2 years in Washington. While in the position, he worked four objectives: (a) increasing the alignment of the policies of the state associations with those of the APA, (b) aiding in the development of graduate education in psychology, (c) strengthening both the scientific and professional aspects of the APA, and (d) cultivating good relations with other organizations, especially the American Psychiatric Association (Darley, 1960). Darley also carried the burden of the early planning of a new headquarters building and was involved in the APA's role in hosting the International Congress of Psychology in Washington, DC, in the summer of 1963.

Arthur Brayfield came from the chairmanship of the Department of Psychology at the Pennsylvania State University to serve for 6 years. He oversaw the significant improvement in the management of APA business affairs that was devised and implemented by Boris Cherney, whom Brayfield hired as the first director of business affairs. This was the first of several actions Brayfield took to supplement a badly overworked staff in the Central Office. He came while final arrangements were being made for the construction of the new headquarters building, and participated heavily in them. Brayfield's annual reports, especially the one for 1965 (Brayfield, 1965), gave insightful and timely commentary on both the operation of the Central Office and the activities of the Association as a whole. He gave frequent testimony before congressional committees and initiated publication of the *Washington Report*, a monthly newsletter, addressed primarily to members of the governance structure, on federal activities affecting psychology. The *Report* was the forerunner of the current *APA Monitor*.

Kenneth Little came from the chairmanship of the Department of Psychology at the University of Denver. He found a strong and functionally organized office, to whose departmental directors he delegated a good deal of authority and responsibility.[8]

Central Office Staff

The growth and differentiation of functions of the Central Office staff parallel the differentiation within the governance structure described above, especially those staff positions in direct support of boards and their associated committees. Growth also took place in administrative and business functions. In 1946, Wolfle assembled a group of 6 people, some of whom had been serving psychological interests during the war at the National Research Council. The staff grew to 13 by 1950, to 30 by 1956, and to 55 in 1961. The substantial increase to a total of 74 in 1963 was the result of the actions that Brayfield successfully recommended, as noted above. By 1966, a total of 93 people were employed, and by 1970 the total complement had reached 141. Thus, from the beginning of the Central Office in 1946 until 1970, the staff increased by a factor of 23, and the Association membership by a factor of 7. Put another way, in 1946 there was one staff member for every 738 members, whereas in 1970 each staffer "served" 218 members. After 1964, the ratio of staff to members grew more gradually, a fact that provided some guidance for projecting space requirements in a new building.

It is not possible to trace in detail here the gradual differentiation of staff or the improvements in the personnel functions of the Central Office. The latter included the development of a salary schedule (patterned after the federal government but not equivalent to it) and a regular procedure for performance evaluation and consultation. In addition, provision for medical insurance and participation in TIAA/CREF retirement programs was made.

Perhaps a summary of the major divisions in the organization chart of 1970 will suggest the principal directions of the differentiation process over the preceding decade. The staff under Brayfield, and later Little in the late 1960s, was organized under three directorates: (a) Communications Management and Development, headed by Harold VanCott, which concerned the publication enterprise and research projects funded by the National Science Foundation; (b) Business Affairs, headed by Boris Cherny, which included accounting, data processing, the financial aspects of publication, and administrative services for the whole office; and (c) Program Administration, headed by the associate executive officer, Charles Gersoni. Included in this last directorate were four offices that supported the four

---

[8]It should be added that the APA Oral History Project has collected recent interviews with Wolfle, Russell, Darley, and Little.

TABLE 5
APA Income, Expenses, and Net Worth

Year	Income	Expense	Net income	Net worth
1945	72	64	8	81
1950	262	239	23	202
1955	437	467	−31	210
1960	905	841	63	412
1965	2,179	2,043	135	827
1970	5,054	5,041	12	1,259

Note: Figures are in thousands of dollars.

boards that then existed (Education and Training, Convention Affairs, Professional Affairs, and Scientific Affairs), Member Services, the Placement Office, and offices of the *Directory* and the *Convention Guide*. Member Services was directed by Jane Hildreth, whose long and effective service in the Central Office was noted earlier. The office handling Public Affairs, headed by Harley Preston, was directly attached to the Executive Office.

Financial Management

Financial history. The opening article in the first issue of the *American Psychologist* stated that the new APA "will cost more because the Association has decided to do more things" (Wolfle, 1946c). His prediction has been amply borne out, as shown in Table 5.

Over the years, the publication of the so-called operating budget has given the membership a very condensed summary of APA activities because many things were included in a single line. The seven categories of income have included six related to publications, whereas the seventh has included income from all other sources: overhead from grants and contracts, receipts from the annual convention, and interest on short-term investments.

Because only the reimbursements for APA overhead from grants and contracts have been counted as income, brief mention should be made of the partial or complete funding of some APA programs by the federal government or private foundations. Such funds were accepted over the whole 25-year period. In 1960, the Council adopted a policy statement that recognized the desirability of performing work that would be helpful to outside organizations or agencies that are of interest to the divisions or state associations. To secure approval by the Board of Directors, proposals had to fall clearly within APA's competence, could not be accomplished by another agency, and could not interfere with ongoing APA activities. Proposals were to be evaluated by the executive secretary and by the board or committee concerned. Between 1960 and 1970, revenue from grants and contracts varied from 7% to 29% of total APA revenue, for an average of 15% (McGeehe, Little, & Cherney, 1971, p. 932).

In these condensed operating budgets, eight categories of expense were shown. Four were related to publications. The other four were (a) total costs of the Central Office, (b) general APA activities, (c) costs of boards and committees (mostly travel expenses of members), and (d) net cost of space occupied. Although this budget format, supplemented by more detailed schedules, yielded useful information and portrayed major changes over the years, it did not provide adequate information for program planning and managerial control.

Program budgeting. As recounted in the treasurer's report for 1965, the Board of Directors and the Council recognized the need for long-range planning, especially in view of the increase in Association activity and its limited cash reserves. As a first step in providing a tool for long-range planning and current cost control, an analysis was made of the 1964 operation that resulted in the identification of 15 programs (Crawford, 1965). Fourteen of them are listed in the first column of Table 6. Each of them is concerned with a particular function of the APA, in support of which certain identifiable expenditures were made. In contrast, those expenditures that were made for general activities that support all the 14 identified programs were spread, in a systematic manner, as indirect costs over each of the 14 programs, as shown in the second column of the table. Some of the 14 programs, notably journals, building operations, and the convention, earned income. This is shown in the next column, and the net cost shown in the fourth column (all but one program showed a deficit). To bring all programs into approximate balance, monies received from member dues were allocated to each program as shown in the fifth column, to produce the results shown in the final column.

On the basis of this analysis of APA activities, the Council adopted a policy statement in 1964; its principal points were as follows: (a) APA affairs should be so managed as to yield, each year, an overall margin of income over expense of 5% to provide for orderly expansion. (b) Each service program that earns direct revenue should be managed to yield an approximate equality of revenue and expense. (c) General service programs should rely on dues income for support.

This general approach facilitated an orderly presentation of the budget to the Board and Council and allowed these bodies to identify and make decisions on expenditures in terms of their judgments of the relative values of each program and to effect trade-offs among them. The budget booklet for 1966 contained 115 pages of detailed, interlocking figures. However, it was not until 1972 that the computerized accounting system was fully

TABLE 6
American Psychological Association Program Budget, 1966

Program	Expenses	Direct program income	Net income before dues allocation	Dues allocation	Net income after dues allocation
State and professional affairs	$ 202,622	$ 0	$ -202,622	$194,136	$ -8,496
Education and training	132,989	0	-132,989	127,422	-5,567
Journals	1,084,690	988,100[a]	-96,590	92,451	-4,139
Convention	101,088	45,500	-55,588	53,216	-2,372
Public information	53,275	0	-53,275	51,046	-2,229
Public affairs	48,395	0	-48,395	46,367	-2,028
Directory	80,174	35,000	-45,174	43,247	-1,927
Manpower	47,803	3,500	-44,303	42,442	-1,861
Scientific information exchange	36,535	0	-36,535	35,011	-1,524
Scientific affairs	26,344	0	-26,344	25,247	-1,097
Building operations	366,566	344,257	-22,309	21,108	-1,201
Employment Bulletin	25,844	12,000	-13,844	13,258	-586
Other publications	28,933	28,200	-733	674	-59
All other	7,982	52,800	44,818	0	44,818
Total	$2,243,240[b]	$1,509,357	$ -733,883	$745,625	$ 11,742

Note: In addition to APA-funded expenses of $2,243,240, it is estimated that there were expenditures of $226,800 for grant- and contract-funded projects. From Crawford, 1965. [a]Includes $250,000 of subscription credits from member dues considered as direct program income. [b]Includes $337,614 of expenses assignable to the Business Affairs Program that were reallocated as indirect expenses to the other 14 programs.

programmed to yield monthly reports providing timely information to program managers with which to exercise cost controls. The system was developed by Boris Cherney with some assistance from the executive officer and the treasurer. With continual refinement, it has served the Association well over the years. When first developed, people from other associations in Washington came to see it and to admire "how the APA does it!"

Successive Locations of the Central Office

When it became clear to the planners of the new APA that an employed, full-time staff would be needed to operate a Central Office, debate ensued about where in the United States it might best be located. During the war years, the extensive psychological activities were centered in Washington, DC. Because the planners forecast that the new Association would have many interactions with the federal government, the choice was Washington, and it has proven to be a wise one.

Renting from the American Association for the Advancement of Science.   After a few months of operations at two sites in the city some distance from each other, the Central Office staff of six or seven was consolidated in the fall of 1947. It moved into the top floor of a large former residence, just off Scott Circle, that had recently been purchased by the AAAS. The space proved to be quite adequate at the time. The AAAS planned to build a new building on that site and to rent space to affiliated societies. The APA planned to occupy one of the suites in it and began making contributions to an AAAS building fund with a check for $5,000.

However, in 1950 Wolfle was authorized to inquire, by mail ballot, about the preferences of the membership for leasing, purchasing, or building to obtain adequate space for the growing Central Office. A strong preference was expressed for some form of ownership—a preference that has been honored ever since. A committee was appointed under the chairmanship of Jerry Clark to look for a suitable purchase. Although he had left the APA by that time, Wolfle was a member of this committee.

The 16th Street residence.   The committee found a fine old residence on 16th Street, also not far from Scott Circle, which was purchased with the help of a building fund—to which contributions by members had been authorized in an earlier year—for about $230,000. The buildings (residence and coach house) were renovated and restored to their original attractive appearance. At that time, when the membership was less than 10,000, these quarters were thought by some to be adequate for the next 50 years (Sanford, 1952)!

The office building on 17th Street.   By 1955, discussion had begun about the foreseen need for more space for the growing staff. In 1959, the Policy and Planning Board made a forecast of staff growth and concluded that the 16th Street building would be outgrown in 2 to 3 years and that the staff would total 100 by 1983. In 1961 the Council "authorized the Board to enter into such obligations as appear desirable to the Board to provide for an adequate headquarters" (Crawford, 1961, p. 775). President Neal Miller appointed an ad hoc Headquarters Committee consisting of Edwin Newman, Ross Stagner, Jack Darley (ex officio), and Meredith Crawford, chairman. The Council had stated that the headquarters should be located in downtown Washington and that it should be adequate for up to 40 years. At the 1961 annual convention in New York, Crawford outlined certain building parameters and stated that the Board would adopt no plan that would increase member dues by as much as $5.00 (Crawford, 1961).

During the following year the Headquarters Committee was shown seven sites in downtown Washington. Only one seemed entirely suitable: a vacant lot of some 17,000 square feet, bounded by Rhode Island Avenue and by 17th and M Streets. The Board authorized its purchase for $1,100,000, to be paid with $350,000 of APA cash and a 3-year note for the remainder. (The revenue from said parking on that lot about equaled the interest on the note.)

The Headquarters Committee then authorized Executive Officer Darley to interview architects and make a recommendation to the Committee. A Washington architect, Vlastmil Koubeck, was engaged. During the next few months he made several concept sketches, and the Committee made several studies of prospects for funding and gaining tenants. The Committee, as amateurs in the construction business, sometimes felt quite overwhelmed by the magnitude of the undertaking. Projections were made of buildings of various sizes that could be built on the newly acquired lot, on the current APA premises on 16th Street, and on another lot of intermediate size. The results of these studies were presented to the Board in May 1962. The Board decided to build a building of maximally allowed size on the new 17th Street site, and presented this plan to the Council in St. Louis in September. Drawings and a model of the new building were on display at that annual convention for attendees to see. The results of financial studies, based on tentative loan commitments and preliminary construction cost estimates, convinced the Council to instruct the Board to go ahead with the construction "of a headquarters building . . . in a manner substantially in accord with the general financial plan and the general architectural concept presented to the Board at its August meeting" and to authorize "the Executive Officer to enter into such obligations as may, with the advice of legal counsel, be deemed wise by the Headquarters Committee" (Newman, 1962, p. 859).

The details of the work of the Headquarters Committee, the surprises and problems encountered, and the necessarily sudden acceptance of building responsibilities by the incoming executive officer, Arthur Brayfield, are recounted in the treasurers' reports for 1962 through 1965. A final summary was presented to the Council and to the membership at the annual convention in Chicago in 1965: The building was complete and fully rented, with the first two floors occupied by the Central Office staff, and the total cost of the land and building was about $4,500,000. Permanent financing for $2,750,000 was furnished by the Morgan Guaranty Company, payable over 25 years at 5%. The Association put about $1,300,000 of its own money into the project. As had been forecast at the previous annual meeting, member dues were increased by $5.00, but it was shown that the action had been taken because of the rapid increase in APA activity over the previous few years and not because of the building project.[9]

POSTWAR INFLUENCE ON PSYCHOLOGY AND ON THE ASSOCIATION

To this point, I have traced how the Association evolved in structure to meet the challenges of the postwar era. In this section, I will discuss certain developments outside of psychology that had a profound influence on the development of psychology and of the Association, especially during the early part of the period under review.

One of these influences was the passage of the "G.I. Bill," which made it possible for at least a million returning service personnel to go to college, and some of those on to graduate school. A new generation of young but mature psychologists entered the Association by this route. Enrollments in higher education swelled, and federal support for education, research, and service became a major factor in providing expanded employment opportunities for psychologists (Darley & Wolfle, 1946).

The experiences of so many members of the Association who served in some capacity during the war expanded their horizons and strengthened their conviction that psychology has an important role to play in practical affairs. In the hands of academic psychologists, operational problems yielded to scientific analysis and reformulation to produce usable results. Accounts

---

[9]The new building was dedicated in a suitable ceremony on October 16, 1965, presided over by APA President Nicholas Hobbs. The speaker was Donald F. Hornig, Special Assistant to President Johnson for Science and Technology.

of this work became part of the literature, as exemplified by the 19-volume report of the Army Aviation Psychology Program (Flanagan, 1946–1947), Bray's account of the work of the Applied Psychology Panel (Bray, 1948), the 4-volume summary of the studies of the motivations and attitudes of service personnel (Stouffer, Suchanan, Devinney, Starr, & Williams, 1949), and the many reports that appeared in the *Psychology Bulletin* and the early volumes of the *American Psychologist*. As will be shown below, the war had an equal or even greater influence on the development of professional psychology.

Donald Marquis was intimately involved in psychological activity in Washington during the war years. He drew on these experiences in preparing his 1948 presidential address, "Research Planning at the Frontiers of Science" (Marquis, 1948). "Psychology has demonstrated its maturity," he stated, and "it can now be expected to be called on to assume the responsibilities of a mature science" (p. 430). His address was about planning large research and development projects that, he said, must occur at three levels: experimental design, program design, and policy design. Psychologists were already good at the first, but few had much experience with the latter two. Such planning, he pointed out, was beginning to be done by psychologists in foundations and in the federal government. These agencies were prepared to fund programmatic efforts in accordance with plans made at the policy level. In sum, Marquis's address painted an enticing picture of a new horizon for psychology.

The National Science Foundation

As the war drew to a close, President Roosevelt, on March 17, 1945, addressed a letter to his director of the Office of Scientific Research and Development, Vannevar Bush, stating that Bush's Office "represented a unique experiment in teamwork and cooperation in coordinating scientific research and applying existing scientific knowledge to the solution of technical problems paramount in war" (Bush, 1945, p. 3). He saw no reason why the lessons learned from that cooperative effort could not be applied in peacetime, and he asked Dr. Bush for recommendations on how to (a) make available much of the new knowledge obtained in wartime, (b) continue the war of science against disease, (c) emphasize and coordinate the roles of public and private agencies in research, and (d) discover and develop scientific talent in American youth.

Dr. Bush's reply constituted the prophetic volume *Science, the Endless Frontier* (1945), which he prepared with the advice of a panoply of prominent scientists and educators with whom he had been associated, including psychologists Walter Hunter and Edwin Land. Its principal recommendation was for the establishment of a new government agency, which turned out to be the National Science Foundation.

In an introduction to the 1960 edition of the Bush report, Dr. Alan Waterman, then director of the Foundation, brought the story up to date, contending that bills authorizing the establishment of the Foundation were introduced in Congress in 1945, but languished for 5 years. During that time, psychologists Walter Miles and Dael Wolfle joined with other scientists on the Intersociety Committee for the Foundation, which urged the passage of enabling legislation. Such legislation was finally passed in May 1960, and provided for the three following divisions of the Foundation: Mathematical, Physical and Engineering, and Scientific Personnel and Education.

Large-Scale Government Funding Begins

The act establishing the Foundation contained the permissive phrase "and other sciences." Under that umbrella, support for psychology began in 1952, although the Office for Social Science was not established until 1958. During the early 1950s, psychology was represented on the Foundation staff by a few psychologists led by John Wilson, who later became assistant director of the Foundation (and, eventually, the president of the University of Chicago).

One of the original responsibilities of the Foundation was to collect and publish, each year, information about federal funding of research by all government agencies. Wilson and his colleagues did this for psychology for the fiscal years 1953 through 1958 (Young & Odbert, 1959), reporting by agency, region, and area of psychology. Expenditures for psychology rose from $10.2 million to $23.9 million over those 6 years. In that time span, the portion of funding supplied by the Department of Defense dropped from 78% to 24%, and that of the Department of Health, Education, and Welfare rose from 15% to 70%. Total funding for psychology by the Foundation itself rose from 0.9% to 4.7% of its total.

Federal funding for psychological research and training continued to rise after 1958, but began to level off in the late 1960s, reaching a point, in 1970, not to be exceeded for some years. The Boards of Scientific and of Professional Affairs, together with Central Office staff, have kept up with developments "on the hill" and have given testimony before congressional committees on funding for psychology.

The Digital Computer

The rapid development of the digital computer from the end of the war through 1970 had a profound effect on many aspects of American life. In the early 1940s, the means of data reduction, test scoring, and other repetitive kinds of operations were revolutionized by punch cards, sorters, machines with hard-wired programs, and other mechanical devices pioneered by IBM. Such equipment became essential to many psychological research and testing operations.

Early versions of the digital computer, using vacuum tubes as relays, were developed during wartime and were installed at large universities and research corporations such as the System Development Corporation, an operational offshoot of the Rand Corporation. With the invention of the transistor to replace vacuum tubes, computers increased in storage capacity and decreased in overall size. In the late 1960s, the IBM 360 series represented the kind of equipment used in psychological research, in business, and in many other applications.

During the late 1950s, a number of articles appeared in the *American Psychologist* on the advantages of computers for data reduction (see Ward, 1955). Computers also came to be useful in the laboratory for timing stimulus presentation and other events. The Association itself, as noted earlier, was able to bring its financial and membership information under immediate control, and its publication operation, especially the extended services of the *Abstracts*, were developed around the computer.

In addition to these uses of the new tool (uses that were not unique to psychology), the advent of the computer was beginning to have an impact on psychological theorizing. The "systems approach" to psychotechnology, as set forth in a volume edited by Robert Gagné (1962) and in its foreword by Arthur Melton, shaped thinking about man–machine relationships. Concepts of input and output, programming, and even mental processes were markedly influenced as psychologists began to use computers, to think in computer terms, and to compare human and computer performance. An early example was Hovland's 1960 paper on attempts to simulate human thinking with the computer. It may be observed that the groundwork was being laid, even in those early years, for the later "cognitive revolution" (Gardner, 1985).

TWO MAJOR FUNCTIONS OF THE ASSOCIATION

Functions are identified by the objective toward which they are directed, and described by the statements of mission that set them up. In the

APA, six major functions can be identified, as well as a number of minor ones that contribute to them. Each of three of these has as its object the accomplishment of one of the three objectives of the Association: the promotion of psychology as a science, as a profession, and as a means of promoting human welfare. These may be called *direct* functions. The other three are *supporting* or *enabling* functions; they support the Association and its members engaged in the direct functions. These are the functions of education and training, conduct of the annual convention, and publication. At various times between 1945 and 1970, boards were established to coordinate the work of existing committees and task forces in five out of the six functional areas (no board primarily concerned with seeing that psychology contributed to the public welfare was formed until after 1970). Only two of the direct functions have been chosen for discussion in this chapter.[10]

Promotion of Psychology as a Science

Scope

As defined in the Bylaws of 1970, the scope of the Board of Scientific Affairs included concern for the continued encouragement, development, and promotion of psychology as a science. In particular, the Board was to guide the scientific programs at the annual convention, maintain liaison with other relevant scientific bodies, cultivate relationships with agencies and organizations that furnish funding for psychological research, and operate a program of awards to members for outstanding scientific achievement. As a further delineation of scope, the following were committees that reported through the Board in 1970 (some of which had been of long standing): Precautions and Standards in Animal Experimentation, Ethical Standards for Research on Human Subjects, Psychological Tests, Educational Uses of Tests With Underprivileged Groups, Family Planning and Population Policy, and Scientific Awards.

Also, the Board had the responsibility of nominating members of the Association to represent it to the following scientific bodies: the AAAS, the National Research Council, the Social Science Research Council, the Intersociety Color Council, and the National Society for Medical Research. A continuing responsibility felt by scientist members has been to explain

---

[10]The Association's concern with the public welfare is treated in Chapter 11, "The American Psychological Association and Social Responsibility." The publication enterprise is discussed in Chapter 12, "The APA Knowledge Dissemination Program." Some aspects of the work of the Education and Training Board will be included in the following section on the profession of psychology, and passing reference to the Board of Convention Affairs will be included later in the section on science.

to the public and to other scientists the nature of psychological research, especially that which supports theory building—as opposed to developmental efforts that produce usable psychotechnology. For example, procedures for using animals have been continually upgraded and publicized (protest groups were active before 1945). Psychological tests also needed explanation and defense before congressional committees and to the public. It should be added that the scientific aspects of the Association's relationships with international bodies has been a responsibility shared by the Board.

Early Science Activities

Because the APA, before it joined with the AAAS, was primarily a scientific society, it is not surprising that concern for science was manifest from the outset of the new Association. In the late 1940s, the Policy and Planning Board devoted a good deal of attention to scientific matters. For example, in 1949, the Board received a report from its subcommittee on science saying that the Association needed a statement "of criteria for examining the state of any research in any field or area of psychology" (APA Policy and Planning Board, 1949, p. 318). The Board perceived an urgent need to review the research responsibilities of all psychologists, because the Association had been "thrown off balance by recent emphasis on professional problems." Many members also felt that more effective use could be made of existing resources of scientific talent, whose work could demonstrate the value of many fields, even some outside of psychology. Finally, the Policy and Planning Board was becoming increasingly aware of the growing amount of funds available for research.

With these considerations in mind, the Board pointed out several things that needed to be done: development of a means of identifying important areas of research, facilitation of the recruiting and training of research talent, and discovery of the factors that promote and those that inhibit research productivity. The Board recommended the appointment of a special committee, with power to appoint subcommittees, to dig into these three areas. Although action by the Council or Board of Directors did not occur immediately, discussion continued.

The Scientific Development Board

In 1954, the Council approved a recommendation of the Board of Directors that a Scientific Development Board be established "to perform such types of activity, as the Council may approve, directed toward the advancement of psychology as a science" (APA Scientific Development Board, 1955, p. 757). Nine prominent scientists were appointed: Arthur

Melton (Chair), Lee Cronbach, Richard Eberhart, Paul Farnsworth, Leon Festinger, Carl Hovland, Lyle Lanier, Kenneth Spence, and Benjamin Underwood. The Council suggested certain methods that might improve the quality and productivity of psychological research for the new Board's consideration.

After two meetings in 1954, between which the Board solicited comments on a draft report from some 300 members of the governance structure, a final report was submitted to the Council (APA Scientific Development Board, 1955). Its first two recommendations seem to have reflected the tenor of the times. One urged the membership to recognize that the development of scientific psychology was a responsibility of the existing Boards— Policy and Planning, Education and Training, and Publications—as well as of the Board of Directors and Council. The other recommended the dissolution of this new Board after the Council meeting at the 1955 Convention, which was done.

The report made the general observation that several psychologists had begun to worry about questionable inferences from the literature of scientific psychology "that have casually been made to support certain types of professional activity" (APA Scientific Development Board, 1955, p. 759). The Board bemoaned what its members believed was the inadequacy of the preparation for scientific work that new PhDs were receiving. However, it did state that the APA was doing what it could to remedy the situation. Interestingly enough, the Board stated that the APA should do nothing to discourage the formation of other psychological societies designed to promote research.

The Board's specific recommendations will be summarized here because many actions of the Council over the next decade can be traced to one or more of them. The first group of recommendations, directed primarily to the Education and Training Board, concerned the means for improving psychologists' competence in research. They included the sponsorship of summer seminars on experimental design and inference, studies of the abilities of applicants for graduate training, and a conference of "pioneer" researchers to estimate the knowledge and skills required to master the literature and to develop scientific psychology over the next decade.

The five recommendations in the second group were directed toward obtaining financial support for research. The editor of the *American Psychologist* was urged to solicit brief articles on sources of support, and the Association's representatives to the National and Social Science Research Councils were urged to advocate increased support for psychology. The Publications Board was requested to consider the issuance of a monograph series presenting critical reviews of areas of research (no mention was made of the *Annual Reviews of Psychology*, which were started by Annual Reviews, Inc., in 1950). The APA was encouraged to affirm the value of special conferences on specific research problems, and the Board of Directors was called on to form a group to advise it on the selection of participants.

A third group concerned methodology, although Board members were cautious about prescribing too rigidly. A list was presented of current research topics the advancement of which would be hastened by conferences on methodology. The 17 areas suggested included mostly laboratory activities current at the time, such as eyelid conditioning, Skinner boxes, stress techniques, and so forth. Another recommendation was to seek support from the National Research Council for the dissemination, through the *American Psychologist*, of information on methods for data reduction. Another suggested that Council support the standardization of laboratory equipment.

A fourth group included the recommendation that APA establish three "Distinguished Scientific Contributions Awards" in the areas of general experimental psychology, social and personality psychology, and psychometrics and methodology.

Distinguished Scientific Contributions Awards Program

The selection of recipients for this award was begun in 1956. The recipients that first year were Wolfgang Kohler, Carl Rogers, and Kenneth Spence. A committee of four was elected each year to make the selections; one member was held over from the previous year to chair the new committee and lend some continuity to the procedures. Former recipients and the current president and president-elect were not eligible. Each year, selection committees have striven to select recipients from different areas of scientific psychology. A total of 45 members were so honored during the period from 1945 to 1970; they are listed in the Appendix.

Projects A and B

In 1952, two years before the Scientific Development Board was appointed, the Policy and Planning Board concluded, from an intensive discussion of the state of psychological science and of research productivity, that the time was ripe for "a major investigation of interrelated questions about psychological personnel, education and employment, including an appraisal of the state of development of the science of psychology" (Wolfle, 1957). This was conceived at the outset as two separate studies, labeled *Projects A and B*, the latter of which was completed before the first product of Project A became available.

This publication, the final report of Project B, was titled *America's*

Psychologists (Clark, 1957). The seven volumes produced by Project A appeared between 1959 and 1963 under the general title *Psychology: A Study of a Science* (Koch, 1963). The committee that was appointed to steer both projects was chaired by Dael Wolfle and included Clarance Graham, Lyle Lanier, Robert McLeod, Elliot Rodnick, Brewster Smith, and Robert Thorndike. The bulk of the funding for both projects was provided by the National Science Foundation, as recommended by psychologist John Wilson, who also gave counsel throughout both projects. The Association added funds for the completion of Project A.

Project B was accomplished under the direction of Kenneth E. Clark, then at the University of Minnesota. The panel that served as consultants included Smith and Thorndike from the Steering Committee, as well as Raymond Bauer, John Stalnaker, and Milton Wexler. The study was devoted to the identification of psychological research personnel and an appraisal of their training. The focus of interest was on how certain scientists are attracted to psychology and what influences in graduate school and subsequent career settings seem to promote creative research and scholarship. Conclusions were carefully drawn from the data gathered, and they were received with little surprise because they seemed to confirm the thinking of the psychologists who were in charge of most of the "good" departments in the country.

Project A was directed by Sigmund Koch of Duke University. His panel of consultants included Lanier of the steering group, Howard Kendler, Conrad Meuller, and Karl Zener. Dael Wolfle set forth the need for Project A with the following words:

> A growing body of empirical information, a serious concern over methodological issues and a variety of efforts to bring a selected body of fact into the organizing framework of theory all emphasize the need for that line of questioning—always going on in science—which explores the shape of knowledge, the range and inner connections of the ideas through which it has been developed and organized, the changing substructures of empirical data, and their emerging relations to each other and to the findings of other sciences. The seven volumes of *Psychology: A Study of a Science* are a response to this need. (Wolfle, 1963, p. vii)[11]

---

[11]A review of the contents of these volumes, written by some 80 authors, is, of course, outside the scope of the present volume. It must suffice to list the titles: Study I. Conceptual and Systematic: Vol. 1. *Sensory, Perceptual and Physiological Formulations*; Vol. 2. *General Systematic Formulations, Learning and Special Processes*; Vol. 3. *Formulations of the Person and the Social Context*. Study II. Empirical Substructure and Relations With Other Sciences: Vol. 4. *Biologically Oriented Fields: Their Place in Psychology and in Biological Science*; Vol. 5. *The Process Areas, the Person, and Some Applied Fields: Their Place in Psychology and Science*; Vol. 6. *Investigations of Man as Socius: Their Place in Psychology and the Social Sciences*. As a postscript to the study, Volume 7 was authored by director Koch alone under the title *Psychology and the Human Agent*. The sale of these volumes was good, and they were used for some years by graduate students. The Association enjoyed some royalties from the publisher, McGraw-Hill.

The Psychonomic Society

The increasing concern about the Association's apparent lack of interest in the scientific aspects of psychology, the relatively low support for it among the Association's programs (see Tables 4 and 6), and the competition for convention time with other interests within the Association led to the establishment of the Psychonomic Society in 1960. A group of 10 prominent research psychologists, including some who were involved in the projects just discussed, formed the organizing committee. They asserted the need of the scientific community, which was not being met by the APA, for more and better communication among themselves. The organizers said that this did not represent a secession from APA, and it is true that many who joined continued their Association membership. Nevertheless, this was an important event in the history of scientific psychology in the APA because it called further attention to the gulf that was widening between professional psychologists and the scientific members.

Focus on Behavior

As indicated above, explanations to a general public audience of what research psychologists were about was part of the mission assigned to the Board of Scientific Affairs, which came into being in 1957. During the early 1960s, the Board persuaded the Association to prepare a television series, "Focus on Behavior," for National Educational Television. At the time, many educational television programs were little more than classroom lectures on film, with perhaps a few demonstrations. This series, by contrast, let the viewer see how psychological data are gathered, and allowed him or her to draw his or her own conclusion. A special advisory committee was appointed to work with some 25 psychologists in the production (by Mayer-Sklar, Inc.) of ten 30-minute programs, which were as follows: "The Conscience of a Child," "A World to Perceive," "The Brain and Behavior," "The Chemistry of Behavior," "Learning About Learning," "No Two Alike," "The Social Animal," "The Need to Achieve," "Of Men and Machines," and "Computers and Human Behavior." John Darley served as an effective moderator of each program. They were shown by more than 80 educational television stations around the country and were distributed to colleges and universities (Sherburne, 1964).

Publication and Scientific Psychology

Although not an area of APA activity directly in the purview of the Board of Scientific Affairs, the APA publication enterprise (see Chapter 12) has provided an essential means of promoting psychology as a science.

Certain important publication activities should be recognized in this section.

In 1955, a new journal of book reviews was launched under the editorship of the eminent psychological scientist Edwin Boring. Although the entire field of psychology has been kept under surveillance for new titles to be reviewed, *Contemporary Psychology* has been especially useful in keeping scientists informed about books that they should know, illustrating the truth of the statement that "a science is its books."

Over the 25 years spanned by this chapter, production of the *Psychological Abstracts* grew from a modest, manual operation in the offices of Walter Hunter at Brown University to a major program of the Central Office, involving a full-time staff, many carefully trained abstractors, and the latest computer-based equipment. Because the *Abstracts* provided such an important service to the scientists in the Association, the National Science Foundation found it appropriate to provide funds to allow for the publication of an accumulated backlog of abstracts to bring the service up-to-date. This subvention was only a relatively small part of a decade of cooperation between the Foundation and the Association toward improvements in the means of communication among scientists. During these years, all sciences were concerned with communication, and steps were being taken at high governmental levels (specifically, the President's Scientific Advisory Council) to develop the National Technical Information Service.

In June 1959, the Board of Scientific Affairs conducted a study of several problems in the promotion of psychological science. The Board concluded that "of all the problems considered, the efficient and effective communication of scientific information presents one of the most critical problems to psychology today" (APA Policy and Planning Board, 1959, p. 267). In planning an attack on this problem, the Board of Scientific Affairs identified needs for (a) rapid communication, (b) opportunities for face-to-face discussions among scientists, and (c) an efficient method of storage and prompt, selective retrieval of research results, as well as location of integrative summaries of an area. It was decided that a comprehensive study of the policies of editors, convention schedulers, graduate faculties, and sponsors of research should be made, including an assessment of the importance of publication in the career progress of psychological scientists.

A proposal was made to the National Science Foundation for support of a "Project on Scientific Information Exchange," to be headed by William Garvey and Belvor Griffith, beginning September 1, 1961. The Board appointed a Project Advisory Panel that included Kenneth E. Clark (chair), Raymond Bauer, Dorwin Cartwright, John Darley (then executive officer), Quinn McNemar, and Donald Taylor.

At the end of the first 2 years, the project had completed a comprehensive description of the mechanisms and flow patterns of information generated by researchers. The relative roles of oral communication, journals, reviews, abstracts, and so on were determined. From these findings, a theory of information flow and a method of measuring the effects, throughout the whole system, of specific innovations were developed. In addition, certain criteria were stated for the selection of innovations to be tried out.

Two new procedures in the APA communication system were tried out. In the first, five journals were selected that had long lead times between acceptance of manuscript and their publication. Each of these journals began to list, in each issue, the manuscripts accepted and their authors. This gave interested researchers a chance to contact authors well in advance of seeing the written report. "Professional courtesy" supplied a good portion of inquirers with information that was much more current than what was reaching the readers of five other journals that did not list manuscripts accepted (the control group). A second innovation was the publication of blocks of scheduled papers in advance of the annual convention. This, too, improved the effective speed of information flow (Garvey & Griffith, 1966).

Based in part on the findings of these studies, and because of the pressure of acute Central Office problems in keeping up with scientific information exchange, a proposal was made by the Association, in February 1967, to the Office of Scientific Information Services of the National Science Foundation for a 2-year effort to develop a National Information System for Psychology, at a cost of $968,000 (Brayfield, 1970). Plans for this big study were summarized by Harold Van Cott, then director of communications and management development in the Central Office (Van Cott, 1970).

These joint explorations and developments make it clear that the productive scientist does not and cannot work alone, but must be able to communicate and interact with scientists of like interests. Thus, the primary function of a scientific organization is to provide a convenient means for achieving that collegial association. Those who joined the Psychometric Society in 1960, as well as those who joined the American Psychological Society 28 years later, must have concluded that the APA could not meet their needs in this matter.

Promotion of Psychology as a Profession

At the outset of this section, a word should be said about terminology. At one time, almost any member of the Association might refer to psychology as a *profession*. Psychologist—scientist Robert M. Yerkes, in describing the work of academic psychologists in World War II, frequently referred to the "profession of psychology" (Yerkes, 1918). The *Random House Dictionary* defines a profession as "a vocation requiring knowledge of some department of learning or science." Any member of the Association could, under that definition, be a *professional.* Over the years, however, the scope of professional psychology has become restricted to the "practice" of psychology.

The mission statement of the Board of Professional Affairs, which was activated by the Council of Representatives in 1957 (APA, 1957a), said that it would be "concerned with all aspects of psychology as a profession and . . . the formulation of recommendations for the Association's policy in professional matters. . . ." These included the establishment of standards for professional practice, the maintenance of satisfactory relations with other professions, and the fostering of the application of psychological knowledge to the promotion of the public welfare at both the state and federal levels. As was prescribed for the Board of Scientific Affairs, the composition of the Board of Professional Affairs should "be broadly representative of all psychology" in all its aspects (APA, 1957b), reflecting, it would appear, the effort of the Policy and Planning Board to maintain some unity of psychology.

In 1957, several groups that had been involved with professional psychology for some years, began to report through this new Board. While one of the Board's committees, that on Academic Freedom and Conditions of Employment, might have met the needs of almost any member of the Association, the remaining seven committees, five task forces, and one advisory panel (see Table 4) limited their concerns to state legislation, insurance reimbursement, standards for psychological service facilities, and participation in national programs for health care. Other committees assigned to the Board were responsible for matters of a more substantive nature, involving aspects of the technology of practice and concerning such topics as clinical assessment, behavior classification, and therapeutic procedures, all in support of clinical-type practice. Little attention seems to have been directed to other areas of applied psychology.

Clinical Psychology: The Prototype Profession

Clinical and counseling psychology had their beginnings at least as early as the 1920s. For the most part, practice was done by individuals, working more or less alone, who had no common definition of their field. Finally, in 1935, a committee was formed that was chaired by Arthur Brown, who defined clinical psychology as "that art and technology that deals with adjustment problems of human beings" (Peterson, 1982, p. 20). As preparation for practice, the Committee favored a 4-year training program leading to the PhD. It would include general education in psychology from its biological through its social aspects, and a year of supervised, practical experience. Not much happened in the definition or promotion of this kind of professional psychology until the mid-1940s.

The remaining part of this chapter will follow some of the major activities of the "new" Association in the promotion of the developing profession. Demonstrations of the competence and usefulness of professional psychologists, especially clinical and counseling psychologists, during the war were noted earlier. Toward the end of the war, the Army, the Army Air Force, and the Navy, together with the Veterans Administration, needed much professional assistance in caring for servicemen and veterans with mental and emotional problems. They, along with the National Institutes of Health, created a demand that university departments training psychologists found hard to meet. In fact, for some years, demand consistently outpaced supply. The government agencies turned to the APA for help.

In responding, an immediate concern of the Association was for the competence of those who would practice and for their selection and training. Purely scientific societies depend on collegial interaction and peer review of writings for quality control, whereas associations whose members offer their services to the public for a fee rely on more formal controls. Within the APA there have been, for many years, two sharply contrasting views of practice. Many of the more scientific members have doubted that the developing science of psychology provides practitioners with enough solidly derived, relevant information. Other psychologists, although aware of the limitations of current science, have felt strongly that psychologists should respond to urgent human need as best they can. Despite these differences of opinion, the Association, in the years immediately following the war, embarked on at least six different efforts to ensure the quality of psychological practice. They will be noted in the following sections.

The American Board of Examiners in Professional Psychology

Almost at the last minute before the new APA Bylaws went into effect, the Council, at its meeting in Columbus, Ohio, in December 1945, voted to put before the membership an amendment authorizing the Association to establish the American Board of Examiners in Professional Psychology (ABEPP). Undoubtedly, the Council recognized the growing demand for professional psychologists and wanted the Association to be prepared for it. The amendment authorized the appointment of a nine-member Board of APA Fellows who were "representative of the areas of psychology that furnish professional services to the public." This Board was to recommend to Council standards for certification, and to administer them "by receiving applications from candidates and examining their training, experience, and demonstrated competence" (APA, 1946a, pp. 38–39). Those meeting the standards would be awarded diplomas naming their area of specialization. The Board could appoint committees of Fellows to advise it on standards and to help in the examination of applicants. The Board was to meet at least annually and to report each year to the Council and the membership. It was authorized to charge a fee for examination; Board expenses were to be met by the Association.

The ABEPP was incorporated as an organization separate from the APA by John Jenkins, Walter Bingham, and Dael Wolfle in April 1947. Even though the Board's members were elected by Council, it was independently incorporated so that the Association would not be liable for actions that might be brought against the Board. The ABEPP began work soon after incorporation. It received many applications from members under the "grandfather" provisions, which expired at the end of 1949. In the APA *Directory* for 1949–1950, a total of 847 diplomates were listed, constituting 12.5% of the Association membership of 6,735. There were 573 diplomates in clinical, 155 in counseling, and 119 in industrial psychology.

During 1950, a group of prominent APA members wrote to the Board asking that it publicize its procedures and the nature of its examinations for all members to see. The principal concern was with some who were certified under the grandfather provisions, which required the doctorate and 5 years of "acceptable" experience, a requirement that the Board found hard to define. The Board replied to the letter, and matters were clarified. Also, in 1950, the question was raised about the desirability of an appeals procedure for ABEPP decisions. Three past presidents sat with the Board during 3 days of deliberations and concluded that such a mechanism was not needed.

An extensive report in 1955 (ABEPP, 1955) furnished information on Board procedures and on the examination, which had written and oral phases. The former involved objective questions in the candidate's field, a lengthy statement by the candidate testifying to his or her competence in the field, and essay questions on clinical and scientific matters and on professional relationships. The oral examination consisted of a required performance in a real-life setting—a clinic or an industrial plant—that called for a diagnosis or evaluation and an appropriate prescription for therapy or recommendation for change. Through July 1955, 72 candidates had been examined; 39, or 54%, passed on the first try, and 7 on the second.

The ABEPP has continued its activity up to the present. Its diplomates are generally recognized as leaders in their professional fields. In many ways, this program is the APA's most valid and reliable method for identifying professional competence, although at a level to which many practitioners do not aspire.

Graduate Education and Accreditation

A second kind of effort by the Association to ensure the quality of psychological practice has been represented by a continuing concern with the nature of graduate education in psychology and the accreditation of programs that prepare students to enter one of the psychological professions. As indicated earlier, governmental agencies needing clinical and counseling psychologists during and immediately after the war turned to the reconstituted Association for guidance about which programs were graduating competent beginning professionals and should thus be given government support.

The view that this constituted a legitimate request was exemplified in the report of the Committee on Graduate and Professional Training, chaired by Sidney Pressy, in 1946 (APA, 1946b). It stated that "programs of graduate and professional training should be a major responsibility for any professional organization." It went on to discuss "the expansion and diversification of psychological work resulting from the war and the increased professional responsibility which the new Association is likely to assume" (APA, 1946b).

Because of the recognition that the selection of components of curricula designed to prepare students for professional work requires an accepted delineation of the area of practice and a statement of the knowledge and skills required to perform, there were efforts in the mid-1940s to examine both the current training programs and the details of professional practice. Calvin Shartle accomplished analyses of several professional and subprofessional positions (Shartle, 1946). Robert Sears chaired a Committee on Graduate and Professional Training, which corresponded with some 45 graduate departments (this committee had begun its work just before the Veterans Administration requested help from the APA). The findings of the Committee on Graduate and Professional Training resulted in a listing of graduate programs and a tabulation of the important features of each (Hilgard & Sears, 1986, p. 11; Sears, 1946). At about the same time, the Committee on Training in Clinical Psychology (1947), chaired by David

Shakow, was at work on its task. Sears's committee issued a more detailed report in 1947 (Sears, 1947).

Space limitations do not permit a detailed account here of the development of the APA accreditation program (see Crawford, 1982; Peterson, 1982). Suffice it to say that there were two kinds of activities undertaken: (a) the development of a definition of *professional psychologist* and the appropriate training for such an occupation and (b) the development of a set of criteria with which to assess such a program and the development and codification of a set of procedures under which the accreditation process should operate.

The first of these undertakings was the subject of several conferences of psychologists of various interests, both professional and nonprofessional. The first of these conferences, held in Boulder, Colorado, in 1947, established the "scientist–professional" model for professional training (Raimy, 1950). This model, which places as much emphasis on education in general, experimental, and theoretical psychology as on training that is specifically professional, was widely accepted at the time and exerted a major influence over the next two decades. Six other conferences were held before 1970, the most influential of which were those held at Stanford in 1955 (Strother, 1956), in Miami Beach in 1958 (Roe, Gustad, Moore, Ross, & Skodzk, 1959), and at the University of Chicago in 1965 (Hoch, Ross, & Winder, 1966).

At the last of these, a substantial movement away from the scientist–professional model was well under way. The concept of the Doctor of Psychology (PsyD) degree had been accepted the year before at the University of Illinois, and a professional curriculum leading to its award was being developed there by Donald Peterson and colleagues. In 1969, apart from any university, the California State Psychological Association, along with other practicing psychologists, organized the California School of Professional Psychology. By 1970, 10 "practitioner/model" programs in professional psychology had been established: four at universities, one each at a medical and a theological school, and four as freestanding, independent institutions (Caddy, 1982).

Before the concept of outright professional training had gained considerable acceptance, the first set of criteria to be used for accreditation purposes was set forth by Shakow's committee, based on a concept that anticipated the scientist–practitioner one. Using these criteria, the APA first undertook the formal process of accrediting doctoral programs in clinical psychology. The process was extended to counseling in 1950 and to school psychology in the late 1960s. The criteria were revised in 1952 and were more formally codified by the Education and Training Board in 1958, not to be revised again until 1973. Toward the end of the 1960s, the Association sought and obtained the approval of its accreditation by the National Commission on Accrediting (which later became the Commission on Postsecondary Accreditation) and, later, the U.S. Office of Education, whose concerns are with the consensus of professional input into the criteria and the fairness of the procedures. A revised set of procedures was approved by the APA Council in 1969 and promulgated in 1970 (Education and Training Board, 1970a).

Practical, hands-on training has always been a part of the training of professionals. In psychology, the distinction was made early between *practicum* and *internship* training. In the former, which usually started in the first year of graduate programs along with classroom work, students learn the techniques of administering tests, taking personal histories, and so forth. In contrast, internship training is a full-time occupation in a hospital, counseling service, school, or commercial establishment. Debate has continued about whether the internship should be done before or after the awarding of the doctorate (the former has long been accepted by the APA). In the early days, most of the internships were completed in the same institution as was the doctoral program, and were known as "captive internships." Soon, however, internships were set up in centers outside of academia. Accreditation of internships by the APA began in 1956 on the basis of criteria developed during the early 1950s.

As of the annual convention of 1970, 81 doctoral programs in clinical psychology were accredited, 22 in counseling psychology, and just a few in school psychology. A total of 97 internships in clinical and 6 in counseling psychology had received APA accreditation (Education and Training Board, 1970b).

A new body, not directly affiliated with the APA, called the National Council on Graduate Education in Psychology had been organized around 1964 (Peterson, 1982). Recognizing that the universities were not turning out enough professional psychologists to meet the demand, especially in clinical psychology, the Council began the promotion of more strictly professional training. The effect of this movement became more and more compelling during the 1970s and 1980s, contributing to the ever-widening scientist–practitioner cleavage. This effect became manifest when the Association's accrediting of university programs began: Some members thought so strongly that it was inappropriate for the APA to be involved in passing judgment on elements of the curricula of universities that they resigned.

Certification and Licensing

Another continuing effort to promote the quality of professional practice has been in the area of the certification and licensing of individual practitioners. This is basically a legal procedure and is a matter of state jurisdiction. Therefore, state psychological associations have been the primary and proper organizations to petition and advise state legislatures on the drafting and enactment of good laws and the constitution of proper boards.

In his article on the first three pages of the new *American Psychologist*, Wolfle accepted as fact that psychologists would have to obtain some legal status if they were to offer their services to the general public (Wolfle, 1946c). As he recognized, the APA was not the proper body to interact with state legislatures, but it did go on to perform a valuable service in providing forums for discussion of the issues and in preparing appropriate models of state legislation.

At the annual convention in Denver in 1949, the Association hosted a symposium arranged by the Conference of State Psychological Associations. Presentations by several psychologists clarified a number of problems to be solved in bringing about adequate state legislation. The Conference defined and contrasted the two forms of legal identification. *Certification* is optional on the part of the practitioner and simply identifies him or her as a competent professional. Obviously, incompetents do not seek certification, but they are not restricted from practice. *Licensing*, on the other hand, is mandatory and offers protection to the public. The Conference recommended the latter but suggested that certification might be a useful first step toward licensing. It was also concluded that licensing should be general, without specification of specialty (the APA Code of Ethics prohibits practicing outside of one's qualified specialty).

The Conference also set forth some responsibilities that organized psychology would have to accept if it was to be licensed as a profession. These responsibilities included the education of students in the requirements of licensing and their indoctrination in the paramount concern they must have as they enter practice: the welfare of the public. The Conference also concluded that organized psychology needed to develop a code of ethics, apparently unaware that the work of the APA committee chaired by Nicholas Hobbs (1948) was already under way. The advantage of having a great deal of uniformity in the legislation of the different states was pointed out (see Wolfle, 1950).

Over the years, the Conference and the staff of the Central Office have guided state associations in the nature of certification and licensing and in the ideal composition and function of state psychological examining boards. The inclusion of general as well as professional psychologists and of a "public" (nonpsychologist) member on the boards was recommended. (Again, Jane Hildreth has played a valuable role in coordinating and disseminating information from the Central Office.) By 1970, acceptable legislation had been enacted in 43 states, 35 of which were licensing and 8 of which were certifying. Of the five provinces of Canada with recognized legislation, all offered only certification.

Two Other Means of Quality Control

Mention should be made of two other ways in which the Association has sought to maintain the quality of psychological services and materials offered to the public. One has to do with the quality of individual and group providers of psychological services and the development of standards for the listing of individuals or centers in a directory of APA approvals. In 1950, the Committee on Standards for Psychological Services reported a discussion of the possibility of such a publication ("Report," 1950). If such a listing was published, the Association would have to accept legal responsibility for the actions of those listed. That the Association should do this was not agreed on, but the Board of Professional Affairs has continued to push the development of criteria by which providers of psychological services should be judged. This concern continued over the years and resulted in the publication of the first edition of "Standards for Providers of Psychological Services" in the early 1970s. This publication evolved into the current "General Guidelines for Providers of Psychological Services," which appears in the front of the APA *Directory*.

Another psychological enterprise that concerns the public is testing. Tests were, of course, used extensively during both world wars by the armed services for selection and classification. A large amount of research and development went into their construction and standardization, and service personnel became accustomed to taking them. After the war, tests proliferated, and thousands of people were required to take them as students or job applicants, or as part of individual assessment procedures. In 1950, President Robert Sears appointed a committee on psychological testing to provide guidelines on the construction and administration of tests, as well as on the proper interpretation of results (Cronbach, 1988). The first set of standards by this committee was published in 1954. These standards have been updated by succeeding committees that have collaborated with similar committees of the American Educational Research Association. The work of these groups has been of vital interest to both scientific and professional members of the Association.

SUMMARY

In this chapter, I have dealt with what was, from many perspectives, the most dynamic 25-year period in the history of the American Psychological Association. This was a time during which psychology began to come of age as a recognized science and as an important resource for the solution of practical problems. The Association grew in membership by a factor of 6, and its budget by a factor of 45. The staff of its Central Office grew from none to 141 persons. The relative homogeneity of the membership in 1945 gave way to increasing differentiation over the years, exemplified by the proliferation of divisions and state associations. These groupings reflected the differences in scientific or professional interests and the diverse nature and locations of members' employment. A marked difference in the points of view of scientific versus professional interests became increasingly apparent as the years went by, portending a real schism among psychologists that has persisted to the present. Despite these differences, however, the basic nature and mode of operation of the Association as an efficient organization unfolded during this period.

REFERENCES

Adkins, D. (1954). The simple structure of the American Psychological Association. *American Psychologist, 9,* 175–180.

American Board of Examiners in Professional Psychology. (1955). The work of the American Board of Examiners in Professional Psychology, 1955 annual report. *American Psychologist, 10,* 773–777.

American Psychological Association. (1946a). *Yearbook for 1946–47.* Washington, DC: Author.

American Psychological Association. (1946b). Report of the Committee on Graduate and Professional Training. *American Psychologist, 1,* 509–510.

American Psychological Association. (1953). *Ethical standards of psychologists.* Washington, DC: Author.

American Psychological Association. (1957a). Proceedings of the sixty-fifth annual business meeting of the American Psychological Association. *American Psychologist, 12,* 696.

American Psychological Association. (1957b). Report of the Policy and Planning Board: 1957. *American Psychologist, 12,* 492.

American Psychological Association. (1960a). Revision of ADA bylaws. American Psychologist, *15,* 135–154.

American Psychological Association. (1960b). Notes and news. *American Psychologist, 15,* 281–282.

American Psychological Association. (1989). *Directory* (1989 ed.). Washington, DC: Author.

American Psychological Association Policy and Planning Board. (1949). Annual report of the Policy and Planning Board of the American Psychological Association: 1949. *American Psychologist, 4,* 317–319.

American Psychological Association Policy and Planning Board. (1957). Proposed changes in the rules for membership in the American Psychological Association. *American Psychologist, 12,* 194–199.

American Psychological Association Policy and Planning Board. (1959). Annual report of the Policy and Planning Board of the American Psychological Association: 1959. *American Psychologist, 12,* 194–199.

American Psychological Association Policy and Planning Board. (1960). Revision of APA bylaws. *American Psychologist, 15,* 135–154.

American Psychological Association Scientific Development Board. (1955). Report of the American Psychological Association Scientific Development Board. *American Psychologist, 10,* 757–766.

Bray, C. W. (1948). *Psychology and military proficiency: A history of the applied psychology panel of the National Defense Research Committee.* Princeton, NJ: Princeton University Press.

Brayfield, A. H. (1965). Report of the executive officer, 1965: Perspectives on APA. *American Psychologist, 20,* 1018–1027.

Brayfield, A. H. (1970). Scientific communication in psychology: Recent history and context. *American Psychologist, 25,* Special insert, i–iv.

Bush, V. (1945). *Science, the endless frontier.* (Reprinted in 1960 by the National Science Foundation with an introduction by Alan Waterman, director)

Caddy, G. R. (1982). The emergence of professional psychology: Background to the Virginia Beach conference and beyond. In R. Peterson & D. Fishman (Eds.), *Professional psychology review: Vol. I. Educating professional psychologists: Proceedings of the Virginia Beach conference on education in professional psychology—and beyond* (pp. 3–18). New Brunswick, NJ: Transaction Books.

Clark, K. E. (1957). *America's psychologists: A survey of a growing profession.* Washington, DC: American Psychological Association.

Committee on Training in Clinical Psychology. (1947). Recommended graduate training program in clinical psychology. *American Psychologist, 1,* 539–558.

Crawford, M. P. (1961). Report of the treasurer. *American Psychologist, 16,* 773–775.

Crawford, M. P. (1965). Report of the treasurer. *American Psychologist, 20,* 1045–1050.

Crawford, M. P. (1982). The accreditation process: Facing new challenges. In D. Peterson (Ed.), *Educating professional psychologists* (Vol. 1, pp. 103–112). New Brunswick, NJ: Transaction Books.

Cronbach, L. (1988). [Interview with Lee Cronbach, by W. E. Wilsoncroft, February 5, 1988]. Presidents Oral History Project, American Psychological Association.

Darley, J. G. (1960). Report of the executive secretary 1959–1960. *American Psychologist, 15,* 746–749.

Darley, J., & Wolfle, D. (1946). Can we meet the formidable demand for psychological services? Editorial comment. *American Psychologist, 1,* 179–180.

Dennis, W., & Girden, E. (1955). Participation in APA voting. *American Psychologist, 10,* 212–214.

Doll, E. A. (1946). The divisional structure of the APA. *American Psychologist, 1,* 336–345.

Education and Training Board. (1958). Criteria for evaluating training programs in clinical or counselling psychology. *American Psychologist, 13,* 59–60.

Education and Training Board. (1970a). Accrediting procedures of the American Psychological Association. *American Psychologist, 25,* 100–102.

Education and Training Board. (1970b). APA-approved accredited doctoral programs in clinical and in counseling psychology. *American Psychologist, 25,* 1049–1050.

Flanagan, J. (Ed.). (1946–1947). *Army Air Force's Aviation Psychology Program research reports* (Vols. 1–19). Washington, DC: U.S. Government Printing Office.

Gagné, R. M. (Ed.). (1962). *Psychological principles of system development.* New York: Holt, Rinehart & Winston.

Gardner, H. (1985). *The mind's new science.* New York: Basic Books.

Garvey, W., & Griffith, B. C. (1966). Studies in social innovation in scientific communication in psychology. *American Psychologist, 21,* 1019–1036.

Hilgard, E. R. (1978). *American psychology in historical perspective.* Washington, DC: American Psychological Association.

Hilgard, E. R., & Sears, B. (1986). *Presidents Oral History Project.* Washington, DC: American Psychological Association. (Available from the Executive Office)

Hobbs, N. (1948). The development of a code of ethics for psychology. *American Psychologist, 3,* 80–84.

Hoch, E. L., Ross, A. D., & Winder, C. L. (Eds.). (1966). *Professional preparation of clinical psychologists.* Washington, DC: American Psychological Association.

Hovland, C. I. (1960). Computer simulation of thinking. *American Psychologist, 15,* 687–693.

Koch, S. (1963). *Psychology: A study of a science: Vol. 6. Investigations of man as socius: Their place in psychology and the social sciences.* New York: McGraw-Hill.

Marquis, D. (1948). Research planning at the frontiers of science. *American Psychologist, 3,* 430–438.

McGeehe, W., Little, K., & Cherney, B. (1971). APA finance (in 5 parts). *American Psychologist, 26,* 658–660, 732–735, 848–854, 931–934, 1085–1088.

McKeachie, W. J. (1971). Proceedings of the American Psychological Association, Inc., for the year 1970: Minutes of the annual meeting of the Council of Representatives. *American Psychologist, 26,* 22–49.

Miller, N. (1986). [Interview with Neal Miller, president, 1961, by M. Crawford, November 28, 1986]. *Presidents Oral History Project*. Washington, DC: American Psychological Association. (Available from the Executive Office)

Newman, E. (1962). Proceedings of the seventieth annual business meeting of the American Psychological Association Incorporated. *American Psychologist, 17*, 843–859.

Peterson, D. (1982). Origins and development of the doctor of psychology concept. In R. Peterson & D. Fishman (Eds.), *Professional psychology review: Vol. I. Educating professional psychologists: Proceedings of the Virginia Beach conference on education in professional psychology—and beyond* (pp. 19–38). New Brunswick, NJ: Transaction Books.

Raimy, V. (Ed.). (1950). *Training in clinical psychology*. New York: Prentice-Hall.

Report of the Committee on Standards for Psychological Service Centers. (1950). *American Psychologist, 5*, 568–571.

Roe, A., Gustad, J. W., Moore, B. V., Ross, S., & Skodzk, M. (Eds.). (1959). *Graduate education in psychology*. Washington, DC: American Psychological Association.

Sanford, F. (1952). Across the secretary's desk: A national headquarters building for APA [with photograph]. *American Psychologist, 7*, 479–483.

Sanford, F. (1955). Annual report of the executive secretary: 1955. *American Psychologist, 10*, 778–792.

Sears, R. (1946). Graduate training facilities: I. General information; II. Clinical psychology. *American Psychologist, 1*, 135–150.

Sears, R. (1947). Clinical training facilities: 1947: A report from the committee on graduate and professional training. *American Psychologist, 2*, 199–205.

Shartle, C. (1946). Occupations in psychology. *American Psychologist, 1*, 559–582.

Sherburne, E. G. (1964). Science and television. *American Psychologist, 19*, 685–687.

Stouffer, S., Suchanan, E., Devinney, L. C., Starr, S., & Williams, R., Jr. (1949). *The American soldier: Adjustment during army life* (Vol. 1). Princeton, NJ: Princeton University Press.

Strother, C. R. (Ed.). (1956). *Psychology and mental health*. Washington, DC: American Psychological Association.

Van Cott, H. P. (1970). National information system for psychology: A proposed solution for a pressing problem. *American Psychologist, 25*, pp. i–xx.

Ward, J. E. (1955). Use of the electronic computer in psychological research. *American Psychologist, 10*, 826–827.

Wolfle, D. (1946a). Across the secretary's desk. *American Psychologist, 1*, 472–473.

Wolfle, D. (1946b). Annual report of the executive secretary, 1946. *American Psychologist, 1*, 537–539.

Wolfle, D. (1946c). The reorganized American Psychological Association. *American Psychologist, 1*, 1–3.

Wolfle, D. W. (1950). Legal control of psychological practice. *American Psychologist, 5*, 651–655.

Wolfle, D. W. (1957). Preface. In K. E. Clark, *America's psychologists: A survey of a growing profession.* Washington, DC: American Psychological Association.

Wolfle, D. W. (1963). Preface. In S. Koch, *Psychology, a study of a science:* Vol. 6. *Investigations of man as socius.* New York: McGraw-Hill.

Wolfle, D. W. (1989). *Reviewing a scientific society: The American Association for the Advancement of Science from WWII to 1970.* Washington, DC: The American Association for the Advancement of Science.

Yerkes, R. M. (1918). Psychology in relation to the war. *Psychological Review, 25*, 85–115.

Young, M., & Odbert, H. (1959). Government support of psychological research: Fiscal year 1958. *American Psychologist, 14*, 497–500.

1 G. Stanley Hall (1844–1924), founder and first president of the APA (1892).

2 J. McKeen Cattell (1860–1944), host of the first regular annual meeting of the APA (December 1892), second secretary of the APA (1894), and fourth president of the APA (1895).

3 The University of Pennsylvania, site of the first regular annual meeting of the APA (December 1892).

4 William James, third president of the APA (1894).

5 Joseph Jastrow (1863–1944), first secretary of the APA (1892–1893).

7 Mary Calkins
(1893–1930),
first woman
president of the
APA (1905).

6 Edward Bradford Titchener
(1867–1927), founder of
the Experimentalists.

9 John B. Watson (1878–1958), founder of behaviorism and president of the APA (1915).

8 Edmund C. Sanford (1859–1924), third secretary of the APA (1895).

11 Robert M. Yerkes (1876–1956), president of the APA (1917). Shown in his World War I uniform as director of psychological testing, U.S. Army.

10 James R. Angell (1869–1949), founder of Chicago functionalism and president of the APA (1906).

12 Committee on the Psychological Examination of Recruits, 1917. Top row, left to right: F. L. Wells (1884–1964), Walter V. Bingham (1880–1952), Robert M. Yerkes (1876–1956), Guy M. Whipple (1876–1941), Lewis M. Terman (1877–1956). Bottom row: Edgar A. Doll (b. 1889), H. H. Goddard (1866–1957), Thomas M. Haines (b. 1871).

14 Francis C. Summer
(1895–1954), the first Black
American to be awarded a
PhD in psychology (1920).

13 Margaret Floy Washburn
(1871–1939), president of
the APA (1921).

15 Howard C. Warren
(1867–1934), founder and
owner of many of the journals
later transferred to the APA.
President of the APA (1913).

16 Walter B. Cannon (1871–1945) and I. P. Pavlov (1849–1936) at the 1929 APA meeting.

17 Kurt Lewin (1890–1947), E. C. Tolman (1886–1959), and Clark Hull (1884–1952) at the 1938 meeting of the APA. The photo was titled "The Three Muses."

18 The Emergency Committee of Psychology of the National Research Council. Top row, left to right: Walter B. Miles, Carol C. Pratt, Robert A. Brotemarkle, Gordon Allport, Kenneth Little, Steuart H. Britt. Bottom row: Leonard Carmichael, Karl M. Dallenbach, Robert M. Yerkes, Walter Hunter.

19 First meeting of the Subcommittee on Survey and Planning (1942). Top row, left to right: R. M. Elliott, Ernest R. Hilgard, Edwin G. Boring. Bottom row: Edgar A. Doll, Robert M. Yerkes, A. I. Bryan, Calvin P. Stone. (Carl R. Rogers is not pictured.)

20 Edwin G. Boring (1888–1967), president of the APA (1928).

22 Dael Wolfle (b. 1906), first executive secretary of the APA after reorganization.

21 Henry Garrett (1894–1973), first president of the APA after reorganization (1946).

23 John Darley (b. 1910), first to hold the title of executive officer of the APA (1959–1962).

24 Colorado Conference on Graduate Education in Clinical Psychology (1949), source of the Boulder scientist-practitioner model of clinical education.

25 First APA building (1952–1965).

26 APA headquarters building (1965–1991).

28 APA medallion celebrating the centennial of Wundt's laboratory (1979).

AMERICAN PSYCHOLOGICAL ASSOCIATION
WILHELM WUNDT

Ψ
1879 1979
A CENTURY OF
SCIENTIFIC
PSYCHOLOGY

27 Artist's rendering of the new APA headquarters building, Washington, DC.

29 Groundbreaking ceremony on the site of the new APA headquarters building, Washington, DC. Left to right: Harry L. Thomas, Raymond D. Fowler, Michael S. Pallak, Janet T. Spence, George W. Albee, Gardner Lindzey, Bonnie R. Strickland, Neal E. Miller, E. R. Hilgard, Florence L. Denmark, Patricia Bricklin, Joseph D. Matarazzo, Jack G. Wiggins, J. McVicker Hunt, Anne Anastasi, Bruce E. Bennett, Nicholas A. Cummings, M. Brewster Smith, Robert Perloff, Stanley R. Graham, Frank Farley, Kenneth B. Little, Patrick H. DeLeon, Steve Morin, Richard M. Suinn, Charles D. Spielberger, Ronald E. Fox.

8

GROWTH, CONFLICT, AND PUBLIC POLICY: THE AMERICAN PSYCHOLOGICAL ASSOCIATION FROM 1970 TO 1985

MICHAEL S. PALLAK

The 15-year period from 1970 to 1985 saw major growth and change for the APA along several dimensions. A major change was represented by the fact that, by 1985, the APA had shifted from an organization with a predominantly internal focus (often on internal conflict) to an organization with an additional substantial public-policy focus enabling it to play a leadership role in several spheres.

The evolutionary shift in the APA developed in roughly three stages.

This chapter is focused on a set of perspectives for the substantial evolution of the APA during 1970–1985. The framework here represents the sort of perspective that, although not often visible in the mix of issues at any given time provided, is a critical ingredient for the the Association at several turning points. I was extremely fortunate and pleased to have played an important role on behalf of my colleagues in that evolution at a critical transition in the history of the Association.

It is impossible to acknowledge individually the substantial number of people on staff and in the governance structure who worked so well and so effectively on behalf of the APA. We made a critical difference in the Association, with a very large array of positive outcomes. We were very fortunate to have had so many good people available and enthusiastic about APA's potential.

During the first stage, approximately between 1970 and 1975, internal political conflicts dominated much of the Association's attention and resources. Several fundamental aspects of that political conflict were not satisfactorily resolved, but at least receded during the 1975–1980 and 1980–1985 periods. Around 1975, the APA began to develop conflict management processes that enabled substantial expansion of programs and outcomes beneficial to psychology, psychologists, and the Association itself. By late 1980 and early 1981, events in the public arena forced a more active role in public policy, facilitated by the base of consensus that evolved in the preceding 5-year period.

Although specific issues have shifted somewhat, one perspective by which to view the Association is evolutionary in terms of growth, diversity, conflict, and accommodation to diversity and conflict. A second, related perspective is the substantial shift in the Association's relationship with the public-policy and political world and with the public on behalf of our collective membership and the public interest.

The shift in the Association's orientation to public policy remains a hallmark of this particular era in APA history. The shift was partly grounded in the sometimes-difficult lessons learned about ourselves as a collective entity and about developing organized, rather than ad hoc, program efforts. By 1985, internal conflict occupied relatively less of center stage, as the APA focused instead on marshalling resources to achieve goals. From my perspective as a social psychologist and as someone involved in the APA for a significant period of time, this set of themes (growth, diversity, and conflict resolution) stand in contrast with other periods and help to provide an interpretive structure for this period.[1]

The record of APA activities during this 15-year period is extensive and often intertwined with multiple groups and levels in the governance hierarchy. Much of what the Association has done is reflected in the minutes of the Council of Representatives and the Board of Directors, as well as in executive officers' reports, reports of the Policy and Planning Board, and treasurers' reports. A lion's share of the Association's efforts month by month and year to year are conducted by boards, committees, task forces, and so forth in an incremental fashion over several years. Summarizing

---

[1]These themes are emphasized in this chapter to a greater extent than other, equally valid themes that might be emphasized by others who played different roles in this period. In that sense, this chapter has the flavor more of an executive officer's report than of a recitation of specific steps by specific people in specific program areas. Part of the "survival" abilities needed by executive officers involve perceiving themes, articulating trends, and proposing future actions. As a result, my intention is to reach out to future members, executive officers, staff, and governance members by conveying a sense of the perspectives and processes that enabled change, so that future transitions in the APA may be productive and more understandable.

these details is well beyond the scope of this chapter in other than a thematic sense.

GROWTH

For any entity, but especially for membership organizations, growth produces strains and inevitable conflict. The transition points in such growth are largely psychological in terms of goals and definitions of purpose, rather than simply numerical. For example, the first transition is always at the point at which purely volunteer efforts are no longer adequate to accomplish desired goals and tasks (in terms of continuity, volume, or desired outcomes). Some form of permanent or full-time staff is delegated responsibility for operating needs. The organization evolves a broader definition of itself and works out role differences and expectations between the "staff" and "policy" functions. For the APA, this step began in the mid-1940s when the modern APA was established (for a detailed account, see Chapter 6).

The next transition point is when significant additions to staff and to volunteer efforts are needed. Typically, the organization needs to expand the scope of its activities in response to the membership or policy structure. I believe that this step began for the APA in the 1975–1980 period.

The third step, however, involves qualitative program and strategic expansion in response to an expanded array of policy goals that reflect a substantially broader definition of purpose and new, additional organizational functions. For the APA, this step had largely been accomplished by about 1985.

Increased Activity by the Governance Structure: 1970–1975

By the beginning of the 1970s and through 1975, the APA had undertaken actions regarding a number of significant issues, many of which are familiar topics for the Association today. A brief overview will be a useful starting point for a perspective on subsequent transitions.[2]

The Board of Scientific Affairs (BSA) was progressing with a task force on family planning and population policy. Members of the Association, under the aegis of the BSA, were involved with DHEW (Department of Health, Education and Welfare) procedures for security clearances for members of scientific review panels—with clear concerns regarding "blacklisting." The Board was monitoring declining trends in research funding,

---

[2]Much of the detail and references are found in Little (1971), McKeachie (1971a, 1971b), and the Proceedings published in 1972, 1973, and 1974 (McKeachie, 1972, 1973, 1974).

distributed several digests noting concerns about these trends, and met with National Institute of Mental Health branch chiefs about the implications of the reductions. Committees were at work on the issues of research involving human subjects and of the conservation of endangered primates. Plans for a task force on Newly Emerging Areas of Research came to fruition in 1973, and the new jointly produced (by the APA, the American Education Research Association, and the National Council on Measurement in Education) *Standards for Educational and Psychological Tests* was published in 1973. Staff and members of the Committee on International Relations in Psychology were involved with planning for the XX International Congress of the International Union of Psychological Science in 1972, as well as for the XII Interamerican Congress and the XVII International Congress of Applied Psychology in 1971.

The APA Board of Professional Affairs (BPA) completed the third draft of a "Guideline Statement on Conditions of Employment of Psychologists," and their policy statement regarding psychology and mental retardation was approved by the Board of Directors in 1970. The BPA advisory panel on children and youth began work on a response to the final report from the Joint Commission on Mental Health of Children. Through the BPA, Tyler (1969) published the statement on psychological assessment and public policy.

The BPA Committee on Health Insurance continued to meet with insurance carriers and health administrators, as well as with federal officials involved with federal health benefits, Medicare, and the Civilian Health and Medical Plan for the Uniformed Services. Efforts in this period continued to focus on obtaining insurance coverage for mental health services and on greater availability of mental health services to the public, as well as on the independent status of psychologists as mental health service providers.

In 1972, the BPA reported discussions with several groups regarding a plan for a directory of psychologists meeting standards that demonstrated competence to provide psychological services. By 1974, the Council for the National Register of Health Service Providers had been established (and separately incorporated) by the American Board of Professional Psychology. By 1989, the "National Register" contained some 16,000 psychologists who applied and met the criteria for inclusion (Council for the National Register of Health Service Providers, 1989). The 1973 Vail Conference (Korman, 1976) shifted training issues to clinicians primarily engaged in practice in nonacademic settings.

Under the Education and Training (E&T) Board, the Commission on Accreditation presented recommendations and various revised procedures to the Council of Representatives in 1970. The E&T Board, with the BPA, formed a joint ad hoc Committee on Professional Training, and the continuing issues of subdoctoral education and the status of service providers received major attention. The E&T Board coordinated the Visiting Psychologist Program (funded by the National Institute of Mental Health [NIMH]), as well as a dual project (funded by the National Science Foundation) comprising the Visiting Scientist Program and an analysis of undergraduate curricula in psychology. At the same time, a precollege project in psychology was funded by the U.S. Office of Education. The E&T Board began to report on job placement activity at the annual convention as part of a developing concern with negative trends in the employment picture for psychologists.

In 1970, the Council of Representatives authorized a $54,000 3-year loan (forgiven in 1972) to enable the Black Students Psychological Association and the Association of Black Psychologists to develop a headquarters office, and agreed to provide free office space for 3 years.

In 1971, the ad hoc Committee on Social and Ethical Responsibility was established, and in 1972 the new Board of Social and Ethical Responsibility was established through a bylaw vote of the APA membership. The Task Force on the Status of Women in Psychology produced several thoughtful reports and recommendations that eventually led to the Committee on Women in Psychology and to a vigorous Women's Program and Office. In 1974, the Minority Fellowship Program was funded by the NIMH and not only evolved substantially in the next 10 years, but also provided a catalyst for training issues and for ethnic minority issues in the APA.

In about this same period (1970–1974), the APA established an ad hoc Committee on Human Resources, which resulted in a special issue of the *American Psychologist* (Perloff, 1972) regarding the education and utilization of psychologists. The developing constriction in the traditional job markets for psychologists (new doctorates followed a steady and rapid increase from 955 in 1965 to 1,883 in 1970 to 2,749 in 1975; Stapp, Fulcher, Nelson, Pallak, & Wicherski, 1981) led to several massive surveys of psychologists (e.g., Boneau & Cuca, 1974) and the beginnings of a large membership data file as part of the continuing concern with the education and employment of psychologists.

The listing of activities above indicates an association carrying out functions needed for organized psychology and acting on behalf of a membership. Those functions included standards setting, commentary on selected public issues, assessing the status of differing subsets of the membership, and generally providing information to our collective selves about our collective selves. In that sense, the Association, in the period from

1970 to 1975, more closely resembled the APA of the late 1960s than the APA of the early 1980s.

However, determinations of appropriate actions in the public sphere were often in reaction to events and often conservative, focused more on the dissemination of APA positions than on an active strategy to shape events. The APA acted in accord with a perception of limited ability and limited options for influencing events (see Tyler, 1969). After the post-Sputnik surge in science and education support (Pallak & Kilburg, 1986), many psychologists in the Association believed that the field enjoyed implicit public support and understanding. In a sense, the APA had little interest or motivation to translate the implications of our knowledge base to public issues, preferring instead to offer advice and comment when asked.

Yet internal pressures had already begun to surface in the 1970–1975 period for more active public policy efforts. On the one hand, issues of professional autonomy for providers of psychological and clinical services had crystallized (see Cummings, 1979), with the attendant sequelae concerning professional standards, ethics, licensure, training models, and accreditation. On the other hand, substantial pressure had developed for public interest activities on behalf of ethnic minorities, women, and gay and lesbian psychologists, along with pressure for the APA to adopt a more publicly visible prosocial role. Similarly, several alarming trends began to crystallize in the science community as "Golden Fleece" awards ridiculed behavioral and social science research and as research and training support diminished (and was impounded at several points). A general shift in science policy began to take shape. Research funding in several agencies (e.g., the NIMH) began shifting from categorical support for basic fields such as psychology to "mission-oriented" and targeted priorities. Psychology needed to justify support in terms of relevance to the stated mission goals (e.g., "psychiatric problems of the elderly").

The traditional APA stance of reacting, or providing information, needed to shift toward the explicit advocacy and definition of issues in advance of policy initiatives. In essence, the eventual policy shift by APA toward a greater involvement in the agendas of the external policy world (cf. Pallak, 1990) represented a transition and turning point, one that would define the Association, by 1985, as something more than a small, homogeneous membership association.

Before that transition could unfold, however, several internal issues had to be resolved and accommodated. In the evolutionary process of organizational transition, demands for services, products, and actions usually reach a point that outstrips available human and financial resources. As pressure or demand increases, forward planning efforts to anticipate the next transition usually lag, and conflict erupts over priorities for attention and resources.

Constricted Finances Hampered Program Development

Organizations at this stage (and in conflict) become inherently reluctant or unable to raise dues or to charge higher prices for services or products. At the same time, because of conflict, the organization is largely unable to agree to maintain limits for programs as competition for program resources increases and as policy becomes dominated by "partisan" (as perceived by nonsupporters) initiatives for action, as a result.

The APA had reached that point by 1974–1975 for three related reasons: (a) growth in numbers, (b) growth in diversity of the membership and consequent diversity of political factions in the Council of Representatives, and (c) limited financial resources to meet demands for program expansion. In general, as a result of these inevitable and naturally occurring events, tendencies to resist certain types of change or expansion end up in conflict with those seeking change. The level of conflict escalates or continues until some new accommodation or redefinition of goals is achieved. The latter is often a painful process, and it was no less so for the APA as a membership association.

Growth in sheer numbers of members complicates organizational function. The amount of mail, requests for information, meetings, and financial accounting (for example) always reaches a point that exceeds resources, especially when revenue per member (dues) is relatively fixed. Although growth in the APA membership was evident (signaled by the doubling of new doctorates between 1965 and 1970; Stapp et al., 1981), the dominant institutional response (often based both on inertia and on conflict) is to handle increased demand with existing resources (which become increasingly stretched). The cumulative impact, depending on rate of increase, is substantial over a 3- to 5-year period and inevitably requires a large infusion of resources, often under crisis conditions.

Although the APA had gone through growth from the mid-1940s to 1970, the 1970–1985 cycle was unprecedented. The APA had about 29,000 to 30,000 members in 1970–1971, about 44,000 in 1975 (approximately a 50% increase), about 55,000 in 1980, and about 70,000 in 1985, representing a 250% increase in this 15-year period (comparable change in the United States would have produced a population of about 450 million by 1985).

Despite modest dues increases and the phasing out of the APA journal credit (in 1974), by 1975 sheer growth in size implied that financial and operating resources needed expansion and different management approaches than in the past. One major index of organizational function and operation is the operating budget. In this regard, the APA had significant financial deficits for the 1971, 1972, 1973, and 1974 operating years. Despite 3 years of deficits, APA entered 1974 with a planned surplus of only $109,000 for a budget of $7,500,000—a tiny margin even under relatively stable conditions—and ended the year with a fourth year of deficit.

Perloff's Treasurer's Report (1975) noted that "APA's appetite for developing programs and services is more voracious than that of most tapeworms." More directly, he also noted that "diffusion of responsibility within APA makes it difficult to hold any one person or body accountable for results." Budget deficits implied chronic organizational dysfunction on the one hand, and, on the other, contributed to a more skeptical and more reluctant approach (by those worried about deficits) to developing or expanding efforts to tackle problems.

GROWTH AND CONFLICT

During the 1970–1975 period, there were two major components relating both to the budget deficits and to a reluctance to move the APA beyond the traditional set of organizational issues and actions noted above. A least part of the problem was (and potentially remained) inherent in the APA governance system centered around the Council of Representatives. The second part concerned the fact that the composition of the APA, and hence political representation in the Council, had begun to shift and diversify in the late 1960s and became an accomplished fact in the 1970–1975 period.

The Council of Representatives, elected by members of divisions and state psychological associations, sets policy for the APA (see Chapter 7 for further details). It is astonishing (but not atypical for membership associations) to realize that this function is handled by a group of approximately 115 (in 1985) members who meet for only about 2 days during the annual convention and for about 3 days in the early part of the following calendar year. From the perspective of the volume of information and activity of the Association, it is difficult to see how Council members can adequately be abreast of all of the issues.

In fact, the system works best by delegating the detailed preparation of issues to an array of groups (boards, committees, and task forces) for deliberation, detailed review, and eventual recommended actions. Although this system tends to produce "checks and balances" for many issues, the Council retains full approval and policy authority; the Council reviews, refers for further study, and changes or overturns recommended courses of actions. In one sense, the Council ensures that past or proposed actions "make sense" and serves as an arena for differences in perspective and for working out compromises.

As with any large group, the Council works most effectively with a good flow of information and with continuity; thus, every issue does not have to be handled *de novo*. When significant proportions of the Council feel that their core issues are being handled inadequately, Council can and has acted on the spot to allocate resources to meet their concerns. In response to acute pressures, the Council often took actions in the 1970–1975 period that contributed to eventual budget deficits (see Perloff, 1975).

The changing membership of the Council also reflects trends in the APA membership. During the 1970–1985 period, the composition of the APA membership also changed dramatically, with increased numbers and percentages of applied- and practice-oriented psychologists. Gottfredson and Dyer (1978), using a stratified random sample, estimated that health service psychologists provided services to some 2 to 4 million people a year. On the basis of a 1977 survey, Mills, Wellner, and VandenBos (1979) reported that 22,588 members (85% of licensed psychologists) reported being trained as health service providers. A total of 15,422 reported involvement with private practice, and 4,683 reported full-time private practice. Regardless of the actual shift in absolute numbers, the perception was that "private practitioners" had come to dominate the APA by 1975.

The Council and the APA found themselves engaged in major conflicts in the period from 1970 to 1975 as the "practitioner" segment moved their agenda regarding professional autonomy to the fore. This agenda took on more urgency as the nation appeared likely to enact some form of national health insurance that, based on the Medicare model, would exclude psychology except under medical supervison (Cummings, 1979; DeLeon, 1977).

As one would expect, decision making and policy development became a more highly charged and politicized process during the 1970–1975 period. Spokespersons adopted more polarized stances in moving their agendas and in reaction to those agendas. The policy process became more openly political on an everyday basis. Limited financial resources relative to demands for programs contributed to the elevation of conflict because the budget had become a "zero-sum" (and deficit-promoting) game. In addition, each new initiative, task force, and office would inevitably try to expand beyond its narrow original mission, lending further tension to budgetary issues. The latter happened, ironically, because initiatives (in most instances) would not have survived the political hurdles and barriers unless there was reasonably widespread consensus about their necessity.

This diversification produced major strains and conflict as it led to an expanded agenda of expectations for the role of the Association on behalf of the membership. It is easy enough to characterize the major conflict as between "scientist" and "practitioner" (these stereotypes, of course, fail to take into account that within each of these and other communities, opinion was often sharply divided among four or five segments—hardly monolithic entities except around core themes). However, discounting the conflict in 1970–1975 as primarily due to these differences tends to trivialize the situation because a more fundamental transition was also in the works—a process of redefining assumptions about the nature and function of the APA in regard to public and policy issues.

On the one hand, one view could be characterized as wanting the APA to remain "the way it used to be," and was usually accompanied by expressions of regret for the passing of a smaller, more closely knit, and more homogeneous Association. On the other, the contrasting view or views could be represented as wanting the APA to engage in the social, professional, science, and education policy issues in the political arena that were intruding into both the APA and society. Inevitably, this clash in orientation would develop as the general membership and the Council shifted and differentiated dramatically.

By 1975, continued growth and continued conflict, coupled with the APA's inability to manage its budget, resulted in the demoralization of the Central Office staff. Depending on the point of view, the Central Office was often characterized as "a series of fiefs in thrall" to various political factions and individuals and as "partisan clerks" rather than as organizational resources. The relative failure of leadership in the Association as a whole was reflected in the Central Office, often taking root as "we versus them" antagonisms and as a cynical, antipsychologist orientation (especially among the various nonpsychology and business-related staff). The staff had difficulty treading among the conflicting groups, further increasing the problems of frustration and morale.

The Association of the 1960s could not easily foresee that growth in diversity would increase pressure for an enlarged and more sophisticated role in relation to the membership and the public. Many of those who could foresee these developing trends were at best ambivalent about the implications for change. In the most extreme characterization of the 1970–1975 period, there were only a relatively few people who seemed to see common goals beyond the immediate conflict. Inevitably, wider diversity implied sharply divergent views of what the Association should be about at a fundamental philosopical and conceptual level.

Recognition of diversity and conflict did produce proposed accommodations to the conflict. But the proposed organizational accommodation suggested that each group should largely go its separate way rather than trying to manage conflict under the broad structure of the APA. For example, the APA Policy and Planning Board (1972) proposed "conversion of the Association from a unified, centralized membership organization toward a diversified, decentralized association of member organizations each formed according to its dominant member needs . . ." (p. 1). This proposal arose from "a review of the serious problems that now beset the association, the range and diversity of functions, often substantially incompatible, that are desired by significant segments of the membership . . ." (p. 1). The Board observed that "with increase in size comes an increase in the power of subgroups that may wish to use the organization as a whole to further their own preferred ends" (p. 2). Finally, "given this totality of problems, it is possible for one to conclude that the Association is creaking along with a management structure less and less capable of making effective decisions and that the variety of incompatible internal pressures makes anything but impotent compromise inevitable" (p. 3).

However, by 1973 (McKeachie, 1973, p. 312), this proposal to restructure the Association failed to achieve enough support to be seriously considered by other than relatively narrow segments, and the issue shifted back to achieving "a unitary voice" (p. 312). Although stepping back to simpler and more homogeneous structures may have been viable in the mid-1960s in response to emerging diversity, it clearly did not represent the evolutionary accommodation of choice for the Association in the early 1970s.

The issue was not which view was "right" in a moral sense, but rather how an association manages political conflict. The process of conflict management, if not conflict resolution, was critical to enhance the Association's effectiveness and to demonstrate effective outcomes from the points of view of the several constituent groups. In turn, conflict negotiation processes are effective only when some sense of shared purpose is evident and when there is some implicit, if not explicit, acknowledgment of the legitimacy of the other's goals. Although the Association could not hold together in the form of the 1970–1975 period, it was possible to build an expanded perspective under which outcomes and progress on issues could be developed.

GROWTH AND CHANGE

Organizational effectiveness and identifying outcomes on behalf of the Association became a major theme for the APA with the new executive officer, Charles A. Kiesler, in 1975. This theme helped bring the political conflict, the diverse groups, and the policy and executive structures into a more coordinated and functioning system. In the context of this change, three policy stances became adopted as routine: (a) a changed approach to Association finances, coupled with the adoption of a 3-year cycle, (b) the establishment of clear accountability and responsibility for the financial implications of APA actions and for the development of alternative actions, and (c) a substantial clarification (and evolution) of staff and governance structure responsibilities.

The theme of outcome and effectiveness (with strong support from the Board of Directors and, eventually, from throughout the governance structure) shifted the policy and management process fundamentally. The general demoralization in the Association and the Council meant that major groups and individual players were ready for a change. By 1974–1975, the policy process in the APA had devolved to a point where few felt that they had much progress to point to or felt much satisfaction with the situation. The specter of yet another deficit for the calendar year 1975 (which would have been the fifth consecutive annual deficit) further reinforced the urgency of beginning some process of organizational evolution and accommodation among groups.

A lengthy series of dialogues with groups became focused on "what are the core issues and goals to accomplish, and what are the outcomes we can agree on that let us assess progress toward those goals?" Although this redefinition of process and focus was not accomplished overnight, the process within the APA began shifting to one of negotiation and consensus building. A key element in disengaging some of the antagonists was the changed perception that progress on particular issues was not at the cost of progress on other issues.

The realization began to develop that the APA could be more effective if it financed itself in a more predictable, responsible, and flexible fashion. The Council had adopted the policy, in 1974, of planned accumulation of operating surpluses (however, it was honored in the breach in 1974; see above), in part to make up for past deficits. This policy became dominant in 1975 on the part of the executive officer, with the result that the APA had a small surplus rather than the expected deficit. The focus on financial responsibility and on demonstrating program outcomes began shifting the policy process in 1975 from one dominated by a "let's get more for our priority" to one of "how can we use our resources more effectively—and what are the goals we want to achieve?" The modest surplus for 1975 suggested that the APA could have flexibility for future, planned expansion under some conditions.

CHANGE IN FINANCIAL POLICY FOR PROGRAMS

Aside from issues of conflict, it also became clear that the APA's financial revenue stream could no longer be perceived or remain in a fixed, constant, or static state. For example, a major reality of the mid-1970s was the inflation—due to sharp increases in fuel costs following the "Yom Kippur War"—that continued rampant throughout the economy as prices for each commodity and service were driven upward cyclicly. At the same time, under the APA Bylaws, any dues increase or price increases for journals had to be announced a year in advance of implementation. As a result, it was impossible to forecast revenue levels to meet expenses in time to implement adequate revenue increases. When implemented, revenues would inevitably lag behind expenses by about 2 years.

The traditional approach to APA budgets and revenue needs (one that, as in most membership organizations, might be characterized as "don't raise dues until it is an absolute crisis; and then when you have to—Duck!") could not keep pace with demand or growth, let alone inflation, by the 1975–1977 period. Further complicating the picture was the fact that adequate dues or price increases, as well as general budget issues, were often colored by the brush of political conflict with the attribution that dues would be going up to support some "other group's" program.

Although some psychologists seem to lapse into a fugue state at the mention of budgets or financial forecasts, the Association budget is a statement of priorities that either restricts or enhances the opportunities to act. It is important to convey some sense of the complexity of the budget task, as well as some sense of the fragility of the outcome even under ideal conditions. The relationship between managing finances and program expansion, and the need for consensus about that process, has been one of the major organizational lessons from the 1970–1985 period. It was small wonder that the Association had difficulty managing the budget, a process that in the best of times needs constant cooperation by all parties, let alone in the midst of political conflict, growth, and staggering inflation.

At any point in time (then or now) the APA's budget is a complex mix of sources of revenue and sources of expense that do not naturally align in terms of causal factors. Sources of revenues include membership dues (with several levels and categories), journal subscriptions (with several levels and categories), rental income received from tenants, various fees (accreditation, continuing education, publication manual, convention registration, convention exhibit rentals), indirect or overhead funds from grants and contracts, short-term interest on cash flow, royalty payments from the PsycINFO system of products, mailing list rentals, *APA Monitor* and journals advertising, and so on. Thus, the exact level of revenue in several categories depends on the numbers of consumers (i.e., the number of members, journal subscriptions, exhibitors, advertisers, and so forth).

Expenses are equally complex, but not all of them follow directly from the size or volume of Association activities. Sources of expenses include journal paper costs, printing costs, utilities, taxes on nonexempt activities, real estate taxes, legal costs, building expenses, the number of governance structure meetings, the number of staff, and so forth. Unlike revenue sources, only some of these are a function of membership size but are instead driven by external factors over which we have little control. Further complicating the picture between 1970 and 1983 was the fact that the accounting and financial tracking system was sufficiently slow that quarterly financial statements were often unavailable until 3 to 6 months after the relevant quarter period of activity.

Perhaps the single most important management step that took place in the period from 1970 to 1985 was the adoption of a "3-year financial cycle" as part of the planning and financial process. At the instigation of the executive officer, the steps began with a series of review and analysis meetings within the senior staff group. The concept was prompted in part by the realization that every 3 years the APA had brought out the *Psychological Cumulative Index*—a major source of revenue and one that established the precedent for a "cycle" approach. The 3-year cycle proposal went through a series of presentations and discussions within the governance structure (the Finance Committee, the treasurer, the boards and committees, and the Board of Directors) and then final discussions and approval by the Council of Representatives in 1977.

The 3-year cycle became part of the fabric and rhythm of the Association. Year I of the cycle envisions a dues increase by a level expected to hold for 3 years. Year II involves price increases for APA publications (journals), also planned to hold for 3 years, and Year III calls for adjustments in a variety of services and products (rents, fees, advertising, etc.). Also, the APA raised various prices that did not impinge on members, such as rent, advertising, and mailing list rentals, as often as the market would bear. Coupled with much more effective monitoring and accountability throughout the staff system, this approach continued as a main underpinning of APA operations of all types.

For those who believed that budgets reflect the enactment of priorities, flexibility for needed programs, and flexibility to meet unforeseeable threats and opportunities, the 3-year cycle was a much-needed masterstroke. Organizational leadership and management involve more than political activity and rely on options provided by financial flexibility. The membership understood the dynamics of inflation and of catching up and "cushioning ahead" for programs. The cycle provided substantial predictability over time without a crisis every year or every few years. The cycle provided the flexibility to facilitate core issues for each of the constituencies in the APA. Finally, it was clear that the membership supported program expansion and would support a rational approach and financial plan toward that end.

From a more psychological perspective, the new financial plan provided a sense of control and a new basis for discussing program needs and limitations on program proposals. The policy structure could discuss the merits and demerits of proposals from an outcome and financial standpoint, as well as from a political standpoint. The new system gave the membership and the policy structure a sense that desired outcomes could happen and that thoughtful programs could be implemented—neither the options nor the discussions were straitjacketed by weak financial underpinnings—because there would be future flexibility.

RESPONSIBILITY FOR FINANCIAL PLANNING, MONITORING, AND PROGRAM DEVELOPMENT

Equally important, responsibility for tracking the budget, for tracking the financial implications of various APA actions, for alerting the governance structure in advance of problems, and for developing appropriate alternative courses of action became an established part of the role and responsibility of the executive officer, with oversight and collaboration by the treasurer, the Finance Committee, the Board of Directors, the Publication and Communications Board, and the Council of Representatives. Crystallization of responsibilty met APA's urgent need for program and financial accountability. In turn, the governance structure could play a much more active role in monitoring programs, in analyzing new proposals, and in maintaining responsibility for policy. The issues of program outcomes, financial status, and availability of flexibility became a routine agenda topic for most groups in the governance and staff structure by 1977.

The outcome orientation was a key component by which (a) conflict resolution or management evolved as a basic organizational expectation, (b) budget and financial responsibility became manageable, and (c) program expansion could develop on a planned basis rather than as an ad hoc response to political cross-pressures in the Council. Finally, the outcome orientation restored, over time, a sense of confidence within the APA because these discussions could be carried out more openly and evaluated on a common outcome-oriented basis regardless of political identity.

STAFF AND GOVERNANCE ROLES CRYSTALLIZED

A further critical component was a clearer set of expectations regarding the Central Office in support of the governance and policy structure. Recognizing that policy development and policy decisions cannot take place in a vacuum, the staff became responsible for gathering and synthesizing information, laying out options, and developing a picture of likely alternative outcomes for the policy apparatus. The staff role evolved from that of a "clerk" mentality during the 1970–1975 period to that of an active colleague playing a critical role on behalf of colleagues in the governance structure and in the membership and on behalf of psychology as a field.

This clarification put the governance structure clearly in charge of policy, priorities, and goals. Operating with an increased flow of quality information, the governance and policy structure played an enhanced and effective role on behalf of the Association. In turn, by 1980, the Central Office became an exciting career path for many people, both psychologists and nonpsychologists. The APA achieved a remarkable array of outcomes as a result of reconfiguring and revitalizing the governance-staff function.

GROWTH AND PUBLIC POLICY

During the late 1960s and early 1970s, the APA adopted a low-key approach to involvement with the external world of policy that reflected conditions within the Association. The Tyler Report (Tyler, 1969) reviewed the conditions under which involvement might be undertaken. It represented a formal benchmark for the late 1960s and early 1970s, in part because the Association clearly felt that some guidelines were necessary. In one sense, "guidelines" implies desire for some involvement. However, as the record suggests, the APA as an organization was reluctant and unable to engage the public policy process on an active, organized, or systematic basis. The Board of Directors' position statement on national health care (cf. APA Board of Directors, 1971) provided some recognition of the need for involvement, but in a limited fashion:

> The APA does not believe it is feasible for psychologists to prepare legislative proposals in regard to overall health care plans, not even for mental health programs. The Association does believe, however, that in concert with other mental health professions it can make a significant contribution to the development of a national health care program, and in particular that portion . . . which deals with coverage of mental health care. (p. 1026)

A circumscribed approach to public policy issues by the Association is understandable in retrospect. The APA had limited resources and a lack of experience, some of the pressure for engagement was seen largely only as a practitioner issue, and the tax code for nonprofit corporate entities contained sharp limitations and constraints for tax exempt activities concerned with advocacy. Within the APA, "advocacy" or "lobbying" was seen as an activity to be undertaken only by those interested, outside of the organizational mainstream.

As a result, in 1972 the professional, or practitioner, group separately incorporated the Council for the Advancement of the Psychological Professions and Sciences (CAPPS) outside of the APA. Furthermore, in response to continuing discussions about the APA's role, the APA actively supported the incorporation of the Association for the Advancement of Psychology (AAP) in 1974 as a separate lobbying organization. Although each of these two groups received some support in some fashion from the APA, both were supported primarily by contributions and dues from their memberships. Within the limits or constraints noted above, including the mix of views, however, it was clear that substantial parts of the Association saw the importance of engaging in the public policy process. The two groups merged in 1976 under the continuing title of the AAP, with an annual (and increasing) subsidy from the Association.

These formal organizational steps took place in the context of a developing consensus about, and a realization of the need for, involvement by the mainstream psychological organization, the APA. As DeLeon (1977) noted,

> This is a most exciting time in Washington, but . . . one that is also frightening and sobering particularly when one realizes the extent to which our profession tends to talk only to itself. . . . At our conventions and in our journals, we pride ourselves on our . . . presentations and . . . research. Unfortunately, very few decision makers ever hear what we have to say. . . . We do not spend the time and the effort necessary to convey effectively the importance of these developments to our public leaders, to those who will ultimately decide whether these discoveries will be incorporated into the mainstream. . . . (p. 263)

By the mid-1970s, it had become clear that psychology should be involved, not only from a guild or self-preservation perspective, but also from the perspective that it had something to offer. Clearly, if we did not build bridges and avenues into the policy process on our behalf, no one else would. The realization crystallized that there were few issues facing the nation that did not involve a psychological or behavioral perspective, and that involvement was a legitimate and necessary role for the Association to play on behalf of psychology and the public interest. In short, we needed the capacity to manage the translation of our collective expertise ourselves.

During 1976 and 1977, the APA developed and intensified relationships with federal agencies important to the development of psychology (see Kiesler, 1977, 1978; Pallak & VandenBos, 1984). These federal liaison activities were organized and centralized in 1979 in the new Office of APA National Policy Studies, which grew from a staff of 6 to a staff of 18 by 1984 (Pallak, 1980; Pallak & VandenBos, 1984). At the outset, it was clear that federal administrators had little information about psychology or about the array of expertise represented by the field.

In 1977, President Carter established the President's Commission on Mental Health. The APA developed a massive report designed to inform Commission members about the views of organized psychology regarding a range of mental health issues. Approximately 50 psychologists (many of whom had been recommended by the APA) became involved in some 30 task panels under the Commission. The role and importance of psychology's contributions were reflected throughout the final report.

Simultaneously, with national discussions focused on national health insurance, the APA developed a general policy stance that still serves as a model, one that also had roots in the Board of Directors statement of 1971 (discussed earlier). Any form of health insurance needed a strong mental health component with three characteristics: (a) Psychologists should be recognized as independent providers of mental health services, (b) the consumer of mental health services should have access to, and choice among, mental health providers and mental health treatment settings, and (c) mental health services should be tied to a strong research and evaluation plan as a means of assessing and evaluating outcomes (see Kiesler, Cummings, & VandenBos, 1979).

This policy stance provided a superordinate goal that helped to shift consideration within APA from more narrowly drawn science, practice, or social responsibility perspectives. This more comprehensive approach also provided a bridge for the several sets of psychological expertise within the Association to a major national issue, thereby underscoring the potential and need for a collective stance. The research and evaluation components were articulated by the APA Task Force on Continuing Evaluation and Accountability Controls for a National Health Insurance Program (1978). In the long run, the policy emphasized the importance of mental health as more than a guild issue relevant to only one political faction within the APA.

By 1979 (when I became executive officer), it seemed that even if the APA had not yet "turned the corner" organizationally, the corner was at least in sight. The APA had achieved a stable accommodation internally that included budget surpluses for 1975 through 1979 (inclusive). New components of the governance structure were being established that included capability for legal issues (and a new half-time "in house" legal counsel), a joint APA–NASP (National Association for School Psychology) task force, the new Public Information Committee, and the ongoing issues regarding appropriate credentialing and designation of programs training psychologists for professional practice.

Also by 1979, the Psychology Defense Fund (funded by voluntary contributions) had been established and made a first contribution to the Virginia Blues suit. The Committee on Research Support, under the Board of Scientific Affairs, was working on (published in 1981) a major compendium of agencies with research support for psychology, providing information about the types of research supported in 150 federal programs (APA Scientific Affairs Office, 1981). The Accreditation Program of the Education and Training Program had been stabilized, the Ethnic Minority Affairs program was coalescing, and the steps leading to the eventual Board of Ethnic Minority Affairs were being taken. The Board of Social and Ethical Responsibility programs were anchored in the mainstream of the APA and had expanded substantially. The special issue of the *American Psychologist* concerning testing was under way, and discussions and planning for the next revision of the "Joint Testing Standards" were developing among the three collaborating organizations (the National Council for Measurement Education, the American Education Research Association, and the APA).

By 1980, APA advocacy efforts had emerged, with APA having major responsibility for interactions with the Executive Branch while the AAP handled and coordinated interactions with Congress. The new State Psychological Association Program had begun to provide assistance to the state associations with capacity building and with legislative, licensure, and regulation issues (often with support from the Psychology Defense Fund). The APA began to coordinate involvement by APA divisions, boards, and committees in regular meetings with congressional policymakers and federal administrators. Together with Division 38 (Health) and Division 12 (Clinical), the APA began a series of evening meetings with legislative, administrative, and other policy officials, chaired by Pat DeLeon, chief legislative assistant to Senator Daniel K. Inouye.

GROWTH AND PUBLIC POLICY: THE REAGAN ONSLAUGHT

The world changed profoundly for psychology, the social sciences, and, most especially, the APA with the advent of the Reagan administration. Despite interactions with various "transition team" officials, the 1981 budget message stated that "support for the behavioral, social and economic sciences is being reduced significantly because much of the support for those sciences is considered of relatively lesser importance to the economy than support of the natural sciences" (Executive Office of the President and OMB, 1981). The Budget Message clearly reflected negative attitudes about the social sciences and psychology that had never been greatly submerged beneath the surface of public opinion. These attitudes, however, had now crystallized at the highest levels of public policy.

The Reagan onslaught moved the APA into a very different focus and accelerated its advocacy involvement. Although this was an acute shock, the APA responded in a magnificent fashion. By the Board of Directors meeting in March 1981, the staff had an organized series of actions approved and a consensus to provide whatever level of resources would be needed, even if the effort resulted in a budget deficit (the policy view was that this was the one time to go all out on behalf of psychology). Although by one reckoning the Association spent about $400,000 (including support for other organizations), it still finished 1981 with a comfortable budget surplus.

The Association played the lead role in managing and coordinating the efforts of a range of other groups. The actions taken in galvanizing the Association and other groups have been amply discussed elsewhere (e.g., DeLeon, O'Keefe, VandenBos, & Kraut, 1982; Pallak, 1982, 1990; Pallak & Kilburg, 1986; Pallak & VandenBos, 1984). The outcome involved a significant vote in 1981 (272 to 165) in the U.S. House of Representatives to restore substantial proportions of the intended cuts in the National Science Foundation research budget for the behavioral and social sciences. For the first time, a significant majority of the House had gone on record as noting the contributions and value of psychologists, of psychology, and of the social sciences.[3]

These efforts were led and coordinated by the APA executive officer and by the APA Central Office with the involvement of the leadership and governance of the Association. The success would not have been possible without the steps and structures that had evolved since the 1975 period. From the perspective of growth, accommodation, and evolution, it seemed clear that the beginning steps of the late 1970s had borne fruit in a capacity for collective action on behalf of the field. The support from all of the political factions of the APA, as well as the support for the extraor-

---

[3]As an aside, the APA had notes on some 20,000 letters written by our members to members of the House of Representatives, a substantial proportion of which had been written by practitioners.

dinary level of effort required, stood in sharp contrast with the APA of the 1970–1975 period.

The APA Develops Long-Term Plans and Programs in the Public Policy Arena

The experience with the Reagan onslaught also made salient the fact that the APA needed another transition in public policy efforts, as well as in efforts devoted to public opinion and public affairs. It became clear that we needed to solidify our capacity on a more programmatic and organized basis, rather than continue advocacy and policy involvement on an ad hoc or crisis-driven basis.

For example, as the APA expanded the range of policy-related efforts, it became clear that it needed to interact with Congress and congressional staff and committees on a more routine and direct basis than previously. The Association found itself most effective—and much more able to anticipate events—when it could interact with both the executive and congressional branches directly. It continued to build the Policy Studies staff group to provide support and information for the governance and policy leadership along with our Governance Affairs staff. As a result, the Association could deal with mental health services, science, training, and employment issues. In coordination with program staff, the APA became more directly involved with issues more directly related to practice, the status of women, ethnic minorities, animal research, testing, children and families, aging, disability determination, the penal system, and early efforts in the AIDS crisis.

Although efforts on Capitol Hill were coordinated with the AAP, the AAP's efforts were limited by a relatively inflexible budget situation despite increases in the annual support from the APA. At the same time, changes in the tax code permitted nonprofit organizations much greater levels of "advocacy" (and all relevant staff, including the executive officer, became registered lobbyists, consistent with the revised regulations). It was also clear that the APA was unlikely to continue delegating responsibility for interactions with Congress to the AAP in light of the level of activity and coordination needed.

Substantial coordination was needed with the state psychological associations. Together with efforts to build capacity, the state associations were critical for increased leverage on an array of training, science, and practice issues. The APA assessed which members of Congress had which interests and how those matched its own interests, and then frequently developed access through state associations. In much the same fashion, the

Council of Graduate Departments of Psychology played a similar role in science and training issues and began meeting routinely with members of Congress—as did an array of APA groups (see Pallak & Kilburg, 1986; Pallak & VandenBos, 1984).

Recognizing that the APA and psychology had fully entered an expanded arena of necessary public policy efforts, uniformly supported by all factions of the APA, the Association borrowed a planning lesson from its own immediate past history. A subcommittee of the APA and the AAP Boards of Directors began meeting routinely; this policy group reviewed, planned, and monitored the burgeoning array of activities by both the APA and the AAP.

In 1983, several divisions, during a joint midwinter conference (dubbed the "Greenbrier" conference), along with the APA and the AAP staffs, developed a strategy for efforts around the issue of psychologists' status in Medicare legislation. Medicare reform became a major priority and added further impetus to an expanded advocacy effort under the same organizational umbrella. Following meetings throughout 1984 and 1985, the merging of the APA staff into the APA took place in January of 1986. This merger signaled that the APA had completed a major transition in the evolution of its role in public policy. No longer the unwanted stepchild of "bothersome groups" of the 1970–1975 period, public policy efforts had become a well-supported mainstream effort within the APA.

GROWTH AND PUBLIC POLICY: PUBLIC AFFAIRS

The second lesson of the Reagan onslaught was the recognized need for a fuller and more extensive approach to public information and outreach on behalf of psychology. In one sense, substantial parts of APA efforts involve interaction with a variety of "publics." Working with the Public Information Committee, staff and governance developed a focus and policy that began to guide, coordinate, and expand APA efforts (Pallak & Kilburg, 1986) for systematic interaction with the public.

In 1981, the *APA Monitor*, the annual convention, and the Public Information programs were organized into the Office of Public Affairs. Several new public-oriented programs for the convention were established, and the APA Separates publishing program, the APA marketing and promotions operations, and the Office of International Affairs were included in the expanded operation. The Office began providing quality information, and sought out opportunities to do so, to a variety of media. A program of monthly news releases began to present basic and applied science and practice in a readable consumer-oriented style to an enlarged network of print and broadcast representatives. Press and media registration for the annual convention exceeded 380 for the 1982 convention. The first public service announcement (PSA) was developed and aired on ABC affiliates through the United States; it highlighted psychotherapy, learning-impaired children, aging, animal behavior, and the workplace.

No attempt to interpret the history of the Association in this 15-year period can be complete without noting the acquisition of the national magazine *Psychology Today*. During the 1976–1977 period, the APA had considered mounting a new magazine for the public. The concept failed, however, because of inadequate planning and finances and a resulting lack of political support. At the same 1977 meeting, the Council voted not to meet in states that had not passed the Equal Rights Amendment, a courageous move that again signaled the Association's strong motivation for involvement in public policy and public affairs on behalf of the public good. Following an extensive (and exhausting) evaluation and planning process during the last half of 1982, the APA Council (following a unanimously positive vote by the Board of Directors to bring the issue to Council) voted in early 1983 to acquire the magazine.

The goals, at least, were straightforward and involved a substantial commitment to improve the editorial content and to enhance the presentation of psychology to the public in a consumer-oriented format. The history and perspectives regarding the acquisition and management of the effort were accurately documented by Kimble (1986) and some of the problems and progress were detailed by Pallak (1985).[4]

In its meeting on October 5, 1983 (a date I remember because our second child was born during the preceding night), the *Psychology Today* Committee came to grips with continuing problems in the management structure (problems that were difficult to grasp because by that time none of us had much line or management authority over the operation). We implemented an altered management plan that reduced expenses by $750,000 annually and established clear lines of authority and accountability. The plan was approved by the Council of Representatives at the January 1984 meeting. By the end of 1984, Pallak (1985) reported, guardedly, that we had achieved some improvement in the operating picture and that the financial shortfall had dropped to between $750,000 and $1,000,000 (in line with the original forecast and plan), with revenue and expense heading slowly in the right directions. However, it was clear that the APA did not

---

[4]At the time of this writing (in 1990), however, as a senior colleague for whom I have great respect noted, "it is hard to see how we bought it, since there aren't but three people on Council who say they voted for it."

have an ongoing management and editorial plan, and policy deliberation led to operating and editorial confusion. The lack of a clearly articulated editorial and conceptual stance, enacted through a more "hands on" management structure, contributed to poor advertising performance and the ultimate demise of the operation several years later.

Psychology Today was a complex undertaking with considerable ground to make up concerning editorial quality, staff quality, management, and advertising volume. The majority of APA members provided support and goodwill between 1983 and 1985–support that came from both those who agreed and those who disagreed with the initial decison by the Council. Without that ground swell, there would have been little hope for stabilizing the operation under any conditions. From the perspective of this chapter, the APA rallied rather than fractionated, so that the modest positive trends that had been achieved seemed stable, at least during 1985.

GROWTH AND THE COMMUNICATIONS PROGRAM

Beginning in 1983 and continuing in 1984 and 1985 (see Pallak, 1985), there were other evolutions taking place in the APA that served to anchor the financial and program underpinnings. In the aftermath of a tiny operating surplus from the 1982 operating year (and the foreseeable financial drain due to the magazine), we began several review processes. On the one hand, responsibilities for the Communications program were reorganized and delegated to a new Office of Communications (including the APA journals, the PsycINFO programs, the Separates programs, advertising, etc). For the first time, the Communications program was no longer under the business office, providing relief for the senior financial staff. On the other hand, the reorganization provided for much greater input and supervision from psychologists and the Publications and Communications Board.

An extensive history of the Communications program and the evolution of the Journals, PsycINFO, and Separates programs (Chapter 12, this volume) documents the substantial growth begun in the 1982–1985 period. A substantial part of the executive officer's effort was concerned with the evolution of each of these areas. Part of the review and reorganization steps of 1983 recognized that APA operations had, again, expanded and differentiated. It was clear that we were due for an internal overhaul because we were outstripping our capacity to handle problems. Similarly, it was clear that we needed more efficient ways of operating to ensure our continued financial surpluses.

Through a series of review and evaluation efforts, the APA was able to continue program expansion despite the *Psychology Today* deficits. The implicit social contract was that, short of a disaster, the magazine ought not to restrict the APA's continued program growth or provide an excuse for restriction. The sobering financial picture due to the magazine clearly implied some necessary overhaul in how we operated several APA programs and, ironically, provided some signposts for appropriate directions. The experience with the poor management and lack of accountability in the magazine operation crystallized several steps that could be taken in APA operations.

Several examples help to illustrate the collaborative problem-solving and review efforts. In concert with the Publications and Communications Board (and in the context of bringing along several new journals), we conducted a needed and overdue review of pricing for institutional subscriptions for our journals. It turned out that we had always underpriced the journals, when one looked at typical ratios between member and institutional subscriptions. The Publications and Communications Board, the Board of Directors, and the Council approved a revised subscription schedule that was worth about $250,000 per year in 1984–85 dollars. As one Board member put it, "our member prices were subsidizing the institutional subscriptions, rather than the other way around."

Similarly, it turned out that there was nothing sacrosanct about the size of journal pages. Journal paper came to the printer in standard magazine size, and the APA had been paying a substantial premium to have the paper cut down to "APA journal" size. Similarly, the paper for the *American Psychologist* was also being trimmed by one eighth of an inch on the top and by a quarter of an inch at the side. For both "trimmings," we could not find a precedent or discover why these decisions had been made (other than because "that was the way it had always been done"). With the strong recommendation of the Publications and Communications Board and concurrence by the Council, we went to the standard paper size for a savings of about $100,000 to $150,000 per year.

Finally, we discovered that the business office, in preparing annual budgets, always included an assumption of a 3% growth in the number of subscriptions (and hence revenue), despite the fact that subscriptions had historically either held level, declined, or increased less than the 3% assumption. This discovery led to efforts to promote journal subscriptions, with a subsequent modest increase in the number of subscriptions in 1984 and 1985.

Although there is some humor in some of these discovered problems (common in any bureaucracy, without periodic attention), program review in terms of outcomes and as a basis for long-term planning had become an institutionalized component of APA staff and governance operations. The additional example below illustrates both the extent of these joint governance and staff efforts and the extent to which a prosocial, public responsibility concern had permeated the Central Office by the 1984–1985 period.

Processing for the PsycINFO system of on-line databases and print products had slowed as the worldwide volume of literature in psychology increased. As a result, the lag between publication and entry in the database increased substantially beyond a year, a major concern for the PsycINFO Advisory Committee, for the Publications and Communications Board, and for the staff. The nature of the operation was such that adding a few staff here and there was not an adequate solution at any given point in time. Rather, staff were needed in functional components of six or seven people, and it was clear that we needed an infusion of several components to catch up.

Once the problem was laid out, discussions with the Investment Committee evolved a plan to invest annual interest from a portion of the APA investment portfolio into program development in the PsycINFO system. This action represented an investment in the association itself, because the interest had never been available for operations, but rather was always simply reinvested. Thus, the APA could expand the program in a timely fashion and increase downstream revenue from an expanded and more timely array of products, as indeed has been the case.

At the same time, the PsycINFO staff proposed a creative and effective solution to a second, related set of problems. The APA had always had difficulty in recruiting ethnic minorities at the middle and senior levels of our technical staff operations, such as PsycINFO. Previous personnel efforts that required these advanced levels of technical competence had the effect of narrowing the pool of ethnic applicants to near zero. The staff proposed that we should target ethnic minorities with a developmental training effort. The core of the plan brought people into the system at entry levels, with 50% of the time (for 6–12 months) spent in learning the components of the system, rather than requiring such credentials before hiring. As openings occurred and as people mastered necessary technical levels of competence, the career path for moving up in the system was clear and open. Because we had a 20% (or greater) turnover rate per year, this internal "cadre" system let us develop a stable staff core with a much higher proportion of ethnic minorities.

In each of these problem-solving and review efforts, the governance structure played a major role because each of these problems and solutions involved shifts in operations that had policy implications for the Association. (There are other examples, although of a less far-reaching policy nature.) One result was that the APA finished 1985 with a $1,200,000–$1,400,000 surplus from operations (other than the magazine) and had about the same projected for 1986 by the time we completed the proposed budget for that year.

A FINAL NOTE: ORGANIZATIONAL EVOLUTION

It also appeared evident by 1981–1982 that regardless of the several Commissions, Task Forces, and so forth, the APA would not easily solve the conflict regarding power sharing within the organization. By the mid-1970s this problem had eased a bit as factions became sufficiently organized to elect "their" representatives to the APA presidency and the APA Board of Directors. Although a workable accommodation through 1985, the process did not satisfy deeper needs by subsets of the membership for more visible symbolic representation of their interests. In 1984–85, a new task force was established for developing alternative forms of organization. Interestingly, the main plan was passed by vote of the Council in 1987 (the first time in modern APA history that the Council had approved a reorganization plan) and referred for a vote of the membership, which failed.

There is no magic solution to the fundamental issues of both symbolic and actual representation. Constituents need to feel that their core issues are being handled by leadership that represents their interests as well as the broader array of APA interests and groups. The APA cannot afford to be perceived as dominated by one particular group for very long; as we have seen, a reaction always develops. Inevitably, without checks and balances among the contending political groups, the worst tendencies of the dominant group often dominate and a reaction occurs. There remain several plausible approaches to accommodation and compromise once the need for action is acknowledged.

Realizing that these issues could not be resolved easily (as, indeed, they had not been in the preceding years), it seemed important in 1980 and 1981 to use strategies to get the Association moving rather than remaining locked in the political conflicts of 1970–1975. Because the policy process moved over time to an outcome orientation, strategies for expanding programs and resources were an effective approach for the Association to play a more publicly responsible role in society.

It seemed clear that the executive officer, as a psychologist, had to play an active role on behalf of psychology and on behalf of the Association to ensure that programs could expand and that the APA developed both flexibility and commitment to take on important issues. On behalf of the

Association, the executive officer is also a strategic planner, a problem solver, an administrator, and, along with presidents and other officers, a representative to the public and the policy world. However, the executive officer has little direct "power," but rather operates only by means of policy consensus and support within the APA.

REFERENCES

APA Board of Directors. (1971). Psychology and national health care. *American Psychologist, 26,* 1025.

APA Policy and Planning Board. (1972). Structure and function of APA: Guidelines for the future. *American Psychologist, 27,* 1.

APA Scientific Affairs Office. (1981). *Guide to research support. First edition.* Washington, DC: American Psychological Association.

APA Task Force on Continuing Evaluation in National Health Insurance. (1978). Continuing evaluation and accountabilty controls for a national health insurance program. *American Psychologist, 32,* 305.

Boneau, A., & Cuca, J. (1974). An overview of psychology's human resources: Characteristics and salaries from the 1972 APA survey. *American Psychologist, 29,* 821–840.

Council for the National Register of Health Service Providers in Psychology. (1989). *National register of health service providers in psychology: 1989.* Washington, DC: Author.

Cummings, N. A. (1979). Mental health and national health insurance: A case history of the struggle for professional autonomy. In C. A. Kiesler, N. A. Cummings, & G. R. VandenBos (Eds.), *Psychology and national health insurance: A sourcebook.* Washington DC: American Psychological Association.

DeLeon, P. H. (1977). Implications of national health policies for professional psychology. *Professional Psychology, 8,* 263.

DeLeon, P. H., O'Keefe, A. M., VandenBos, G. R., & Kraut, A. G. (1982). How to influence public policy: A blueprint for activism. *American Psychologist, 37,* 476.

Executive Office of the President and OMB. (1981). *Additional details on budget savings: Fiscal year 1982 budget revisions.* Washington DC: U.S. Government Printing Office.

Gottfredson, G. D., & Dyer, S. E. (1978). Health service providers in psychology. *American Psychologist, 33,* 314.

Kiesler, C. A. (1977). Report of the Executive Officer: 1976. *American Psychologist, 32,* 390.

Kiesler, C. A. (1978). Report of the Executive Officer: 1977. *American Psychologist, 33,* 529.

Kiesler, C. A., Cummings, N. A., & VandenBos, G. R. (Eds.). (1979). *Psychology and national health insurance: A sourcebook.* Washington, DC: American Psychological Association.

Kimble, G. A. (1986). *The APA–PT connection.* Washington, DC: American Psychological Association.

Korman, M. (Ed). (1976). *Levels and patterns of professional training in psychology (Vail conference).* Washington, DC: American Psychological Association.

Little, K. B. (1971). Report of the Executive Officer: 1970. *American Psychologist, 26,* 1.

McKeachie, W. J. (1971a). Proceedings of the American Psychological Association, Inc. for the year 1970: Minutes of the annual meeting of the Council of Representatives. *American Psychologist, 26,* 22.

McKeachie, W. J. (1971b). Report of the Recording Secretary. *American Psychologist, 26,* 19.

McKeachie, W. J. (1972). Proceedings of the American Psychological Association, Inc. for the year 1971: Minutes of the annual meeting of the Council of Representatives. *American Psychologist, 27,* 268.

McKeachie, W. J. (1973). Proceedings of the American Psychological Association, Inc. for the year 1972: Minutes of the annual meeting of the Council of Representatives. *American Psychologist, 28,* 312.

McKeachie, W. J. (1974). Proceedings of the American Psychological Association, Inc. for the year 1973: Minutes of the annual meeting and special meeting of the Council of Representatives. *American Psychologist, 29,* 381.

Mills, D. H., Wellner, A. J., & VandenBos, G. R. (1979). The National Register Survey: The first comprehensive study of all licensed/certified psychologists. In C. A. Kiesler, N. A. Cummings, & G. R. VandenBos (Eds.), *Psychology and national health insurance: A sourcebook.* Washington, DC: American Psychological Association.

Pallak, M. S. (1980). Report of the Executive Officer: 1979. *American Psychologist, 34,* 488.

Pallak, M. S. (1982). Report of the Executive Officer: 1981. *American Psychologist, 37,* 488.

Pallak, M. S. (1985). Report of the Executive Officer: 1984. *American Psychologist, 40,* 605.

Pallak, M. S. (1990). Public policy and social psychology: Bridging the gap. In J. E. Edwards, R. S. Timdale, L. Health, & E. J. Posavak (Eds.), *Social influence process and prevention.* New York: Plenum Press.

Pallak, M. S., & Kilburg, R. R. (1986). Psychology, public affairs, and public policy. *American Psychologist, 41,* 933.

Pallak, M. S., & VandenBos, G. R. (1984). Employment of psychologists in the U.S.A.: Responses to the crises of the 1970's. *Journal of the Norwegian Psychological Association, 21,* 65–73.

Perloff, R. (Ed.) (1972). Psychology's manpower: The education and utilization of psychologists [Special issue]. *American Psychologist, 27*(5).

Perloff, R. (1975). Report of the APA Treasurer: 1974. *American Psychologist, 30,* 616.

Stapp, J., Fulcher, R., Nelson, S., Pallak, M. S., & Wicherski, M. (1981). The employment of recent doctorate recipients in psychology: 1975 through 1978. *American Psychologist, 36,* 1211.

Tyler, L. (1969). An approach to public affairs: Report of the ad hoc Committee on Public Affairs. *American Psychologist, 24,* 1.

9

THE AMERICAN PSYCHOLOGICAL ASSOCIATION: 1985 TO 1992

RAYMOND D. FOWLER

As the American Psychological Association approached its centennial year, the organization was changing rapidly, and a number of problems were beginning to converge. The second half of the 1980s began with many unsolved issues left from earlier years, and there were growing tensions among various factions within the Association. The sources of these tensions were structural, demographic, political, and financial. Although some appeared to be new problems, most reflected historical trends and can only be understood in that context. Before the end of the decade, they came together in a major upheaval that threatened the future of the Association.

THE APA IN 1986

At the beginning of 1986, the APA showed many signs of health. With more than 60,000 members and 30,000 affiliates, the APA was by far the largest national association for behavioral and social sciences. With annual revenues of $23 million, less than one third of which came from dues, the Association seemed prosperous as well. The APA Central Office owned and occupied three buildings in the District of Columbia and northern Virginia. Michael Pallak, who had completed a 6-year term as executive officer, was succeeded by Leonard Goodstein in late 1985.

The Association had 336 employees, more than half of whom were engaged in a highly successful information dissemination program that made the APA the largest single publisher of psychological literature and the owner of a sophisticated database of the world's behavioral science literature. The policies of the Association were determined by the membership through an elected Council of Representatives and an extensive network of boards, committees, and task forces composed of members and supported by Central Office personnel. Forty-two divisions represented the special interests of the members, and 52 state and provincial psychological associations represented psychology at the state level. The annual convention, one of the largest in the United States, drew 12,000 to 18,000 participants each year.

The discipline also seemed healthy. Unemployment among members was virtually nonexistent, and psychology was still among the most popular majors and elective courses throughout the country. The post-1970s contraction that had hit most other doctoral programs had not happened to psychology: Most graduate programs rejected many applications for each one they could accept, and the minimum standards for admission continued to rise. Consultants and practitioners were well compensated, and agencies and institutions in the public sector were actively recruiting psychologists. As a flourishing discipline and a national association, psychology and the APA were the envy of many.

How could an organization that seemed so healthy in 1986 face dissolution and financial ruin only a year or so later? In retrospect, it is apparent that not all of the signs were as healthy as they appeared. From a financial standpoint, the existing management systems were inadequate to deal with a multimillion-dollar corporation, and warning signs that change was needed were being ignored. Organizationally, a number of serious, long-standing conflicts among groups of members that had never been resolved were reaching a state of active conflict. A structure designed 45 years earlier for a smaller and very different organization was no longer satisfactory to a substantial minority of the membership. To understand the pressures for change, it is useful to examine the APA's structure as a membership organization and how that structure evolved over time.

THE APA AS A LEARNED SOCIETY AND A PROFESSIONAL ORGANIZATION

Part of the difficulty in making the APA work derived from the different expectations of various subsets of the members. Disciplinary membership organizations perform a variety of functions. Some have to do with promoting the discipline, and others with promoting opportunities for members of the organization. Those associations that are made up of practitioners tend to emphasize regulatory, standard-setting activities as well as the advancement of professional opportunities.

Membership organizations that are primarily devoted to the advancement of the discipline are referred to as *learned societies*, and those that exist primarily to promote the applications of the discipline are called *professional associations*. Learned societies exist primarily for informaiton exchange among their members. Annual meetings are held for the presentation of scholarly papers and to give members the opportunity to meet colleagues and hold informal discussions. Journals are published to provide outlets for scholarly work, to extend the frontiers of the discipline, and to advance the careers of members. Placement services at the annual meetings and newsletters advertising the availability of positions help new members of the discipline find suitable positions.

Small learned societies tend to be simple in their organizational structure. As they grow larger, they may differentiate and establish sections or divisions to recognize specialized areas of interest within the discipline. Most of the members of learned societies are academicians employed as faculty members in colleges and universities; they tend to be relatively homogeneous in their activities and their values. Prestige and power are distributed along lines of seniority, institutional prestige, and national visibility within the discipline.

For most of its first century, the APA was clearly a learned society. The activities of the Association were similar to the activities of other learned societies, such as those for philosophy, history, and anthropology. The members were primarily teachers, some of whom managed laboratories for their students and some of whom did original research. The leadership of the Association included some of the more prestigious members of the discipline. The presidency, a largely honorary position, was a recognition of outstanding contributions to psychology, and an individual who had reached the peak of discipline in terms of scholarly contributions was likely also to be elected APA president.[1]

From the beginning, applied psychologists were an awkward fit into the traditional academic structure of the APA. Recognition was difficult to achieve, their values and priorities were not the same as those of the

---

[1] Some psychologists still feel bitter that the achievements of B. F. Skinner were never recognized by election to the APA presidency. In fact, he was nominated often but always declined to be a candidate for personal reasons.

academicians, and the goals they wanted to attain were foreign and sometimes objectionable to the academic members.

A *discipline* attains its definition by what the members of that discipline know and do. For example, the founders of the APA included philosophers, educators, and physicians, few of whom would be currently recognized as "psychologists." They were brought together by a common interest in psychology, and thus became identified as psychologists. (See Chapters 1, 2, and 3, for further discussion.)

A *profession* may initially be defined in a similar way, but eventually, as a consensus is reached, certain boundaries are established and only those who fall within those boundaries are recognized as members of the profession. The scope of practice and the nature of training are established by the profession, publicized, and, eventually, recognized by law. In the early stages of a profession, admission tends to be by self-definition. Thus, lawyers were originally individuals who had "read the law" and offered legal services to others. Later in the development of a profession, standards of training and practice are defined that determine who can be called a member of the profession and that establish the limits of that individual's practice.

Professional organizations define a profession by establishing criteria of competence, establishing educational requirements for entry into the profession, defining the scope of practice, and setting standards of practice such as ethical codes. They also establish regulatory mechanisms, including accreditation of educational programs, screening of applicants, and enforcement of standards of practice. Because they are usually regulated by law, professions actively advocate at the state and national levels for laws that promote, enhance, and protect the profession. They may lobby, contribute to the campaigns of receptive lawmakers, and develop model laws that define and regulate the profession.

Professional organizations often provide services that their members cannot easily provide for themselves. For example, a professional organization may provide insurance programs, develop methods to promote and publicize the services of the members of the profession, and conduct public relations campaigns to influence the public's understanding and acceptance of the profession. Members of learned societies rarely, if ever, need such services. When those services are needed, the colleges and universities supply them.

THE ROLE OF DIVISIONS AND STATE ASSOCIATIONS IN THE APA

The difficulty of operating a membership organization that is simultaneously both a learned society and a professional association is magnified by the APA's unusual system of representation. Members of the Council of Representatives, the APA's legislative and policy-making body, are elected by divisions, which represent substantive interests and state and provincial associations, which represent geographic units. Divisions are the primary vehicle for the representation of academics, whereas practitioners are represented by state associations as well as by divisions. State associations have always been primarily associated with applied interests, and their increased influence in the Association was seen by some academicians as further erosion of their influence. The growth of these two major forces in the APA, the divisions and the state associations, provides an interesting contrast.

Divisions

Divisions have been part of the APA structure for about half of the life of the organization. In the early years of the Association, most APA members were academicians whose interests were relatively homogeneous. By 1910, the increasingly diversified interests of psychologists were expressed first in the organization of convention program sessions under distinctive topics, and then by the evolution of several interest groups (Fowler, 1989).

The divisions were established in 1945 to facilitate the grouping within the larger organization of psychologists with similar interests. The APA, in its current form, resulted from the 1945 merger with the American Association for Applied Psychology (AAAP), about which more will follow later in this chapter. Thus, although the divisions represent the diversity of the APA, they have been an important element in promoting its unity.

To determine which divisions were needed to represent the range of interests in psychology, the membership was surveyed in 1944 with a questionnaire that suggested 19 possible divisions and provided spaces for write-ins (Hilgard, 1945; see also Chapter 6, this volume). An analysis of the primary and secondary interests of the members as reflected by the survey resulted in combining some divisions that had large overlaps (physiological and comparative, for example). Others were combined to reach a membership of 50, the minimum then required to form a division.

Among the 19 charter divisions shown in the first bylaws of the new APA, five (Divisions 12, 13, 14, 15, and 19) were sections of the AAAP. Two were independent groups, the Society for the Psychological Study of Social Issues (SPSSI) and the Psychometric Society. SPSSI became Division 9, but the Psychometric Society, which was to be Division 4, did not become a division. Division 11 (Abnormal and Psychotherapy) decided to combine with Division 12 (Clinical) to form a single division. Positions

4 and 11 were thus left unfilled, which has resulted in the mystification of many APA members and even the dark suspicion that some divisions had somehow been expelled from the APA or otherwise lost their charter.

It was generally assumed at the outset that the initial array of divisions would change as weaker divisions died out and were replaced by new ones reflecting current interests. In fact, the charter divisions have proved quite hearty, and new interests have been reflected by new divisions. There has been some regrouping and a few name changes, but no division has ever been dissolved: All of the original divisions are currently active, and the Council has never considered dissolving any of them.

Over the years, divisions have grown and receded for various reasons. At the present time, some divisions are growing, a few are shrinking, and most are keeping pace with the growth of the APA (Fowler & VandenBos, 1989). Some that are shrinking appear to be victims of changes in specialization by members. For example, some members who might once have seen themselves as educational psychologists now prefer the designation *cognitive psychologist* and may thus be less likely to join the Division of Educational Psychology.

It does not appear that the loss of members in any division has been primarily attributable to members of the division leaving the APA. Because most people who belong to any division belong to more than one, it appears that people who leave a division simply shift their primary focus to another division.

An issue frequently raised in the Council of Representatives as well as by various members is the "proliferation" of divisions. Some Council proposals to place a moratorium on new divisions have gained considerable support, but all have ultimately been defeated. Most of the reasons presented to justify a moratorium have been countered by more persuasive arguments to the contrary. For example, one argument for a moratorium has been that there are too many divisions. The current list of 47 divisions seems bewilderingly large to many members, but the total membership has increased by 1,500% since divisions were first established in 1945. If the ratio of membership to the number of divisions had remained constant, there would now be close to 300 divisions.

Some of the new divisions reflect areas of interest hardly represented in the membership in 1945, such as Consumer Psychology (23) and Media Psychology (46). Others grew out of existing divisions, such as Psychotherapy (29) out of Clinical (12) and Psychoanalysis (39) out of Psychotherapy (29). Some, such as Psychologists in Independent Practice (42), evolved from interdivisional interest groups as increasing numbers raised these groups to division size. What appears on the surface to be a pointless proliferation of new divisions is rather an expression of the expanded interests of a growing discipline.

Another argument against new divisions is that they might tend to fractionate the Association. But experience has shown that the primary point of contact with the APA for many people is their division affiliation, and some might not want to be a member of a generic psychological organization if their interest areas were not specifically represented. Certainly, many would not be able to participate as actively as officers and committee members if a divisional structure did not exist.

Some members oppose the establishment of new divisions because they dilute the voting power on the Council of the smaller divisions, some of which have largely academic memberships. It is often argued that the new divisions tend to be predominantly practice oriented, but this is not the case: Most of the new divisions reflect public interest concerns, such as Psychology of Women (35) and Ethnic Minority Interests (45); new areas of application, such as Consumer Psychology (23) and Health Psychology (38); and subject matter areas that were small or nonexistent in 1945, such as Experimental Analysis of Behavior (25) and Psychopharmacology (28).

The relationship between the APA and its divisions is still evolving. According to Dael Wolfle (1946, p. 5), the APA's first executive officer, the relation of the divisions to the APA was to be similar to the relation of the states of the union to the United States, with the divisions retaining a high degree of internal autonomy yet conceding certain authority to the central organization. In practice, the divisions have been granted much greater autonomy than a strict reading of the bylaws would permit, and some would prefer even more latitude to function independently.

The establishment of divisions probably played a significant role in keeping the APA together and in developing psychology as a discipline. Just as the founding of the APA created a critical mass of scholars who then established and cultivated the discipline, the founding of a division creates a critical mass of specialists who work together to develop that subfield. An equally important function of the divisions is to bridge the research–practice gap by bringing together, through common interest in a specific area, researchers, teachers, and practitioners who otherwise might not make contact. This is particularly true of some divisions that are almost equally dedicated to scientific, applied, and public interest concerns. But almost all divisions contain an element of diversity, and they provide an opportunity for interaction between academicians and practitioners.

State Psychological Associations

The expanding role of practitioners in the APA has been paralleled by the increasingly active role played by state and provincial psychological associations (SPPAs). Unlike the APA divisions, which are an integral part of the Association, the SPPAs are independent entities that voluntarily associate themselves with the APA. For affiliation, the APA bylaws require only that membership not be restricted on any basis other than psychological interests and qualifications or place of residence or work, that the name shall be the name of the state or province followed by the words "Psychological Association," and that at least 10 of its members be members of the APA (see Chapter 6 for further information).

No formal history has been written of the SPPAs. In their early days, the SPPAs tended to be informal groups of psychologists for whom record keeping was not a high priority, and few accounts of their origins and development have been published. Soon after the APA was established, members in the larger cities began to hold meetings, and the bylaws were changed to permit the establishment of "local sections," which, in practice, came to be called "branches." The Chicago and New York branches, which were organized by academics and existed primarily for the presentation of papers, evolved into the Midwestern and Eastern psychological associations, and the APA recognized them as regional affiliates.

The SPPAs, which grew more out of the activities of applied psychologists, evolved quite independently of the regional associations. Some groups had organized themselves as state associations as early as 1930 (the New York and Colorado branches, established much earlier, were predecessors of regional associations, not of state associations). In 1946, Wolfle noted that there were then 14 associations, and predicted that "because of the interest in state laws to regulate professional standards, state societies may become increasingly important" (Hamlin & Habbe, p. 17).

That prediction was confirmed. Executive Officer Fillmore Sanford, noting that in 1954 there were 46 state associations, initiated a section on "Psychology in the States" in the *American Psychologist*. He observed that when psychology was almost entirely confined to the academic environment, no need was felt for state psychological associations. But "as society began to get the notion that psychologists were useful as well as scholarly, psychology began to have increasing contact with the outside world and with events and problems that are geographically sliced" (Sanford, 1954, p. 808). Sanford observed that the 46 state associations appeared to be stable and active bodies that are "concerning themselves most vigorously with such problems as legislation, public relations, and ethics. . . . The activities of these psychological organizations, though not now of explicit interest to all psychologists, are steadily determining the position of psychology in American life, are gradually helping to shape the pattern of opportunities and responsibilities of anyone who bears the psychological label" (p. 808). Sanford predicted that "as psychology develops and as the number of psychologists increases, local and state organizations will probably become more stable, more active and more numerous" (p. 808). Sanford captured, even in the early days of SPPAs, much of the essence that still characterizes them. Although they include academicians among their members, they are primarily concerned with psychology's relationship with the "outside world," especially events at the state level.

Typically run entirely by volunteers, the state associations in small states existed primarily to hold an annual meeting, to elect officers, and to appoint committees. The lack of effective associations in some states became a source of concern to the practice community because the restrictive or inappropriate laws passed by one state could establish a precedent and threaten practice in other states.

It had long been apparent that the APA could not effectively advocate at the state level: That requires citizens of the state who can build ongoing relationships of mutual understanding and support with legislators. But many states had state associations that were not capable of responding to threats at the state level or, sometimes, even knowing that they existed. The APA recognized the importance of helping all of the states build resources to monitor state affairs and to respond to threats to psychology, which cannot be done effectively by volunteers who have other full-time responsibilities. Paid staff, even if on a part-time basis, is essential to carry out basic administrative functions and to coordinate the essential work of volunteers.

Over the years the SPPAs have evolved from small groups of volunteers into fairly complex professional organizations with central offices, executive officers, and active programs of advocacy for professional psychology. Grants from the APA, along with consultation with and national coordination from the Practice Directorate, accelerated that evolution and helped to create a powerful national network to promote the applications of psychology.

ORGANIZING AND REORGANIZING THE APA

Calls for organizational changes that would permit greater autonomy for the major constituencies began to come from some academic–research psychologists as early as the 1970s. More specifically, they wanted a separation of the administrative and policy-making aspects of the Association that would permit the academic members to manage their own affairs and pay for only the limited services they thought were sufficient to meet their needs. Nor did they want to be tied to policies with which they might not agree.

Organizational change is hardly a novel experience for the APA. As early as 1901, a group of philosopher–psychologist APA members left the APA to form the American Philosophical Association (Hilgard, 1987, p. 740; see also Chapter 2, this volume). The separation was apparently precipitated by a decision that philosophical papers would no longer be presented at the annual meeting. The decision stood, and the philosophers went their own way.

Throughout most of the APA's first century, however, the central conflict has been between basic and applied psychology and the values associated with each. This schism, which Spence (1987) referred to as psychology's "fracture line," has been the boundary along which the APA's most critical battles have been fought.

The major function of the academic psychologist is the transmission of knowledge (teaching) and the generation of new knowledge (research). The central value associated with these endeavors is academic freedom. The teacher determines the material to be taught and the interpretations to be conveyed; the researcher is led into areas of inquiry by the data, not by instructions from others. The APA's founders were brought together by a common interest in the subject matter of psychology and a common set of values associated with the importance of scientific inquiry. Some of the founders were personally interested in the applications of psychology, but most were fundamentally academics for whom teaching and research held the highest priority.

If scientific psychology may be said to have found its first expression in Wundt's laboratories in Leipzig, applied psychology may be said to have grown out of the work of James McKeen Cattell, who received his doctorate with Wundt in 1886. The scholarly German and his brash American student differed in many ways, but especially in how they viewed individual differences. Wundt, concerned with the elements and structure of the mind, believed that individual differences were little more than random variations that should be eliminated as sources of error. For Cattell, the measurement of individual differences, through what he came to call mental tests, offered an opportunity not only to understand the mind in general but to describe the functioning of an individual and to predict future performance.

Thus, even before the founding of the APA, the science–practice dichotomy, which would enrich and endanger both the new discipline and the Association, had expressed itself in the contrasting orientation of the first experimental psychologist and his American student. Laboratory experimentation became the hallmark of the scientific psychologist, and psychological tests became the key that opened the doors of factories, hospitals, and schools to psychologists. The attitudinal differences between the scientist and the practitioner have been a constant for more than a century, and are the source of many of our internal tensions.

In a 1984 *American Psychologist* article, "Psychology's Two Cultures," Kimble attempted to define this basic dichotomy in terms of attitudes and values. Kimble pointed out that the conflict is by no means unique to psychology. C. P. Snow (1964) originated the concept of the two cultures when he described his scientific colleagues and his literary colleagues as being so different in intellectual, moral, and psychological orientation that they could have been residents of different societies. In psychology, Kimble pointed out, these conflicting cultures exist within a single field, and this is the source of a bitter and continuing family feud.

By the beginning of the 20th century, many of the tensions that currently characterize the discipline were already appearing in the APA. There were, according to Hilgard (1987), serious debates about what psychology should be, power struggles within the organization, and concerns that the papers at the annual meeting were not scientific enough. Disagreements over basic versus applied psychology were already in the air. Along with growth came more and more specialization, but most psychologists still shared the hope of maintaining psychology as a unified science and the APA as a unitary organization.

Altman (1987) viewed the history of psychology in terms of centripetal and centrifugal factors, which also characterize higher education and American society in general. Centripetal factors consolidate and unify, whereas centrifugal factors differentiate and separate. A society, an institution, or a discipline may display at one time centripetal and at another centrifugal tendencies. Centripetal qualities may result in stagnation and resistance to change, but they provide organization and structure. Similarly, centrifugal qualities may polarize and divide, but they can result in new ideas and creative change.

Altman (1987) characterized the period before 1890 as a predominantly centrifugal, nonunified stage in the history of psychology. Before the last quarter of the 19th century, psychology did not exist as a discipline. People interested in psychological phenomena were identified with other disciplines and had little communality or identification with each other. This separation had its disadvantages, but also its advantages: The emerging psychology was enriched by its immersion in other related disciplines.

With the establishment of the first psychological laboratories and the founding of the APA in 1892, American psychology entered a long unifying period in which centripetal, organizing forces gained strength. Schools of psychology—such as structuralism, functionalism, and behaviorism—pulled together groups of psychologists, and eventually a broad, behaviorist perspective emerged that brought some unity to the various theoretical perspectives.

According to Altman (1987), the period from the early 1900s to the 1960s was one in which psychological theory and research were increasingly centripetal. The field defined itself, its topics, its content, and its approach to psychological phenomena. There was broad agreement on the necessity for rigorous quantification and measurement, and experimental, laboratory-oriented research methodologies prevailed as an idealized methodological strategy. The tensions between researchers and practitioners existed during the 1900–1960 period and centrifugal forces emerged, but they were eventually resolved in a centripetal direction that maintained a unified national organization.

An example of the resolution of centrifugal trends may be found in the emergence of applied psychology from 1910 to 1920. Neither the universities nor the APA was supportive of practitioner needs, and this reluctance led to increasing frustration on the part of the small cadre of applied psychologists in the APA. When a group of dissatisfied clinicians got together and founded the American Association of Clinical Psychologists (AACP) at the 1917 APA convention, this centrifugal action was countered by a centripetal action on the part of the Association: The APA created a clinical section, admitted the members of the AACP as members of the APA, and changed the bylaws to read that the APA's purpose was to advance psychology as both a science and a profession. The AACP was formally dissolved. In 1937, after a period of unity during and after World War I, applied psychologists again felt that the APA was not meeting their needs. They founded the American Association for Applied Psychology (AAAP), and the APA's clinical section dissolved.

The approach of World War II provided a centripetal force that brought psychologists together once again. In 1941, meetings between representatives of the APA and the AAAP resulted in recommendations for a number of changes in the APA structure to encourage the participation of applied psychologists. Membership standards were changed, and applied psychologists who had been associates were granted full membership and the right to vote and hold office. By 1945, new bylaws had been approved that reorganized the APA in ways that were supportive of practitioners. The establishment of a central office with an executive director and staff made the APA more able to provide the kinds of services that the practitioners needed.

The crowning centripetal action was probably the development of the

Boulder Model of training in clinical psychology. This scientist–professional model, in which the clinical psychologist was trained as both a scientist and a practitioner, was generally accepted by other areas of specialization. This resulted in a unified conception of the professional–applied psychologist and a clear overlap with the traditional scientific psychologist.

The reorganization of the APA reduced the concerns of applied psychologists, but some academic–research psychologists felt that the APA was moving in a direction that threatened psychology as a science. With the rapid growth of psychology that began in the 1960s, other centrifugal forces began to prevail. Psychology departments became large and subdivided into areas of specialization. Core curricula tended to weaken as specialty courses proliferated. Faculty members within a department began to have less and less in common with each other, and students became more identified with their specialty areas than with psychology. As APA members became more specialized in their interests, their involvement with divisions increased and affiliation with the national organization, or even with psychology, weakened.

The 1945 reorganization of the APA had established a hybrid organization: The APA became both a learned society and a professional association. As long as the needs of the professionals in the APA were not great and the numbers were small, the hybrid organization worked well. However, as the demographics began to change and an increasingly powerful minority demanded more support for professional activities, many academic members began to look for a different structure that would allow the learned society members and the professional association members some degree of autonomy and separation from each other.

The Growth of Professional Advocacy

The growth of professional psychology as a major force in the APA resulted in increased demands for more vigorous advocacy for practitioner interests and to more resistance from nonpractitioners to the expenditure of general dues money for such specialized purposes. The demands that the APA be more proactive in the public arena had always come from the practitioners (although the APA's first major effort at public advocacy came when it mobilized its resources to counter the Reagan administration's cutbacks in funding for research and training in the social and behavioral sciences; Pallak, 1990; Pallak & Kilburg, 1986).

The first organized effort by practitioners to establish their own advocacy for practitioner concerns was the founding of the Council for the Advancement of Psychological Professions and Sciences (CAPPS) in 1972

("United Council," 1975). Funded by voluntary contributions and formed as an independent corporation entirely separate from APA, the CAPPS formed a political action committee (PAC) that permitted contributions to the campaigns of political candidates.

Establishing a psychology advocacy organization outside of the APA, managed entirely by practitioners, was viewed by some APA leaders as dangerously centripetal. After prolonged discussion, the Council of Representatives authorized the formation of an alternative advocacy organization, the Association for the Advancement of Psychology (AAP), with equal representation on its Board of Trustees going to practice, science, and public interest. Negotiations between the leadership of the AAP and the CAPPS led to the merging of the two organizations (Cummings, 1979).

For a time, the AAP, as an independent organization, was the major advocacy voice for psychology, but the APA began to develop its own advocacy operation, and the two groups did not always work in coordination. AAP contributions dwindled as the APA played an increasingly visible role in advocacy. The AAP's primary activity became the management of its PAC, called Psychologists for Legislative Action Now, and advocacy increasingly moved into the jurisdiction of the APA.

By the 1980s, some practitioner groups had begun to believe that neither the AAP's nor the APA's advocacy efforts were doing enough to meet practitioners' needs. The widespread availability of third-party payments through health insurance that had attracted so many young psychologists into private practice in the 1970s had begun to contract, and shifts toward managed care, especially the health maintenance organizations, threatened the livelihood of practitioners. The pressure of the health care dollar had grown considerably with federal budget deficits, and business and government purchasers of health care were drastically reducing expenditures. The impact of these reductions fell most heavily on mental health care. These pressures also increased the belligerency of medical groups toward their nonmedical health care competitors. For example, in December 1984, the American Medical Association House of Delegates passed a resolution aimed at curtailing the independent practice of all allied health professionals, and established a political war chest to fight what they referred to as incursions of psychologists and others into medical practice by way of prescribing privileges, independent practice, mandated third party reimbursements or other expansion of their scope of practice.

Confronting these new challenges would require additional funds, but many academicians were already frustrated by APA dues that they felt were too high and unfairly distributed. It was becoming increasingly difficult for the Association to attract and retain academic–research psychologists, and raising dues could only make matters worse. The practitioners conceived of a plan designed to let health care providers assess themselves to fund the new programs that they felt were needed, without further affecting the academic–research members. The new funds were to be sequestered and used to supplement, not to supplant, existing APA support for practice.

In August 1985, the Council of Representatives unanimously approved a proposal by practitioner groups that would permit the Association to levy a special assessment to fund such expenditures as state advocacy, hiring experienced professional advocates, and developing a grass roots network. The implementation of the special assessment was approved at the next meeting of the Council in February 1986. With certain exceptions, all licensed members of the Association who provided health care services were assessed an additional $50 in annual dues, with practitioners at the upper income levels asked to pay an additional $50 or $100. A new Office of Professional Practice (OPP) was established to carry out the special assessment initiatives. Some of the funds raised by the special assessment were funneled back to the states through grants. The highest priority was given to helping state associations establish stable central offices with paid staffs. This was sometimes done with matching grants that required state associations to increase their dues from the token amounts necessary to operate a small organization to amounts that were double, triple, or more what they were. Although raising dues increased the effectiveness of the SPPAs, it had an unfortunate side effect: Most academic members, unwilling to pay the larger dues, left the SPPAs, with the result that most became entirely practitioner groups.

The vast majority of members on whom the special assessment fell seemed to accept it willingly. The rate of compliance was quite high, and many made additional voluntary contributions to support the work of the OPP. The Committee for the Advancement of Professional Psychology was established as an ad hoc committee to advise the Board of Directors on the expenditure of the special assessment funds and to oversee the operation of the OPP.

The reaction of academic members was ambivalent. Academic members had often advocated a differential dues system that would allow those who wanted more services to pay for them. Although they were pleased not to have to pay for the new activities through increased general dues, some academic members strongly questioned the appropriateness of some of the new initiatives. Others worried about the increased power to influence the Association that would come with the increased funds. Of particular concern to some was the plan to greatly expand the activities and effectiveness of the state psychological associations. It had long been the position of many academicians that representation in the Council of Representatives should only be through divisions, an organizational structure characteristic of learned societies, whereas practitioners supported representation through the state associations, a kind of representation more characteristic of professional associations. Thus, the special assessment, although solving some problems for the association, focused attention on two new issues: the organizational structure of the APA and the relative roles of state associations and divisions in setting the agenda of the Association.

The willingness of practitioner groups to assess themselves to pay for additional services was intended as a centripetal move, and the unanimously favorable vote by the Council of Representatives reflected that it was seen in that way by the members of the various factions. However, the implementation of the special assessment aroused great concern on the part of many academicians that the image of the Association was changing to that of a professional association. More than $1.5 million a year in new funds was brought in by the special assessment, and the OPP began to be viewed by some as a powerful and dangerous new force in the APA. Members who were already uncomfortable with the APA's professionally related activities focused their attention on the new activities and were not happy with what they saw.

GROWING PRESSURES FOR REORGANIZATION

Operating a highly complex, hybrid organization became increasingly difficult as the disparate elements began to compete for resources and control. As the number of applied psychologists approached the number of academic psychologists, the pressure for reorganization of the APA increased. Indeed, the changing demographics of the Association became a major source of tension. Changes in the kinds of psychologists graduating from doctoral programs were reflected in APA membership. Poor employment prospects for academic psychologists and rapidly developing opportunities for psychologists in private practice led to more and better applicants to clinical programs and fewer applicants for the traditional nonapplied areas: New graduates were overwhelmingly oriented toward providing clinical services. In addition, professional schools of psychology, both university based and freestanding, emerged, and their graduates, who were not trained in the Boulder Model, were even more different from the traditional academics. The numerical power of academic psychologists, who had been the major force in the Association for most of its existence, was declining, and their ability to influence events seemed threatened.

Demographic Changes

The changes in psychology were part of a nationwide trend. As the country shifted from an agricultural and industrial economy to a service economy, the predominant locus of employment of graduates of scientific programs shifted from the university to business, government, consulting, and the delivery of services. It would have been remarkable if psychology had been untouched by these national trends.

The steady growth in psychology as a whole masked important changes in the distribution of psychologists in the specialty areas. Up to 1940, almost 70% of new PhDs in psychology were in experimental psychology. By 1960, only 25% of PhDs were in experimental, physiological, and comparative psychology combined. By 1984, more than one half of all PhDs were awarded in health service provider areas, with all other areas accounting for 47% of the new PhDs. Doctoral production in the academic–research areas peaked in the mid-1970s, and by 1984 had declined to its 1968 level (Howard et al., 1986). The growth of professional psychology took place during a period in which most of the new opportunities for employment occurred outside of academic settings, especially in the health care sector.

By the 1970s, it was clear that the changing demographics of the APA meant that political control of the Association was shifting from the academic to the applied psychologist. Many psychologists became alarmed about the increasing disaffection of the academic psychologists and sought to find ways to make the Association more attractive to them, to preserve unity. However, the early efforts to change the Association into a loose federation were seen by some as dangerously centrifugal and weakening and were strongly resisted by clinicians and by many other psychologists as well.

In 1985, the APA's Committee on Employment and Human Resources published "The Changing Face of American Psychology," a report prepared to brief the Board of Directors of APA and other interested parties on some recent trends of importance in psychology's human resources. The report, subsequently published in the *American Psychologist* (Howard et al., 1986), used national statistics and various APA surveys to demonstrate that an increasing proportion of students going into psychology were choosing the health provider subfields (clinical–counseling–school) over the traditional academic–research subfields of psychology (experimental–comparative–physiological; social–personality; developmental; and psychometrics). Psychology, one of the fastest growing fields in the production of doctorates since 1945, did not experience as great a decline in the 1970s and 1980s as did other disciplines because of the increasing numbers of students interested in the health provider fields.

Unlike human resource surveys that excite little interest, "The Changing Face" became a major political issue. It was extensively cited by people who favored a reorganization of the APA and who interpreted it in ways that accentuated the "negative" aspects of the situation. For example, the report noted that the annual production of traditional academic/research psychologists, which had peaked in the 1970s, had subsequently declined by more than 40%. It concluded that this decline could erode the scientific knowledge base for our understanding of human behavior. The fact that large numbers of psychologists are being trained primarily for applied positions rather than academic–research positions, however, does not mean that psychology will be less able to develop as a scientific discipline. The discipline is currently producing enough academic–research PhDs to fill all of the available positions, and the number of positions is not likely to increase for another decade or so. The reduced number of graduates in the traditional areas reflected not a lack of interest in science, but a shortage of academic positions.

The report also noted that the proportion of new psychology PhDs graduating from the top-ranked research departments had declined. It suggested that this raised questions about the quality of training that students were receiving and that it might impair psychology's continued standing as both a science and a profession. In fact, the proportion of scientists who graduate from the major research institutions has not decreased, and the absolute number of scientist–practitioners who graduate from those same institutions has remained constant. The increase of new doctorates outside of the major research institutions is of professional psychologists. They are coming, as one might expect, from professionally oriented programs and professional schools, not from the major research departments, many of which do not provide training programs for practitioners.

The report further noted that psychology had become less attractive to men, as evidenced by the data showing an increasing proportion of women entering the field. For years, the APA had been working to reduce the barriers to women who wanted to enter the field of psychology. The dramatic increase in the number of women graduate students, which could have been interpreted as evidence that the field had become increasingly attractive and accessible to women, was instead interpreted to mean that psychology had become unattractive to men.

These interpretations of the demographic data were accepted uncritically by many readers and became part of the political dispute on reorganization. Interpreting the decrease in the ratio of students attracted to academic careers in psychology relative to those going into applied areas ignored the marketplace factors. Society had great demands for applied psychologists, and, at that particular time, most academic positions were filled and were likely to remain so for many years.

A Plan for Reorganization

Membership surveys conducted in 1987 (Howard et al.) indicated an increasing dissatisfaction with the APA on the part of some members. More than half of the members surveyed indicated that they knew reorganization was being discussed and that they intended to vote on the issue when it was presented to the membership. Most felt that some organizational changes were needed, but members identified as scientists were more likely to favor change, especially major change, than were scientist–practitioners or practitioners. Members were more than twice as likely (49%) to believe that the APA was serving the needs of practitioners than that the needs of researchers were being well served (22%). Among the survey respondents who indicated they were likely to vote, 47% favored a major reorganization: too few to pass a reorganization, because a two-thirds vote is needed for approval. The authors noted that the results of the survey indicated that most members would vote on the issue, and counseled that any proposed plan be simple to understand.

In 1984, the Board of Directors established a Task Force on Reorganization to examine ways in which the Association might organize itself to better represent all constituencies. The Task Force, recognizing the primacy of the academic-versus-practitioner split, worked toward the establishment of a bipartite structure with semiautonomous science and practice units and no role for divisions (Task Force, 1987). Many psychologists saw that as too simple a structure to represent the variability of interests of 70,000 psychologists.

In 1987, the Council of Representatives rejected the plan submitted by the Task Force and two other plans submitted by the Board of Directors, and appointed the Group on Restructuring of APA (GOR) to succeed the Task Force. The GOR also tried a bipartite structure, but, by that time, three other groups had gathered strength and were demanding inclusion. Because the goal of the Association is to promote psychology as a science and a profession in the public interest, a tripartite structure including science, practice, and public interest was proposed and accepted by the GOR. Most of the supporters of reorganization in the science community accepted the tripartite structure, and even clinicians who were not enthusiastic about changing the APA were not strongly opposed to the arrangement.

The next group to be heard from, however, greatly complicated the mix. A scientist–practitioner group, which primarily represented the Boulder Model, research-oriented clinicians, asserted that none of the three assemblies represented them, and demanded to be included. Both science-oriented and practice-oriented groups were alarmed by the prospect of this new group, both because it could, in terms of size, become the dominant group and because each group had assumed that scientist–practitioners would choose to affiliate with them.

Still another group, the state psychological associations, which had gained strength with the growth of professional psychology, asserted that the practice section did not fully represent their interests, and they also demanded representation. This was resisted by scientists who had never believed that state associations should be represented in the governance structure and by some practitioners who had assumed that state association members, being primarily practitioners, would add to their numbers.

The restructuring plan submitted by the Group on Restructuring was the result of many compromises. It was a delicately balanced response to a network of political pressures within the formal and informal governance structure of the APA. Essentially, it permitted the emergence of up to five semiautonomous units representing science, practice, public interest, scientist–practitioners, and state associations. Many of the activities of the Central Office would be carried out autonomously by the separate units.

THE EMERGING FINANCIAL CRISIS

As the politics of the Association grew more tense, financial problems were building as well. Annual deficits in the APA's operation had absorbed most of the equity in the APA's three buildings and eventually forced their sale. The organizational problems were even more threatening to the APA's future than the financial problems, but deficit financing led to further erosion in the confidence that members felt in the management of the Association. The financial problems of 1986 cannot be understood without looking back at *Psychology Today*.

From the beginning, *Psychology Today* generated controversy in the APA. Many believed that purchasing a well-established national magazine was the APA's finest opportunity to communicate psychology to the public and that it could be a respected and profitable addition to the APA's journals and other publications. To others, the management by the APA of a popular magazine seemed an exercise in folly, and these opponents cited lack of expertise on the part of the APA's Central Office, unknown financial risk, questions about the usefulness of "pop psychology," and many other arguments against the venture.

The possibility of purchasing *Psychology Today* was first presented to the Board of Directors in the fall of 1982. The magazine, extremely poplar in the late 1960s, had declined in popularity and quality. Most Board members were interested in the possibility of owning a major magazine, but some were uncomfortable about the risks involved. After considerable discussion, the Board voted in February 1983 to submit the question of purchasing the magazine to the Council of Representatives. The Council authorized the Board of Directors to proceed with negotiations to buy the magazine if satisfactory terms could be reached. The Board held many special meetings and conference calls during the Spring of 1983. As more information about the magazine was obtained, positions for and against the purchase on the part of the various Board members began to emerge. By the time of the final vote in March 1983, the Board was evenly split, and the vote of President Max Siegel, in favor, broke the tie.

During the years the magazine was published under APA ownership, opposition grew among the membership as various groups objected to advertisements they considered offensive. Tobacco advertisements took the brunt of the criticism, but there were also objections to advertisements for alcohol and subliminal learning and some specific advertisements seen as offensive to women or to religious groups. The volume of mail in opposition to the magazine increased, and open forum meetings at the convention were dominated by the topic.

By 1986, the substantive debate over whether the operation of a popular magazine was appropriate or useful for the Association had been overshadowed by the increasing financial burden of the magazine. With each year, the deficits grew; the losses to the association were $3.6 million in 1986 alone. Some members of the Board favored putting the magazine up for sale, whereas others held out for more time to see if a financial turnaround would occur. Finally, abandoning hope that the magazine's finances would ever improve, the Board of Directors in 1987 authorized the chief executive officer to seek possible buyers, but there was still considerable ambivalence: Some Board members believed that the worst losses were past and that a turnaround was possible. As 1987 ended, an active search for a buyer began.

A YEAR OF CRISIS

The crisis year for the APA was 1988. It began with a serious confrontation between the APA and the National Register of Health Service

Providers that threatened to lead to litigation. A bitter discussion at the January 1988 Council of Representatives meeting culminated in a conflict-of-interest resolution prohibiting members of the National Register governing body from service in any part of the APA governance system, including boards and committees.

The National Register debate was followed by an equally intense debate on the merits of the reorganization plan submitted by the Group on Restructuring, which was ultimately approved to be submitted to the membership for a vote (Fisher, 1988c). The GOR's efforts to satisfy everyone had resulted in a plan that was unsatisfactory to most members. Disagreements among the leaders of the opposing groups became distinctly uncordial, and the bitterness that characterized the debate among the membership was reflected in strong disagreements among members of the Board of Directors.

A new group called the Assembly of Scientific and Applied Psychologists (ASAP) was established to promote reorganization. As the election grew closer, the ASAP stated its intention of being the focal point for a new national organization to be formed if reorganization failed, and the APA members most directly involved in the ASAP predicted that if reorganization failed the Association would irrevocably split. Many Council members who voted in favor of submitting the plan to the membership were deeply opposed to the plan, but felt that the issue should be resolved in one way or another. Many supporters of reorganization had misgivings about the plan that finally went to the membership, but supported it in the belief that it might be the last hope for reorganization. The months preceding the May vote saw what was surely the most intense political campaigning in the history of the Association. Proponents of the plan promoted it through universities and the more academically oriented divisions. The opponents solicited the practice divisions but focused their attention on mobilizing the state associations in opposition to the plan. The long-festering conflict between the two sides—those members who favored a reorganization of the APA and those who opposed it—erupted into a bitter, internecine political battle. The fault line between academicians and practitioners had never been more clear.

As tensions built within the Association, the Board of Directors learned that the final accounting of the previous year, 1987, showed a deficit of $6.2 million (Fowler, 1988b). In addition to a deficit of $4.5 million in *Psychology Today* operations, there was a deficit in normal APA operations of $1.7 million, more than all of the previous deficits in the Association's history combined.

APA President Raymond Fowler, Treasurer Charles Spielberger, and the Board of Directors moved rapidly to take control of a financial system that had gone awry (Fowler, 1988b, Spielberger, 1988, 1989). Emergency actions were taken to decrease the anticipated deficits for 1988, and a new chief financial officer was employed to take charge of the Association's finances and to develop a new financial management system. Chief Executive Officer Leonard Goodstein resigned, the Board appointed Gary VandenBos, executive director of the Office of Communications, as acting chief executive officer, and a search began for a permanent chief executive officer.

In the summer of 1988, as the Board worked to stabilize the finances of the Association, the news came that reorganization had been rejected by the membership (Fisher, 1988b). As predicted, the vote was heavy: Nearly 40% of the membership voted, compared with the usual 25%. The reorganization plan, a product of extensive compromises, had been complex, difficult to understand even by the leadership, and presented in the form of extensive bylaws changes. It received only 42.8% of the votes cast, far less than a two-thirds majority. Reports from the state associations indicated that many had organized to defeat the plan and that the vote from SPPA members had been very heavy.

The controversy left many members, particularly those who had led the reorganization effort, feeling battered, bruised, and alienated. The ASAP, which had formed to support reorganization, metamorphosed into what ASAP leaders described as an alternative organization, the American Psychological Society (APS). The leadership of the new organization included many people who had long been active in the APA governance structure, including three past-presidents and a past-executive officer. Strong and sometimes intemperate statements were made by proponents of both the APA and the APS, and the relationship between the two organizations began in a climate of anger and suspicion. The APA Board of Directors voted that the APS was a competing organization, and declined to rent them an exhibit booth for recruiting new members at the convention. A move at the August 1988 Council of Representatives meeting to disqualify APS leaders from service in the APA leadership narrowly failed when time ran out on a crucial vote (Fisher, 1988a).

The bitterness that had characterized the reorganization campaign continued to influence the relationships among various APA constituencies. The leadership of some of the more science-oriented divisions began to doubt that there was a future for them in the APA and to look for possible affiliation with the APS or, alternatively, status as independent associations. Some academic psychologists believed that the vote against reorganization was antiacademic, and began to feel more unwelcome in the APA.

By the end of 1988, the finances of the Association had been stabilized. In May 1988, *Psychology Today* was sold to PT Partners, a group made up of Owen Lipstein, a magazine entrepreneur, and T. George Harris, an early and highly successful editor of the magazine in better days. A projected loss of $2.6 million for the year turned into a surplus of more than $400,000. Gary VandenBos served as acting chief executive officer from October 1988 until Raymond Fowler; the immediate past-president, became chief executive officer in June 1989.

However, 1989 began with some major uncertainties for the Association, the first of which was financial. The new financial management system had performed well in 1988 by means of drastic cutbacks, including salary and hiring freezes and fewer board and committee meetings, but no one could be sure that the new system could also assure a surplus with a return to normal services and staffing. Fortunately, it was able to do so. A predicted modest surplus for 1989 turned into one of $1.6 million, larger than all previous surpluses combined. This substantially increased the APA's net worth, demonstrated the success of the new management system, and provided the assurance that the Association was once again responsibly managing its finances.

The defeat of reorganization and the formation of the APS, whose stated goal was to recruit 10,000 to 20,000 members, raised the specter of the loss of many APA members. It was by no means certain that the APA could maintain its membership level in the face of these challenges. To guard against the possibility of membership loss, the Membership Office coordinated a major campaign to recruit and retain members. This campaign showed impressive results, and the membership of the APA continued to increase. There was no evidence of a substantial loss of members in any category, and more than 5,000 psychologists joined or rejoined the APA, making it the best year ever for new memberships. The student affiliate category grew rapidly with the development of an active student association, the APA Graduate Students Association. By the end of 1989, more than 103,000 individuals were members, fellows, associates, student affiliates, and high school teacher affiliates of the APA. There was no evidence that the APS had negatively affected APA membership: Apparently, most of the members of the APS are also members of the APA, as is the case with most of the 100 or so other psychology-related organizations in the United States (VandenBos, 1989).

Although many feared that there would be major confrontations between the APA and the APS, no serious conflicts materialized. In various discussions that were held with representatives of the APS, both parties attempted to minimize conflict and to seek out cooperation and collaboration on issues whenever possible (Fowler, 1988a). For example, the Board of Directors authorized APA President Fowler and Executive Director of Communications VandenBos to negotiate with the APS for the APA to become the publisher of the new APS journal, *Psychological Science*. Although the APS ultimately contracted with another publisher, collegial interaction on this matter reduced friction between the APA and the APS (VandenBos, 1989). A letter from APS past-president Charles Kiesler noted, "We in APS appreciate very much the good faith effort of the American Psychological Association to cooperate with APS and to consider a collaborative business venture with us. We appreciate as well the congenial and collegial tone of all our interactions" (C. A. Kiesler, personal communication, February 14, 1989).

Another uncertainty that faced the APA in 1989 was the relationship between the APA and its divisions, which had become strained through neglect and misunderstanding. Some divisions reported a loss of membership, and some division officers felt that they were getting little, if any, support from the APA. In the summer of 1989, the Central Office launched a major initiative to provide support and communication. The Division Services Office was expanded, and the Membership Office began to work closely with the divisions to retain and increase their members. Increased communication with the membership about the contributions of the divisions and a redesigned membership interest form resulted in a 144% increase in the total number of members expressing interest in joining divisions, as well as an increase in the membership of every division. The response of the divisions to this demonstration of support was very positive, and losing divisions began to seem less likely.

Finally, the APA faced the problem of finding a permanent home. The financial losses engendered by *Psychology Today* had required the sale of the APA buildings and relegated the Association to the status of a tenant in the buildings it had formerly owned. The Association began an active search for a new building. Preliminary efforts resulted, by the end of 1988, in the formation of a partnership with Trammell Crow, a nationally prominent building development firm. During 1989, the building development program went into high gear. The result was the purchase, under very favorable terms, of an excellent building site near Capitol Hill. On December 2, 1989, 12 past presidents of the APA joined the current officers and members of the Board of Directors for a formal groundbreaking ceremony on the building site (Photo 29).[2]

---

[2]Past presidents in attendance were George W. Albee, Anne Anastasi, Nicholas A. Cummings, Florence L. Denmark, E. R. Hilgard, J. McVicker Hunt, Gardner Lindzey, Neal E. Miller, Robert Perloff, M. Brewster Smith, Janet T. Spence, and Bonnie R. Strickland.

THE APA'S ROLE IN ORGANIZED PSYCHOLOGY

Most of the groups that had wanted more separation and autonomy still wanted to retain a unitary APA. For most APA members, the advantages of a single, strong voice to represent psychology was apparent, but there were growing doubts that the APA could continue to provide that single voice. In fact, the general perception of a single voice for psychology had long since ceased to be accurate. In his annual report for 1988 titled "Loosely Organized 'Organized Psychology,'" VandenBos (1989) identified more than 100 organizations that in one way or another speak for psychology (see Figure 1). VandenBos observed that although about half of the psychologists in the world reside in North America, and although the APA is the largest of the world's psychological associations, it is only one of many organizations that play a role in defining and promoting psychology in the United States and the world. The need to exchange information in specialized areas has resulted in the development of many psychology-related groups that overlap with each other and with the APA. The need to join forces with other associations and other disciplines has resulted in an elaborate network of national and international psychological organizations.

International Organized Psychology

There is scarcely a country in the world without psychologists. Indeed, the APA has members and affiliates in 105 countries, many of which also have national psychological associations. The largest international psychological association is the International Union of Psychological Science (IUPsyS), which represents scientific psychology in 50 countries. The APA nominates some of the members of the U.S. National Committee, which, in turn, represents U.S. psychology in the IUPsyS. The IUPsyS sponsors an international congress of psychology every 4 years and, through its Executive Committee, serves as a United Nations of psychology, facilitating an exchange of views and information. Other international organizations include the International Association of Applied Psychology, the International Society of Psychology, and the European Federation of Professional Psychologists Association.

Multidisciplinary Groups

APA members belong to many groups that also include members of other disciplines. Participation in such groups encourage collaboration among the disciplines and helps to place psychology in the context of broader

AMERICAN PSYCHOLOGICAL ASSOCIATION

1. General Psychology	18. Psychologists in Public Service
2. Teaching of Psychology	19. Military Psychology
3. Experimental Psychology	20. Adult Development and Aging
4. Evaluation, Measurement and Statistics	21. Applied Experimental & Engr. Psy.
5. Physiological and Comparative	22. Rehabilitation Psychology
6. Developmental Psychology	23. Consumer Psychology
7. Personality and Social	24. Theoretical and Philosophical Psy.
8. Psychological Study of Social Issues (SPSSI)	25. Experimental Analysis of Behavior
9. Psychology and the Arts	26. History of Psychology
10. Clinical Psychology	27. Community Psychology
11. Consulting Psychology	28. Psychopharmacology
12. Industrial and Organizational	29. Psychotherapy
13. Educational Psychology	30. Psychological Hypnosis
14. School Psychology	31. State Psychological Assn. Affairs
15. Counseling Psychology	32. Humanistic Psychology

33. Mental Retardation & Develop. Disabilities
34. Population and Environmental Psychology
35. Psychology of Women
36. Psychologists in Religious Issues (PIRI)
37. Child, Youth and Family Services
38. Health Psychology
39. Psychoanalysis
40. Clinical Neuropsychology
41. Psychology-Law
42. Psychologists in Independent Practice
43. Family Psychology
44. Psy. Study of Lesbian and Gay Issues
45. Psy. Study of Ethnic Minority Issues
46. Media Psychology
47. Exercise and Sports Psychology

STUDENT ORGANIZATIONS
Amer. Psychological Assn. of Graduate Students (APAGS)
Psi Chi
Psi Beta

EDUCATION AND TRAINING GROUPS
Council of Graduate Departments of Psychology (COGDOP)
National Council of Schools of Professional Psychology (NCSPP)
Assn. of Psychology Internship Centers (APIC)
Council of Training Directors (CTD)
Council of Undergraduate Psychology Programs (CUPP)
Assn. of Medical School Professors of Psychology (AMSPP)
Council of Teachers of Undergraduate Psychology (CTUP)
Joint Council on Professional Education in Psychology (JCPEP)

CREDENTIALING AND LICENSING ORGANIZATIONS
Amer. Assn. of State Psychological Boards (AASPB)
Amer. Board of Professional Psychology (ABPP)
National Register of Health Service Provider in Psychology

ETHNIC MINORITY PSYCHOLOGICAL ASSOCIATIONS
Asian Amer. Psychological Assn.
Assn. of Black Psychologists
National Hispanic Psychological Assn.
Soc. of Indian Psychologists

OTHER PSYCHOLOGICAL ASSOCIATIONS
Psychonomic Soc., Inc.
Soc. of Experimental Psychologists
Soc. for Multivariate Experimental Psychology
Soc. for Computers in Psychology
Soc. for Mathematical Psychology
Amer. Psychological Society (APS)
Psychometric Soc.
Nat. Academy of Practice in Psychology
Nat. Assn. for School Psychologists (NASP)
Amer. Assn. for Correctional Psychologists
Assn. of Practicing Psychologists
Soc. of Psychologists in Addictive Behaviors
Amer. Academy of Forensic Psychology
Nat. Organization of VA Psychologists (NOVA Psi)
Soc. of Psychologists in Substance Abuse
Psychologists in Long-Term Care
Soc. of Air Force Clinical Psychologists
Assn. for Jungian Psychology
North Amer. Soc. of Adlerian Psychology
Soc. of Psychologists in Management
Assn. of Applied Social Psychologists
Assn. for the Advancement of Applied Sports Psychology
Psychologists for Social Responsibility
Assn. of Women in Psychology
Assn. of Lesbian and Gay Psychologists
Soc. of Experimental Social Psychology

CANADIAN PSYCHOLOGICAL ASSOCIATION
Psychologists Assn. of Alberta
British Columbia Psychological Assn.
Psychological Assn. of Manitoba
Manitoba Psych. Soc., Inc.
Psych. Assn. of Nova Scotia
Assn. of Psychologists of Nova Scotia
Assn. of Psychologists of the NW Terr.
Ontario Psychological Assn.
Corp. Prof. des Psychologues du Quebec
Saskatchewan Psychological Assn.
Coll. of Psychologists of New Brunswick Psych. Soc. of Saskatchewan
Assn. of New Foundland Psychologists
Psych. Assn. of Prince Edward Is.

AFFILIATED REGIONAL PSYCHOLOGICAL ASSOCIATIONS
Eastern Psychological Assn.
Midwestern Psychological Assn.
New England Psychological Assn.
Rocky Mountain Psychological Assn.
Southeastern Psychological Assn.
Southwestern Psychological Assn.
Western Psychological Assn.

AFFILIATED STATE PSYCHOLOGICAL ASSOCIATIONS

Alabama	Louisiana	Oklahoma
Alaska	Maine	Oregon
Arizona	Maryland	Pennsylvania
Arkansas	Massachusetts	Puerto Rico
California	Michigan	Rhode Island
Colorado	Minnesota	South Carolina
Connecticut	Mississippi	South Dakota
Delaware	Missouri	Tennessee
District of Columbia	Montana	Texas
Florida	Nebraska	Utah
Georgia	Nevada	Vermont
Hawaii	New Hampshire	Virginia
Idaho	New Jersey	Washington
Illinois	New Mexico	West Virginia
Indiana	New York	Wisconsin
Iowa	North Carolina	Wyoming
Kansas	North Dakota	
Kentucky	Ohio	

INTERNATIONAL PSYCHOLOGICAL ASSOCIATIONS
Intl. Union of Psychological Science (IUPsyS)
Intl. Assn. of Applied Psychology (IAPP)
European Federation of Professional Psychologists Assn. (EFPPA)
Interamerican Soc. of Psychology (ISP)
Intl. Council of Psychologists (ICP)

INTERDISCIPLINARY GROUPS WITH STRONG PSYCHOLOGICAL INTERFACE
Amer. Assn. for the Advancement of Science (AAAS)
Amer. Education Research Assn. (AERA)
Soc. for Research in Child Development (SRCD)
Gerontological Soc. of America (GSA)
Cognitive Science Soc.
Soc. for Neuroscience
Human Factors Soc.
Nat. Mental Health Assn. (NMHA)
World Federation for Mental Health (WFMH)
Soc. for Psychotherapy Research

Acoustical Soc. of America
Amer. Pain Society
Behavior Genetics Assn.
Intl. Soc. of Hypnosis
Amer. Correctional Assn.
Assn. for Behavior Analysis
Intl. Brain Research Orgn.
Amer. Psychopathological Assn.
Amer. Orthopsychiatric Assn.
Amer. Evaluation Assn.

Academy of Management
Soc. for Clinical and Experimental Hypnosis
Amer. Assn. for Marriage & Family Therapy
Assn. for the Psychophysiological Study of Sleep
Soc. for the Advancement of Field Therapy
Amer. Soc. of Group Psychotherapy & Psychodrama
Assn. of Business Simulation & Experiential Learning
Assn. of Mental Health Administrators
Biofeedback Soc. of America
Comm. on Rehabilitation Counselor Certification

Intl. Soc. for Research on Aggression
Intl. Soc. for Psychological Research
Intl. Soc. for Research on Emotion
Soc. for Clinical & Experimental Hypnosis
Soc. for Exploration of Psychotherapy Intervention
Soc. for Reproductive & Infant Psychology
Soc. for the Scientific Study of Sex
Intl. Soc. for Mental Imagery Techniques in Psychotherapy & Psych.
Soc. for Professionals in Dispute Resolution
Assn. for Gifted-Creative Children

Figure 1: Organizations that make up organized psychology (an illustrative sampling; from *The American Psychologist,* Vol. 44, p. 982).

concerns. Examples of such organizations are the American Educational Research Association, the Society for Research in Child Development, the National Mental Health Association, and the American Orthopsychiatric Association.

Interdisciplinary Coalitions

Participation in interdisciplinary coalitions helps to amplify the APA's voice and make advocacy efforts more effective. The APA participates in many such coalitions and, because of its size and experience, frequently plays a leading role. Academic–research interests are represented through the Consortium of Social Science Associations, which advocates federal funding of the social sciences and humanities, and the Federation of Behavioral, Psychological, and Cognitive Sciences ("the Federation"), which has the goal of familiarizing government officials with the substance of research on behavioral, psychological, and cognitive processes. Other coalitions with practice or public interest implications include the Coalition for Health Funding, the Mental Health Leadership Forum, the Joint Commission on Interprofessional Affairs, the Federation of AIDS-Related Organizations, and the National Child Abuse Coalition.

Specialized Psychological Organizations

The diverse and specialized interests of psychologists have spawned a variety of associations that represent particular content areas; address particular research, practice, or public interest initiatives; and coordinate administrative responsibilities. Examples of such organizations, of which there are dozens, are the Psychonomic Society, the Association of Practicing Psychologists, the Association of Women in Psychology, the Society of Psychologists in Management, and the Association of Black Psychologists.

The APA's Complex Structure

Because of its size and diversity, the APA is itself a complex entity. Each of its 47 divisions operates to some extent as a psychological organization and may have sections, interest groups, task forces, committees, and publications. There are more than 50 affiliated state and provincial associations, some of which are larger and more complex than the APA itself was in 1945. Several hundred APA members serve as members of the boards, committees, and task forces that make recommendations to the Council of Representatives that determine the functions and policies of the

Association. The APA speaks for psychology through its office of public affairs, through an active program of communication with Congress and virtually all relevant government agencies, and through *amicus curiae* briefs filed in the Supreme Court and other appellate bodies.

The APA's Role in Organized Psychology

No single organization can represent all of the needs of every psychologist. The great diversity of organizations that have emerged to meet special needs attests to that fact and to the ingenuity of psychologists in finding ways to meet those needs. The APA maintains relationships with virtually all national and international psychological and behavioral organizations. In contrast with the other groups described above, the APA functions as a generic, umbrella organization whose size, experience, and complex structure contributes to national and international coordination and collaboration.

THE STATUS OF THE APA IN 1990

The return to financial health in 1989 permitted the APA to return to active programming throughout the Association. Restructuring the Central Office in 1987 had placed many programs in one of three Directorates— Science, Practice, and Public Interest—leaving others in the Executive Office, the Office of Financial Affairs, or the Office of Communications. The Education Directorate was established in January 1990. A description of these departments provides a cross-sectional view of the APA Central Office structure in late 1990 (see Figure 2 for an organizational chart).

Science Directorate

The Science Directorate is the focal point of the APA's efforts to expand the recognition—in Congress, federal agencies, and the larger scientific community—of psychology's scientific achievements. The 26-person directorate staff is the most visible national group advocating on behalf of the science of psychology. The directorate advocates a national science policy consistent with the interests of the psychological research– academic community and seeks to bring the contributions and future promise of psychological research to the attention of national policymakers and the general public.

In response to the concerns of academic members that too little at-

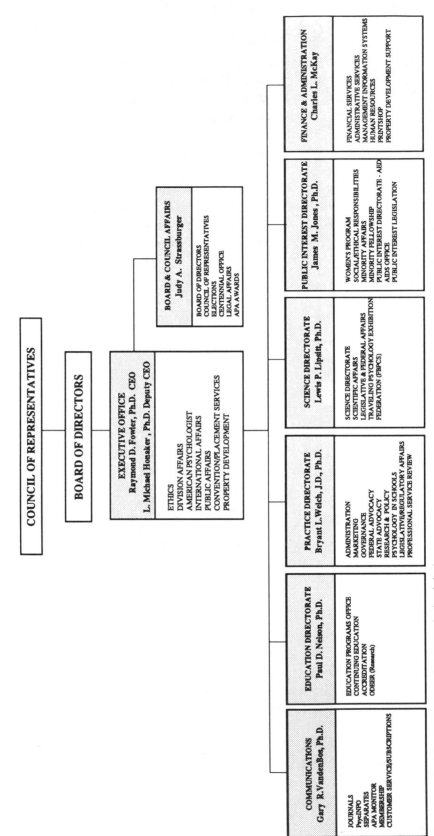

Figure 2: American Psychological Association organizational chart.

tention had been directed to science in the APA, some major steps were taken to expand the activities of the Science Directorate: A Science Advisor was appointed in 1986, and the Council of Representatives voted in 1987 to increase funds to the Science Directorate by $500,000. In 1988, President Joseph Matarazzo appointed an ad hoc Science Advisory Committee to advise the Board of Directors on science initiatives that should be undertaken. The appointment in 1990 of Lewis Lipsitt, a highly regarded research psychologist, as Executive Director for Science was widely applauded by academic–research psychologists.

The Science Directorate has successfully promoted legislation that increased research funding for the major federal agencies that support psychological research. The staff also promotes the development of federal guidelines on animal and human research standards that are consistent with APA policy, and develops coalitions with other professional science organizations to advance common legislative interests. The directorate is playing a major role in the development of an exhibition about psychology that will travel to science museums around the United States beginning in 1992, the centennial year. New directorate programs include support for university-based research conferences that result in published volumes (see Chapter 12), two graduate student awards programs, and substantive science programs at the annual APA convention. The directorate keeps the research community informed through the quarterly *Science Agenda* newsletter, a research support network, and electronically delivered research funding information.

Practice Directorate

The Practice Directorate was established by combining the Office of Professional Practice and the Office of Professional Affairs under a single executive director, Bryant Welch, an independent practitioner. Its purpose is to promote the practice of psychology through legislative and judicial advocacy, education, and public relations and marketing efforts. The directorate also helps to develop the policies, standards, and guidelines for the delivery of psychological services, as well as educational documents about the profession for psychologists and the public. The work of the directorate focuses on three areas: federal advocacy, state advocacy, and public awareness.

Staff and volunteers of the Federal Advocacy Program work directly with members of Congress and the administration to develop the role of psychologists in the provision of health–mental health services. The directorate played a major role in the passage of federal legislation in 1989 enabling Medicare beneficiaries to receive psychological care under the Medicare program, as well as in increasing opportunities for psychologists to participate in the health care arena.

The Practice Directorate provides extensive assistance to state and provincial psychological associations through its state association development and legislative advocacy programs. These include on-site consultation and workshops with governing boards and an annual State Leadership Conference. The State Grant Program assists state associations in developing the resources necessary to better serve members and to promote psychology at the state legislative level.

Marketing and public relations programs are designed to convey the value of psychological services to consumers and businesses. The quarterly newsletter *Practitioner Focus* keeps practitioners informed about new developments and about the activities of the APA and the Practice Directorate.

Public Interest Directorate

The mission of the Public Interest Directorate is to promote the application of the science and profession of psychology in the public interest. Priority issues include the psychological impact of discrimination, poverty, mental illness, victimization, violence, and homelessness. The programs of the directorate focus on children, families, and life-span development. An active Public Interest Legislative Office informs Congress and federal agencies of psychology's concerns and influences legislation and regulations on behalf of underrepresented groups.

The directorate has outreach programs that are designed to promote the use of psychological knowledge and services in addressing pressing social issues. Examples include operating a program to train service providers working with AIDS patients, providing financial support and professional guidance to ethnic minority graduate students through the Minority Fellowship program, coordinating a Congressional Science Fellowship program to place psychologists in congressional offices, and convening a panel of expert psychologists to write a state-of-the-art paper on psychological responses to abortion that served as the basis for testimony in Congress and for an *amicus curiae* brief to the U.S. Supreme Court. The Public Interest Directorate was headed by James M. Jones until he was succeeded by Henry Tomes, formerly Massachusetts Commissioner of Mental Health.

Education Directorate

The Education Directorate was established in 1990, 3 years after the other directorates. Its purpose is to develop policy in education and training for the science and practice components of psychology. Paul Nelson, the APA's accreditation officer, was acting executive director until Joanne Callan was appointed to that position in October 1991.

Shortly after the directorate was established, the Education and Training Board was replaced by the Board of Educational Affairs, with a broad mandate to oversee the programs of the directorate. A major activity is the accreditation of doctoral training programs in professional psychology and predoctoral internship programs. Through the Office of Continuing Education, the Education Directorate approves sponsors of continuing education nationally, develops continuing education policy, and promotes continuing education activities at the annual convention.

The Office of Demographic, Employment, and Educational Research conducts extensive research on the activities of psychologists, including an annual survey of graduate departments and schools of psychology. The directorate plays a major role in planning national conferences on psychology education, including undergraduate and postdoctoral education in psychology and in the practice specialties.

Communications

The Office of Communications, with oversight by the Publications and Communications Board, publishes books, journals, and computer data bases that are distributed throughout the world. The largest of the Central Office operations, Communications, directed by Gary VandenBos, employs more than half of the APA's staff and utilizes the services of more than 7,000 psychologists in the writing, review, and editorial process.

The APA publishes 21 major national journals and five secondary databased journals (*Psychological Abstracts* and six *PsycSCANS*). Other publications include *PsycBooks*, professional and scholarly books, and an annual membership directory. APA publications reach almost 300,000 individuals and institutions worldwide. (See Chapter 12 for further discussion of the Office of Communications.)

Office of Finance and Administration

The Office of Finance and Administration develops and manages the APA budget and coordinates all financial and business affairs, including administrative services, property development, management information services, human resources, and printing and duplication support. Charles L. McKay, who directed APA business operations from 1974 to 1983, was appointed Vice President for Financial Affairs and Chief Financial Officer in 1988.

Executive Office

Raymond Fowler, the chief executive officer (CEO), is responsible for the operation of all aspects of the Central Office and for coordinating the activities of the directorates and other APA programs. The CEO serves as a nonvoting member of the Board of Directors and the Council of Representatives, is a member of all divisions, and regularly participates in the meetings of all boards and committees.

The CEO has special responsibility for oversight of the following association offices: Board and Council Operations, which conducts the Association's elections and arranges and manages the meetings of the Board and the Council; International Affairs, which coordinates the APA's relations with psychology organizations in other countries, participation in international meetings, and the APA's involvement in international issues related to human rights and the role of scientists and professionals; the Centennial Office, which works with the Task Force on Centennial Celebrations in planning for the APA's 100th anniversary in 1992; and Legal Affairs, which provides in-house legal services and consultation, coordination with outside counsel, review of documents for legal implications, staff support for the Committee on Legal Issues, and oversight of *amicus* briefs and other legal projects.

Michael Honaker, appointed deputy chief executive officer in January 1990, has special responsibility for the following offices: Division Affairs, which is the interface between the APA and its 47 divisions, with their legal, structural, and policy matters, and which provides support in such areas as membership, publications, awards, and meetings; Ethics, which administers the ethics adjudication system, supports the Ethics Committee, and responds to questions from members and the public on ethical issues; Convention Services, which manages the arrangements for the annual convention; and Public Affairs, which serves as the official voice of the APA to the news media and the general public.

LOOKING TO THE FUTURE

By late 1990, the mood of the APA had become noticeably less contentious. A few valued leaders had left the Association or were deeply alienated, and others watched the activities of the Association, and particularly the Practice Directorate, with distrust. The active belligerence among various constituencies had diminished, however, and there were increasing signs that the APA was beginning to be seen as responsive and supportive to some groups that had almost given up on the Association. No division had left the Association, and the leadership of some of the science divisions began assuring their members of the support the APA was providing for science and encouraging their members to respond to this by giving support to the APA. The 1990 convention in Boston and the 1991 meeting in San Francisco were among the best attended ever, and there was general agreement that the scientific aspects of the programs were excellent. Some members began to believe that perhaps there was, after all, a possibility that a unified, balanced APA could work.

However, the Association still faces some long-unresolved problems, perhaps the most fundamental of which involves the distribution of power in the Association. Although there is increasing acknowledgment on the part of academicians that the APA is working on behalf of their issues, many see the Association as dominated by practitioners. Many academicians doubted that they retained any power to influence events except through the goodwill of the practice group. Even those enthusiastic about the activities of the APA on behalf of the research–academic psychologist believed that it might be impossible for nonpractitioners to be elected to the Board or to the presidency in future years, and worried about how that might affect the willingness of academicians to be members of an organization led entirely by representatives from constituencies other than their own. The observation that this state of affairs had existed in reverse for most of the APA's history may not have been comforting to academicians, but the election of Frank Farley as president-elect suggested that the recent tradition of alternating academic and practitioner presidents continues.

BEGINNING A NEW CENTURY

The Centennial year began with the occupancy, in January 1992, of the APA's new headquarters building at 750 First Street, NE. For the first time in 15 years, all of the APA's 450 employees were under one roof. The attractive 11-story building permitted expanded and more efficient work space near Capitol Hill and adjacent to Union Station, Washington's major transportation hub.

From a fiscal standpoint, the new building completed a three-year recovery process. As the major partner in a building already 98% leased, the Association is assured of a steady income that will reduce the need for normal adjustments for inflation. Eventual ownership of the building, which should be worth over $200 million in 20 years, will provide the Association with a handsome endowment for its second century.

Projecting the future is hazardous under any circumstances, and projecting the future of the APA is no exception. The crisis faced by the Association in 1988 seems well resolved, but the rapidly changing demographics of the Association suggest that changes in the distribution of power and in the focus of APA programs and policies will continue to change. The Association has been surprisingly flexible in adjusting to change and in modifying its structure to maintain the unity of psychology. Keeping the organization strong, united, and broadly representative will be a worthy challenge as the APA moves through its second century.

REFERENCES

Altman, I. (1987). Centripetal and centrifugal trends in psychology. *American Psychologist, 42*, 1058–1069.

Cummings, N. A. (1979). Mental health and national health insurance: A case history of the struggle for professional autonomy. In C. A. Keisler, N. A. Cummings, & G. A. VandenBos (Eds.), *Psychology and national health insurance: A sourcebook* (pp. 5–16). Washington, DC: American Psychological Association.

Fisher, K. (1988a, October). Council tackles conflicts, budget. *APA Monitor*, pp. 3–4.

Fisher, K. (1988b, September). GOR plan fails: Other avenues of unity sought. *APA Monitor*, pp. 1,4.

Fisher, K. (1988c, March). Reorganization plan to be sent to members. *APA Monitor*, p. 1.

Fowler, R. D. (1988a, December). After a difficult year, answers to some persistent questions. *APA Monitor*, p. 4.

Fowler, R. D. (1988b, June). Message from the president. *APA Monitor*, p. 1.

Fowler, R. D. (1989, October). Federal model works for APA and divisions. *APA Monitor*, p. 3.

Fowler, R. D., & VandenBos, G. V. (1989, October). Divisions reflect APA's diversity. *APA Monitor*, pp. 4–5.

Hamlin, R. M., & Habbe, S. (1946). State psychological societies. *American Psychologist, 1*, 17–21.

Hilgard, E. R. (1945). Psychologists' preferences for divisions under the proposed APA by-laws. *Psychological Bulletin, 42*, 20–26.

Hilgard, E. R. (1987). *Psychology in America*. New York: Harcourt Brace Jovanovich.

Howard, A., Pion, G. M., Gottfredson, G. D., Flattau, P. E., Oskamp, S., Pfafflin, S. M., Bray, D. W., & Burstein, A. G. (1986). The changing face of American psychology: A report from the Committee on Employment and Human Resources. *American Psychologist, 41*, 1311–1327.

Howard, A., Pion, G. M., Sechrest, L. B., Cordray, D. S., Kaplan, L., Hall, J., Perloff, R., & Molaison, V. (1987). Membership opinions about reorganizing APA. *American Psychologist, 42*, 763–779.

Kimble, G. A. (1984). Psychology's two cultures. *American Psychologist, 38*, 833–839.

Pallak, M. S., & Kilburg, R. K. (1986). Psychology, public affairs, and public policy: A strategy and review. *American Psychologist, 41*, 933–940.

Pallak, M. S. (1990). Public policy and applied social psychology. In J. Edwards, R. S. Tindale, L. Heath, & E. J. Posavac (Eds.), *Social influence, processes, and prevention*, New York: Plenum Press.

Sanford, F. H. (1954). Psychology in the states. *American Psychologist, 12*, 808–810.

Snow, C. P. (1964). *The two cultures and a second look*. London: Cambridge University Press.

Spence, J. T. (1987). Centrifugal versus centripetal tendencies in psychology: Will the center hold? *American Psychologist, 42*, 1052–1054.

Spielberger, C. D. (1988, December). Turning the deficit around. *APA Monitor*, p. 6.

Spielberger, C. D. (1989). Report of the treasurer: 1988. Turning the deficit around: Better days ahead. *American Psychologist, 44*, 987–992.

Task Force on the Structure of APA. (1987). *Final report of the Task Force on the Structure of APA*. Washington DC: American Psychological Association.

United Council urges AAP–Capps merger. (1975, March). *APA Monitor*, pp. 1,7.

VandenBos, G. V. (1989). Loosely organized "organized psychology": 1988 Executive Officer's report. *American Psychologist, 44*, 979–986.

Wolfle, D. (1946). The reorganized American Psychological Association. *American Psychologist, 1*, 3–6.

II

ESSAYS ON THE AMERICAN PSYCHOLOGICAL ASSOCIATION AT 100

10

WOMEN IN THE AMERICAN PSYCHOLOGICAL ASSOCIATION

ELIZABETH SCARBOROUGH

The purpose of this chapter is to trace the history of women psychologists in the context of their participation in the national professional association. The focus, therefore, is on the American Psychological Association and those women who have played particularly prominent roles in its history, rather than on women psychologists as such. Actually, the history of "women in psychology" would cover the same time period as the history of "women in the APA" because the first women qualified as psychologists at almost precisely the same time as the founding of the APA a hundred years ago. However, the history of women in psychology would require a different approach and would extend well beyond this selective

I thank Marion White McPherson and John A. Popplestone, directors of the Archives of the History of American Psychology, for their generous assistance in locating and providing reference materials.

Some research was conducted in the APA collection located at the Library of Congress, but pertinent records of later years, relating both to the APA and to Division 35 and destined for archival deposits, were not yet available for use.

A portion of this chapter is based on a paper presented at the annual meeting of the American Psychological Association, Montreal, September 1980, titled "Women in APA: The first 30 years, 1892–1921."

presentation. Nor is the intent here to deal with women's biographies, their contributions and experiences, though it must be recognized that only by doing so can we fully appreciate the circumstances that provide the context for women's participation in psychology and the APA.

What follows is a portrayal of the roles that women have played in the APA and the way organized psychology has responded to the challenge of its women members. The 100 years of APA history, when viewed from women's perspective, seems to divide into three periods, unequal in time and unequal in the opportunities for women to function as full participants. The first 20 years, 1892–1921, were a time of growth for the APA and of eager entrance by women. This was followed, however, by a half-century, 1922–1971, during which women, though increasingly attracted to psychology, found their professional opportunities sharply limited and their status as professionals seriously questioned. The last period, 1972–1991, shows promise of moving toward a time, still to be realized, of parity in status and opportunity.

THE EARLY YEARS: 1892–1921

There were no women included in the first meetings when the APA was formed in 1892. By 1921, when the professional organization celebrated its 30th anniversary, however, 79 women had been admitted as members (along with a total of 457 men). Here we examine the characteristics of those early women and their participation in the APA.

Several considerations suggest the choice of this 30-year period as a special time for psychology and for women. Psychology was rapidly establishing itself as a discipline and as a profession, self-consciously marking its boundaries in the 1890s and then in the next two decades confidently exploring extensions in various directions. By the 1920s, psychology had emerged from the laboratory and was becoming a pervasive influence in education, government, industry, and clinical practice. The early years, then, were a time when the new field was being created and was striving to establish itself. At first relatively sex-neutral and open, it became increasingly sex-segregated as it gained prominence and confidence. This trend was clearly under way by the early 1920s and strongly influenced participation by women.

Another justification for using 1921 as a breaking point is that this was a transition year for APA membership elections. Important organizational changes took place with the adoption of bylaws relating to membership qualifications. During the early years, the criteria applied to candidates shifted a bit, as discussed later. After 1921, however, the qualifications clearly emphasized training over academic or professional position; for the first time, published scientific research was required for election to membership. The decade of the 1920s saw other significant modifications in the character and functions of the APA; Fernberger's history (1932) discusses those changes in detail.

The year 1921 also marks a transition for women in society at large, particularly for college-educated women, the group from which psychology drew recruits. This transition involved a subtle shift starting earlier and extending into the 1920s and beyond. Historians have varied in their interpretations of the changes that occurred in the decade following the winning of the vote for women, but there now seems to be general agreement that the political victory marked an apex in the long struggle of 19-century women for "woman's rights," even as progressive women began identifying an expanded agenda (Cott, 1987). However, the success of the suffrage movement did not result in a greatly improved situation for women, even for those aspiring to professional careers (Chafe, 1972).

But to return to the beginnings: Although no women were included in the 1892 meetings and the charter membership of the APA, there were women "in the wings," poised to make their entry into a field that held as much inherent interest for women as for men. It was a time when some women were beginning to eschew the traditional feminine role of wife— mother in favor of the challenge of a career. Educational institutions were beginning to respond by providing both the advanced training necessary to pursue such a path and employment possibilities for those who chose academic careers, then the only choice for persons who aspired to become psychologists (see Scarborough & Furumoto, 1987, for a discussion of the earliest women psychologists).

Among those women who were ready to enter psychology in 1892 were Mary Whiton Calkins, Christine Ladd-Franklin, and Margaret Floy Washburn. Calkins had already begun her formal study with E. C. Sanford at Clark and William James at Harvard, while concurrently holding her position as instructor at Wellesley College (her study on dreams was presented by Sanford at the first APA meeting). Ladd-Franklin had become interested in the field some years before and in 1891–92 studied abroad at Göttingen and Berlin with G. E. Muller and H. Helmholtz. Washburn had spent one year with James McKeen Cattell at Columbia and then transferred to Cornell to study under E. B. Titchener in 1892. These three became the first "women of the APA." Calkins and Ladd-Franklin were elected to membership in 1893 at the second meeting, which Calkins attended. Washburn was elected a year later upon receipt of her PhD in 1894.

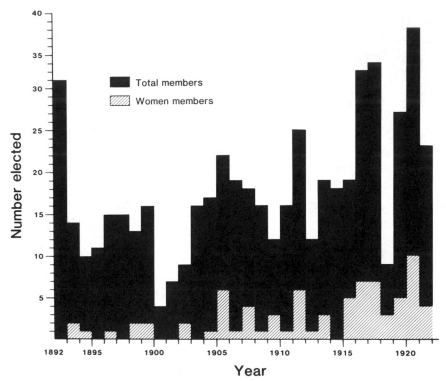

Figure 1: Members elected to the APA by year, 1892–1921.

It was Cattell, a member of the first Council, who nominated Calkins and Ladd-Franklin, presumably on the basis of their having already contributed to the literature through journal publications. He was apparently aware that he was proposing an unusual precedent and wrote to G. S. Fullerton, another Council member, "I suppose we psychologists ought not to draw a sex-line." In his formal proposal to Joseph Jastrow, secretary of the association, Cattell added, "Please let me know whether you favor the election of these (especially the women)" (cited in Scarborough & Furumoto, 1987, p. 172). Later he commented, "We were thus tolerably prompt to recognize equality of opportunity for the sexes, and this record we have maintained, for we now have 39 women among our members" (Cattell, 1917, p. 278).

Between 1893 and 1921, the APA elected 79 women (14.7% of the total elected). For 7 of these 30 years, no women were elected. The percentage of women elected during the other 23 years ranged from 6% to 33%, with 1918 having the highest percentage and 1920 having the greatest number of women elected. Figure 1 presents the comparative membership data for this period.

Throughout this time, nomination to membership was the responsibility of the Council, composed of the president and secretary–treasurer along with six members. Fernberger (1932) detailed the shifting criteria that were used. Periodically these became more stringent, resulting in a decreased number of new members for a given year. By 1921, the qualifications clearly emphasized training and research contributions (i.e., publication) over academic or professional position. Fernberger suggested that a 1906 statement of qualifications "had the function of henceforth making eligible for election only individuals who were primarily and professionally interested in psychology and who were sufficiently well placed academically so that there was reasonable assurance that their interest would be permanent" (p. 9). We do not know how women as individuals or as a "class" were discussed in the Council's deliberations, but subsequent records do indicate that the women's interests tended to be permanent, though their "placement," particularly in academic positions, was problematic (Furumoto & Scarborough, 1986).

Data on the variables reported below for the women elected during the APA's first three decades were obtained primarily from the annual proceedings of APA meetings (published regularly in *Psychological Bulletin*), APA membership directories, and the *Psychological Register*, Volume 3 (Murchison, 1932). All but 15 of the 79 women were included in the *Register*, indicating that they were still affiliated with the field around 1930.

The institutions from which the women received their baccalaureate degrees are known for 72 of the 79 individuals. Six types of institutions are noted: women's colleges (34% of the women psychologists), state universities (28%), private universities (14%), private coeducational colleges (9%), state normal schools (4%), and foreign colleges (4%). Those institutions that produced three or more women baccalaureates who joined the APA before 1922 were Vassar (9), Nebraska (6), Smith (5), Wellesley (5), Chicago (4), and Mt. Holyoke (3). Fernberger (1921) referred to baccalaureate origins as sources of "first psychological inspiration." Tabulation by decades indicates the shifting importance of the women's colleges, where students might expect to encounter a woman psychologist as professor, as sources for recruiting women psychologists. During the first decade (1892–1901), seven of the eight women elected were graduates of Vassar (3), Wellesley (2), or Smith (2); the eighth was from Ohio State. The prominence of the eastern women's colleges declined, however, over the next two decades, so that the state universities of the Midwest and western regions produced 38% of those who joined during the third decade (1912–1921), compared with the 24% who then came from the women's colleges.

Concerning their degree status at the time of election, 71 of the 79 women held the doctorate. Christine Ladd-Franklin and Lillie Martin had completed doctoral-level studies at Johns Hopkins and Göttingen, respectively, prior to their election but were denied the degree because of their gender. Mary Calkins was engaged in such study at Harvard and completed her work two years after election, but she, too, was denied the degree. Ethel Puffer (Howes) was elected in 1898 without the degree but having completed doctoral work under Hugo Münsterberg at Harvard; she received a PhD from Radcliffe in 1902. Three later women (Grace Kent, Rose Hardwick, and Frances Lowell) held M.A.s at the time of election but were granted PhDs shortly after. Only Margaret Prichard, elected in 1905, did no doctoral-level work (she studied at the University of Pennsylvania, but at a time when women were not accepted as degree candidates even at the baccalaureate level). Thus, 99% of the women completed doctoral training.

Of the 20 graduate degree-granting institutions represented, 4 contributed 47 women doctorates, or 60% of those who received the PhD: Chicago (19), Columbia (12), Cornell (10), and Clark (6). These four universities, plus Harvard, were clearly the most productive for PhDs in psychology during this period—for all psychologists (Fernberger, 1921). Radcliffe College produced four women doctorates; Johns Hopkins and Pennsylvania each had three; Brown, George Washington, Illinois, Yale, and Zurich, two. Eight institutions produced one doctorate in this cohort: Bryn Mawr, California, Indiana, Iowa, Minnesota, Nebraska, Ohio State, and Wurzburg.

Comparisons across this time period reflect two trends: the geographic dispersion of graduate training sites and the increased accessibility of graduate-level education for women, each an important characteristic of this period for both the history of psychology and the history of professional women. Cornell was the only degree-granting institution for women who joined the APA before 1902. Chicago was preeminent in the second decade, producing 42% of the women who joined then. In the third decade, 1912–1921, Columbia was most heavily represented (22%), with Chicago in second place (18%).

While discussing degrees, it might be noted that two of the women (Mildred Scheetz and Olga Bridgman) held M.D. degrees prior to receiving the PhD and APA membership. Three others (Clara Jean Weidensall, Anna Rogers, and Mabel Goudge-Crane) received medical degrees subsequent to their PhDs and APA election. Each of these received the M.D. from a Midwestern institution and joined the APA in the third decade.

Analysis of employment status at time of election indicates that 67% of the women were engaged in academic positions, nearly half of these (45%) at women's colleges. The other academics were at teachers colleges (19%), private universities (13%), state universities (9%), and private coeducational colleges (8%). Four women (6% of the academics) were listed as holding fellowships at the time of election; these were people who would not have been eligible for regular membership after the tightening of membership qualifications in the 1920s, the group for whom the associate status was provided in 1926. Twenty-five percent of the total group of women were in applied settings at the time of their election, with half of those in clinical psychology and the remaining in social work, applied education, and industrial psychology. It is important to point out that academic employment was predominant even for women up to 1921. Also, it is noteworthy that 8% of the group were apprarently unemployed at the time of their election, despite the fact that holding a "psychological position" was a primary membership requirement during this early period. A reasonable assumption is that these women were sponsored by their graduate school mentors, men who were well placed and influential in the APA political hierarchy.

Concerning the areas of research interest, Boring (1920) presented an analysis of the 61 women and 332 men listed in the *1920 Year Book*. He used 21 categories for "field of research" and showed that women were represented in all but anthropology, psychiatry, statistics, social, and miscellaneous. Fernberger (1928) later published a statistical analysis of APA membership and reported comparisons between 1920 and 1928. For this purpose, he collapsed Boring's 21 categories into 5: *experimental* (animal behavior as well as all kinds of experimental psychology), *applied* (abnormal, psychopathology, applied, tests, industrial, clinical, vocational, educational, genetic, and child psychology), *theoretical* (general, theoretical, social, and religious psychology), *not psychology* (philosophy, aesthetics, statistics, education psychiatry, physiology, and neurology), and *no research*. Fernberger converted to percentages and showed that women and men expressed almost equal interests in *experimental*, *not psychology*, and *no research*. They differed in that women were more highly represented in *applied* and less represented in *theoretical* fields.

Most people listed more than one field of research (one as many as eight). For the 61 women members in 1920, the most representative fields were tests and experimental psychology, these being reported by 25 (41%) and 22 (36%) of the women, respectively. Less than half as many women (10) were involved with research in educational psychology, and an even smaller number (5) were in clinical. Only nine women (15%) reported no research. (Of these nine, none appears to have been located in a situation supporting scientific research work: Four were married and listed home addresses in the *Year Book*, suggesting that they were not employed; another listed a home address but is not known to have been married; two were involved in instruction at institutions; one listed a company business address; and one was an administrator in a public school system.) Thus, most of these women were perservering in their discipline, with research interests spread across the spectrum of work then being conducted in psychology, although most heavily concentrated in testing and experimental topics.

Regarding participation in APA affairs by women, they were most active in presenting papers at annual meetings. Over the first 30-year period, 105 papers by women (10% of the total number presented) were listed in the proceedings, with the numbers doubling by decade. A classification by title suggests that overall, 53% of these dealt with experimental psychology, 29% with testing, 8% with theoretical and philosophical topics, and 10% with miscellaneous topics. In the first decade, experimental and theoretical papers were equally represented. Experimental topics dominated in the second decade, accounting for 69% of the women's papers. In the third decade, however, the papers were almost equally divided between experimental and testing, these two categories encompassing 88% of the papers given by women during this period. Certain women tended to be repeaters, presenting a number of papers during the time surveyed. Several were students when their presentations were made, and some of these did not later join the APA.

The presidential addresses delivered by Calkins in 1905 and Washburn in 1921 are notewothy in that each examined the possibility of a rapprochement between opposing factions at the time, Calkins (1906) dealing with "A Reconciliation of Structural and Functional Psychology" and Washburn (1922) considering "Introspection as an Objective Method." Washburn received further attention in another presidential address when Harvey Carr (1927) focused on a critique of the position she espoused in her book *The Animal Mind* (1908), which came out in its third edition in 1926.

In addition to paper presentations, Ethel Puffer and Margaret Washburn served as early discussants of sessions, and Mary Calkins delivered tributes to Josiah Royce and Hugo Münsterberg at the 25th anniversary meeting of the Association. Christine Ladd-Franklin, Kate Gordon, and Helen Grace Kent provided apparatus exhibits at meetings.

Participation by women in the APA governance was more limited. The significant fact here, of course, is that two women served as president of the Association during its first 30 years. Calkins was chosen as the 14th president by the eight-man Council, which included Hugo Münsterberg while William James was president, these two men having been her mentors at Harvard. Washburn was elected by a mail ballot of all of the members and served as the 30th president. That these women were so honored is remarkable, given the general status of women in science during this early period, as documented by Margaret Rossiter (1982). However, it is also significant that there then followed a hiatus of 50 years in which the APA, using more democratic procedures than in its earlier years, elected only men as presidents. Moreover, during that time, women came to represent a third of the field.

Calkins and Washburn were also the only women to serve on the Council during the first 30 years, Calkins from 1906 to 1908, just after her presidency, and Washburn from 1912 to 1914, some years prior to hers. Lillie Martin is the only other woman mentioned by name in the proceedings as having taken an active part in business meetings. These three plus two others also served on APA ad hoc committees prior to 1921. Fernberger (1932) discussed the work of these committees, which were generally appointed by the president, but did not always identify the members. Calkins was appointed to the Committee on Methods of Teaching Psychology in 1908 and was also a member of the Committee on Terminology, which functioned intermittently through 1921. Martin served on the Committee on the Relation of the Association to American Psychological Journals in 1910. As a member of the Committee on the Academic Status of Psychology, Washburn wrote the report on the status of psychology in normal schools, which was distributed in 1915 and referred to by Fernberger (1932) as an excellent statistical summary. In 1917, Mabel Ruth Fernald, Leta S. Hollingworth, and Helen T. Woolley were appointed to an eight-person committee charged to report on the qualifications for "psychological examiners and other psychological experts," and Hollingworth and Woolley served on a committee established in 1919 to consider methods for certifying consulting psychologists. The resulting Standing Committee on Qualifications and Certification of Consulting Psychologists, established in 1920, included Woolley. In addition, Washburn served as member-at-large to the Division of Anthropology and Psychology of the National Research Council for 1919 and 1920.

The picture that emerges from this description of early women psychologists is a familiar one: Women were attracted to the field, sought and obtained the necessary training through graduate study, regularly contributed to the knowledge base of the discipline, and were admitted without prejudice to the national association. Full participation in governance, however, was realized by only a very few of them. Explanations for these findings, as well as their importance for the history of American psychology and for the APA, must be developed with care.

One factor was undoubtedly the impact of marriage on a woman's career, discussed in some detail in Scarborough and Furumoto (1987).

Almost half of the women who joined APA in its first 30 years were married at some time; almost a third were married at the time they became APA members. The percentages of those both ever-married and later-married increased across the three decades. Of the women who did marry, 31% married psychologists, some before and some after doctoral study and APA election. During this period, middle-class married women were considered ineligible for employment; their lives were home centered and devoted to domesticity. For those who had sought and obtained the educational training that specifically prepared them for intellectual work outside of the home, this was a painful limitation (Scarborough & Furumoto, 1987, Chap. 3).

Another factor had to do with the limited opportunities for even unmarried women to engage in the kind of work that promoted careers and reputations. Women were barred from positions in the research universities, where psychology was building its research base, because social and cultural conventions assumed that women were incapable of instructing men. Those women who were determined to pursue their research interests did so under the limitations of teaching at women's colleges and normal schools, where laboratory facilities were meager or nonexistent. A few did obtain positions in coeducational institutions, but they almost always held the lower professorial ranks or functioned as "assistants." Thus, women were handicapped by location and heavy teaching demands; they also lacked the opportunity to build up a cadre of graduate students whom they could promote as protégés, a disability shared by women in other professions (see Glazer & Slater, 1987). A further limiting factor was women's exclusion from the social and professional networks that fostered career advancement and the building of national reputations (see Furumoto, 1988; Scarborough & Furumoto, 1987, Chap. 5).

NADIR FOR WOMEN: 1922–1971

American women born after 1900 seemed generally less eager than a somewhat older cohort to act as reformers and pioneers. They pursued college degrees in increasing numbers into the 1920s but overwhelmingly chose marriage and homemaking as careers. For them, the home-economics movement effectively portrayed homemaking as a socially desirable "profession" for the educated woman. Those who rejected marriage or attempted to combine that traditional role with a profession outside of the home became increasingly clustered in the "female" occupations: teaching, nursing, and social agency service. Professionally minded women continued to be attracted to psychology, and in record numbers. But in psychology, also, women became clustered, and concentrated in the applied areas: testing, child welfare, school psychology, and clinical work. Their status in the field actually declined before it improved.

Women earned 22.7% of the doctorates in psychology between 1920 and 1974, with the percentage of degrees earned by women decreasing irregularly from a high of one third in 1920–1924 to one eighth in the period immediately following World War II and rising again to about one fifth during the 1960s (Women's Programs Office, 1988). Harmon (1964) reported that "these proportions of women PhDs are higher than in most fields. . . . In the physical sciences, by contrast, the percentage of women doctorates has declined more or less steadily for 40 years, from 7½% in the early 1920s to 2½% over the past decade" (p. 629). Women psychologists did not, however, gain status and recognition in the field or in the APA proportional to their numbers (see Mitchell, 1951, for a painstaking analysis of women's status between 1923 and 1949). As noted previously, following Margaret Washburn's presidency, it was a full half-century before the APA elected the next woman to that position.

In the decades spanning 1922 to 1971, the APA underwent a number of changes, each of which had important implications for women psychologists: a rise in the attraction of applied work, the splitting off of applied psychologists to form their own association, a reorganization of the APA that reunited the academics and practitioners, and the first concerted effort of women psychologists to band together to improve their lot. The first three of these developments are discussed elsewhere in this volume. Here, we will emphasize their implications for women and give major attention to the emergence of a nascent woman's movement in the APA of the 1940s.

The successful efforts of psychologists to find practical applications had an important effect for women entering the field, because they found these areas more congenial to their career aspirations than was traditional academia. Finison and Furumoto (1980) argued that a tracking system that channeled women into testing and mental measurement began to operate in graduate education as early as the 1910s. Furthermore, Napoli (1981), a historian of applied psychology, reported that in the 1920s, "women came to comprise a growing percentage of applied psychologists. . . . Many women psychologists found themselves in applied work because academic careers that were open to men remained closed to them" (p. 47). So rare was the presence of women in academe that a former APA secretary, when confronted by a woman graduate student who asserted that as many as 250 of the 688 women members of the APA were in some kind of academic position, went to membership statistics to examine the employment pattern, possibly to determine whether indeed there could be so many women and, if so, where they might be employed (Fernberger, 1939).

Just as academic psychology was "men's work," so in the 1930s applied psychology was "women's work": In 1932, 63% of all of the United States' clinical psychologists were women (Napoli, 1981), and by 1938 women outnumbered men by three to one in school psychology (Finch & Odoroff, 1939). The female dominance of psychological practice apparently had negative consequences for both applied psychology and women; applied work was regarded as second-rate. Napoli (1981) suggested that "even without consciously discriminating against them men may have categorized applied psychologists as sub-professionals like social workers and elementary school teachers simply because most practitioners were women" (p. 47).

The APA, dominated by men academicians, showed little interest in the concerns of applied psychologists. Given the elitist attitudes of its leaders, it is not surprising that women figured very little in the affairs of the Association. Prior to the 1946 APA reorganization, which replaced the eight-person Council with a Board of Directors, only three women had served on the Council: June E. Downey in the 1920s, Florence L. Goodenough in the 1930s, and Edna Heidbreder in the early 1940s. Each of these women held a secure academic position and was a respected contributor to the science of psychology, characteristics that were implicitly necessary (if not sufficient) conditions for such recognition.

Lack of attention in the APA to applied psychologists created strained relations between them and the academics and led finally to the establishment of the American Association for Applied Psychology (AAAP), which in 1937 became the organizational base for professionals who had previously been members of the Association of Consulting Psychologists and the Clinical Section of the APA (see Napoli, 1981, for a full discussion of this development). Despite their greater proportional representation in applied work, however, women were not granted equity in leadership positions in the AAAP. Only 2 of the 29 members of the influential organizational committee were women, and none of the 8 AAAP presidents, who held office between 1938 and 1945, were women. However, women were better represented in the AAAP than in the APA: In 1943, with 33% of the membership of the AAAP, women received 25% of the administrative appointments (one of the most influential women was Harriet O'Shea, chair of the AAAP's Board of Affiliates). In the same year, women represented 18% of the members eligible for holding office in the APA (many of the women were associate members and therefore ineligible); 10% of the administrative appointments were held by women (Bryan & Boring, 1944).

It was during this period, however, that the first efforts of women psychologists to act collectively in their own behalf got under way, spurred by the wartime crisis that escalated between 1939 and 1941 and by the blatant exclusion of women from mobilization plans being formulated by psychologists representing several psychological associations (see Walsh, 1985). Gladys Schwesinger spoke out at state meetings and at the annual conventions of the APA in favor of a women's organization; Clairette Armstrong wrote the surgeon general about the omission of women in governmental appointments of psychologists (Portenier, *n.d.*). In the fall of 1941, the National Research Council's Emergency Committee in Psychology (ECP), which had no women members, was coordinating the response of psychologists to the threat of war. The ECP appointed a Subcommittee on the Services of Women Psychologists (SSWP), with Ruth Tolman as chair (Tolman, 1943a). This group, which first met in January 1942, defined its mission as coordinating and distributing information about women's work in connection with the war, and recommended its own discontinuance 19 months later, asserting that the needs of women psychologists were being met by existing organizations (Tolman, 1943b).

One of these existing organizations was the newly established National Council of Women Psychologists (NCWP). Pearl Harbor and the declaration of war by the United States had produced a sense of great urgency. On December 8, 1941, a group of women who had been meeting informally in New York City, eager for action after months of being put off, sent out a call for a meeting that drew an enthusiastic response from women who then voted to organize on a national scale. Five of the women on the SSWP, including Tolman, were elected to NCWP leadership positions in 1942. A contemporaneous record of the early years and the activities of the NCWP was provided by the group's first executive secretary, Gladys C. Schwesinger (1943). Capshew and Laszlo (1986), in an article that was both informative and speculative, examined the events, people, and contributing factors that shaped these women's efforts to participate fully in wartime professional activities.

The NCWP was established to promote and develop emergency services for the duration of the war and to utilize the energies of women psychologists—academicians and practitioners alike—who "felt baffled and frustrated in the early days of the war [and were] eager to discover the fields in which their energy and patriotism could find outlets, impatient with the difficulties and delays which prevented their prompt and useful functioning" (Tolman, 1943b). In addition to the projects sponsored by the NCWP itself, the organization called attention to women's need to be recognized in their professional role. Alice Bryan (executive secretary of the AAAP and a member of both the NCWP and the SSWP) was elected as representative to the ECP and was then invited to serve on the ECP Subcommittee on Survey and Planning. In that capacity, she came into contact with E. G. Boring, who was prominent in all of psychology's organized affairs. Capshew and Laszlo (1986) gave a carefully crafted account of how these two unlikely collaborators (see Boring, 1961) then coauthored a series of papers that brought the issue of women's status in psychology into sharp focus (Bryan & Boring, 1944, 1946, 1947; see also Boring, 1951, Bryan, 1986, for their "last words"). Through her various connections, Alice Bryan was particularly well placed and effective in representing women. The Subcommittee on Survey and Planning engineered a reorganization of the APA that brought the various psychological associations back together in 1946 after the schisms of the 1930s; Bryan played a significant role in mustering support for this reunification plan (Bryan, 1983; Napoli, 1981).

Women figured more prominently in the new APA, although still not with parity in status and leadership positions (Mitchell, 1951). From 1947 through 1971, eight women served on the Board of Directors (including Dorothy C. Adkins and Anne Anastasi, who, along with Helen Peak, were elected recording secretary of the Association in the years from 1947 to 1955). During 11 of those 25 years, there was at least one woman on the Board of Directors; for 10 years, there were two women; and for 1 year, there were three. The years between 1959 and 1969 were the most bleak: In 1960, 1961, and 1962, there were no women on the Board, and in the other years, only one.

This low period coincided with the time when women made their first drive to become a division of the APA, divisions having been provided in the reorganization to incorporate the special interests of the previously separate psychological organizations. Mary Roth Walsh (1985) recounted the efforts of the leaders of the NCWP (renamed the International Council of Women Psychologists to reflect a somewhat different vision after the war ended) to raise the status of women psychologists by establishing a women's division. In 1958, with a "handful of male members," the organization applied for division status, but did not receive a formal response. The name was changed again in the hope that deleting the word "women" would remove the stigma that offended, and again the group petitioned for division status, only to be denied then because of the international focus.

Capshew and Laszlo (1986) concluded that despite some gains made during the war years, the failure of women to change the status quo of gender imbalance in psychology was due to the cultural milieu (which favored the masculine nature of science), to women's acceptance of a false professional ideology of meritocratic reward, and to women's ambivalence about feminist activities. In her commentary on Capshew and Laszlo's article, Alice Bryan (1986), who played an influential role in the activities that they described, acknowledged "the state of ambivalence that probably affected the thinking and behavior of some of the women" (p. 183).

Cynthia Deutsch (1986), who came to psychology later than Bryan, observed, "What now seems to be a shameful disregard for the contributions of women was apparently tolerated with only limited anger by the women" (p. 186). Commenting on Capshew and Laszlo's observation that "very few women at the time of World War II had the consciousness or the will to step outside the prescribed female role and form an organization that would persist in working for the attainment of academic and professional parity" (Deutsch, p. 187), Deutsch concluded that "undoubtedly, some of the women involved did have the consciousness but lacked the social support to act on their true understanding of the prejudice and the status relationships that were the source of their exclusion" (p. 187).

THE FEMINIST SURGE: 1972–1991

The past two decades have seen an impressive shift toward more equitable representation in the APA governance structure and increased recognition for women. The "social support" required for women to act effectively on their own behalf and to institutionalize these changes depended heavily on the national women's movement that emerged with renewed vigor in the 1960s. Women in the APA, as in other professional organizations, learned the value of joining together to act on their feminist convictions, with the goal of bringing about organizational reform designed to improve their status and recognition. Although many psychologists may still have felt ambivalent, a large enough group of clearly determined women coalesced to form a critical mass and devised successful strategies.

Between 1968 and 1971, 44 organizations were formed by academic women (Walsh, 1985). One of these was the Association for Women in Psychology (AWP), which grew into a vigorous organization, sponsoring both an annual national conference for the presentation and examination of research, therapy, and theory, and also regional group conferences. These meetings provided a vital mechanism for women psychologists to engage in mutual support and celebration. Avowedly feminist and politically activist in stance, the AWP's purpose was, in part, "to expand women's role in psychology as well as to increase sensitivity within the field to women's concerns" (Walsh, 1985, p. 23). The AWP gained early attention when, outraged by discriminatory employment practices fostered by the APA, its members demonstrated at the 1969 APA convention (Mednick, 1978).

In October 1970, the APA Council of Representatives established a task force to prepare a position paper on the status of women in psychology. This eight-person task force, chaired by Helen S. Astin, took as its responsibility a three-pronged mission: to identify problems, to advocate, and to facilitate constructive change in psychology. The overarching goal was to "ensure that women would be accepted as fully enfranchised members of the profession" (Task Force, 1973, p. 611). During its 2-year life, the task force collected information to document the status of women in academe (faculty and graduate students), in clinical settings, in the federal government, in applied areas, and in the school system. Going further, the group provided detailed recommendations in each of these categories and challenged "the policy-making bodies of the APA [to] use all their designated powers to institute the changes recommended by the Task Force" (Task Force, 1973, p. 615). The Board of Directors and the Council were requested to transmit specific recommendations to the appropriate governance units. Recognizing that many of the problems called for continuing attention, the final request was that a Committee on the Status of Women be established within the APA.

In December 1972, the APA provided for continuation of the work begun by the task force by appointing an Ad Hoc Committee on the Status of Women in Psychology, chaired by Martha T. Mednick, to report to the newly established Board of Social and Ethical Responsibility for Psychology. This ad hoc committee was granted continuing status in 1973 and continued as the Committee on Women in Psychology (CWP), charged with functioning as a catalyst for change. Since then, the CWP, holding a special position within the APA governance structure, has been signally significant, influencing both psychology and the APA by the creation and review of publications, by affecting the governance structure, and by providing public information and education. The work of the CWP and its accomplishments is summarized in a biennial report (see Women's Programs Office, 1988), in which it is clear that issues related to minority women have been given prominent attention.

A visible structural element that reflects the APA's response to women's concerns is the Women's Programs Office, now located in the Public Interest Directorate. Established in 1977, this office functions as a resource on women's issues, distributes information about psychology and women, develops special projects, and provides staff support for the CWP and other APA units. Two PhD psychologists have served the Women's Programs Office as administrative officer for extended periods: Nancy Felipe Russo, from its inception to 1984, and Gwendolyn Puryear Keita, who was a member of the CWP, from 1987 to the present.

Another highly visible and immensely significant achievement was the establishment of an APA division dedicated to addressing women's issues. Division 35, the Division of the Psychology of Women, was approved by the APA Council in 1973, coincident with the granting of continuing committee status to the CWP. Most of the division's members had received their doctorates in clinical, counseling, and developmental psychology, but it attracted members from every other division as well (Mednick, 1978). The division quickly became one of the largest ones. In 1990, there were 2,884 members (2,245 APA members, 316 associates, and 323 affiliates), with academicians and private practitioners equally represented (Lott, 1990). A 1989 APA membership survey indicated that over 50% of the division's members were involved in research, over 60% were involved in education, approximately 63% were involved in health and mental health services, and 65% were licensed, certified, or both (P. Carr, 1990).

Consistent with its feminist orientation, the division developed an egalitarian mode of operation, encouraged student involvement, and used an ad hoc committee/task force model to address issues and make recommendations for action. Subsequently, Division 35 evolved a complex structure consisting of sections on Black women and feminist professional training and practice, 11 standing committees, an array of task forces and awards, and an extensive set of liaisons and monitors working with other organizational units (primarily but not exclusively APA governance groups). The establishment in 1976 of the division's journal, *Psychology of Women Quarterly*, initially under the editorship of Georgia Babladelis, represented a major accomplishment because the journal provided "a symbol of the legitimacy of the field as well as a publication resource and outlet for researchers" (Mednick, 1978, p. 128).

The activities and accomplishments just described—establishment of the CWP, Division 35, and the Women's Programs Office—all took place in the 1970s. That decade saw definite improvement in the status of women in the APA, because of the specific efforts of these organizational units and also because of the wider societal supports that helped produce them. A major disappointment, however, came late in 1981, when a Council amendment to establish a permanent Board of Women's Issues was soundly defeated by a membership vote.

Nevertheless, the effects of improved possibilities for women are clear, at least in terms of election to high office. During the APA's first 80 years, only 13 women served on the executive body (the Council prior to the 1946 reorganization, the Board of Directors later), two as president. During its past 20 years, however, 15 women have served as members of the Board of Directors, one as the first woman treasurer, Judith Albino. Five women have held the office of president during this period: Anne Anastasi in 1972,

Leona E. Tyler in 1973, Florence L. Denmark in 1980, Janet T. Spence in 1984, and Bonnie R. Strickland in 1987. With the exception of Strickland, each was elected president after having served on the Board of Directors. Representation on the Board, even during this period, however, achieved a level commensurate with the proportion of women members of APA (about a third) only in 1984 and 1988, and in 1975 there was no woman on the 12-person Board of Directors.

Other indicators—election to the Council of Representatives and to Fellow status, selection for participation through governance units, and receipt of outstanding awards—present an uneven record. In 1975, 20.2% of the 124 Council members were women. By 1985, the percentage had risen to 38.6%, but in 1988 it stood at 27.8%. From 1975 to 1988, representation on boards, committees, and task forces varied widely across years and governance units; there was some modest gain on most, with the exception of Scientific Affairs. Gains in women's participation were very slight among the Publications and Communications, Professional Affairs, and Education and Training boards. The greatest increase was in two boards, Policy and Planning and Social and Ethical Responsibility for Psychology, and their associated committees and task forces (Women's Programs Office, 1988).

Election to Fellow status in the APA is an honor signifying "unusual and outstanding contribution or performance in the field of psychology." In 1980, the CWP targeted the underrepresentation of women as Fellows of the APA as an area of concern. In that year, 22.3% of the Fellows elected were women, up from 8% in 1970. In 1989, 23.4% of the elected Fellows were women.

In 1956, the APA instituted an awards program, with the first award designated for Distinguished Scientific Contributions. Through 1990, nine women (8% of the 115 total) had received that signal honor, only two of these (Nancy Bayley and Eleanor J. Gibson) being recognized prior to 1972. However, other award programs were established in later years, and women received proportionately better recognition in one of the other categories: Distinguished Professional Contributions, for which women received 6 of the 53 awards between 1972 and 1990 (see Table 1 for a list of APA awards to women through 1990).

In addition to increased participation in governance and the recognition of women, the range of women's issues that have received attention includes, for example, sexist language in APA publications, the ethics of therapist–client sexual intimacy, sex bias and sex-role stereotyping, women's research needs, the inclusion of gender-related content in graduate education, the APA accreditation criteria, women's mental health needs,

TABLE 1
Women Receiving Awards From the American Psychological Association
Through 1990

Year	Name of winner
	Distinguished Scientific Contributions
1990	Frances K. Graham
	Anne Treisman
1989	Mary D. Salter Ainsworth (with John Bowlby)
1988	Eleanor E. Maccoby
1976	Beatrice C. Lacey (with John Lacey)
1973	Brenda Milner
1972	Dorothea Jameson (with Leo Hurvich)
1968	Eleanor J. Gibson
1966	Nancy Bayley
	Distinguished Scientific Award for Applications in Psychology
1981	Anne Anastasi
	Distinguished Scientific Award for an Early Career Contribution to Psychology
1989	Ruth Kanfer
1988	Barbara Boardman Smuts
1985	Nancy E. Cantor
	Linda B. Smith
1984	Marta Kutas
1983	Carol L. Krumhansl
1982	Martha McClintock
1981	Lyn Abramson
1980	Lynn Cooper
	Shelley Taylor
	Camille Wortman
1977	Judith Rodin
1976	Sandra Bem
	Rochel S. Gelman
	Distinguished Professional Contributions
1989	Florence W. Kaslow
1987	Mary D. S. Ainsworth
	Lenore Walker
1986	Nadine Lambert
1982	Carolyn R. Payton
1981	Jane W. Kessler
	Distinguished Contributions to Psychology in the Public Interest
1988	Ellen Langer
1979	Marie Jahoda
	Distinguished Contributions to Research in Public Policy
1988	Sandra Scarr
	Distinguished Education and Training Contributions
1987	Florence L. Denmark

employment opportunities for women, nonsexist guidelines for research, and the visibility of ethnic minority women in psychology.

An issue of increasing concern, under study as the APA approaches its centennial, is the so-called "feminization of psychology," a phrase that would have seemed oxymoronic to earlier generations of psychologists. During the 1970s and 1980s, the percentage of PhDs in psychology received by women increased dramatically and in a steady pattern, from 30.8% in 1974 (Women's Programs Office, 1988) to 56% in 1988–89 ("Fact File," 1991). Segregation by subfield decreased: Women accounted for 50% or more of the the doctorates granted between 1984 and 1987 in 7 of the 16 subfields of psychology (Women's Program Office, 1988). Tipping the percentage of the total in favor of women would produce several positive effects (Ostertag & McNamara, 1991). However, in other professions and occupations, movement toward predominance by women has been associated with a loss of occupational prestige and earnings, so this phenomenon is of special concern for psychologists, women and men alike. In 1991, the APA Board of Directors appointed an ad hoc Task Force on the Feminization of Psychology.

CONCLUSION

Women have been active participants in the APA since its inception in 1892. On the eve of the APA centennial, 39% of the 70,266 members of the APA are women. The distribution across membership categories, however, is skewed: Women comprised 18.2% of the Fellows, 38.6% of the Members, and 52.5% of the Associate members (American Psychological Association, 1990). These statistics demonstrate one of the striking features of the history detailed in this chapter: the underrepresentation of women at the highest levels. That state of affairs reflects a continuing problem regarding the status of women. It has practical implications in that the status of women psychologists is directly related to the seriousness and vigor of the attention paid to issues of special importance to them. Given the present situation, however, it appears that the American Psychological Association itself is in small danger of becoming feminized in the near future.

REFERENCES

American Psychological Association. (1990). *1990 APA membership register*. Washington, DC: Author.

Boring, E. G. (1920). Statistics of the American Psychological Association in 1920. *Psychological Bulletin, 17,* 271–278.

Boring, E. G. (1951). The woman problem. *American Psychologist, 6,* 679–682.

Boring, E. G. (1961). *Psychologist at large.* New York: Basic Books.

Bryan, A. I. (1983). Alice I. Bryan. In A. N. O'Connell & N. F. Russo (Eds.), *Models of achievement: Reflections of eminent women in psychology* (pp. 69–86). New York: Columbia University Press.

Bryan, A. I. (1986). A participant's view of the National Council of Women Psychologists: Comment on Capshew and Laszlo. *Journal of Social Issues, 42*(1), 181–184.

Bryan, A. I., & Boring, E. G. (1944). Women in American psychology: Prolegomenon. *Psychological Bulletin, 41,* 447–454.

Bryan, A. I., & Boring, E. G. (1946). Women in American psychology: Statistics from the OPP questionnaire. *American Psychologist, 1,* 71–79.

Bryan, A. I., & Boring, E. G. (1947). Women in American psychology: Factors affecting their professional careers. *American Psycologist, 2,* 3–20.

Calkins, M. W. (1906). A reconciliation between structuralism and functionalism. *Psychological Review, 13,* 61–81.

Capshew, J. H., & Laszlo, A. C. (1986). "We would not take no for an answer": Women psychologists and gender politics during World War II. *Journal of Social Issues, 42*(1), 157–180.

Carr, H. (1927). The interpretation of the animal mind. *Psychological Review, 34,* 87–106.

Carr, P. (1990). Division 35 1990 membership survey. *Psychology of Women, Newsletter of Division 35, American Psychological Association, 17*(4), 18–19.

Cattell, J. M. (1917). Our psychological association and research. *Science, 45,* 275–284.

Chafe, W. H. (1972). *The American woman.* New York: Oxford University Press.

Cott, N. F. (1987). *The grounding of modern feminism.* New Haven, CT: Yale University Press.

Deutsch, C. P. (1986). Gender discrimination as an intergroup issue: Comment on Capshew and Laszlo. *Journal of Social Issues, 42*(1), 185–189.

Fact file: Earned degrees, by field of study, 1988–89. (1991, February 20). *Chronicle of Higher Education,* p. A42.

Fernberger, S. W. (1921). Further statistics of the American Psychological Association. *Psychological Bulletin, 18,* 569–572.

Fernberger, S. W. (1928). Statistical analyses of the members and associates of the American Psychological Association, Inc. in 1928. *Psychological Review, 35,* 447–465.

Fernberger, S. W. (1932). The American Psychological Association, a historical summary, 1892–1930. *Psychological Bulletin, 29,* 1–89.

Fernberger, S. W. (1939). Academic psychology as a career for women. *Psychological Bulletin, 36,* 390–394.

Finch, F. H., & Odoroff, M. E. (1939). Employment trends in applied psychology. *Journal of Consulting Psychology, 3,* 118–121.

Finison, L. J., & Furumoto, L. (1980, June). *Status of women in American psychology, 1890–1940, or on how to win the battles yet lose the war.* Paper presented at the meeting of the Cheiron Society, New Brunswick, ME.

Furumoto, L. (1988). Shared knowledge: The Experimentalists, 1904–1929. In J. G. Morawski (Ed.), *The rise of experimentation in American psychology* (pp. 94–113). New Haven, CT: Yale University Press.

Furumoto, L., & Scarborough, E. (1986). Placing women in the history of psychology, the first American women psychologists. *American Psychologist, 41,* 35–42.

Glazer, P. M., & Slater, M. (1987). *Unequal colleagues: The entrance of women into the professions, 1890–1940.* New Brunswick, NJ: Rutgers University Press.

Harmon, L. R. (1964). Production of psychology doctorates. *American Psychologist, 19,* 629–633.

Lott, B. (1990). Message from the new president. *Psychology of Women, Newsletter of Division 35, American Psychological Association, 17*(4), 2.

Mednick, M. T. S. (1978). Now we are four: What should we be when we grow up? *Psychology of Women Quarterly, 3,* 123–138.

Mitchell, M. B. (1951). Status of women in the American Psychological Association. *American Psychologist, 6,* 193–201.

Murchison, C. (Ed.). (1932). *Psychological Register* (Vol. 3). Worcester, MA: Clark University Press.

Napoli, D. S. (1981). *Architects of adjustment: The history of the psychological profession in the United States.* Port Washington, NY: Kennikat Press.

Ostertag, P. A., & McNamara, J. R. (1991). "Feminization" of psychology. *Psychology of Women Quarterly, 15,* 349–369.

Portenier, L. G. (Ed.). (n.d.). *The International Council of Psychologists, Inc.: The first quarter-century, 1942–1967.* (Booklet printed by ICP)

Rossiter, M. W. (1982). *Women scientists in America: Struggles and strategies to 1940.* Baltimore: Johns Hopkins University Press.

Scarborough, E., & Furumoto, L. (1987). *Untold lives: The first generation of American women psychologists.* New York: Columbia University Press.

Schwesinger, G. C. (1943). The National Council of Women Psychologists. *Journal of Consulting Psychology, 7,* 298–301.

Task Force on the Status of Women in Psychology. (1973). Report of the Task Force on the Status of Women in Psychology. *American Psychologist, 28,* 611–616.

Tolman, R. (1943a). Some work of women psychologists in the war. *Journal of Consulting Psychology, 7,* 127–131.

Tolman, R. (1943b). Subcommittee of the Emergency Committee on the Services of Women Psychologists. *Journal of Consulting Psychology, 7*, 296–297.

Walsh, M. R. (1985). Academic professional women organizing for change: The struggle in psychology. *Journal of Social Issues, 41*(4), 17–28.

Washburn, M. R. (1908). *The animal mind, a textbook of comparative psychology.* New York: Macmillan.

Washburn, M. F. (1922). Introspection as an objective method. *Psychological Review, 29*, 89–112.

Women's Programs Office. (1988). *Women in the American Psychological Association, 1988.* Washington, DC: American Psychological Association.

11

THE AMERICAN PSYCHOLOGICAL ASSOCIATION AND SOCIAL RESPONSIBILITY

M. BREWSTER SMITH

Were this chapter to deal with American *psychology* and social responsibility, it could appropriately begin—like most historical reviews of American psychology—with our culture hero William James, who was publicly critical of the new American imperialism displayed in the Spanish–American War (Allen, 1967, p. 389) and who, in his famous essay on "The Moral Equivalent of War" (James, 1910/1982), provided a psychologically astute text that is still rightly honored in the peace movement. But my assignment is limited to the APA, which was a firmly academic–scientific organization not appreciably involved in social issues until its reorganization after World War II. My scanning of Hilgard's (1978) roster and sampling of APA presidential addresses turned up only two possibly relevant ones in the years before World War II. One was John Dewey's on "Psychology and Social Practice" (Dewey, 1900), essentially a rationale for his approach to educational psychology, in which, however, he gave articulate expression to the dialectical relation between theory and practice that Lewin (1948) promoted much later on as "action research." The other was A. J. Poffenberger's (1936) Depression-era address, in which he deplored the lack of representation of psychologists in the new agencies that President Franklin D. Roosevelt had set up to combat unemployment and encourage economic recovery.

By way of setting the scene for the APA's involvement with social issues and social responsibility, I must nevertheless venture some initial comments about the participation of American psychology in matters of social controversy. From our retrospective standpoint, the psychology we "gave away" (Miller, 1969) in the 1920s as our main public contribution was an ambiguous gift: the testing movement as it was commonly promoted in racist, eugenicist terms (Kamin, 1974; Keveles, 1985; Sokal, 1987). Carl Brigham (1923) had organized the Army testing data to raise an alarm about the intelligence of Negroes and of southern and eastern European immigrants; Robert Yerkes, the wartime president of the APA who had directed the Army testing program, gave his enthusiastic endorsement in a foreword that ended,

> The volume . . . which I now have the responsibility and satisfaction of recommending is substantial as to fact and important in its practical implications. . . . [I]t is better worth re-reading and reflective pondering than any explicit discussion of immigration which I happen to know. The author presents not theories or opinions but facts. . . . [N]o one of us as a citizen can afford to ignore the menace of race deterioration or the evident relations of immigration to national progress and welfare. (p. vii)

Brigham, Yerkes, and other respected psychologists of the time certainly thought that they were showing good social responsibility and contributing to the public interest in their advocacy of restrictionist immigration policy and their supposed documentation of Negro racial inferiority. According to their lights, they were public-spirited citizens, not evil men. But what a responsibility American psychology incurred to make up for this ill-conceived offering! Some of psychology's principal contributions to the public interest in the 1930s were devoted to undoing the earlier damage (e.g., Klineberg, 1935). By the end of the decade, the scientific consensus in psychology and related disciplines had changed, and psychology joined the other social sciences in promulgating quite a different story.

During the Great Depression, the APA remained a detached academic—scientific organization, little involved in the social crises of the time, in spite of Poffenberger's (1936) presidential address. The APA's unresponsiveness to the social turmoil, including its unwillingness to become organizationally concerned with the employment problems of psychologists, led David Krech, Goodwin Watson, and Ross Stagner to organize the Society for the Psychological Study of Social Issues (SPSSI), which held its first meeting in association with the annual APA convention at Dartmouth College in 1936. Lois Murphy (1990), in her carefully researched biography of Gardner Murphy, described the instigation of SPSSI as follows:

> In Chicago, a brilliant young psychologist, Isadore Krechevsky (later, David Krech) began to relate his failure to get an academic job not only to difficult times, but to an unenlightened society. . . . The psychologist Ross Stagner was also unemployed in Chicago at the time and he, with Krech and others, circulated a petition asking the American Psychological Association (APA) to respond to unemployment. This led the APA to appoint a Committee on Standard Requirements for the Ph.D. in Psychology, which discussed the desirability of finding ways of "straining out weak brothers and sisters" (who do not have an adequate ground in the natural sciences). A new concern about the possibility "that professional psychological service can make increasing contributions to community life" was included in the instructions to the committee chairman, A. T. Poffenberger, in 1934, but he reported that the committee did not touch this task, believing "that to tamper too much with the laws of supply and demand even in psychology may be a precarious business." (p. 137).

Krech and Watson came from New America, a socialistically oriented movement at least partly inspired by John Dewey; Stagner was a Norman Thomas socialist. They were joined early on by G. W. Allport, E. R. Hilgard, G. Murphy, T. M. Newcomb, and E. C. Tolman, all of whom were to become presidents of both SPSSI and the APA (Finison, 1986; Stagner, 1986). Hilgard (1986) reminisced that many of the early leaders of SPSSI were recruited to the liberal study of human relations by their involvement in Christian youth activities inspired by the "social gospel." Several of them (R. Likert, D. O. Cartwright, R. MacLeod, T. M. Newcomb, and Hilgard himself) had known each other as Kent Fellows, whose graduate study was supported in Depression times by the National Council of Religion in Higher Education. SPSSI also attracted various brands of Marxists and "fellow travellers" during the Popular Front period of the Spanish Civil War; a more Stalinist perspective predominated in the New York-based Psychologists League, which was established about the same time and composed mainly of clinical psychologists, most of them at the master's level (Finison, 1986). These organizations provided channels for American psychologists' social concerns in the years before World War II.

It was not only the social activists who were discontent with the scientific academicism of APA leadership: Also in 1936, the clinical and industrial psychologists split from the APA to form the American Association for Applied Psychology (AAAP; Stagner, 1986). Neither the AAAP nor SPSSI strayed very far from the fold, however: Both established affiliation with the APA in 1937. Plans to reorganize the APA were begun during World War II, motivated especially by a concern for retaining the participation of the applied professionals. In the new postwar APA, SPSSI continued as Division 9 to prod the APA toward involvement with social issues.

In what follows, I note some salient controversies and turning points, leading to an appraisal of the APA's stance in regard to social responsibility and social controversy as it enters its second century. I do not attempt to provide a systematic or definitive history, although I have checked the factual accuracy of my selective account.

ACADEMIC FREEDOM

Issues of academic freedom came before the new APA early on, as American universities confronted the rise of McCarthyism with the onset of the Cold War. The Board of Directors established the Committee of the Association on Academic Freedom and Civil Liberties in 1949. Two years later, the committee was reorganized under its present name, Academic Freedom and Conditions of Employment (CAFCOE). CAFCOE was seldom able to give real help to psychologists at risk, although the APA did indeed try. Two distinguished psychologists, Edward C. Tolman and Nevitt Sanford, were among faculty members who refused on principle to sign a noncommunist loyalty oath required by the regents of the University of California. The Board of Directors and the Council of Representatives voted to put the University of California on notice that no psychologist should take a position at Berkeley so long as the oath was required and until the nonsigners were rehired. This action took the lead in inspiring other national scientific and professional associations to follow suit. The Board also decided in 1952 not to invite the International Congress of Psychology to meet in New York City in 1954, because of the McCarran Act, which subjected international visitors to a political test ("Across the Secretary's Desk," 1952). The same Board meeting concurred with a resolution of the American Association for the Advancement of Science deploring interference with scientific travel under the McCarran Act.

RACIAL JUSTICE

The APA has been actively concerned with racial justice since the earliest years of its postwar rebirth. In 1950, the Council established the policy that the APA would hold its meetings only in educational institutions, hotels, or other establishments in which the meetings could be held with no discrimination on the basis of race or religion. That policy was soon tested at the 1952 meeting in Washington, DC. In his summary report on the meeting then Executive Secretary Fillmore Sanford (1952) wrote,

> Although the Association appears to move with great care and deliberation toward the formulation of policy, it demonstrated at the Washington Meeting that it can act with great dispatch on the basis of policies already adopted. [This is a principal rationale for sometimes divisive resolutions proposed to Council.] The Association has a policy that it will not hold conventions in settings where discrimination against any of our members is practiced. There was discrimination in Washington. Very quickly the Association drew up and passed a resolution commending those hotels in which no discrimination was practiced but stating calmly that we would not meet again in Washington until there has been more progress toward equal treatment of minority groups. (p. 640)

Soon, the issue of racial discrimination at conventions arose again. The APA had planned to hold its 1957 meeting in Miami Beach, but in 1956 the Board of Directors was told that 178 signed members would not attend a meeting in Miami Beach because of the indignities to which Negro (the language of the time) members would predictably be subjected. The Board appointed Stuart Cook, then a Board member, and S. Oliver Roberts, a Black psychologist from Fisk University, to visit Miami Beach to explore the situation. The pair used the approach established by the Committee on Racial Equality, presenting themselves to register at hotels, be served at restaurants, and transported by cabs. According to Cook (personal communication, November 28, 1990), without exception they were never refused, much to Dr. Roberts's surprise (Cook noted that all their trials were as an interracial pair). Cook reported this experience to the Board, but President Theodore Newcomb called attention to the fact that services in Miami Beach were only part of the significant considerations. Negro members would have to travel to Miami through the South, perhaps by car, and because they might suffer, or decide on consideration not to attend, the Board was persuaded to cancel plans for the meeting. The APA met in New York City instead.

Those were the years in which psychologists (but not the APA as such) made a significant contribution to the case for school desegregation, culminating in the landmark Supreme Court decision *Brown v. Board of Education* (Kluger, 1976). Kenneth B. Clark had played the central role in developing the psychological argument presented in the Appendix to the

Appellants' Brief, that legally imposed educational segregation was inherently discriminatory against Negroes. It was a legacy of his year as president of the APA, in 1971, that at his initiative the Board of Social and Ethical Responsibility for Psychology (BSERP) was established, putting in institutional place organizational commitments of long standing. For the next 20 years, BSERP, the committees that reported to it, and, in the second decade, also its offspring, the Board of Ethnic Minority Affairs (BEMA), were the institutionalized base from which social issues of justice and social responsibility got on the APA's complex agenda.

In 1968, the Board of Directors asked George Albee to chair a conference on the recruitment of Black and other minority students and faculty. This conference brought together leaders of American White and Black psychology (Albee, 1969). The Board of Directors of the Association of Black Psychologists descended upon the APA Board meeting in San Francisco in 1968 (Albee, personal communication to Theodore Baroody, April 12, 1991). The APA Board invited the Black Psychologists' board to send a delegation to Washington to negotiate, which they refused to do, so, at their demand, George Miller (then APA president) and George Albee flew to Watts and hammered out an agreement. In 1969, at the peak of the years of student protest, representatives of the Black Students' Psychological Association presented to Council a series of demands for APA financial support and support in student and faculty recruitment and program development. With the leadership of President George Miller and the Board of Directors, what began as a confrontation turned into supportive dialogue, with a joint committee of Council, the Association of Black Psychologists, and the Black Students Psychological Association being charged to develop plans to help Black students attain their objectives.

Nearly a decade later, during my own presidency in 1978, the time seemed ripe for the APA to take an active role in involving psychologists from all ethnic minorities. I remember engaging in long and difficult telephone appeals, attempting to reassure distrustful leaders of the ethnic psychological organizations that had formed outside of the APA that the APA was acting in good faith (Smith, 1987). All of the ethnic minorities in psychology were indeed represented in the Dulles Conference that met that year, and among other proposals recommended the creation of a Board of Ethnic Minority Affairs (BEMA). Progress that seems rapid in retrospect felt glacially slow at the time. In 1978, Council rejected the proposal of a new board but established an Ad Hoc Committee on Cultural and Ethnic Affairs, as well as a Cultural and Ethnic Affairs Program Office (by 1979, the Ethnic Minority Affairs Program Office), which began functioning at the beginning of 1979. Predictably, the 1979 report of the Ad Hoc Committee again recommended the appointment of a board in its stead, and perhaps just as predictably, the Board of Directors proposed instead the establishment of a standing bylaws committee. However, Council overturned the Board of Directors' proposal and put the bylaw amendment for a Board of Minority Affairs before the membership. The amendment was indeed passed, and BEMA began its activities in 1981. Meanwhile, with financing from the National Institute of Mental Health, the APA had initiated in 1974 its long-term Minority Fellowship Program, which over the years has been a major source of support for the doctoral training of minority psychologists.

In the governance of the APA, divisions present an alternative route of representation and policy development to the board-and-committee system. Partly in response to the complaint that Council was at risk of becoming lily-white, Division 45, the Society for the Psychological Study of Ethnic Minority Issues, was organized in 1987.

THE EQUAL RIGHTS AMENDMENT

If the active role of the APA in ethnic minority affairs reflected national developments spanning the civil rights movement and the subsequent stridency of "Black power," its concern with women's rights similarly emerged with the national women's movement. Feminist issues were included in the agenda of the Committee on Equal Opportunity in Psychology, established in 1963 long before BSERP, to which it was assigned (other bodies took over its functions later on). A separate Committee on Women in Psychology was launched in 1973, backed administratively in 1977 by a Women's Programs Office in the APA central headquarters. Many of the activities that the Committee catalyzed in the APA and American psychology proceeded without controversy as a matter of course. However, two were targets of controversy: the APA's support of the eventually failed Equal Rights constitutional amendment (ERA) and its support of women's rights to free choice with respect to abortion.

In 1975, Council voted to support the ERA with a resolution worded carefully to allay predictable misgivings about endorsements of politically sensitive issues:

> WHEREAS, psychological theories and research should have no bearing upon the desirability of the Equal Rights Amendment, which is a matter of human rights rather than of scientific fact; and WHEREAS, unfortunately, unsubstantiated psychological theories and research have, nevertheless, been misused to justify discrimination against women and to oppose the Equal Rights Amendment; BE IT RESOLVED, that the

American Psychological Association (a) asserts that arguments linking sex differences and their origins to the desirability of the Equal Rights Amendment are specious and without foundation; (b) deplores these misuses of psychological theories; (c) supports the passage of the Equal Rights Amendment.

The framers found in alleged misuses of psychology the context in which endorsement of the amendment itself seemed palatable.

Then, in 1977, the APA took a risky and controversial step to back up its support. Advocates of the ERA proposed that the APA refuse to hold conventions in any state that had not ratified the ERA. Because the APA had contractual obligations to meet in Atlanta, New Orleans, and Las Vegas, all in nonratifying states, the Board of Directors recommended against the proposal. However, Council overturned the Board's recommendation, and Executive Officer Charles Kiesler, who had previously advised in favor of the legally cautious position, carried out a strategy that managed to save the APA from potentially very expensive legal consequences and at the same time publicized the APA's case for being the first major national organization to take such a principled stand for the ERA. He drew heavily on the precedent of the APA's withdrawal from the Miami convention site on the grounds that many members would be morally bound not to attend even if the APA were to honor its contracts (Kiesler, 1989).

Although the APA's ERA policy was carried out without damaging legal consequences, APA members were not of one mind about the issue, and considerable bad feeling resulted. Perhaps this indirect cost was involved when, in 1981, the membership voted down Council's proposal to elevate the Committee on Women in Psychology to a statutory Board of Women's Issues in Psychology, following the example of the recent creation of the Board of Ethnic Minority Affairs. Nevertheless, the Committee on Women in Psychology was given autonomy in essential respects, even though it was formally subsidiary to BSERP.

ABORTION RIGHTS

The APA's actions concerning abortion rights followed quite a different pattern. As early as 1969, Council had endorsed a resolution urging the repeal of criminal statutes pertaining to abortion, noting that "termination of unwanted pregnancies is clearly a mental health and child welfare issue, and a legitimate concern of APA." With that policy firmly established, APA staff could take various initiatives adapted to the changing legal and political context of abortion issues. In the wake of recent challenges to the standing national policy embodied in *Roe v. Wade*, the APA assembled the best research expertise available in its membership to advise Surgeon General Everett Koop on the psychological effects of abortion in the first trimester of pregnancy (no strong evidence for substantial adverse effects; indications that effects are probably mostly minor and transitory). Subsequently, a peer-reviewed article by the psychological experts whom the APA had brought together was published in *Science* (Adler et al., 1990), and a packet of materials including a reprint of the article was made available for use by psychological organizations, individual psychologists, and other advocates. Although APA members can obviously never attain unanimity about abortion issues, this research-based approach (which will not always be available for issues of equally deep and urgent concern to APA members) has definite advantages in drawing on psychologists' greatest strength and minimizing disruptive controversy in the APA.

Members concerned with women's issues used the divisional route to strengthen their influence in the APA earlier than did those concerned with ethnic minority affairs. Division 35, Psychology of Women, was established in 1973.

SEXUAL ORIENTATION

Issues relating to homosexuality followed closely behind those of race and gender in the APA's social agenda. In 1975, by action of Council, the APA endorsed the 1973 action of the American Psychiatric Association removing homosexuality from that association's official list of mental disorders. The APA adopted a resolution that stated in part,

> Homosexuality, per se, implies no impairment in judgment, stability, reliability, or general social or vocational capabilities; . . . Further, the American Psychological Association urges all mental health professionals to take the lead in removing the stigma of mental illness that has long been associated with homosexual orientations.

The resolution went on to oppose all forms of discrimination against persons who engage in homosexual activities, to support civil rights legislation protecting such persons, and to urge the repeal of discriminatory legislation singling out homosexual acts by consenting adults in private. It provided the basis for many related staff initiatives, including participation in relevant court cases with *amicus curiae* briefs.

From my years on the Board of Directors in the 1970s, I remember session after session of the annual Town Meetings (scheduled at the APA convention as a device to draw off steam from member discontent) being dominated by gay and lesbian spokespersons who wanted the APA to take a stronger role in support of their cause. In 1975, a Task Force on the Status of Lesbian and Gay Male Psychologists was initiated at the instigation of BSERP. It was not until 1980 that a continuing Committee on Gay and Lesbian Concerns was formed under BSERP, and from its inception this Committee played an active and constructive role in the APA (it was renamed the Committee on Lesbian and Gay Concerns in 1985). Because of the Committee's integration into the APA policy process, the APA was able to take the lead among organizations in the social and behavioral sciences and the mental health professions in marshaling an appropriate response to the AIDS crisis along behavioral lines.

As in the case of ethnic and feminist issues, gay and lesbian concerns found their representation in the divisional structure of APA as well as in the board-and-committee system of governance. Division 44, the Society for the Psychological Study of Lesbian and Gay Issues, was established in 1985.

DISABILITIES AND HANDICAPS

A smaller but no less intensely concerned disadvantaged minority among APA members are psychologists with various disabilities. As in the previous cases, concerns of disabled psychologists for justice for themselves extended to their wish that the resources of psychology be made available to citizens at large who suffer from similar problems. The APA has had a good record of pressuring convention hotels to provide adequate facilities for physically disabled psychologists. The Committee on Disabilities and Handicaps was established under BSERP in 1985 as a focus for APA concerns for persons with disabilities. There is no parallel component of the divisional structure, because Division 22, Rehabilitation Psychology, is concerned with research and practice from the standpoint of the *treatment* of disability, not from that of disabled persons.

EXTERNAL CONTROVERSIAL ISSUES

All of the foregoing areas of social action in the APA had in common a concern with rectifying injustice to a particular category of disadvantaged APA members, as well as with extending the resources of psychology to the corresponding category in society at large. As we have noted, the APA's role in these areas was by no means free of controversy—of "divisiveness," in the terminology of members who did not like it. But the fact that fairness to particular sets of members was intrinsically involved made the APA's concern legitimate, even in the eyes of members who disapproved of the actions taken. And there was a dependable constituency to keep each set of issues salient. These advantages were not shared by another set of issues, which involved the APA in political controversies of the "outside" world. The classic cases touched on matters of violence: How should the APA stand in relation to the Vietnam War, to proposals for a nuclear testing freeze, and to policies regarding corporal punishment in the schools and handgun control? These issues proved more seriously divisive in Council debate, with principled opposition dependably forthcoming from spokespersons for a hard-science perspective, who would rule out advocacy on such matters and restrict the APA's role, and the role of individual psychologists qua psychologist, to the reporting of "data," and principled support often coming from psychologists in the activist tradition of SPSSI, with which I have been identified.

The APA did not involve itself directly in controversy about the Vietnam War, but many members so interpreted its action in cancelling plans to hold the 1969 convention in Chicago because of the shock felt at the 1968 San Francisco APA meetings because of the police brutality against peace activists visible on TV across the nation from the Chicago Democratic Convention. Shortly thereafter, Council commended "the willingness of the [Chicago] hotel managers to join with the APA and the Chicago Convention Bureau to seek an improvement in the conditions which caused us to move our Convention from Chicago." It asked the Board of Directors to be responsive to the Chicago initiative and to publicize its actions "in the hope that it may serve as a model to be followed by businessmen and psychologists alike in other cities where similar conditions exist."

The resolution adopted in 1975 opposing "the use of corporal punishment in schools, juvenile facilities, child care nurseries, and all other institutions . . . where children are cared for or educated" on psychological grounds was worth some organizational strain in debate, at least from the standpoint of its proponents, even though it did not lead to such consequential action by the APA as changing a convention site or mobilizing Central Office staff toward advocacy roles. It provides a clear example of the utility of a resolution when an outside organization is prepared to undertake the advocacy and can make effective use of it: EVAN-G (End Violence Against the Next Generation) put the APA's policy position to good use in its continuing campaign against corporal punishment in the schools.

In the case of the 1982 resolution supporting legislation to control the availability of handguns, a critic could question whether APA endorsement of gun control made any practical difference—apart from aligning the APA on the side of the angels, as perceived by a majority of the Council. The balance of the costs and benefits to the APA of taking an official position was debatable, given the strong feelings of a minority of members who subscribed to the position of the National Rifle Association. Similar misgivings are probably warranted about another 1982 resolution, which called "upon the President of the United States to propose to the U.S.S.R. that together both countries negotiate an immediate halt to the nuclear arms race," including a testing freeze and the development of plans to convert the nuclear arms industry to civilian production. Perhaps the strongest justification for this resolution was in potential educational influences on APA members.

As I write this chapter, the arms race between the U.S.A. and the U.S.S.R. is at an end, although not the dangerous stockpiles of nuclear arms—and the APA has not been asked to comment on our controversial military policy in the Persian Gulf. Since 1990, however, Division 48, Peace Psychology, has provided a focus for research and discussion of applications of psychology to the attainment and maintenance of peace, working in cooperation with a more activist group outside of the APA (one that involves many of the same people), Psychologists for Social Responsibility.

THE PERENNIAL CONFLICT AND ATTEMPTS AT RESOLUTION

I have alluded to the persistent conflict in APA politics between those who are ready to lead the APA into advocacy roles in behalf of what they see as the public interest, and those who would limit the APA to the support of psychology as a science and as a profession, with the public interest role confined to the reporting of data and scientific conclusions. The controversy goes back to the discussions during World War II in which the construction of the postwar and present APA was determined. Theodore Newcomb, an early SPSSI president who subsequently became president of the APA, wrote Lois Murphy as follows regarding the part played by Gardner Murphy, a leading mid-century social and personality psychologist (Murphy, 1990):

> [In] a typical, and unforgettable, event in New York over a 48-hour session in what was then the Pennsylvania Hotel, the clinical members of APA together with some nonmembers were threatening to create a rival organization. Forty-odd APA members were invited to what turned out to be a critical decision. Until then the purposes of APA were

described as follows: "The object of the APA shall be to advance psychology as a science." Gardner argued eloquently, passionately and effectively, that we should add the phrase "and as a means of promoting human welfare." The latter phrase remains, today, exactly in his wording. He was not the only one to advocate this, but it was he who turned the tide. (p. 151)

The phrase in the preamble to the Bylaws has not obviated debate, because some would put the emphasis on advancing *human welfare* in a broad construction, whereas others would emphasize advancing *psychology as a means*, narrowing the APA's warrant to contributions closely rooted in psychology as a science or a profession.

The most serious attempt to deal with this recurring conflict was by an Ad Hoc Committee on Public Affairs chaired by Leona Tyler, then a member of the Board of Directors, later president. The so-called Tyler Report (Tyler, 1969) that the committee produced was never officially adopted as APA policy, but its frequent citation thereafter has given it the status of *de facto* policy, subject to later elaboration and amendment. The Tyler Report was organized around two aspects of the decision process, vested in the Board of Directors, as to what action the APA should take with respect to a particular issue of public policy:

1. A graded series of actions that might be taken, ranging from a high level of political involvement to no action at all.

2. A graded series of types of issues ranging from those on which action by APA is most relevant or most urgent to those involving little or no relevance or urgency for APA as a national association. (p. 1)

Among types of issues, those affecting the science were assigned highest priority, on the grounds that they affect all psychologists, be they researchers, teachers, or practitioners, and if action is to be taken, the APA must take it. Professional issues were set a little lower on the scale because they do not affect all psychologists, and there may be other organizations besides the APA prepared to act on them. Social problems were put at the lower end in terms of relevance or urgency: "Only if there is a considerable quantity of research-based information and value consensus is high, for example, would an attempt be made to influence legislation" (p. 3). Underlying any of the types of action discussed should be the development of an explicit policy position by means of the careful preparation of position papers.

In the spirit of the Tyler Report, Council adopted guidelines in 1984 for the introduction of resolutions in the Council agenda. Council was mainly concerned with resolutions in the area of social issues, but the guidelines apply to all resolutions.

Before formulating a resolution for presentation to the Council, the issue to which it pertains should be evaluated against five criteria:

1. Its relevance to psychology and psychologists, or of psychology to it.

2. Its importance to psychology or to society as a whole.

3. The quality and quantity of psychological data, and conceptualization relevant to them.

4. The likely degree of consensus within the membership.

5. The likelihood of the resolution's having a constructive impact on public opinion or policy.[1]

In the event of a favorable evaluation, further requirements were set for the introduction of the resolution as new business, emphasizing explicitness of rationale and citation of relevant research. These provisions still stand as Association Rules. My earlier comments on the merits of various APA initiatives in causes of justice and social advocacy reflect my own long-term socialization to the perspective of the Tyler Report and of the present guidelines, which do not downgrade social issues as automatically as the Tyler Report seems to require (I have been an advocate of modifying the Tyler recommendations in that direction).

The focus on resolutions in the foregoing would seem to imply that resolutions are the primary channel of advocacy for the APA. Such an assumption is definitely wrong, but I think it has been widely shared by members of Council, perhaps because resolutions that appear on the Council agenda have been a conspicuous source of annoyance to many members. As I suggested earlier, resolutions are essential to establish new APA policy, especially in important and controversial areas. But as public documents they are likely to have little influence outside of the APA, except in special circumstances.

The actual influence of the APA on public policy has sometimes been directed by resolutions, but quite different strategies have been the focus of attention since the APA became a major player in national policy during the administration of Charles Kiesler as executive officer (1975–1979), to a considerable extent guided by his leadership (Kiesler, 1989). Since Kies-

---

[1]These guidelines were influenced by the fuller discussion in the final report of the Task Force on Psychology and Public Policy, appointed by BSERP in 1980 (Task Force, n.d.), and presumably reporting in 1984. The published summary of the report (Task Force, 1986) contained a valuable discussion of psychologists' roles in public policy but did not include the proposed criteria for APA involvement in public policy issues.

ler's time, APA staff have stayed in close touch with the executive and legislative branches of the federal government. Much staff activity has focused on central guild issues of the profession and of psychological science—thus, participation in Medicare on the one hand and federal funding of behavioral research and training programs on the other. But the connections and experience produced by efforts inspired by these legitimate guild concerns have been turned to good use in the service of public interest matters. Even with its spectacular growth, the APA is hardly a mass organization that can deliver significant numbers of votes, so it has found its effectiveness mainly in getting appropriate dependable information and expertise to the right place at the right time—and is having friends on Capitol Hill and in the agencies who have learned to value the APA's input and who can alert the APA about the time and place of issues that concern psychologists. The APA's effective participation in issues of abortion rights, as noted above, exemplifies this general approach. The 1969 resolution endorsing abortion rights was important for the instructions that it gave to APA staff, not as a public document. Recently, expert information got to the attention of the Surgeon General, and, later, of players in the policy process who take seriously articles published in *Science*.

The courts are another major channel with which the APA has become increasingly involved, both in protecting professional guild interests and in more disinterested concerns, especially with patients' rights. The APA typically avoids the risky and expensive role of litigant, but participates often as *amicus curiae*, "friend of the court," presenting the APA's perspective on issues under litigation. Because the Board of Directors was being asked more and more often to make rapid judgments about *amicus* participation and other complex legal matters beyond its own professional competence, in 1979 it established an ad hoc Committee on Legal Issues (COLI), including members with both psychological and legal training, to provide competent advice. Since its inception, COLI has played an increasingly central role in delicate policy questions arising in APA governance, substantially increasing the APA's effectiveness in these areas of concern.

CREATION OF BAPPI: 1991

I have now completed my cursory review of the APA's involvement with social responsibility—up to *almost* the time of writing. This centennial history comes at an especially propitious time, however, because the APA is about to enter a new era in its involvement with social responsibility. In 1991, the Board for the Advancement of the Public Interest in Psychology

(BAPPI) replaced BSERP and BEMA, which had been central to the story that I have been telling. I therefore conclude the chapter with a brief account of the process by which BAPPI was conceived and brought to birth, and my own perspective on the challenges that it will face.

A major feature of the restructuring of the APA Central Office under Chief Executive Officer (and former President) Raymond Fowler was the establishment of four major directorates: Scientific Affairs, Professional Affairs, Educational Affairs, and Public Interest. Each of these directorates needs policy guidance from appropriate structures of governance, but Public Interest was represented in two boards, BSERP and BEMA, with the Committee on Women in Psychology reporting through BSERP but enjoying relative autonomy. Could a single board be created to guide the directorate? The political problem seemed almost insuperable, because BEMA had attained its status as an independent board with such difficulty; it could not be asked to make itself subsidiary to BSERP once more.

James Jones, the executive director of the Public Interest Directorate, who had early won the enduring respect of the APA and of minority psychologists for his role as director of the Minority Fellowship Program, rose to the challenge. In the course of two summit conferences in 1988 and 1989 in which he took the lead, the plan to "sunset" both BSERP and BEMA in favor of the new BAPPI was developed, and a working consensus was solidified to support it. As a bystander to this process, I continue to be amazed at the achievement.

The summit meetings included appropriate representatives of the groups and constituencies affected by the restructuring: BSERP and its committees, including the Committee on Women in Psychology and the Committee on Lesbian and Gay Concerns, and BEMA, with the leadership of ethnic minority psychologists. An important aspect of the negotiations that produced support for BAPPI was commitment to a particular balance of ethnicity, gender, and sexual orientation in the initial composition of BAPPI—a matter requiring trust, because it was understood that writing such a provision into the proposed revision of APA Bylaws would be inappropriate. On the basis of that trust, there was no opposition to the bylaw amendment creating BAPPI, which the APA membership accepted in the spring of 1990. Proposals for the initial slates of candidates to compose BAPPI according to the agreement were developed by the executive committees of BSERP and BEMA meeting jointly in the fall of 1990. The Board of Directors, which had responsibility for the nominations, made no changes in the slates, so BAPPI began in 1991 with the composition agreed on at the summit meetings.

I have noted elsewhere (Smith, 1990) that the APA has a very strong record of supporting the public interest when concern with social equity and justice coincides with advancing equity and justice toward disadvantaged categories of APA membership; we have reviewed some of that history here. As a result of the negotiated summit agreement, BAPPI starts out very well constituted to continue this record of effectiveness. What of its prospects with respect to conceptions of the public interest in more general terms not linked to particular group interests, where, I have also noted, the APA's record of effectiveness has been less impressive? Here lies the immediate challenge to BAPPI and to the APA.

Of course, the public interest in this broader sense cannot be determined objectively; establishing it is a matter for democratic political process at its best (when it goes beyond mere horse trading of group interests; Smith, 1990). No category of psychologists, no component of APA governance, can claim to "know" the public interest in this sense, although all can, and at times do, advocate their own conceptions of a public interest that goes beyond their own legitimate self-interested concerns. Over the two decades since its establishment, BSERP has not only stood for justice for disadvantaged categories of members and other people, but it has kept broader conceptions of the public interest in view. Like SPSSI among the divisions, BSERP in the board-and-committee structure has risen well to its responsibility as a kind of institutionalized superego of the APA. BAPPI has now inherited BSERP's charge. As (at the end of 1990) I read the list of the initial members just elected to BAPPI by APA Council, I am encouraged to hope that BAPPI will serve the APA well in keeping public interest issues of human welfare before the APA, issues that transcend the guild interests of psychology as a science and as a profession and the special group interests of particular categories of APA members. That is an essential part of its charge, and that is its difficult challenge.

REFERENCES

Across the secretary's desk. (1952). The March meeting of the Board of Directors. *American Psychologist*, 7, 162–166.

Adler, N., David, H. P., Major, B., Roth, S. H., Russo, N. F., & Wyatt, G. E. (1990). Psychological responses after abortion. *Science*, 268, 41–44.

Albee, G. W. (1969). A conference on recruitment of black and other minority students and faculty. *American Psychologist*, 24, 720–723.

Allen, G. W. (1967). *William James: A biography*. New York: Viking Press.

Brigham, C. C. (1923). *A study of American intelligence*. Princeton, NJ: Princeton University Press.

Dewey, J. (1900). Psychology and social practice. *Psychological Review, 7,* 105–124.

Finison, L. J. (1986). The psychological insurgency: 1936–1945. *Journal of Social Issues, 42*(1), 21–33.

Hilgard, E. R. (Ed.). (1978). *American psychology in historical perspective: Addresses of the presidents of the American Psychological Association, 1892–1977.* Washington, DC: American Psychological Association.

Hilgard, E. R. (1986). From the social gospel to the psychology of social issues: A reminiscence. *Journal of Social Issues, 42*(1), 107–110.

James, W. (1982). The moral equivalent of war. In *Essays in religion and morality* (pp. 162–173). Cambridge, MA: Harvard University Press. (Original published 1910)

Kamin, L. J. (1974). *The science and politics of I.Q.* Potomac, MD: Erlbaum.

Keveles, D. J. (1985). *In the name of eugenics: Genetics and the uses of human heredity.* Berkeley and Los Angeles: University of California Press.

Kiesler, C. A. (1989). [Unpublished interview by M. Brewster Smith, August 12, 1989]. Presidents' Oral History Project, American Psychological Association, Washington, DC.

Klineberg, O. (1935). *Negro intelligence and selective migration.* New York: Columbia University Press.

Kluger, R. (1976). *Simple justice: The history of Brown vs. Board of Education and Black America's struggle for equality.* New York: Knopf.

Lewin, K. (1948). *Resolving social conflicts: Selected papers on group dynamics.* New York: Harper.

Miller, G. A. (1969). Psychology as a means of promoting human welfare. *American Psychologist, 24,* 1063–1075.

Murphy, L. B. (1990). *Gardner Murphy: Integrating, expanding, and humanizing psychology.* Jefferson, NC, and London: McFarland.

Poffenberger, A. T. (1936). Psychology and life. *Psychological Review, 43,* 9–31.

Sanford, F. H. (1952). Summary report on the 1952 annual meetings. *American Psychologist, 7,* 634–644.

Smith, M. B. (1987). [Unpublished interview by Ernest R. Hilgard, May 25, 1987]. Presidents' Oral History Project, American Psychological Association, Washington, DC.

Smith, M. B. (1990). Psychology and the public interest: What have we done? What can we do? *American Psychologist, 45,* 530–536.

Sokal, M. M. (Ed.). (1987). *Psychological testing and American society, 1890–1930.* New Brunswick, NJ: Rutgers University Press.

Stagner, R. (1986). Reminiscences about the founding of SPSSI. *Journal of Social Issues, 42*(1), 35–42.

Task Force on Psychology and Public Policy. (n.d.). *Final report of the Task Force on Psychology and Public Policy.* Washington, DC: American Psychological Association. (Mimeograph)

Task Force on Psychology and Public Policy, Board of Social and Ethical Responsibility for Psychology. (1986). Psychology and public policy. *American Psychologist, 41*, 914–921.

Tyler, L. (1969). An approach to public affairs: Report of the Ad Hoc Committee on Public Affairs. *American Psychologist, 24*, 1–4.

12

THE APA KNOWLEDGE DISSEMINATION PROGRAM: AN OVERVIEW OF 100 YEARS

GARY R. VANDENBOS

Scientific and professional societies have existed historically to define a field and facilitate communication within it. Two major information dissemination channels have been the hallmark of these activities by societies: annual conventions and publications. The publications developed and disseminated through such societies may be pamphlets intended for use

The author gratefully acknowledges the assistance of many APA staff in the preparation of this chapter. Elizabeth Bulatao of the Office of Communications deserves particular acknowledgment for her extensive research, fact checking, and editorial support in the refinement of this chapter. Barbara McLean, formerly with APA's PsycINFO unit, provided an extensive 130-page source document of dates, facts, figures, names, and text that provided the initial structure of the section of this chapter covering the *Psychological Abstracts* and PsycINFO. Other APA staff who provided assistance include Rick Sample and Laura Dworken of the APA Library; Janet Cole of the Office of Communications; Leslie Cameron, Lee Cron, and Susan Knapp of the Journals Office; Candace Won of Convention Affairs; Sarah Jordan of Division Services; and Susan Bedford of APA Books.

The author is also grateful for the substantive comments that the following individuals provided in reviewing the draft manuscript: Norman Abeles, Earl Alluisi, Ludy Benjamin, Brenda Bryant, Meredith Crawford, Anita DeVivo, Howard Egeth, the late Jane Hildreth, Ernest Hilgard, Alan Kazdin, Gregory Kimble, Patrick Miyamoto, Walter Mischel, Helen Orr, J. Bruce Overmier, Cecil Peck, Robert Perloff, Barbara Ross, Marion Russell, Michael Sokal, Warren Street, Martha Storandt, and Carl Thoresen.

347

by the public, newsletters intended for specialists, scientific journals, or professional and scientific books. Publications provide a vital and invaluable record of the growth and intellectual development of the field, and of the social and economic forces affecting the discipline through time.

Exchange of scientific information was one of the primary objectives for which the American Psychological Association (APA) was established. This exchange was achieved initially through an annual meeting, which can be viewed as the first component of the APA knowledge dissemination program. Later, the APA acquired several journals and established an abstract periodical—the second and third components, respectively. After World War II, the APA began publishing occasional books, and book publication could be viewed as the fourth component of the APA knowledge dissemination program. In 1970, the APA monthly newspaper, the *APA Monitor*, was established—the fifth component. In the mid-1980s, the APA purchased and for 5 years published *Psychology Today* as a public information effort. This chapter traces the development and growth of the knowledge dissemination program of the APA.

THE APA CONVENTION

Before the APA became a formal publisher, the annual meeting was the vehicle provided by the Association for the exchange of scientific information. The APA convention, then and now, constitutes a major component in the APA's overall efforts in the dissemination of scientific and professional knowledge.

It could well be argued (Sokal, 1973) that the first publication by the APA was the *Proceedings of the American Psychological Association, 1892–1893*. The proceedings were developed as a 29-page pamphlet that was separately published for the Association by Macmillan and Company. A complete photo reproduction of this pamphlet was reprinted for historical purposes in the April 1973 issue of the *American Psychologist* (AP). Subsequent to this, the APA "proceedings" (i.e., program listing and abstracts of presented papers) were published in scholarly journals for the next 70

A final note on the preparation of Appendix B on the publication history of the division journals: The table was initially prepared on the basis of records in the APA Journals Office and the APA Library. After identifying the relevant information and drafting the proposed historical descriptions, copies of the draft table were sent to current and former editors of each of the journals, as well as current and some past officers of each of the relevant divisions. The author greatly appreciates the feedback provided by these individuals, because it would not have been possible to verify the accuracy of the data presented without their assistance.

years, appearing sequentially in the *Psychological Review* (1895–1903), *Psychological Bulletin* (1904–1945), and *AP* (1946–1964).

The first annual meeting of the American Psychological Association was held in December 1892. The Association has held an annual meeting since. In 1929, the annual meeting regularly scheduled for December was omitted because of the convening of the Ninth International Congress of Psychology in New Haven. However, arrangements were made by the International Congress to receive the presidential address of the APA during the Congress (Fernberger, 1929, p. 127). Through 1930, all annual meetings of the Association were held between Christmas and New Year's Day. Since 1931, all annual APA meetings have been held in late summer or early fall (i.e., a few weeks before or after the Labor Day weekend). Karl Dallenbach was primarily responsible for proposing this change. Between 1942 and 1945, the regular meetings were modified to adapt to the conditions of war. The name "annual meeting" was changed to "annual convention" in 1946.

For at least the first 30 years of the APA's existence, the APA annual meeting was one of the central vehicles for the exchange of the latest and most timely research and theoretical discussions within psychology. From 1892 through 1896, the entire APA meeting was a single continuous session, with all attendees hearing all papers. In 1897, a portion of the meeting was divided into simultaneous sections. Judging from available records, it appears that until about 1910 all papers submitted for presentation were accepted (Fernberger, 1932, p. 60). Between 1912 and 1927, the Convention Program Committee struggled with managing the increasing number of submissions while minimizing the number of simultaneous sessions and maximizing discussion. By 1927, it was clear that there had to be procedures for accepting and rejecting submitted papers, limits to the length of most convention presentations, and simultaneous sessions.

During the early APA years, annual meetings were usually held in conjunction with other scientific groups. Before 1900, the membership of the APA averaged less than 100; a viable meeting was not possible without the presence of a majority of members. Travel to professional meetings was more difficult then, and it took longer. Thus, several professional meetings were frequently held in the same town, either simultaneously or sequentially. Sometimes, when different associations met in an overlapping manner, there would be a day of joint sessions. Between 1892 and the mid-1920s, APA meetings were most frequently held in conjunction with the meetings of the American Association for the Advancement of Science (AAAS). However, annual APA meetings were also held in association with the meetings of the American Society of Naturalists, the American

Philosophical Association, the American Anthropological Association, the American Political Science Association, the American Physiological Society, and other regional societies or sections of other associations (Fernberger, 1932, pp. 63–64). The close relationship with the AAAS was loosened in 1914 when the APA decided to meet with AAAS on alternate years, and after 1929, APA conventions were primarily independent scientific and professional meetings (Hilgard, 1987, p. 740).

Beginning with the 1939 annual meeting, a program and abstracts of papers were published in the *Psychological Bulletin* before the meeting. The proceedings, containing transactions of the annual business meeting, committee reports, and financial reports, were published in the *Psychological Bulletin* following the meeting. This publication pattern continued in the *Psychological Bulletin* through 1944. It was carried over to the *AP* in 1946, so that the official program with abstracts appeared in the *AP* through 1967.

As APA annual conventions grew in size and complexity, the official program reflecting the substantive content of the convention also expanded, ultimately including abstracts of individual papers; a list of symposia and scientific and professional meetings; and official notices and announcements. Starting in 1958, a separate "Convention Guide" was published, consisting of a chronological listing (without abstracts) of all programs and functions. The guide, which is now called the "Convention Program," has continued to be a separate annual publication that is now sent to convention registrants prior to the convention and is used solely as a chronological guide to the convention. This "Convention Guide" is essentially the same as the convention program published today. (The role, value, and utility of publishing abstracts of the APA convention presentations would continue to evolve.) In 1965, the APA Project on Scientific Information Exchange in Psychology (PSIEP) began a separate publication of abstracts of contributed convention papers selected by the convention program committees of various APA divisions. The PSIEP publications of proceedings (i.e., abstracts) ceased with the 1973 convention, when the PSIEP lost its funding support. In 1974 and 1975, the abstracts appeared in a separate publication within the *Journal Supplement Abstract Service* (*JSAS*, a short-lived document delivery service that the APA provided from 1971 to 1985) but was discontinued after 1975 because of poor sales of published convention abstracts. Since 1975, no comprehensive publication of convention abstracts has been undertaken, although some APA divisions have published their abstracts in either newsletters or journals.

As noted earlier, publication of the official program (with abstracts) in the *AP* ceased in 1967. Starting in 1968, the *AP* began publishing a corrected version of the convention guide program listing (without abstracts) in the December issue, with the minutes of the annual business meeting being published in a later *AP* issue. This practice continued until 1973, when the archival listing of the convention program was dropped, although the minutes of the Board of Directors and the Council of Representatives sessions continue to be published in the *AP*.

The annual APA convention continues to be an important vehicle for scientific and professional information exchange in psychology. However, its centrality, although still high, is less critical today than 50 or 100 years ago, a reflection of the availability of numerous other vehicles for obtaining information on the latest advances in psychology, such as other specialized conferences, journals, books, and electronic media.

THE APA'S KNOWLEDGE DISSEMINATION PROGRAM

The APA Journals Program

Although various early APA leaders were individually active in the creation of several psychology journals in the United States, publication of journals in psychology was not central to APA organizational activities at least at the time of the 1892 founding of the Association. Rather, the earliest APA efforts focused on defining the discipline of psychology, and the convening of the annual meeting was the major vehicle for scientific information exchange within the Association. However, as psychology evolved as a distinct discipline, psychologists needed their own journal outlets to report their research and theories. The *American Journal of Psychology* (AJP) was created by G. Stanley Hall in 1887. In part because of claims of editorial bias and undue influence by *AJP* on American psychology, the *Psychological Review* was started in 1894, edited by James McKeen Cattell and James Mark Baldwin (Hilgard, 1987, p. 741). These and other psychology journals published in the late 1880s through the early 1900s were privately owned by individuals.

The first formal consideration within the APA governance structure of possible APA involvement in publishing is dated by Fernberger (1932, p. 72) as 1909, when Robert M. Yerkes inquired about possible APA financial support of a journal of animal behavior and asked that the APA Council of Representatives consider providing $1 per member toward its establishment. The request for financial subsidy was declined, the reason given being that because all then-existing American journals in psychology were privately owned, financial support of a private journal by the Association was inappropriate and potentially unfair. However, the request stimulated a broader question, namely, what was the relationship of the Association to American psychological journals, which led to the creation in 1910 of a committee to examine this question. The committee consisted of Frank Angell, J. Carleton Bell, James McKeen Cattell, G. Stanley Hall, Morton Prince, Edmund C. Sanford, Howard C. Warren, Frederick J. E. Woodbridge, and Robert M. Yerkes, all editors of major psychology journals. The committee existed for several years and was then discharged. The issue seemed to lie dormant for several years, until a similar committee operated in 1920 and 1921, but that committee also generated no significant change.

However, a third committee (consisting of Margaret Floy Washburn, S. I. Franz, and Herbert S. Langfeld) was established immediately thereafter. Opinions about the need for editorial turnover and for other mechanisms to assure fair and unbiased editorial selection practices were evolving. There was a growing sentiment that such practices could best be achieved if the APA were more directly involved with journal operations, perhaps even becoming the owner and publisher of some journals. This new committee quickly reported (in 1922) that Howard C. Warren was prepared to sell to the APA all shares of stock in the Psychological Review Company and its five journals (*Psychological Review*, *Psychological Bulletin*, the *Journal of Experimental Psychology* [JEP], *Psychological Monographs*, and *Psychological Index*). In 1922, the APA Council voted to accept the opportunity (Fernberger, 1932, p. 73).

APA Primary Journals

The APA became involved in the administration of these journals in 1923, and the formal purchase by APA was accomplished when the first payment toward purchase was made on January 1, 1925. It was originally agreed that annual payments would be made through 1936, but in 1929, when APA had paid approximately 64% of the original $5,500 purchase price, Warren canceled the balance of the unpaid note and the purchase was completed.

The efforts of the 1921–1922 "journal committee" and the events of 1922 and 1924 involving the journals of the Psychological Review Company influenced other journal owners. In 1925, Morton Prince wrote to the APA and offered to donate the *Journal of Abnormal and Social Psychology* (JASP) to the APA (Fernberger, 1932, p. 76). The APA Council voted to accept the journal. In 1926, it was formally announced that *JASP* had been transferred to the APA (with APA publication beginning in 1927). The journal had been called the *Journal of Abnormal Psychology* from its founding in

1906 until 1921, at which time Prince expanded the name to include social psychology. Prince continued to edit *JASP* until his death in 1929.

By 1930, scientific publishing had become a significant formal APA activity. The APA owned 7 of the 17 publications appearing in the directory of psychological publications printed on the back of the journals. Relatively little formal APA action occurred related to journal publications during the 1930s, although new psychological journals were being published. Rather, Osier and Wozniak (1984, p. xxix) reported that 77 new serials in psychology were inaugurated in the United States between 1930 and 1939 (and that these serials represented only 43% of all new psychology periodicals launched worldwide during the 1930s). They reported that the subject matter of these new journals changed relatively little from the subject matter addressed in the previous decade, with 26.3% being in the area of general psychology, 35.7% in various "applied" areas (almost equally distributed among educational, abnormal/clinical, and applied psychology), and 8.4% related to children and their development. The publication of new psychological journals continued to increase in the 1940s, with 85 new serials being established in the United States during this period (which represented only 40% of the worldwide total). Not surprisingly, most of these journals were inaugurated in 1945 or later, concomitant with the post-World War II boom in interest and research in psychology.

The 1940s saw the APA purchase or establish four journals. The *Journal of Applied Psychology* was purchased from James P. Porter in 1943 for $10,000 (Peak, 1949, p. 467), and the Association assumed publication in the same year. The APA purchased the *Journal of Comparative Psychology* from the Williams and Wilkins Company and began publishing it as an APA journal in 1947. This latter acquisition was noteworthy because it represented the continuation of the *Journal of Animal Behavior* (published 1911–1917) and *Psychological Biology* (published 1917–1920), which had been combined to form the *Journal of Comparative Psychology* in 1921: in other words, the journal about which Yerkes had first approached APA in 1909. When the APA acquired this journal, the title was expanded to the *Journal of Comparative and Physiological Psychology* (in 1983, the APA split the journal into *Behavioral Neuroscience* and the *Journal of Comparative Psychology*, thus reestablishing the title used from 1921 through 1946). When the American Association for Applied Psychology merged with the APA in 1946 to form the "modern APA," the *Journal of Consulting Psychology* was acquired through the merger (and in 1968 the APA changed the title to the *Journal of Consulting and Clinical Psychology*). The *American Psychologist* was established as the official journal of the Association in 1946 by the reorganized APA.

In 1947, the APA Council voted to merge *Psychological Monographs* and *Applied Psychology Monographs* into one journal called *Psychological Monographs: General and Applied* (Peak, 1947, p. 476). *Psychological Monographs: General and Applied* was the successor to the *Archives of Psychology*, *Applied Psychology Monographs*, and *Psychological Monographs*. The *Archives of Psychology* was founded in 1906 by James McKeen Cattell and Robert S. Woodworth of Columbia University as a forum for publishing doctoral dissertations of their students (Hilgard, 1987, p. 742). The *Archives* were merged with *Psychological Monographs* in 1945. The publication of the *Archives of Psychology* terminated with the publication of Monograph No. 300 in 1945, *Applied Psychology Monographs* with the publication of Monograph No. 17 in 1948. *Psychological Monographs* ceased publication on December 31, 1966 (Newman, 1966, p. 1137), with the publication of No. 287 (Volume 61, No. 6, 1947). In seriation or numbering, *Psychological Monographs: General and Applied* was continuous with *Psychological Monographs*; that is, the new series started with No. 288 (Volume 62, No. 1, 1948; Conrad, 1949, p. 112) and continued through No. 633 under Volume 80 in 1966.

Major expansion in the publication of scientific knowledge in psychology occurred worldwide between the late 1950s and the mid-1970s. The APA journals program was part of that expansion. *Contemporary Psychology*, a journal of book reviews, was created in 1956 with E. G. Boring as founding editor, and the *Journal of Educational Psychology* was purchased from Warwick and York Company in 1957. However, the relative proportion of psychology journals published by the APA decreased during this period of expansion.

In 1965, when the *Journal of Personality and Social Psychology* was established, the title of JASP was changed to the *Journal of Abnormal Psychology*. At the end of 1966, *Psychological Monographs* became the first serial publication to be terminated by the Association (Newman, 1966, p. 1137). The APA acquired the *Journal of Counseling Psychology* in 1967 and established *Developmental Psychology* and *Professional Psychology* in 1969.

Throughout the 1960s, the process of scientific information exchange in psychology was the subject of extensive examination and controversy (see Clark, 1971). In 1961, the APA submitted a proposal to the National Science Foundation (NSF) seeking funding for a "coordinated study of information exchange in psychology," which was ultimately funded by NSF as the PSIEP. The *Journal Supplement Abstract Service* (JSAS) was established in 1971 as an outgrowth of the *Experimental Publication System*. JSAS became *Psychological Documents* in 1983; the change in title was intended to project more clearly its status as a psychological journal, albeit with a different mode of publication. However, as a result of a continuing decline in submissions and subscriptions, JSAS ceased publication in 1985. Another significant development in 1963 was the introduction of author abstracts at the head of all articles published in APA journals. In addition, the abstracts were taken verbatim from the articles and printed in *Psychological Abstracts* (*PA*). Also, the APA urged all non-APA journals to include abstracts.

In 1975, the Publications and Communications (P&C) Board members realized that the size of *JEP* was getting out of hand and that something had to be done. Largely on Arthur Melton's initiative (then a P&C Board member), the *Journal of Experimental Psychology* was split into four journals: *JEP: General*, *JEP: Animal Behavior Processes*, *JEP: Human Learning and Memory* (now *JEP: Learning, Memory, and Cognition*), and *JEP: Human Perception and Performance*. These four journals in core research areas in psychology now publish a total of 2,800 pages annually.

As noted earlier, in 1983, the *Journal of Comparative and Physiological Psychology* was split into two journals, *Behavioral Neuroscience* and the *Journal of Comparative Psychology*. This action allowed the APA to maintain its historical recognition of the comparative area while simultaneously more effectively recognizing psychology's growing involvement in neuroscience research (Eichorn & VandenBos, 1985).

In 1986, the APA began publishing *Psychology and Aging*, the first completely new journal launched by the Association in 17 years. The establishment of an APA journal in the area of psychology and aging was one of the recommendations of the Conference on Training Psychologists for Work in Aging ("older Boulder") held in Boulder from June 14 to 18, 1981 (Santos & VandenBos, 1982). Finally, in 1989, the *Journal of Counseling and Clinical Psychology* (JCCP) was split, segregating articles on assessment into a journal called *Psychological Assessment* and maintaining JCCP as a journal of techniques of diagnosis and treatment in disordered behavior of clinical interest. Appendix A summarizes the publication history of APA journals. By 1990, the APA published 20 primary journals, 2 special journals (*AP* and *Contemporary Psychology*), 7 secondary journals (*PA* and six *PsycSCANS*, which are print derivatives from the PsycINFO database), and one newsletter, the *Clinician's Research Digest* (*CRD*), which was purchased on July 1, 1988, from Clinical Information Services. The first APA-published issue of *CRD* began with the July 1988, Volume 6(7) issue.

In 1990, 7,023 psychologists and other behavioral scientists—22 regular APA journal editors, 54 associate editors, 838 consulting editors, and 6,109 reviewers—helped to either review or select material for the APA journals. The APA's 22 regular editors operate separate editorial offices, which are located throughout the country, usually at the university with which the editor is affiliated. Each regular journal editor and associate editor receive honoraria and office support funds from the APA. They work with a full-time journal production staff of 31.

In 1990, APA journal editors received 6,291 new manuscripts and book reviews for possible publication. They rejected nearly three fourths of the manuscripts submitted in 1990; only a few of the book reviews (which are mostly invited) were rejected. A total of 1,766 articles were published in 19 journals, along with 1,166 book reviews in *Contemporary Psychology*. The number of pages published in APA journals has increased from 5,015 "standard size" (7 × 10 in.) pages in 1959 to 16,507 pages (plus 80 additional pages for *CRD*) in 1990. The number of published pages for 1991 was 16,899.

Division Journals

Divisions have been a part of the APA structure for about half of the APA's existence. They were designed in the early 1940s to preserve the APA as a unified association representing all of psychology. Then as well as now, the role of the divisions is to promote the diverse areas of psychology and to assure that all of the legitimate areas of interest of the members are recognized and accommodated. The relation of the divisions to the APA is similar to the relation of the states of the union to the United States, with divisions retaining a high degree of internal economy yet conceding certain authority to the central organization (Fowler & VandenBos, 1989).

There are currently 48 divisions. Eighteen of these divisions publish their own journals; Division 12, Clinical Psychology, in addition to its main division journal, has two other journals published by its two sections. Divisions without journals publish newsletters, and a majority of the divisions with journals also have newsletters. The earliest division journal published was that of the Society for the Psychological Study of Social Issues (Division 9), *Journal of Social Issues*. Some journals evolved from the divisions' newsletters. Division 2's *The Teaching of Psychology* evolved from the "Teaching of Psychology Newsletter" in 1974. Division 12, Section I's *Journal of Clinical Child Psychology* started as a newsletter, became a journal in 1971, and was recognized by the Council as a division journal in 1977. Some division journals underwent name changes through the years, and in some cases, a transfer of ownership of a division journal to the APA was undertaken, as was done recently with the *Journal of Family Psychology*. Appendix B is a list of divisions with their respective journals.

Division journals are official publications but are published by outside publishers and funded by the respective divisions. The P&C Board acknowledges the value of the diversity of journals sponsored by APA divisions and encourages divisions to continue these publication activities. The APA bylaws charge the P&C Board with the supervision of the managing and editing of division journals. To implement this mandate, the P&C Board delegates the management and editing of each division journal in full to the relevant division and vests the majority of responsibility for the journal in the executive committee of that division. The P&C Board reaffirms the importance of editorial freedom of division journal editors. The divisions, through their executive committees, maintain and manage their journals in a manner comparable to the way in which the APA maintains and manages its primary journals. To foster communication, the executive committee of any division that publishes a journal incorporates in the annual report of the division a statement of editorial operations comparable to the statements prepared by APA journal editors for the P&C Board, and the Board receives a copy of this report. Divisions that wish to create new journals must obtain formal approval from the Council of Representatives through the P&C Board. Because the intent of the P&C Board is to foster scientific communication, the Board will normally recommend to the Council that the new journal be authorized.

Because a division is a constituent part of the APA, any publishing arrangement for a journal by a division that involves a contract for joint publishing or joint ownership of a journal with a non-APA publisher requires review and recommendations for approval by the P&C Board prior to signing a contract. Because division journals are official APA publications, they are required by the Council to participate in the APA liability insurance program. Division journal editors are encouraged to seek advice from the APA Central Office and the P&C Board on matters of mutual concern, such as printers and printing costs, postal regulations, advertising, accounting systems, copyright, and permission practices.

The APA Abstract Program[1]

The history of APA's concern with abstracting the journal literature in psychology spans 70 to 80 years. The first effort to index the psychological literature was begun in 1890 by H. Ebbinghaus and A. Koenig with the publication of the first volume of *Zeitschrift fur Psychologie und Physiologie der Sinnesorgane*, in which the literature for 1889 was classified. In 1895, the *Année Psychologique*, edited by H. Beaunis and A. Binet, published a

---

[1]Most of the historical material in this section was condensed from a summary document compiled by Barbara E. McLean (1990) describing the history of the APA PsycINFO program as reflected in the historical files of that program.

classified bibliography of titles only; publication of annual volumes continued until 1905, when the *Année Psychologique* began publishing classified abstracts in addition to title citations. Also in 1895, bibliographic services in the United States were initiated with the publication of the annual *Psychological Index* (*PI*) under the joint editorship of H. C. Warren and L. Farrand. The first *PI* volume contained 1,312 article titles from 1894. *PI* continued publication until 1935.

By 1910, the demand for information on psychological research was greater than what could be provided by citations alone. An APA Bibliography Committee was formed to support the publication of "resumes" of psychological investigations and to urge authors to furnish abstracts of research results to psychological journals as soon as these studies appeared in print. In 1919, the APA, in cooperation with the AAAS, began arranging for an abstract journal in psychology. An initial step was the publication of abstracts in one issue a year of the *Psychological Bulletin* from 1921 through 1926.

In 1926, the Laura Spelman Rockefeller Foundation provided a grant of $76,500 (over an 11-year period) to the APA to finance *Psychological Abstracts* (*PA*). The first volume of *PA* was published in 1927 and used essentially the same classification scheme as *PI*. In the first year, under the dedicated editorship of Walter S. Hunter, 2,730 abstracts from 165 journals were published in 12 monthly issues. Abstracting was done almost entirely by volunteer psychologists in the United States and abroad. The editor and his assistants did the indexing, using only the abstract and title of the document (the volunteers retained the journals they abstracted). Index terms (an average of 2.5 per abstract) were written on 3-by-5-inch cards. The cards were sorted to produce the annual subject index. During its first 10 years, when the psychological literature was growing but still manageable, the materials abstracted in *PA* included journals, books, proceedings, bibliographies, obituaries, and, for several years beginning in 1934, films.

By 1937, 6,000 abstracts from 380 journals and other sources were published, and the first major revision of the subject classification also appeared that year, mirroring the growth of and changes in the field. World War II significantly affected *PA*: Scholarly publishing in psychology decreased worldwide, and the number of articles available to abstract, as well as access to them, diminished while subscriptions to *PA* increased. As a result, only 3,500 abstracts were published in *PA* in 1945.

After World War II, there was enormous growth in the demand for psychological knowledge. In 1947, to make *PA*'s classification system useful and to reflect changes in the field, significant changes were again made to the system. In 1949, 6,530 abstracts were published, providing strong evidence of the beginning of the worldwide, post-World War II emergence of psychological science and the attendant journal publication boom and the gradual reestablishment of foreign publishing houses. In addition, the field of psychology was also taking a borderline position overlapping the biological and social sciences and having tangential or material relations with more than a dozen other fields. Five years later, there were 9,120 abstracts published, a 39.7% increase over 1949. This increase prompted the APA Publications Board to set an artificial annual page limit for *PA*. Soon, *PA*'s dilemma became the problem of communicating all of the world's relevant literature in psychology in a timely manner within the cost limitations set by the APA's budget.

As noted earlier, in 1961, the APA submitted a proposal to the NSF for a "coordinated study of information exchange in psychology." This resulted in an initial NSF grant of $167,700 for the PSIEP. The project, which was concerned chiefly with the behavioral study of scientific information dissemination, conducted a series of studies between 1961 and 1965. In addition to the 1961 grant, seven annual grants were obtained for the PSIEP from 1962 through 1968. Two of those grants were devoted to *PA* operations.

Prior to 1963, editors of *PA* operated from university offices, whereas *PA* business operations were managed from the APA Publications Office. In 1963, the editorial and operations offices of *PA* were combined into the APA Central Office, and a new *PA* executive editor, Philip J. Siegmann, was selected. In the same year, *PA* entered the computer age with the addition of an IBM 1401, which was applied to sorting terms for the 1963 volume index (as well as making possible a modified and early form of a brief subject index).

In 1968, the APA embarked on a major undertaking that would occupy a significant portion of the organization's attention for almost 6 years, involve large expenditures of funds, and have an enormous positive impact on the future of *PA*. The APA established the Office of Communication Management and Development (OCMD, later to become the Office of Communications). All major APA activities concerned with scientific and professional information exchange were brought together for management purposes as a total Communications Program under the OCMD. Belver Griffith served as Acting Director, Helen Orr as managing editor, Estelle Mallinoff as Separates editor, and Philip J. Siegmann as executive editor. The OCMD's charge was to set up and oversee the PSIEP's main program, the National Information System for Psychology (NISP). The NISP project sought to introduce major innovations in the APA Communications Program (which might serve as a prototype for other disciplines) and to evaluate their effects (Brayfield, 1968). The NSF supported the NISP effort for 5 years, from 1968 to 1972, providing about $2 million during that period. Because the *PA* computerized system was the initial pivot point of the entire NISP system, it was the target for the largest amount of reorganization and expansion.

The NISP/OCMD's plans for *PA* included the installation of in-house keyboarding facilities; investigation of the sale of *PA*'s magnetic tapes to other organizations; production of standardized vocabulary, input, and bibliographic control (to take advantage of machine records produced by other systems, joined to the rest of the world's psychological literature); distribution of *PA* in "sections" as well as in a complete set; and development of a psychological thesaurus. Considerable controversy existed during the NISP's existence from 1968 until it lost its funding in 1973. However, even in the absence of outside funding, the OCMD managed to press on with planned changes for the growth and expansion of *PA*, all of which were integral to the development of the PsycINFO system as it is known today. The successes and positive results of the PSIEP and the NISP, although limited, were most notable in their effects on *PA* and in the impetus they provided for moving the APA more swiftly into the modern communications era.

In 1965, as a result of the PSIEP studies, the APA Publications Board approved an experimental study of the feasibility of producing *PA* by the Photon process, which incorporates the use of a computer, and investigation of possibilities of improving information retrieval by computer and magnetic tapes (which were available as a by-product of the Photon process). This process was tested with the publication of Volume 40, 1966, of *PA* and brought considerable changes to *PA* production. The *PA* staff in the APA Central Office was increased from 5 to 12 members. The number of core and peripheral journals regularly searched more than doubled. *PA* went from bimonthly to monthly publication. The "lag time" for the appearance of abstracts in *PA* from "core journals" was reduced from between 12 and 18 months to between 3 and 4 months (and for peripheral journals from 2 to 3 years to 6 to 10 months). The number of abstracts printed in *PA* increased from 8,381 in 1963 to 13,622 in 1966 and to 18,068 in 1969.

In 1966, the National Clearinghouse for Mental Health Information (NCMHI) of the National Institute of Mental Health (NIMH) expressed interest in purchasing selected abstracts on magnetic tape created during the *PA* process, beginning with the 1967 volume. The APA, believing that the income from the sale of abstracts would make *PA* almost self-supporting, concluded a contract with the NIMH–NCMHI in 1967 that called for the delivery of approximately 10,000 abstracts at $22.00 per abstract. However, because of PA start-up problems, the APA delivered less than it promised and realized only a small portion of the expected income. Other prospective customers (ERIC and EDUCOM, for example), although interested, were not in a position to buy tapes. The first APA-produced 3-year *PA Cumulative Index* (1969–1971), a by-product of the computerized database, was planned during the NISP period but was not identified directly with the NISP. Other cumulative indexes to *PI* (1894–1935) and *PA* (1927–1960) had been published by Hall and Company of Boston.

In the early 1970s, several services were designed and initiated in the PA system, under the title of *Psychological Abstracts* Information Services (PAIS). Using the *PA* tape database, the Mead Data Central System, and a local terminal, a group of psychologist users in the Washington, DC, area participated in a 6-month pilot test of the potential of the system to provide computer aid; this test demonstrated the value of the system.

In 1971, PADAT (*Psychological Abstracts* Direct Access Terminal), PASAR (*Psychological Abstracts* Search and Retrieval), and PATELL (*Psychological Abstracts* Tape Edition Lease and Licensing) were introduced. With PADAT, subscribers could perform interactive searches of the *PA* database (then containing more than 75,000 records) using a terminal located in the researchers' own facilities. PATELL made *PA* tapes available to academic institutions capable of using them, and by 1971, Syracuse University, the University of Georgia, and the Karolinska Institute in Sweden had expressed an interest in leasing the tapes. PASAR was accessible to psychologists by mail. For a fee, a psychologist could have a literature search made by a member of *PA*'s in-house staff. The APA switched system contractors for the *PA* "user services" from Mead to Lockheed's system, DIALOG, so that by 1973, the *PA* database was offered on a royalty basis to any qualified information analysis center, and the Information Sciences Department of the Lockheed Missiles and Space Company agreed to run PADAT.

From the earliest days of *PA*, it was recognized that there was a need for techniques to arrange by content the masses of citations, annotations, and abstracts of psychological literature to make finding desired material easier. The earliest arrangements were merely by broad areas of psychology. As the field grew, so did the classification system, enabling more and more specific classification of information. The advent of the computerized database radically changed the way in which indexing and retrieval systems were viewed. Thus, in 1969, a major project was the development of a "thesaurus of behavioral terms." In 1970, the development of a Controlled Indexing Vocabulary was undertaken. A first draft of the resulting 3,033 candidate indexing terms was completed in 1972. The first edition of the

Thesaurus of Psychological Index Terms (PsycINFO, 1974) was published in 1974. The sixth edition was released in 1991.

Between 1972 and 1973, APA acquired a Burroughs 2500 mainframe computer system to serve as a multipurpose general processor for the production of *PA* and to use with the PAIS database. George Thomson was hired as programmer for the *PA* project. In 1974, Robert G. Kinkade resigned as *PA* editor, and Boris Cherney, then head of the Office of Business Affairs (and soon to be head of the Office of Communications), recruited Lois Granick as, initially, acting head of the program and, then, after January 1975, as executive editor of *PA* and director of the computer-based abstract initiative. Granick's time was spent in designing, programming, and testing elements of the new computer system and in planning for extensive internal changes.

For several years, the name used for the entire family of information services derived from *PA* had been PAIS, which appeared widely in a variety of publications and advertisements. In the spring of 1975, the APA was notified by the Public Affairs Information Service that the acronym was illegally being used by the APA. After obtaining legal advice, the APA decided on "PsycINFO" as the new department name in November 1975, and, in December 1975, the first advertisement using the PsycINFO name appeared in *PA*.

Early in Granick's directorship, a major PsycINFO concern was the need for realistic guidelines for the coverage of psychological literature. *PA* staff were forced, on a daily basis, to make pragmatic decisions about what constituted PsycINFO's universe of coverage. Throughout *PA*'s history, several ad hoc committees and task forces had been formed under the aegis of the Publications Board to advise on *PA* and its concerns. For the most part, these groups discharged their responsibilities well. However, Granick realized the need at this juncture for a group who would work *with* the *PA* staff as well as *for* them. An ad hoc *PA* coverage subcommittee of the P&C Board composed of Lorraine Bouthilet, Michael Wertheimer, and Arthur Melton met to discuss the practicality of a *PA* coverage advisory board. On the basis of this committee's recommendations to the P&C Board, in 1976, the Board authorized the creation of an Advisory Editor Committee for *PA*, the expansion of *PA* to cover the world's literature in psychology and related disciplines, and the appointment of Foreign Language Cooperating Editors. In October 1976, the first PsycINFO Advisory Editors Committee (PIAC) members were named: Lorraine Bouthilet (chair), Earl Alluisi, Stephen Worchel, Meredith Crawford, Arthur Melton, and Cecil Peck. The PIAC has continued as a permanent group charged with providing long-range policy and planning recommendations for the PsycINFO system.

In 1977, PsycINFO could be searched through DIALOG and Bibliographic Retrieval Services (new in 1977) in the United States and through overseas distributors in Germany, Sweden, Canada, and South Africa. In 1978, the APA acquired a new building in Arlington, Virginia, to house parts of its overcrowded Central Office. PsycINFO, the rest of the Office of Communications, and most of the Office of Business Administration moved to these new quarters.

PsycINFO, under Granick's leadership and with policy guidance from the PIAC and the P&C Board, evolved into a computer-based system for acquisition, storage and retrieval, and dissemination of information on the world's literature in psychology. The printed *PA* slowly became "derivative" products of this computerized system. This change has evolved gradually over the past few years and is the most significant development since the founding of *PA*. Recognition of this change in perception and function in PsycINFO policy implied that increasing the amount and kind of information in PsycINFO does not necessarily increase the size of printed volumes of *PA*, because certain information could be available only as computer output and not in published form.

With increased services available to PsycINFO users, the APA realized the need for educating the community of information users about these products and services, as well as instructing them on how to find needed information in the electronic database. The *PsycINFO Users Reference Manual*, a loose-leaf publication with semiannual updates included in the subscription, was developed in 1975 and released in 1976. Tutorials and workshops were initiated in 1975 by PsycINFO. They attracted the attention of the professional community using computerized techniques for searching, and requests for workshops and seminars accelerated from 1976 onward.

As *PA* grew in size (and price), it became clear that it was rapidly becoming primarily a "library product." However, individual psychologists still desired easier printed access to abstracts related to their specialty area. The issue of how to supply such selected information to individual users had repeatedly been discussed and explored by the Publications Committee, the PIAC, and various research project staff. Finally, in 1977, the APA authorized an extensive survey of the membership to determine what they would most like to see in the "derivative" *PA* products. On the basis of member responses, it was decided to publish derivatives in three topic areas as a "first offering": clinical, developmental, and general psychology. The general psychology derivative was eventually dropped. The first *PA* derivatives quarterlies were introduced in 1980: *PsycSCAN: Clinical Psychology* and *PsycSCAN: Developmental Psychology*. Subscriptions were adequate, and *PsycSCAN: Applied Psychology* was introduced in 1981 and *PsycSCAN:*

Learning Disabilities/Mental Retardation appeared in 1982. As recognition of the utility of the derivatives began to spread among the APA membership, PsycINFO received requests from special interest groups of psychologists for PsycSCANs in their areas. In 1982, contacts were made with APA Divisions, inviting them to participate in planning specific PsycSCAN publications supported by the divisions and directed toward their interests. In 1986, *PsycSCAN: Psychoanalysis* appeared, developed in collaboration with Division 39 (Psychoanalysis). *PsycSCAN: Applied Experimental and Engineering Psychology*, developed in collaboration with Division 21, began publication in 1987.

The emergence of a new technology in the 1980s gave rise to a new medium through which PsycINFO could deliver its information, the Compact Disk—Read Only Memory (or CD-ROM). When Gary VandenBos became the head of the APA Office of Communications in 1984, he and Lois Granick immediately began exploring the technology and the newly emerging companies utilizing it. They selected SilverPlatter, Inc., as the commercial firm with which the APA would first develop a CD-ROM product, because of the quality of their search software and disk production capacity. After a year and a half of developmental work, the new product, PsycLIT, was ready for distribution, and the APA signed the first CD-ROM licensing agreement for PsycLIT with Indiana University at Bloomington on September 17, 1986. The response to PsycLIT was tremendous. By December of 1986, there were 16 PsycLIT leases, and the number increased to 274 by the end of 1988 and 774 by the end of 1990.

In January of 1990, Lois Granick stepped down as the head of PsycINFO to work on a major overhaul of the PsycINFO operating system. VandenBos recruited Dennis Auld, previously the head of Data Courier in Louisville, KY, to replace her as the director of PsycINFO. The PsycINFO staff today totals approximately 95 abstractors, indexers, analysts, editors, marketers, managers, and coverage specialists.

PsycINFO today is a greatly expanded *system* of databases, publications, and services. The PsycINFO database is a computerized file of over 750,000 references (most with abstracts) to the international literature in psychology and related fields, cumulated since 1967. The database is updated monthly. The print publications include *PA*, the annual index to the serial literature; *PsycSCANs*, subject-oriented current awareness publications for special audiences; *PsycBOOKS*, an annual publication providing access to books and book chapters in psychology; and the *PsycINFO User Manual* and the *Thesaurus of Psychological Index Terms*. Currently, PsycINFO data enjoy a diverse audience that includes the users of the 3,400 print subscriptions; the customers of six online data vendors (DIALOG and

Maxwell Online/BRS Search Services in the United States, DIMDI in Germany, Data-Star in Switzerland, SASDI in South Africa, and the University of Tsukuba's online distribution system in Japan); and the faculty, staff, and students of over 700 institutions who either lease magnetic tape versions of the database or subscribe to the CD-ROM version, PsycLIT. Although the majority of the user community consists of patrons of academic libraries, PsycINFO data are also accessed extensively in medical, public, national, special, and corporate libraries and research centers throughout the world.

The APA Book Program

As noted earlier, Sokal (1973) argued that the first "separates" publication of the APA was the combined 1892–1893 proceedings. From his perspective, the second separates publication of the APA was probably the 1914 APA membership directory, which was actually a 16-page pamphlet listing the officers of the Association, the constitution, and all members' names and institutional affiliations. Beginning in 1916, the APA regularly published a *Yearbook* (or *Directory*, or *Membership Register*) on a continuing basis. However, it also could be argued that these publications were routine association documents, not APA books per se.

When the APA acquired *Psychological Monographs* in 1925, it might be argued that the APA began publishing "separates"—if "separates" are defined as bookletlike reports that are separately available and that appear irregularly. However, although each *Psychological Monograph* supplement had a separate whole number and was published (and obtainable) on a separate basis, the reports were promoted and distributed to institutional libraries and individuals under the concept of a volume number. In addition, they were all published with a lightweight paperback cover, similar to the cover of a journal issue, in the same size and format. Thus, everything about them encouraged libraries to bind them as annual volumes of a scientific periodical. Moreover, the majority of these monographs averaged slightly fewer than 50 pages. In short, there was little about *Psychological Monographs* that would qualify them as APA "book" publications.

The publication with the strongest claim for marking the beginning of book publication by APA is *Ethical Standards of Psychologists* (APA, 1953a). This 171-page "casebook" on ethical standards was published by the APA in 1953, after they were provisionally approved as a policy statement by the Council of Representatives in 1952. This book included consideration of an array of general problems, with descriptions of incidents illustrating each of the problems and articulation of some general principle related to expected behavior or conduct in such situations. This book was the outgrowth of 15 years of deliberation and discussion. A special committee had been formed in 1938 to consider the advisability of drafting an ethical code and to informally resolve complaints of unethical conduct. In 1940, a standing Committee on Scientific and Professional Ethics was created to handle charges of unethical conduct, but it was not until 1947 that this committee recommended that work begin on a formal code of ethics. The Committee on Ethical Standards of Psychology was created to develop a code. It used a highly participatory process, receiving actual examples of ethical problems from members, publishing partial draft statements of standards in the *American Psychologist*, and receiving feedback from psychology departments, psychological societies, and individual psychologists (Golann, 1970). The actual "principles," without case examples or discussion, were published as *Ethical Standards of Psychologists: A Summary of Ethical Principles* (APA, 1953b), a 19-page pamphlet. The basic code was revised many times over the next 35 years, with the various revisions appearing in either the *AP* or the *APA Monitor*. From time to time, article-length "casebooks" related to specific principles appeared in the *AP*. In 1987, the APA again published, in book form, a *Casebook on Ethical Principles of Psychologists* (APA Ethics Committee, 1987).

In 1954, the APA released a 38-page pamphlet, the *Technical Recommendations for Psychological Tests and Diagnostic Techniques* (APA Committee on Test Standards, 1954), which would eventually develop into an APA-published book. Based in part on this initial APA work, in 1955 the *Technical Recommendations for Achievement Tests* was developed by the American Educational Research Association and the National Council on Measurements Used in Education, endorsed by the APA, and published by the National Educational Association (1955). Later, through the efforts of a joint committee on test standards, these two pamphlets were combined into a single 40-page booklet, *Standards for Educational and Psychological Tests and Manuals* (APA, 1966), and a formal "second edition," *Standards for Educational and Psychological Tests* (APA, 1974a), was later released. Between 1977 and 1984, the APA, the American Educational Research Association, and the National Council on Measurement in Education undertook a joint project to review and restructure the standards, which resulted in the eventual publication of a 100-page book titled *Standards for Educational and Psychological Testing* (APA, 1985).

In 1952, the APA published, in the *Psychological Bulletin*, a 60-page "article" that would eventually become an important APA book publication. The article was a journal supplement titled "Publication Manual" (APA Council of Editors, 1952). It was also available as a separate pamphlet/reprint. This was not, however, the first appearance of such an article or statement from the APA. In 1928, a Committee on Form of Manuscript, chaired by Madison Bentley (and comprising editors and business managers of anthropological and psychological journals), had met to discuss the form of journal manuscripts and to write instructions for their preparation. The Committee's report was the forerunner of the current *Publication Manual*. The Committee agreed that it would not dictate to authors, but it recommended a "standard of procedure, to which reference might be made in cases of doubt" ("Instructions," 1929, p. 57). The effort was intended for science writers, who were cautioned that "the writer who is incompetent in spelling, grammar, or syntax should seek help. . . . A badly prepared manuscript always suggests uncritical research and slovenly thinking" ("Instructions," 1929, p. 58). The report was published as a 7-page article in the February 1929 issue of the *Psychological Bulletin*. Four subsequent guides were specifically aimed at assisting authors writing for APA journals (DeVivo, 1975, pp. 37–38): In 1944, a 32-page guide appeared in the *Psychological Bulletin* as an article by John Anderson and Willard Valentine (1944). In 1952, the APA Board of Editors (now called the Council of Editors) expanded the 1944 article into the 60-page supplement of the *Bulletin*, which carried the title "Publication Manual" for the first time (APA Council of Editors, 1952) and marked the beginning of a recognized "APA style." Two revisions, in 1957 and in 1967, followed as small booklets (APA, 1957, 1967). The APA published the "second edition" of the APA *Publication Manual* in 1974, a 136-page book (APA, 1974b), with change sheets issued in 1975 and 1977. It was still directed to the authors of the APA's journals, but it also recognized the growing number of other psychology journals that had adopted the *Publication Manual* and the students in both graduate and undergraduate psychology who relied on it as a reference or a text (DeVivo, 1975, p. 38). Between 1975 and 1982, an average of 76,712 copies of the APA *Publication Manual* were sold each year, with sales from year to year being almost identical. In 1983, in response to users' suggestions for improvements, a 208-page third edition was issued. To ensure that standards were met on all levels, the 1983 edition added a section on grammar (APA, 1983; Bazerman, 1988, p. 262). From 1983 through 1986, an average of 124,653 copies of the APA *Publication Manual* were sold per year, again with little variation from year to year. A promotional campaign was carried out by Gary VandenBos in 1986 and 1987 to introduce the APA *Publication Manual* to undergraduate English instructors, teachers in undergraduate journalism and communications departments, and faculty members in nursing and social work. This campaign was apparently quite successful, because

APA *Publication Manual* sales rose to 144,576 in 1987, 154,675 in 1988, 181,565 in 1989, and 202,325 copies in 1990.

In 1955, the APA published its first hardcover book related to education and training, *School Psychologists at Mid-Century* (Cutts, 1955). It was a well-developed monograph based on the "Thayer Conference" on the functions, qualifications, and training of school psychologists, which was held at the Hotel Thayer, Westpoint, New York, from August 22 to 31, 1954. This was followed by two more education and training volumes in 1956: *Psychological Aspects of Aging* (Anderson, 1956) and *Psychology and Mental Health* (Strother, 1956). The former contained the proceedings of a conference held under the auspices of Division 20 and the National Institutes of Health in April 1955 in Bethesda, Maryland, and the latter was a training-related report on psychological contributions to mental health derived from a conference that had been held in August 1955 at Stanford University, California. These three books were of a type often expected from a scientific and professional association: volumes related to the education and training of individuals in that discipline.

In 1957, the APA published *America's Psychologists: A Survey of a Growing Profession* (Clark, 1957). When the Association reorganized at the end of World War II, a Policy and Planning Board was created with a mandate to periodically review the major problems and trends that affected psychology. In 1952, the Policy and Planning Board recommended a major investigation of a number of interrelated questions on psychological personnel, education, and employment, and an appraisal of the state of development of the science of psychology. The NSF agreed to provide financial support for the study, which involved two projects. Project A, under the direction of Sigmund Koch, dealt with substantive questions about psychology as a scientific discipline and resulted in a series of six books published by McGraw-Hill Company (Koch, 1959–1963). Project B, under the direction of Kenneth E. Clark, was devoted to matters of psychological personnel and training.

In 1959, APA published *Research in Psychotherapy, Volume 1* (Rubinstein & Parloff, 1959). This APA book represents the first truly substantive book published by the APA—that is, it was not a reference work, not a volume on the education and training of psychologists, and not a volume on the status and future of the discipline. It was an edited volume assessing the current status of methodology and research findings in the area of psychotherapy research. The chapters in the book were based on presentations made at an NIMH-funded Conference on Research in Psychotherapy held in Washington, DC on April 9–12, 1958.

Appendix C presents data on APA book publication between 1946 and 1990. The data are presented in 5-year intervals and organized by type of publication (e.g., directories, proceedings, training aids, substantive books, etc.). Between 1946 and 1965, the APA averaged 2 or 3 such "book" publications per year, generally directories, proceedings, and training aids. Between 1966 and 1980, the average was 5 or 6 books each year. This increased to 10 per year between 1981 and 1985, and averaged over 15 titles each year between 1986 and 1990. In 1991, the APA published 32 book titles, with 45 books expected in 1992.

The APA did not regularly publish what most psychologists would think of as books until 1965, when the APA Separates Office took over the production of the proceedings of the annual APA convention. In 1966, the Council authorized the president of the APA to appoint an ad hoc Panel on Occasional Publications to make recommendations about the format and management of a Separates program by the Association (Newman, 1966, p. 1137). In 1970, the Council of Representatives created a Separates Committee that consisted of the executive officer, the managing editor, and the chair of the Publications Board (McKeachie, 1970, p. 25), and the following year the executive officer was granted authority to publish up to three "separates" each year (McKeachie, 1971, p. 37). In 1973, the APA Council indicated its expectation that separates publications would have the same excellence of content and editorial quality control as the Association's journals, and the Council gave final authority for accepting or rejecting manuscripts for the Separates program to the executive officer (APA, *Rules of Council*, 1973, p. 60). In 1974, the Council formally established the Separates Advisory Committee (SAC) as a subcommittee under the P&C Board as a source of advice and consultation to the executive officer on the overall goals and guidelines for the Separates program (McKeachie, 1974, p. 400).

In 1977, David Rosenthal proposed to the P&C Board that the APA create an "APA Press" to publish books written by members of the APA. The P&C Board discussed the matter but took no formal action. However, in 1979, some heightened interest in expanded book publishing activities began to develop. The P&C Board considered a broader initiative for the book program and in 1982 developed a 3-year plan for the expansion of the APA Separates program, authorizing $90,000 of research and development funds to underwrite the expansion. This action led to a modest increase in book titles from the APA in the early 1980s.

In 1984 and 1985, the P&C Board and the SAC further reviewed and discussed the APA book program at the urging of Gary VandenBos, newly appointed as the overall head of the APA knowledge dissemination program. At the suggestion of Charles Spielberger, the P&C Board established a Practitioner's Publication Committee specifically to consider the book publication interests and needs of practicing school psychologists, clinical and counseling psychologists, and industrial/organizational psychologists. This Committee, working with APA staff, conducted a series of surveys of the views and opinions of practitioner members about whether there was a need for a major expansion in the publication of books from APA. Respondents overwhelmingly encouraged significant expansion, identified potential topic areas, and suggested specific titles. The P&C Board approved plans for further expansion for several reasons. First, although the number of publications produced by other organizations, including commercial publishers, was large, the quality of many of those products was not viewed as particularly high; it was thought that the APA's well-established standards for substantive quality could be applied if the APA itself directed the production of books. Second, some types of products, such as those that would support psychology students in their development, were not being produced at all by any publisher or were of poor quality. Third, there were also areas of professional interest that were not being covered by other publishers. Between 1986 and 1990, this further expansion of the APA book program became more evident.

The APA Book Program is currently the fastest growing component of APA's knowledge dissemination activities, with more than 100 titles currently available. The program's "list" includes books and materials on scientific, theoretical, and professional advances in psychology, professional development and practice issues, educational and training programs, and student services; style manuals and instructional materials; and bibliographies. In general, the APA's goal is to publish books of theoretical and research value, with strong practical applications. The Association encourages novice and seasoned authors to consider the APA as the first-choice publisher for their books. The APA Book Acquisition and Development Office coordinates the acquisition and review of proposals, as well as the development and review of manuscripts. Once the substance of each new product is completed, the APA Book Production Office takes over, and it technically edits, typesets, and prints the book, which is then distributed through the APA's warehouse facilities. Promotional campaign efforts are designed to give the widest appropriate exposure through the use of space ads, targeted mailings, exchange ad programs, and conference displays.

OTHER APA PUBLICATION EFFORTS

The APA Monitor

In October of 1970, the APA began publishing a monthly newspaper on an experimental basis (McKeachie, 1971, p. 47), the APA Monitor. In

1971, it became a permanent part of the APA operation, and the *Monitor* was designated as the APA's official newspaper (McKeachie, 1972, p. 295). The need for the *Monitor* grew out of organizational growth in the late 1960s and the need to communicate with an increasingly diverse membership on a more timely basis than could be afforded by a scholarly journal such as *AP* (Preston, 1975).

The concept of the *Monitor* was that of a publication with distribution to all APA members to provide them with "monthly news about the APA, the operations of the Central Office, the progress of various boards and committees, and news about what APA members are saying and doing" (Little, 1970). The "Washington Report," a 6-year-old small-circulation newsletter geared to providing federal officials with information about the behavioral sciences, was integrated into the APA *Monitor*. The "Notes and News" section of *AP*, which published brief, nonarchival information about individual members and psychology programs, was also transferred to the *Monitor*. A special announcement in *AP* articulated the initial thoughts about what material would appear in *AP* and what material would appear in the *Monitor* ("Announcement," 1970). A special "Interaction" page was created to include signed editorials and letters to the editor as a vehicle for discussion of Association activities and initiatives and as a forum for expressing dissenting views. It was believed that such an opinions page was vital to open discussion within the Association and as a means for ensuring that all views were expressed. The *Monitor* also carried display advertising and classified ads.

The *Monitor* was, in many respects, an initiative of the APA Central Office staff, developed with the support and approval of both the Board of Directors and the Council of Representatives (Preston, 1975). It developed and appeared during the presidency of George Albee and while Kenneth Little was the APA Executive Officer and Alan Boneau was Director of Programs and Planning. The first editor was James Warren (Mervis, 1986). It was specifically decided that the newspaper's editor should be a full-time APA employee, selected and supervised by the APA Executive Officer, to keep the position somewhat isolated from political pressure to shape or censor the reporting (Albee, 1980). Warren had come to the APA in 1969 as a public information officer after previously working for the National Mental Health Association. Warren, with the support of Harley Preston, Director of the APA Office of External Affairs, developed the first 4-page mock-up for such a paper, which was presented to the Board of Directors in the summer of 1970. Warren wrote the entire first issue, handling all the technical production details as well (Mervis, 1986).

The original model for the *Monitor* assumed that it would be an 8-

page monthly newspaper. The model quickly proved far too small. Only two issues of the *Monitor* ever appeared within the initially conceived 8-page model. By the end of 1971, the monthly issue was averaging 18.6 pages. By the time the *Monitor* was five years old, in 1975, a monthly issue averaged 32.7 pages. In its 10th year, in 1980, the "Employment Bulletin," previously published and distributed separately, was folded into the *Monitor* (Pallak, 1979, p. 492), which now averaged 48.8 pages. In 1990, its 20th year, the *Monitor* averaged 82 pages per issue.

Psychology Today

The public image of psychology has long been an issue of concern among psychologists. Over the years, there have been considerable discussion and debate within the APA on the need to educate the general public about psychology as a science—its materials and methods of study, its findings, and its relevance to society. Members like Joseph Jastrow and Hugo Münsterberg mounted public psychology exhibitions at the world's fairs in 1893 and 1904 in an attempt to educate the public about the new science (Benjamin, 1986). Psychologists described their work in popular magazines like *Harpers*, *Forum*, *Atlantic Monthly*, and *Colliers*. Psychological advice columns appeared, written by both psychologists and nonpsychologists. Joseph Jastrow's daily column "Keeping Mentally Fit" was syndicated and appeared in more than 150 newspapers, and Albert Wiggam's (a nonpsychologist author) newspaper column on psychology was popular in the 1920s.

In the early 1930s, upon a request from the National Advisory Council on Radio in Education, an advisory Committee on Psychology was created, which organized the participation of psychologists in a large-scale experiment in educational broadcasting, in collaboration with the University of Chicago. A series of weekly 15-minute lectures on psychological topics, preceded by talks on economics, were broadcast by several stations across the nation between October 1931 and April 1932 (Bingham, 1932; Samelson, this volume). Before the broadcasts, the University of Chicago distributed listener notebooks together with a request for audience feedback (Lumley, 1932). These sets of lectures were subsequently published by the University of Chicago under the title *Psychology Today* (Bingham, 1932). In addition, three popular psychology magazines emerged in the 1930s—*Modern Psychologist*, *Practical Psychology Monthly*, and *Psychology Digest*—but all ceased publication by 1939 (Benjamin, 1986).

Although the idea of the APA publishing a popular magazine was mentioned in the official archives of the APA as early as 1941, the Association took no steps in that direction until the 1970s. The following was one of the items considered at the 1940 annual convention:

> The APA has a responsibility to the public. There is a tremendous popular interest in psychology at this time. It needs directing. A magazine along the lines of *Hygeia* or *Parents* might prove one answer. . . . The interest and curiosity of the layman in things psychological needs to be properly attended, not ignored or merely criticized, by the APA membership. (Habbe, 1941, p. 231)

In August 1940, the Emergency Committee in Psychology was established to prepare the profession for national defense, as discussed earlier in this volume by Hilgard and Capshew. The Emergency Committee soon established a number of standing subcommittees, one of these being a Subcommittee on a Textbook in Military Psychology, chaired by E. G. Boring. The Subcommittee worked to produce a popular paperback on military psychology aimed at the soldier in the field. The book, *Psychology for the Fighting Man* (Boring & Van de Water, 1943), appeared initially in serialized chapters in the fall of 1942. By the summer of 1943, 250,000 paperback copies of the completed book were distributed. Boring also produced a college textbook suitable for use at West Point titled *Psychology for the Armed Services* (Boring, 1945).

The APA published a *Public Information Guide* (APA, 1954) in 1954, and it was distributed to all members to assist those engaged in public information activities. With the establishment of a Central Office, APA gradually developed organizational and systematic capability to provide information about the field when asked by the public. For example, in 1963, with NSF funding, the APA sponsored the production of 10 educational films about areas of psychology for classroom use, for National Educational Television. The APA also produced a series of 12-minute radio programs dealing with a wide array of topics ranging from energy conservation to children's reaction to death (Pallak & Kilburg, 1986; Pallak & VandenBos, 1984).

In 1960, the APA Publications and Communications Board stated that "it would look with favor on proposals for media providing the public with information on psychology, but believes that such media should be other than the present APA journals" (Kimble, 1987, p. 1). However, it was not until 1974 that the P&C Board decided to explore publication of an APA magazine directed to a science-oriented lay public. On the recommendation of Robert Perloff, treasurer of the APA, the Board allocated $5,000 of its 1975 research and development budget to fund a Magazine Task Force charged with the responsibility of studying the feasibility of publishing such a magazine (Kimble, 1987, pp. 10–11). A prototype magazine, *Psychology*, was produced, and in January 1977 Council authorized the distribution of the magazine to all APA members and psychology students, with the understanding that members would be invited to comment on the magazine. Council was to be informed of the results of this mailing and membership response, and, if appropriate, Council would consider the desirability of publishing it as a regular magazine in 1978 (Conger, 1977, p. 423). At its June 1977 meeting, the Board of Directors received the results of the survey of member and student opinion on *Psychology* magazine. After analyzing the advantages and disadvantages of publishing the magazine, the Board recommended going ahead with the concept for a magazine, and the decision was reaffirmed at the August 1977 meeting of the Board of Directors. The Council, however, at its August 1977 meeting, by a vote of 63 to 44, opposed its publication.

Psychology Today (*PT*), a monthly magazine, came into existence in 1967, around the time when the discipline of psychology was gaining public prominence. *PT* was founded and originally edited by a psychologist, Nicholas Charney. For a while, the magazine served as an excellent dissemination medium for presenting psychology to the public. Kimble (1987) noted that

> *Psychology Today* presented psychology as scientific, intelligent, idealistic, and relevant. It treated psychology with interest, respect, and enthusiasm, everything that the public and the discipline could want. Even for psychologists who were uncomfortable with the notion of popularizing psychology, the magazine was hard to resist. Many of us subscribed to it and recommended it to our students" (p. 8).

However, around 1969, the number of quality articles appearing in the magazine decreased and sensationalistic journalism began replacing them. In 1969, *PT* began emphasizing sexuality, and there was coverage of nudity and ESP. Some psychologists theorized that America's involvement in the Vietnam War and its corrosive effects on American society, namely social protest, an expanding drug culture, disillusionment, and noninvolvement, resulted in a negative image for psychology and made *PT* irrelevant.

PT was sold, first to Boise-Cascade, a large wood products conglomerate, and then in 1973 to Ziff-Davis Publishing Company, a publisher of numerous consumer magazines. These developments had further negative effects on *PT*: It lost most of its staff, its identity, and its mission (Kimble, 1987, p. 9). In the late 1970s, Ziff-Davis increased the rate base (subscribers plus newsstand sales) of the magazine to over one million, a rate base Ziff-Davis had difficulty maintaining. As profitability declined, the magazine likewise declined in quality both in production and in content. The magazine had difficulty attracting advertisers: Of the top 100 magazines in the United States, *PT* was second highest in loss of advertising pages in 1982

(Kimble, 1987). Attempts were made by Ziff-Davis to remedy *PT*'s situation by redesigning the total editorial package and by cutting back the magazine's base rate to 850,000, but these changes failed in regaining its image as a respectable psychology magazine for the lay public.

In January 1982, a member of the Council of Representatives requested the APA Central Office to explore the feasibility of launching a magazine about psychology targeted to the lay public. At its March 1982 retreat meeting, the Board of Directors encouraged staff to proceed with the exploration. The issue was also referred to the P&C Board, and they concurred with the Board of Directors. In June 1982, Michael Pallak, the APA's Executive Officer, and Virginia O'Leary, Director of Public Affairs, met with Alan Hammond, editor of *Science 83*, to discuss the process through which AAAS launched *Science 80*. In the course of the conversation, Hammond mentioned the possibility of *PT* being sold. Hammond thought that an acquisition was a more appropriate move for a member association than a launch, particularly for economic reasons. He further suggested that the APA retain a magazine consultant to explore the feasibility of a launch and the potential acquisition of an existing magazine (APA Board of Directors memorandum to the Council of Representatives, January 17, 1983, unpublished).

In January 1983, the APA Council of Representatives voted (75 for, 27 against, and 5 abstentions) to acquire the magazine *Psychology Today* (Abeles, 1983, p. 661), with the intended goal of providing communication to the U.S. public. Although the Council vote was 3 to 1 in favor of acquisition, the Board of Directors had been almost evenly split (5–5) on the question of acquisition, and President Max Siegel's tie-breaking vote led to the magazine's purchase. The APA Board of Directors was given the authority to negotiate and consummate the final contract, with a four-person committee consisting of William Bevan, Max Siegel, Raymond Fowler, and Michael Pallak to oversee the negotiations.

On February 18, 1983, after a protracted debate within the Board of Directors (following a tentative, partial agreement on January 28, 1983, on the terms of the purchase), final agreement was reached to purchase *PT*. The Association paid $3.8 million to Ziff-Davis to buy the 15-year-old magazine. The APA also acquired $8 million in deferred subscription liabilities (the amount of money paid by subscribers for future issues of the monthly publication), and the APA took out a loan to borrow as much as $2.5 million to cover transition costs in acquiring the magazine. The Association's officers hoped that the 1.1 million circulation magazine could be used to educate the public about psychology without losing its popular appeal (*APA Monitor*, March 1983, p. 1).

From the moment of acquisition, *PT* was controversial within the Association—in terms of the acquisition process itself (and the lack of input from the membership), the nature of the advertising appearing in the magazine (particularly advertisements for subliminal learning, as well as those for tobacco and alcohol), the quality and content of the editorial material appearing in the magazine, and its financial losses.

Immediately after acquiring the magazine, the Board of Directors appointed a *Psychology Today* Advisory Board, which was to report directly to the Board of Directors so as to insulate *PT* from interference from routine APA governance processes and other monitoring needs of the Association. This initial transition team was chaired by Gregory Kimble (Abeles, 1984, pp. 617–618). Raymond Fowler, Ronald Fox, and Eugene Shapiro concentrated on financial aspects of *PT*, and Mildred Katzell, William Prokasy, and Kimble dealt primarily with substantive matters related to editorial content. The question of whether to involve the APA Public Information Committee in the oversight of the *PT* operations was deferred. The APA P&C Board was also not involved in the operation of *PT*. The Board of Directors spent extensive amounts of time on *PT* issues during their April, June, August, and December 1983 meetings.

The *PT* odyssey lasted for slightly over 5 years, when it ended with the sale of *PT* in May of 1988 (Fox, 1989, p. 1028; Spielberger, 1990, p. 807). During the period of time that the APA owned and operated *PT*, it lost $15,771,000 (Spielberger, 1989, p. 991; 1990, p. 807), despite the best efforts of many individuals.

CONCLUSION

Knowledge exchange is the foundation of successful science, and knowledge application is critical to a successful field of practice. One of the key reasons for the existence of the APA since its founding in 1892 has been the exchange of scientific and professional information in psychology. In the past 100 years, the APA's knowledge dissemination program has gradually evolved from a single annual event of the Association—the annual meeting—to a highly respected international publication and abstracting network for psychology.

The journals program, the PsycINFO abstract program, the book program, and the annual convention have all contributed to producing one of the most successful knowledge dissemination programs in the scientific and professional community. The journals program, begun in the mid-1920s with 7 publications, has now expanded to 23. Since the inception of *Psy-*

chological Abstracts in 1927, the quantity of psychological research conducted and published each year has mushroomed, necessitating the development of the APA PsycINFO system. PsycINFO products and services now include *Psychological Abstracts*, PsycSCAN periodicals, PsycINFO online, PsycLIT CD-ROM, PsycBOOKS, and other derivative products. The book program is currently the fastest growing component of the APA's publishing efforts. APA publications reach almost 300,000 individuals and institutions worldwide. Attendance at the APA annual meeting has grown tremendously, but, although it remains a major APA activity, its centrality as a vehicle for scientific and professional information exchange is less critical today because of the advent of mass media, both printed and electronic.

The APA knowledge dissemination program endeavors to maintain its vital role through the publication of new research in its journals covering various aspects of psychology, through the expansion of its book publishing efforts, and through increased coverage and updates of the PsycINFO system. Given the advantages of new electronic technologies, the APA aims to improve and broaden scientific interchange among psychologists, other scientists, and its expanding constituency of readers and user groups.

REFERENCES

Abeles, N. (1983). Proceedings of the American Psychological Association, Incorporated, for the year 1982. *American Psychologist, 38,* 649–682.

Abeles, N. (1984). Proceedings of the American Psychological Association, Incorporated, for the year 1983. *American Psychologist, 39,* 604–638.

Albee, G. (1980, September–October). Happy birthday *Monitor. APA Monitor,* p. 2.

American Psychological Association. (1953a). *Ethical standards of psychologists.* Washington, DC: Author.

American Psychological Association. (1953b). *Ethical standards of psychologists: A summary of ethical principles.* Washington, DC: Author.

American Psychological Association. (1954). *Public information guide.* Washington, DC: Author.

American Psychological Association. (1957). *Publication manual of the American Psychological Association* (rev. ed.). Washington, DC: Author.

American Psychological Association. (1966). *Standards for educational and psychological tests and manuals.* Washington, DC: Author.

American Psychological Association. (1967). *Publication manual of the American Psychological Association* (rev. ed.). Washington, DC: Author.

American Psychological Association. (1973, January). *Rules of Council* (rev. ed.). Washington, DC: Author.

American Psychological Association. (1974a). *Standards for educational and psychological tests* (2nd ed.). Washington, DC: Author.

American Psychological Association. (1974b). *Publication manual of the American Psychological Association* (2nd ed.). Washington, DC: Author.

American Psychological Association. (1983). *Publication manual of the American Psychological Association* (3rd ed.). Washington, DC: Author.

American Psychological Association. (1985). *Standards for educational and psychological testing*. Washington, DC: Author.

American Psychological Association Committee on Test Standards. American Psychological Association, American Educational Research Association, & National Council on Measurements Used in Education. (1954). *Technical recommendations for psychological tests and diagnostic tests*. Washington, DC: Author.

American Psychological Association Council of Editors. (1952). Publication manual of the American Psychological Association. *Psychological Bulletin, 49*, Part 2, July 1952 supplement, 389–449.

American Psychological Association Ethics Committee. (1987). *Casebook on ethical principles of psychologists*. Washington, DC: Author.

Anderson, J. E. (Ed.). (1956). *Psychological aspects of aging: Proceedings of a conference on planning research* [Bethesda, MD, April 24–27, 1955]. Washington, DC: American Psychological Association.

Anderson, J. E., & Valentine, W. L. (1944). The preparation of articles for publication in the journals of the American Psychological Association. *Psychological Bulletin, 41*, 345–376.

Announcement. (1970). *American Psychologist, 25*, 986.

APA Monitor. (1983, March). APA buys *Psychology Today*. p. 1.

Bazerman, C. (1988). *Shaping written knowledge: The genre and activity of the experimental article in science*. Madison: University of Wisconsin Press.

Benjamin, L. T., Jr. (1986). Why don't they understand us? A history of Psychology's public image. *American Psychologist, 41*, 941–946.

Bingham, W. V. (Ed.). (1932). *Psychology today*. Chicago, IL: University of Chicago Press.

Boring, E. G. (Ed.). (1945). *Psychology for the Armed Services*. Washington, DC: Infantry Journal.

Boring, E. G., & Van de Water, M. (Eds.). (1943). *Psychology for the fighting man*. Washington, DC: Infantry Journal.

Brayfield, A. H. (1968). The APA Central Office: 1968. *American Psychologist, 23*, 603–611.

Clark, K. E. (1957). *America's psychologists: A survey of a growing profession*. Washington, DC: American Psychological Association.

Clark, K. E. (1971). A critical examination of the national information system for psychology. *American Psychologist, 26*, 325–348.

Conger, J. J. (1977). Proceedings of the American Psychological Association, Incorporated, for the year 1976. *American Psychologist, 32,* 408–438.

Conrad, H. S. (1949). Comment: The new *Psychological Monographs: General and Applied. American Psychologist, 4,* 112.

Cutts, N. E. (Ed.). (1955). *School psychologists at mid-century: A report of the Thayer conference on the functions, qualifications, and training of school psychologists.* Washington, DC: American Psychological Association.

DeVivo, A. (1975, October). A new publication manual for psychologists. *Scholarly Publishing,* pp. 37–47.

Eichorn, D. H., & VandenBos, G. R. (1985). Dissemination of scientific and professional knowledge: Journal publication within the APA. *American Psychologist, 40,* 1309–1316.

Fernberger, S. W. (1929). Proceedings of the thirty-seventh annual meeting of the American Psychological Association, Incorporated, New York, NY, December 27, 28, 29, 1928. *Psychological Bulletin, 26,* 121–184.

Fernberger, S. W. (1932). The American Psychological Association: A historical summary, 1892–1930. *Psychological Bulletin, 29,* 1–89.

Fowler, R. D., & VandenBos, G. R. (1989, October). Divisions reflect APA's diversity. *APA Monitor,* pp. 4–5.

Fox, R. E. (1989). Proceedings of the American Psychological Association, Incorporated, for the year 1988. *American Psychologist, 44,* 996–1028.

Golann, S. E. (1970). Ethical standards for psychology: Development and revision, 1938–1968. *Annals of the New York Academy of Sciences, 169,* Article 2, 398–405.

Habbe, S. (1941). A comparison of the American Psychological Association memberships of 1929 and 1939: An analysis of changes during the past decade with a few suggestions for the next decade. *Psychological Record, 4,* 215–232.

Hilgard, E. R. (1987). *Psychology in America: A historical survey.* San Diego, CA: Harcourt Brace Jovanovich.

Instructions in regard to preparation of manuscript. (1929). *Psychological Bulletin, 26,* 57–63.

Kimble, G. A. (1987). *The APA–PT connection.* Unpublished manuscript.

Koch, S. (Ed.). (1959–1963). *Psychology: A study of a science* (Vols. 1–6). New York: McGraw-Hill.

Little, K. B. (1970, October). Introducing—the APA Monitor. *APA Monitor,* p. 1.

Lumley, F. H. (1932). An evaluation of fifteen radio talks in psychology by means of listeners' reports. *Psychological Bulletin, 29,* 753–764.

McKeachie, W. J. (1970). Proceedings of the American Psychological Association, Incorporated, for the year 1969: Minutes of the annual meeting of the Council of Representatives. *American Psychologist, 25,* 13–37.

McKeachie, W. J. (1971). Proceedings of the American Psychological Association,

Incorporated, for the year 1970: Minutes of the annual meeting of the Council of Representatives. *American Psychologist, 26,* 22–49.

McKeachie, W. J. (1972). Proceedings of the American Psychological Association, Incorporated, for the year 1971: Minutes of the annual meeting of the Council of Representatives. *American Psychologist, 27,* 268–299.

McKeachie, W. J. (1974). Proceedings of the American Psychological Association, Incorporated, for the year 1973: Minutes of the annual meeting and special meeting of the Council of Representatives. *American Psychologist, 29,* 381–413.

McLean, B. E. (1990). *A history of* Psychological Abstracts *and of* PsycInfo, *the* Psychological Abstracts *Information Services.* Unpublished manuscript.

Mervis, J. (1986, January). Fifteen years of the *Monitor:* Up through the years with the *Monitor. APA Monitor,* pp. 38, 42.

National Educational Association. (1955). *Technical recommendations for achievement tests.* Washington, DC: Author.

Newman, E. B. (1966). Proceedings of the American Psychological Association, Incorporated, for the year 1966: Minutes of a special meeting of the Council of Representatives. *American Psychologist, 21,* 1125–1153.

Osier, D. V., & Wozniak, R. H. (1984). *A century of serial publications in psychology, 1850–1950: An international bibliography.* Milwood, NY: Kraus International.

Pallak, M. S. (1979). Report of the Executive Officer: 1979. *American Psychologist, 35,* 485–496.

Pallak, M. S., & Kilburg, R. R. (1986). Psychology, public affairs, and public policy. *American Psychologist, 41,* 933–940.

Pallak, M. S., & VandenBos, G. R. (1984). Employment of psychologists in the U.S.A.: Responses to the crisis of the 1970s. *Journal of the Norwegian Psychological Association, 21,* 65–73.

Peak, H. (1947). Proceedings of the fifty-fifth annual business meeting of the American Psychological Association, Inc., Detroit, Michigan. *American Psychologist, 2,* 468–510.

Peak, H. (1949). Proceedings of the fifty-seventh annual business meeting of the American Psychological Association, Inc., Denver, Colorado. *American Psychologist, 4,* 443–485.

Preston, H. O. (1975, June). Interaction: A success story. *APA Monitor,* p. 2.

PsycINFO. (1974). *Thesaurus of psychological index terms.* Washington, DC: American Psychological Association.

Rubinstein, E. A., & Parloff, M. B. (Eds.). (1959). *Research in psychotherapy* (Vol. 1). Washington, DC: American Psychological Association.

Santos, J. F., & VandenBos, G. R. (Eds.). (1982). *Psychology and the older adult: Challenges for training in the 1980s.* Washington, DC: American Psychological Association.

Sokal, M. M. (1973). APA's first publication: Proceedings of the American Psychological Association, 1892–1893. *American Psychologist, 28,* 277–292.

Spielberger, C. D. (1989). Report of the treasurer: 1988. *American Psychologist, 44*, 987–992.

Spielberger, C. D. (1990). Report of the treasurer: 1989. The 1980s: A roller coaster decade for APA finances. *American Psychologist, 45*, 807–812.

Strother, C. R. (Ed.). (1956). *Psychology and mental health*. Washington, DC: American Psychological Association.

APPENDIX A

Publication History of APA Journals By Date of Publication

Journal	Date of 1st publication	Date of first APA publication	Acquisition
Psych. Review	Jan 1894	1925 (1938)[a]	Purchase.
Psych. Monographs	Feb 1895	1925–1966 (1938)[a]	Purchase; discontinued 1966.
Psych. Bulletin	Jan 1904	1925 (1938)[a]	Purchase.
J. of Experimental Psych.	Feb 1916	1926 (1938)[a]	Purchase[a]; split into four journals in 1975 under the general title of JExP. The sections were JExP: General, JExP: Learning & Memory, JExP: Perception & Performance, and JExP: Animal Behavior Processes. (See listing of four JExPs below for details.)
J. of Abnormal Psych.	Apr 1906	1927 (1929)	Gift, Morton Prince. Vols. 1–15 were published under this title from 1906 through March 1921. Vols. 16–19 were published from April 1921 through March 1925 as the J. of Abnormal Psychology and Social Psychology.[b] The title was shortened in April 1925 to the J. of Abnormal and Social Psychology, and it continued under this title through 1964 (spanning Vols. 20–69). Prince gave the journal to the APA in 1926. The journal continued to be published by the Boyd Printing Company for the APA until the APA undertook publication in 1929. In 1965, the J. of Personality and Social Psychology was split out of the J. of Abnormal and Social Psychology. JPSP began as Vol. 1. The J. of Abnormal and Social Psychology continued (as Vol. 70) under the title of J. of Abnormal Psychology.
J. of Applied Psych.	Mar 1917	1943	Purchased from J. P. Porter.
J. of Consulting Psych.	Jan 1937	1946	Transferred to APA during merger with the American Assn. for Applied Psychology; title changed to J. of Consulting & Clinical Psychology in 1968.
American Psychologist	Jan 1946	1946	Created by APA.[c]
J. of Comparative & Physiol. Psych.	1911	1947	Purchased from Williams & Wilkins Co. in 1947[d]; the journal was split into Behavioral Neuroscience and the J. of Comparative Psychology in 1983, both of which continued the volume numbering of JCPP. This journal is now just known as the J. of Comparative Psychology.
Contemporary Psych.	Jan 1956	1956	Created by the APA.
J. of Educational Psych.	Jan 1910	1957	Purchased from Warwick & York Co.

Journal	Date	Year	Notes
J. of Personality & Social Psych.	Jan 1965	1965	Created by the APA. Split out of the *J. of Abnormal & Social Psych.* and started with Vol. 1 in 1965. In April 1980 (Vol. 38), *JPSP* was sectioned into three separately edited sections, all contained within one journal.
J. of Counseling Psych.	Feb 1954	1967	Gift from J. of Counseling Psych., Inc.; price: $1.00.
Developmental Psych.	Jan 1969	1969	Created by the APA.
Professional Psych.	Nov 1969	1969	Created by the APA in 1969; title changed to *Professional Psychology: Research & Practice* in 1983.
Journal Supplement Abstract Service: Catalog of Selected Documents in Psych.	Fall 1971	1971–1986	Adopted when NSF grant funds for support of an experimental journal/document delivery system were discontinued; title changed to *Psychological Documents* in 1983; sold to Select Press in 1986.
JExP: Human Learning & Memory	Jan 1975	1975	These four *JExPs* were created by splitting the *J. of Experimental Psychology* into four journals. *JExP: General* continued the volume numbering of the original publication (publishing Vol. 104 in 1975); the other three began Vol. 1 in 1975. *JExP: Human Learning & Memory* changed its title to *JExP: Learning, Memory, & Cognition* in 1982.
JExP: Animal Behavior Processes	Jan 1975	1975	
JExP: Human Perception & Performance	Feb 1975	1975	
JExP: General	Mar 1975	1975	
Behavioral Neuroscience	Feb 1983	1983	Created by the APA. Split out of the *J. of Comparative & Physiological Psychology* (see above); continued the volume numbering of *JCPP*.
Psychology & Aging	Mar 1986	1986	Created by the APA.
Psychological Assessment	Mar 1989	1989	Created by the APA. Split out of the *J. of Consulting & Clinical Psych.*; Vol. 1, No. 1 published in 1989. Published as *Psychological Assessment: A J. of Consulting & Clinical Psychology* until 1992, when the name changed to *Psychological Assessment*.
Neuropsychology	Jan 1987	1991	Purchased from Taylor & Francis on Dec. 31, 1990.
J. of Family Psychology	Sep 1987	1992	Created by Division 43 as a division journal. Published by Sage through June 1992. Ownership of journal transferred from Division 43 to the APA by way of a within-Association transfer agreement signed on June 29, 1990; transfer became effective on December 28, 1990. The APA will begin publishing in September 1992.

[a]On January 1, 1925, the APA took title to the Psychological Review Company's stock. The Psychological Review Company continued to publish four journals for the APA until the APA undertook publication of the *Review, Psych. Monographs, Bulletin,* and *Experimental* in 1938.
[b]This journal was the "official organ" of the American Psychopathological Association from 1910 to 1925, and of the Psycho-Medical Society of England from 1914 to 1921.
[c]Serves as the official journal of the APA.
[d]Represents the continuation of the *J. of Animal Behavior* (1911–1917), *Psychobiology* (1917–1920), and the *J. of Comparative Psychology* (1921–1946). The APA purchased this journal and began publishing it under the title *J. of Comparative & Physiological Psychology* in 1947.

APPENDIX B

Publication History of Division Journals

Division number and name	Journal	Date of first publication as a journal
2 Teaching of Psychology	*Teaching of Psychology*	1974

2 Teaching of Psychology   *Teaching of Psychology*   1974
Division owned; copyrighted and published by Erlbaum. Continues the *Teaching of Psychology* newsletter. Became an APA division journal starting with Volume 1(1), October 1974. First 11 volumes (1974–1984) were published privately and supported by the division. Erlbaum became the publisher in 1985. Published quarterly.

8 Society of Personality &   *Personality & Social Psychology*   1975
   Social Psychology   *Bulletin*
Division owns journal and copyright; published by Sage. Initially published quarterly by the Society of Personality and Social Psychology, Inc. In January 1977, the APA Council gave approval for the division to operate the *Bulletin* as an official APA division journal. Starting with Volume 6(1) in March 1980, the *Bulletin* has been published by Sage, initially on a quarterly basis and then switched bimonthly beginning with Volume 17(1) in February 1991.

9 Society for the Psycho-   *Journal of Social Issues*   1945
   logical Study of Social
   Issues
Division owns journal and copyright; published by Plenum. Initially published by the Society for the Psychological Study of Social Issues. In January 1977, the APA Council gave approval for the division to operate *JSI* as an official APA division journal. Starting with Volume 38(1) in 1982, the quarterly publication of *JSI* was contracted to Plenum.

12 Clinical Psychology   *Clinical Psychology Review*   1981
Pergamon owns, copyrights, and publishes the journal. In 1987, the division established an official relationship with *Clinical Psychology Review* and, combined with a bulk purchase agreement, designated the *Review* as its official "all divisional" division journal. Pergamon allowed inclusion of the division's quarterly newsletter, *The Clinical Psychologist*, at the back of the *Review* beginning with Volume 8(1) in 1988 (first publication as the official APA division journal). (The *Clinical Psychologist*, in an earlier version, became *Professional Psychology* in 1970.) Published bimonthly.

   Division 12, Section 1   *Journal of Clinical Child Psychology*   1971
   Owned by Section 1, copyrighted and published by Erlbaum. Started by Section 1 as a newsletter; became a journal beginning with Volume 1(1), Winter 1971–72, published 3 times a year. Recognized by the APA Council in January of 1977 as an official APA division/section journal. Erlbaum started publishing the journal, as a quarterly publication, beginning with Volume 14 in 1985.

Division number and name	Journal	Date of first publication as a journal

Division 12, Section 5   *Journal of Pediatric Psychology*   1976

Owned by Section 5; copyrighted and published by Plenum. Journal began as *Pediatric Psychology* (the newsletter of the Society of Pediatric Psychology) with the March 1969 issue. The newsletter gradually expanded and became the official *Journal of Pediatric Psychology* in 1976. In 1980, the Society of Pediatric Psychology officially became Section 5 of Division 12 (Clinical Psychology) of the APA. Published quarterly through 1989, then switched to bimonthly publication in 1990.

13 Consulting Psychology   *Consulting Psychology*   1992

Division owned, copyrighted, and published through the APA's EPF specialty journal program. The APA Council approved in August 1991 conversion of the division's official newsletter, *Consulting Psychology Bulletin*, into journal status and for it to serve as the official journal of the division. It started as a newsletter and has been published by the division for 42 years. Conversion of the publication to journal took place in January 1992. Published quarterly.

15 Educational Psychology   *Educational Psychologist*   1963

Division owned; copyrighted and published by Erlbaum. In January 1977, the APA Council gave approval for the division to operate the *Educational Psychologist* as an official APA division journal. Initially published by the division 3 times a year (except that Volumes 11 and 12 were published over 2-year periods, in 1975–76 and 1977–78, respectively); switched to a once-a-year publication for Volumes 13 and 14 (1978 and 1979). Switched back to a 3-times-a-year publication with Volume 15 in 1980. Became quarterly with Volume 19 in 1984. Starting with Volume 20 in 1985, the journal has been published quarterly by Erlbaum.

16 School Psychology   *School Psychology Quarterly*   1986

Division owns journal and copyright; published by Guilford. Division got approval in 1983 to establish *Professional School Psychology* as the official division journal; first publication did not start until 1986, with Erlbaum as publisher. In 1990, Guilford took over publication beginning with the Volume 5(1) spring 1990 issue; the journal title also changed to *School Psychology Quarterly*.

17 Counseling Psychology   *The Counseling Psychologist*   1969

Division owns journal and copyright; published by Sage. In January 1977, the APA Council gave approval for the division to operate the *Counseling Psychologist* as the official APA division journal. Journal was initially published by the division (through Volume 12 in 1984); Sage became the publisher starting with Volume 13 in 1985. Published quarterly.

19 Military Psychology   *Military Psychology*   1989

Division-owned; copyrighted and published by Erlbaum. Contract took effect in 1987 but initial publication started in 1989. Published quarterly.

Division number and name	Journal	Date of first publication as a journal
22 Rehabilitation Psychology	*Rehabilitation Psychology*	1972

Division owns journal and copyright; published by Springer. Started as a mimeographed *Newsletter* in 1953 and grew to a *Bulletin* published by the division. The *Bulletin's* title was changed to *Psychological Aspects of Disability* in 1969. In 1972, the journal acquired official division journal status and the title was changed to *Rehabilitation Psychology* beginning with the Volume 19(1), spring issue. The publication was temporarily suspended after Volume 26(4) in 1979. Springer began publication of the journal with Volume 27(1) in spring 1982. Published quarterly.

27 Society for Community Research and Action	*American Journal of Community Psychology*	1973

Plenum Press owns, copyrights, and publishes the journal. Initially published quarterly until 1977, then switched to bimonthly publication beginning with Volume 6 in 1978. In 1987, Division 27 entered into an agreement with Plenum to make a bulk purchase of copies for division members as a benefit of division membership (and the division guaranteed a minimum of 500 member subscriptions per year), with the agreement becoming operational in 1988.

29 Psychotherapy	*Psychotherapy*	1964

Division owns, copyrights, and publishes the journal. Initially published under the title *Psychotherapy: Theory, Research, & Practice* by Psychologists Interested in the Advancement of Psychotherapy (PIAP) and printed by George Banta Company in Menasha, Wisconsin. Beginning with Volume 5(1) in 1968, the PIAP imprint was changed to the current division's name. The journal title was changed to *Psychotherapy* in 1984, beginning with Volume 21. Published quarterly.

32 Humanistic Psychology	*The Humanistic Psychologist*	1973

Division owns, copyrights, and publishes the journal. Initially started as a division bulletin in 1973; acquired division journal status in August 1989, starting with Volume 17(3). Published 3 times a year.

34 Population & Environmental Psychology	*Population & Environment: Behavioral & Social Issues*	1978–1987

No longer a division journal. Created as the official publication of Division 34 in 1978 under the title *Journal of Population: Behavioral, Social, & Environmental Issues* and published quarterly by Human Sciences Press. The title was changed to *Population & Environment: Behavioral & Social Issues* in 1980. Ceased as a division-sponsored journal on December 31, 1987, although quarterly publication by Human Sciences Press continues.

35 Psychology of Women	*Psychology of Women Quarterly*	1976

Division owns journal and copyright; published by Cambridge. In January 1977, the APA Council gave approval for the division to operate the *Quarterly* as the official APA division journal. Initially published by Human Sciences Press until Volume 8(4) in summer 1984. Cambridge took over publication starting with Volume 9(1) in January 1985.

Division number and name	Journal	Date of first publication as a journal
38 Health Psychology	*Health Psychology*	1982

Division owned; copyrighted and published by Erlbaum. Approved by the APA Council as the official APA division journal in January 1981 and initially published quarterly. Switched to bimonthly publication starting with Volume 3(1) in 1984. In 1991, journal expanded to an 8½ × 11 format starting with Volume 10(1).

39 Psychoanalysis	*Psychoanalytic Psychology*	1984

Division owned; copyrighted and published by Erlbaum. Approved by the APA Council as the official APA division journal in August 1982. Volume 1(1) published in 1984. Published quarterly.

41 American Psychology– Law Society	*Law & Human Behavior*	1977

Plenum owns, copyrights, and publishes the journal. Approved by the APA Council in August 1984 as the official division journal. Official division relationship with the journal, and bulk purchase of subscriptions for division members, began with Volume 9(1) in 1985. Initially published quarterly by Plenum with the assistance of students at the Law School, University of Virginia, and the College of Law, University of Arizona, and in cooperation with the American Psychology–Law Society. Starting in 1980, Plenum published the journal solely in editorial cooperation with the American Psychology–Law Society. Became a bimonthly publication beginning with Volume 14(1) in 1990.

43 Family Psychology	*Journal of Family Psychology*	1987–1992

No longer a division journal. Division originally owned journal and copyright, and it was published by Sage. Approved by the APA Council, at its January–February 1986 meeting, as official division journal. First issue published in September of 1987. Transferred ownership of journal from Division 43 to the APA on December 28, 1990, with quarterly publication by Sage continuing through Volume 5(4) in June of 1992. Published as an all-APA journal starting in September of 1992.

Note: See footnote on p. 348 regarding the preparation and verification of this appendix.

APPENDIX C

Number of Publications by Type and Period in the APA Book Program[a]

Type	1951–55	1956–60	1961–65	1966–70	1971–75	1976–80	1981–85	1986–90
Membership directories	3[b]	4[c]	5	5	5	5	5	5
Convention programs	—	3[d]	5	5	5	5	5	5
Graduate study	—	—	—	4[e]	4	5	5	5
Proceedings	1	4	1	2	3	—	2	4
Standards & guidelines	2	—	—	2	1	—	2	2
Manuals & users' aids	—	1	—	1	2	3	5	2
Users' directories	—	—	—	1	1	1	3	8
Education & career aids	—	—	—	—	1	4	1	9
Bibliographies	—	—	—	—	—	—	2	8
Content-oriented books	—	3	2	4	3	7	11	22

[a]Titles under each heading appear below.
[b]Not published in 1952 and 1954.
[c]Not published in 1956.
[d]Started with 1958.
[e]Started with 1967.

Titles by Type in 5-Year Intervals

Proceedings

1951–55   *School Psychologists at Mid-century*

1956–60   *Psychological Aspects of Aging; Graduate Education in Psychology; Psychology and Rehabilitation, 1959; Psychological Research and Rehabilitation, 1960*

1961–65   *Preconference Materials (Chicago Training Conference)*

1966–70   *Professional Preparation; Program On Teaching of Psychology*

1971–75   *Rehabilitation Psychology; Master's Level Education in Psychology; Levels and Patterns of Professional Training*

1981–85   *Psychology and the Older Adult; Issues in Cognition*

1986–90   *Quality in Professional Training; Service Needs of the Seriously Mentally Ill; Improving Psychological Services for Children; Toward Ethnic Diversification*

Standards and Guidelines

1951–55   *Ethical Standards, 1953; Technical Recommendations for Tests, 1954*

1966–70   *Casebook On Ethical Standards, 1967; Publication Manual, 1967*

1971–75	*Standards for Educational and Psychological Tests* (2nd edition)
1981–85	*Standards for Educational and Psychological Tests* (3rd edition); *Ethical Principles With Human Subjects*
1986–90	*Casebook of Ethical Principles; Professional Liability*

Manuals and Users' Aids

1956–60	*Publication Manual* (1957 revision)
1966–70	*Publication Manual* (1967 revision)
1971–75	*Publication Manual* (2nd edition); *Thesaurus* (1st edition)
1976–80	*PsycINFO Users' Reference Manual* (1st edition); *Publication Manual* (1977 edition); *Thesaurus* (2nd edition)
1981–85	*PsycINFO Users' Reference Manual* (2nd edition); *Thesaurus* (3rd & 4th editions); *Publication Manual* (3rd edition); *Library Use*
1986–90	*Thesaurus* (5th edition); *PsycINFO Users' Manual: 1987*

Users' Directories

1966–70	*International Opportunities for Advanced Training*
1971–75	*Consolidated Roster for Psychology*
1976–80	*Teaching Innovations*
1981–85	*Guide To Research Support* (1st & 2nd editions); *Ethnic Minority Human Resources*
1986–90	*Guide To Research Support* (3rd edition); *Latin American Psychology; Computer Use* (1st & 2nd editions); *Journals in Psychology* (1st, 2nd, & 3rd editions); *Ethnic Minority Professionals* (2nd edition)

Education and Career Aids

1971–75	*Psychology Teacher's Resource Book* (2nd edition)
1976–80	*Career Opportunities; Psychology Teacher's Resource Book* (3rd edition); *The Psychology Major; Preparing for Graduate Study*
1981–85	*Activities Handbook, Vol. 1*
1986–90	*Activities Handbook, Vol. 2; Is Psychology the Major for You?; Search PsycINFO; Teaching a Psychology of People; Is Psychology for Them?; Invertebrate Learning; Mastering APA Style: Students; Mastering APA Style: Instructors; Activities Handbook, Vol. 3*

Bibliographies

1981–85   *Learning and Communication Disorders; Mental Retardation*

1986–90   *AIDS* (1st & 2nd editions); *Black Males; Alzheimer's Disease; Black Females; Environmental Toxins; Hispanics; Homelessness*

Content-Oriented Books

1956–60   *Psychology and Mental Health; America's Psychologists; Research in Psychotherapy, Vol. 1*

1961–65   *Soviet Psychology; Research in Psychotherapy, Vol. 2*

1966–70   *Interoceptors; Research in Psychotherapy, Vol. 3; William James; Psychology and the Problems of Society*

1971–75   *Environment and the Social Sciences; Psychology of Adult Development and Aging; Undergraduate Education in Psychology*

1976–80   *Behavioral Instruction; APA Commission Report On Behavior Modification; American Psychology in Historical Perspective; Psychology and National Health Insurance; Resources in Environment and Behavior; Who Is the Client?; Aging in the 1980s*

1981–85   *G. S. Hall Lecture Series, Vols. 1,2,3,4, & 5; Master Lecture Series, Vols. 1,2,3, & 4; Psychology and Union Mental Health Benefits; Gifted and Talented*

1986–90   *Professionals in Distress; G. S. Hall Lecture Series, Vols. 6,7,8, & 9; Law and Mental Health Professionals: Arizona; Law and Mental Health Professionals: Texas; Master Lecture Series, Vols. 5,6,7,8, & 9; Handbook for Clinical Memory Assessment; 14 Ounces of Prevention; Self-Esteem; Sleep and Cognition; Taste, Experience, and Feeding; Women and Depression; Psychology Aweigh; Child's First Book of Play Therapy; Organ Donation; Researching Community Psychology*

APPENDIX

STATISTICAL DATA ON THE AMERICAN PSYCHOLOGICAL ASSOCIATION

ELIZABETH Q. BULATAO and ROBERT FULCHER, American Psychological Association, and RAND B. EVANS, East Carolina University

Presidents of the American Psychological Association

1892	G. Stanley Hall	1910	Walter B. Pillsbury
1893	George T. Ladd	1911	Carl E. Seashore
1894	William James	1912	Edward L. Thorndike
1895	J. McK. Cattell	1913	Howard C. Warren
1896	G. S. Fullerton	1914	Robert S. Woodworth
1897	James M. Baldwin	1915	John B. Watson
1898	Hugo Münsterberg	1916	Raymond Dodge
1899	John Dewey	1917	Robert M. Yerkes
1900	Joseph Jastrow	1918	John Wallace Baird
1901	Josiah Royce	1919	Walter D. Scott
1902	Edmund C. Sanford	1920	Shepherd I. Franz
1903	William L. Bryan	1921	Margaret Washburn
1904	William James	1922	Knight Dunlap
1905	Mary Calkins	1923	Lewis M. Terman
1906	James R. Angell	1924	G. Stanley Hall
1907	Henry R. Marshall	1925	I. Madison Bentley
1908	George M. Stratton	1926	Harvey A. Carr
1909	Charles H. Judd	1927	Harry L. Hollingworth

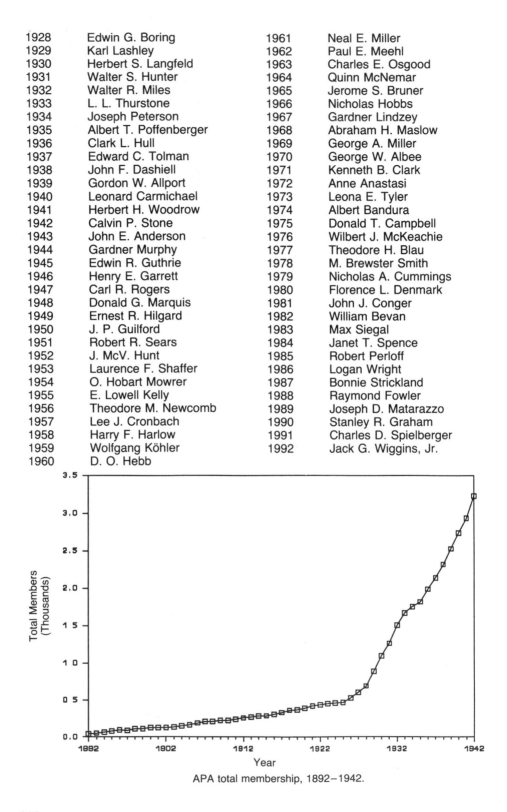

1928	Edwin G. Boring	1961	Neal E. Miller
1929	Karl Lashley	1962	Paul E. Meehl
1930	Herbert S. Langfeld	1963	Charles E. Osgood
1931	Walter S. Hunter	1964	Quinn McNemar
1932	Walter R. Miles	1965	Jerome S. Bruner
1933	L. L. Thurstone	1966	Nicholas Hobbs
1934	Joseph Peterson	1967	Gardner Lindzey
1935	Albert T. Poffenberger	1968	Abraham H. Maslow
1936	Clark L. Hull	1969	George A. Miller
1937	Edward C. Tolman	1970	George W. Albee
1938	John F. Dashiell	1971	Kenneth B. Clark
1939	Gordon W. Allport	1972	Anne Anastasi
1940	Leonard Carmichael	1973	Leona E. Tyler
1941	Herbert H. Woodrow	1974	Albert Bandura
1942	Calvin P. Stone	1975	Donald T. Campbell
1943	John E. Anderson	1976	Wilbert J. McKeachie
1944	Gardner Murphy	1977	Theodore H. Blau
1945	Edwin R. Guthrie	1978	M. Brewster Smith
1946	Henry E. Garrett	1979	Nicholas A. Cummings
1947	Carl R. Rogers	1980	Florence L. Denmark
1948	Donald G. Marquis	1981	John J. Conger
1949	Ernest R. Hilgard	1982	William Bevan
1950	J. P. Guilford	1983	Max Siegal
1951	Robert R. Sears	1984	Janet T. Spence
1952	J. McV. Hunt	1985	Robert Perloff
1953	Laurence F. Shaffer	1986	Logan Wright
1954	O. Hobart Mowrer	1987	Bonnie Strickland
1955	E. Lowell Kelly	1988	Raymond Fowler
1956	Theodore M. Newcomb	1989	Joseph D. Matarazzo
1957	Lee J. Cronbach	1990	Stanley R. Graham
1958	Harry F. Harlow	1991	Charles D. Spielberger
1959	Wolfgang Köhler	1992	Jack G. Wiggins, Jr.
1960	D. O. Hebb		

APA total membership, 1892–1942.

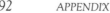

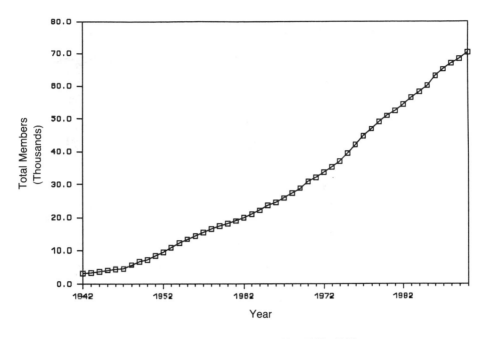

APA total membership, 1942–1990.

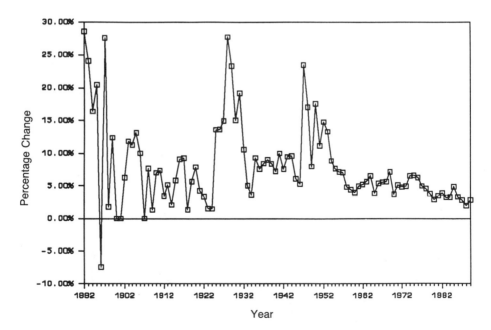

APA membership rate of growth, 1892–1990.

APA Income and Expenses, 1940–1990 (in thousands)

Year	Income	Expenses	Net income
1940	50	44	6
1945	72	64	8
1950	262	239	23
1955	437	467	−31
1960	905	841	63
1965	2,178	2,043	135
1970	5,054	5,041	12
1975	7,308	7,245	63
1980	13,097	12,765	332
1985[a]	22,932	21,312	1,620
1985[b]	33,745	35,412	−1,370
1990[c]	36,661	36,867	−206

Source: APA Financial Services.
[a]Excludes *Psychology Today* operations.   [b]Includes *Psychology Today* operations.   [c]Projected.

INDEX

logical *Review*, 58–61; and public affairs, 254–56; reorganization of, 76, 149, 153, 158–60, 163–72, 243–44, 256, 259, 271–75, 278–86; rules of, 194; structure of, 178–90, 263–71, 278, 290–91; and testing, 54–57, 81–82; and wartime, 96–97, 100–102, 105–8, 111–14; and women, 303–22

American Psychological Society (APS), 219, 285–87

American Psychologist, 185–86, 209, 257, 279, 348–49, 353, 366; and APA, 194–95, 200, 270; and *APA Monitor*, 371; and computers, 211; and ethics, 181, 366; and human resources, 237; and research funding, 214; and testing, 251

American Society for Psychical Research (ASPR), 46–47, 49

American Society of Naturalists, 44–45, 48, 53, 58, 65, 349

American Teachers Association, Department of Psychology, 157–58, 165

Anastasi, Anne, 316, 319

Anderson, J. E.: *Psychological Aspects of Aging*, 368; quoted, 127

Anderson, John, 164–69, 367

Angell, Frank, 30

Angell, James R., 30, 52, 76, 81–82, 84, 93, 121

Angier, Roswell P., quoted, 99

animals, and research, 133–34, 213, 236, 293

Année Psychologique, 357–58

Annual Report (1884), of Johns Hopkins University, 23

Annual Reviews, Inc., 215

Annual Reviews of Psychology, 215

anthropologists, 50, 52

APA. *See* American Psychological Association

APA Insurance Trust (APAIT), 186–87

APA Monitor, 254, 348, 366, 370–72

Appel, T. A., quoted, 44–45

Applied Psychology Panel, 209

APS. *See* American Physiological Society; American Psychological Society

Armstrong, Clairette, 315

Army Aviation Psychology Program, 209

Assembly of Scientific and Applied Psychologists (ASAP), 284–85

Association for the Advancement of Psychology (AAP), 249, 253–54, 276

Association for Women in Psychology (AWP), 290, 317

Association of Black Psychologists, 237, 332

Association of Consulting Psychologists, 135, 137

associations: professional, 264–66; regional, 166–67. *See also* state psychological associations; *names of associations*

Astin, Helen S., 318

Atlantic Monthly, 131

Auld, Dennis, 364

Aviation Examining Boards, 111

awards: APA, 215, 320–21; "Golden Fleece," 238

AWP. *See* Association for Women in Psychology

Babladelis, Georgia, 319

Bacon, Francis, 6

Bain, Alexander, 13

Baldwin, Bird T., 84–85, 123

Baldwin, James Mark, 33; and APA, 54, 75; *Dictionary of Philosophy and Psychology*, 83; journals of, 51–52, 58–59, 126, 351; *Mental Development in the Child and the Race*, 55; quoted, 19; and testing, 54–56, 81

Bauer, Raymond, 216, 218

Bayley, Nancy, 320

Beaunis, H., 357

Behavioral Neuroscience, 353, 355

behaviorism, 74, 121, 130–31, 274

Bentley, Madison, 100, 367

Bevan, William, 375

Bibliographic Retrieval Services, 363

authority of, 240–41; and dues for practitioners, 277; election of, 267; and ERA, 333; functions of, 247; and proposed reorganization, 281; and *Psychology Today*, 375; and research, 213–14; and state associations, 190, 192; and women in psychology, 317–18

counseling, doctoral programs in, 224–25

courts, and APA, 341. *See also* U.S. Supreme Court

Cousin, Victor, 8, 14

Cowles, Edward, 24, 31, 49–51

Crawford, Meredith, 362

Creighton, J. E., 63, 83

Cronbach, Lee, 201, 214

Cultural and Ethnic Affairs Program Office (APA), 332

curricula: 19-century, 8–14, 22; for professional psychologists, 223–25; undergraduate, 84

Cutts, N. E., *School Psychologists at Mid-Century*, 368

CWP. *See* Committee on Women in Psychology

Dallenbach, Karl, 153–54, 349

Darley, John (Jack), 201, 207, 218

Darwin, Charles, 61

data reduction, and computerization, 211

Davenport, Charles B., 93

Davis, W. H., quoted, 56

Dearborn, W. F., 85

debate, over professional issues, 130–32, 152

defense, national: and psychology, 153; and scientific community, 152. *See also* military

degrees, 19-century, 4–5, 9–11, 17, 34. *See also* doctorates

Delabarre, E. B., 18

DeLeon, P. H., 251; quoted, 249

democratization, and APA governance, 139

Denmark, Florence L., 320

desegregation, school, 331–32

Deutsch, Cynthia, quoted, 317

Dewey, John, 11, 29, 54, 84, 92; and APA, 31, 49; "Psychology and Social Practice," 327–28

DIALOG, 361, 363–64

dichotomy, academic–professional, 266–67, 271–81, 284–85, 297. *See also* factionalism

Dictionary of Philosophy and Psychology, 58

Directorates (APA), 202–3, 291–95, 342. *See also names of directorates*

Directory (APA), 186, 203, 222, 227

disabilities, 336

Disability Boards, 110

discipline, academic, 266

discrimination: and disabled, 336; investigation of, 186; racial, 328, 331–32; and sexual orientation, 335; against women, 317, 333–34

Division of Anthropology and Psychology (NRC), 151, 311

Division of the Psychology of Women (APA), 319

Division Organization Committee (APA), 171

Divisions (APA), 166–67, 170, 187–89, 264; and APS, 285; functions of, 266–69, 290; growth of, 172; journals of, 356–57; and membership, 184–85, 188–89, 287; power of, 278; and PsycSCANS, 364; and women, 316, 319

Division Services Office (APA), 287

doctoral programs, and professional psychologists, 224–25

doctorates: psychology, 17, 34, 84, 224–25, 279–80; and APA membership, 78, 126, 182–83; granting of, 4–5, 9–12; for women, 307–8, 313, 322

doctors, medical, 106–7

Dodge, Raymond, 96, 101, 105, 111

Doll, Edgar, 154–55, 165, 167, 188

Donaldson, Henry H., 24, 31–32

Downey, June E., 314

dues, APA, 51, 58–60, 122, 125, 179,

183–86, 207–8, 263; associate, 127; and Bylaws, 245; and service provision, 271–72, 276–77

Dummer, Jeremiah, 6

Dunlap, Knight, 78, 111, 127; quoted, 83, 136

Eastern Psychological Association, 56

Ebbinghaus, Hermann, 27, 30, 357

Eberhart, Richard, 214

education: and APA, 212; and broadcast media, 133, 217; graduate, 4, 9–12, 19–20, 33, 44, 134–35, 201, 214, 223–25; and licensing, 226; medical, 9; 19-century, 4–5, 8–10, 17–31; physical, 54; psychological, 84–86, 88, 123, 131, 162–63, 214, 221, 223–25, 237; and psychological testing, 113–14, 121; undergraduate, 14, 84; for women, 307–8. *See also* training

Educational Affairs Directorate (APA), 342

Educational Division (APA), 166, 189

Education and Training Board (APA), 197, 224–25, 236–37, 295

Education and Training Office (APA), 203

Education and Training Program (APA), 251

Education Directorate (APA), 295

educators, 50

Edwards, Jonathan, 6–7

Eisenberg, P., quoted, 136

elections: ICC, 158; NAS, 65

elections, APA: and Bylaws, 191, 196; of Council, 139–41; Council of Representatives, 267; of members, 76–78, 120; of officers, 75–76, 87, 133, 139, 191–92, 199–200; participation in, 185; and women members, 304–7

Eliot, Charles W., 13

Elliott, Richard M., 122, 154–55

Emergency Committee (APA), 151

employment, 64, 97, 136, 199, 236–37, 264, 278–81, 328–29; in Great Depression, 132, 134–35; for women psychologists, 140, 308–10, 312–14; and World War II, 152, 208

"Employment Bulletin," 372

End Violence Against the Next Generation (EVANG), 337

Equal Rights Amendment (ERA), 255, 333–34

equipment, psychological, 27–28, 55, 82, 215

Ethical Standards of Psychologists: A Summary of Ethical Principles, 365–66

Ethical Standards of Psychology, 181–82, 184

ethics, 140, 162, 179–82, 184, 226, 237–38, 251, 365–66

Ethics Committee (APA), 196

Ethnic Minority Affairs Program (APA), 251

Ethnic Minority Affairs Program Office (APA), 332

Ethnic Minority Interests Division (APA), 269

Europe: graduate education in, 9; as model for intellectual life, 44; psychological laboratories in, 27

European Federation of Professional Psychologists Association, 288

examinations, 138, 222–23

examining boards, state psychological, 226

Executive Committee, Western Philosophical Association, 63

Executive Office (APA), 203

Experimental Analysis of Behavior Division (APA), 269

Experimentalists, 80, 122, 128, 132, 140; and World War I, 95–96, 112

Experimental Publication System, 354

factionalism, within APA, 51–52, 65, 86–88, 122–24, 139–40, 142, 239, 259, 264–66, 271–73

Farley, Frank, 297

Farnsworth, Paul, 214

Farrand, Livingston, quoted, 53–55, 63

Fay, J. W., 7–8; *American Psychology Before William James*, 15

Fechner, Gustav Theodor, influence of, 4–5, 11, 14–17, 34, 80; *Elements of Psychophysics*, 4

membership: Council of Representatives, 241; NAS, 65, 92–93; of psychological societies, 123, 137, 159–61, 165

membership, APA, 76–80; benefits of, 183–87; categories of, 80, 126–27, 138, 165–66, 179, 182–83; diversity of, 67, 239, 241–43, 266–67, 269, 279–82; divisional, 188–89, 287; and elections, 51, 75–76, 133; employment of, 136; and ethical standards, 180–81; growth of, 114, 120, 149–50, 172, 177, 183, 196, 228, 239; obligations of, 183–85; and policy, 264; and proposed reorganization, 285; requirements for, 53, 62, 64, 76–78, 124, 126–27, 132, 140, 180, 305; trends in, 241; and World War I, 105–6

membership directory, APA, 295, 365

Membership Office (APA), 286, 287

Memoirs of the National Academy of Sciences, 23

methodology: and computers, 211; development of, 130; and scientific psychology, 215; standardization of, 274

Meuller, Conrad, 216

Miami Beach, as proposed site for 1957 APA meeting, 331

Midwestern Psychological Association, 56–57, 137

Miles, Walter R., 151–52, 210

military: and applied psychology, 88, 100–104, 107, 109–11; and psychological testing, 121, 328; and psychology, 95–96, 98, 151–52, 154, 171, 209; textbooks for, 373

Military division (APA), 189

Miller, George, 332

Miller, Neal, 207; quoted, 195

Millikan, Robert, 93

Mills, T. W., 32

minorities: and APA, 237–38, 251, 269, 294; and PsycINFO system, 258; and racial justice, 330–33; and testing, 328

Minority Fellowship Program (APA), 237, 294, 333, 342

Mitchell, S. Weir, 32

mobilization, wartime, 94–106, 150–53, 315

Monitor (APA), 201

Morris, George S., 21–24, 47

Münsterberg, Hugo, 18, 49, 76, 83, 87–88; quoted, 50

Murphy, Gardner, 141, 163, 329, 338–39

Murphy, Lois, 338; quoted, 329

Murray, Nicholas, 24

Napoli, D. S., quoted, 313–14

NAS. *See* National Academy of Sciences

Nation, The, 15–16

National Academy of Sciences (NAS), 15, 34, 65, 131, 154; and World War I, 92–94

National Advisory Council on Radio in Education, 133, 372

National Clearinghouse for Mental Health Information, 360–61

National Commission on Accrediting, 225

National Council of Women Psychologists (NCWP), 138, 315–16; and professional reform, 155, 157–58, 160–61, 165

National Council on Measurements Used in Education, 236, 366

National Education Association (NEA), 48, 366

National Information System for Psychology (NISP), 219, 359–60

National Institute of Mental Health (NIMH), 236–37, 333, 360–61

National Institute of Psychology, 127, 136; and professional reform, 157, 158, 160

National Institutes of Health, 221

National Mental Health Association, 290

National Register of Health Service Providers, 236, 283–84

National Research Council (NRC), 94, 153, 199, 212, 311; Division of Anthropology and Psychology, 121, 125, 129, 140; Emergency Committee, 141, 151–54, 156–57, 373; and psychology, 121, 131; Psychology Committee, 94–95, 98–99, 105–9; and women psychologists, 315; and World War I, 97–99, 102, 105–8

National Science Foundation (NSF), 142, 192, 209–10, 214; and APA publications, 218; divisions of, 210; and information exchange, 359–60; and journal funding, 354; and psychology funding, 216, 219; and research projects, 202, 252

Nelson, Paul, 295

Newcomb, Theodore, 165, 329, 331, 338

Newman, Edwin, 193, 207

newsletters, 201, 293, 294, 348, 355–56, 371–72

New York Academy of Sciences, 56

New York Association for Applied Psychology, 155

New York Association of Consulting Psychologists, 123, 137

New York University, 8, 10

Nichols, Herbert, 26

Nominating Committee (APA), 76

North American Review, 16

Noyes, A. A., 93

Noyes, William, 31, 49, 51

NSF. *See* National Science Foundation

O'Donnell, J. M., 61; quoted, 50

Office of APA National Policy Studies, 250

Office of Communication Management and Development (APA), 359–60

Office of Communications (APA), 256, 295, 359

Office of Continuing Education (APA), 295

Office of Demographic, Employment, and Educational Research (APA), 295

Office of Finance and Administration (APA), 295–96

Office of International Affairs (APA), 254

Office of Professional Affairs (APA), 293

Office of Professional Practice (APA), 277, 293

Office of Psychological Personnel, 152, 156, 171

Office of Public Affairs (APA), 254

Office of Scientific Research and Development, 209

officers: ICC, 162; Western Philosophical Association, 63

officers, APA, 52, 150, 190–92, 199–202, 319; election of, 51, 75–76, 87; executive, 199–202, 244, 247, 252, 259–60, 264, 296. *See also names of individuals*

Ogden, R. M., 96

O'Leary, Virginia, 375

Olson, W. C., 141, 199; quoted, 140, 142

organizations: for academic women, 317; African–American, 157–58; lobbying, 249; psychological, 135–137, 290; scientific, 44–45. *See also names of organizations*

Ormond, A. T., 63

Orr, Helen, 359

Osborn, Henry F., 19

O'Shea, Harriet, 169–70, 314

Osier, D. V., 353

Pace, Edward A., 49

PA Cumulative Index, 361

PADAT, 361

Paley, William, *Evidences of Christianity*, 12

Pallak, Michael S., 255, 264, 375

Palmer, George Herbert, 14

papers, at APA meetings, 50, 79, 112, 122, 139, 140, 272, 310, 349

PASAR, 361

PATELL, 361

Paterson, Donald G., quoted, 137

Patrick, George T. W., 31; quoted, 28

Pavlov, I. P., 128, 130

Peace Psychology Division (APA), 338

Peak, Helen, 316

Peck, Cecil, 362

Peirce, Charles S., 13, 15–16, 21–24, 34, 47

Perloff, Robert, 240, 373

Personal and Social division (APA), 189

ligence, 131; mental, 53–57, 85–86, 121, 272–73; military, 100–101, 103–4, 110–11, 113–14, 121; and racism, 328

tests: administration of, 85, 227; standardization of, 81–83

textbooks: for military, 373; philosophy, 7; psychological, 12, 132. *See also titles*

theory, psychological, 130–32, 274

Thesaurus of Psychological Index Terms, 361–62, 364

Thilly, Frank, 63

Thompson, George, 362

Thorndike, E. L., 76, 93–94, 100, 105, 122–23; quoted, 110, 113

Thorndike, Robert, 216

Titchener, E. B., 30, 49, 62, 93, 132; and APA, 86–87; and Experimentalists, 80, 95, 122, 127–28; *Experimental Psychology*, 83; quoted, 61, 74

Tolman, Edward C., 329–30

Tolman, Ruth, 315

Tomes, Henry, 294

training: accreditation of, 295; and APA, 212, 307; and Boulder Model, 278; clinical, 221, 275; professional, 223–25, 237, 266

Trammell Crow firm, 287

Trendelenberg, Adolf, 11

Truman, Harry S., 142

Tyler, Leona E., 236, 320, 339

Tyler Report, 248, 339–40

Underwood, Benjamin, 214

unemployment, 328–29

United States, International Congress of Psychology in, 86, 128, 131

universities, 4–5, 8, 10, 20, 44, 64, 138, 150; German, 20, 27, 44; and women psychologists, 307–9

University of California, 330

University of Chicago, 44, 48, 133, 307, 308, 372

University of Colorado, 140

University of Iowa, 28

University of Minnesota, 122, 154

University of Nebraska, 30, 307

University of Pennsylvania, 9, 29, 46, 50, 54, 308

University of Wisconsin, 29–30

Upham, Thomas: *Elements of Intellectual Philosophy*, 7; *Elements of Mental Philosophy*, 7

U.S. Congress, 210, 253–54, 291, 293–94

U.S. Department of Agriculture Division of Program Surveys, 156

U.S. Department of Defense, 210

U.S. Department of Health, Education, and Welfare, 210, 235

U.S. House of Representatives, 252

U.S. Office of Education, 225, 237

U.S. Supreme Court, 294, 331–32

U.S. War Department, and psychologists, 110

utilitarianism, 74, 88

Valentine, Willard, 199, 367

Van Cott, Harold, 202, 219

VandenBos, Gary R., 285–88, 295, 364, 369

Vienna, International Congress in, 138, 140

Vietnam War, 337

Vineland Training School, 154–56

violence, opposition to, 337–38

Visiting Psychologist Program, 237

Visiting Scientist Program, 237

volunteers, 235, 271, 358

voting procedures, APA: and APA reform, 158, 169–71, 285; and Bylaws, 179; and certification, 125, 129; and Council of Representatives, 193; and officer election, 76, 133, 139–40, 191, 199–200; participation in, 185

Walker, James, 12

Wallin, J. E. Wallace, 123

Walsh, Mary Roth, 316